D1528335

CELEBRATING

50 YEARS

Texas A&M University Press
publishing since 1974

THE TEXAS
LOWCOUNTRY

Prairie View A&M University Series

THE TEXAS LOWCOUNTRY

∼

Slavery and Freedom
on the Gulf Coast,
1822–1895

John R. Lundberg

TEXAS A&M UNIVERSITY PRESS
COLLEGE STATION

∞ This paper meets the requirements of ANSI/NISO Z39.48–1992
(Permanence of Paper).
Binding materials have been chosen for durability.
Manufactured in the United States of America

Library of Congress Cataloging-in-Publication Data

Names: Lundberg, John R., author.
Title: The Texas lowcountry: slavery and freedom on the Gulf Coast,
    1822–1895 / John R. Lundberg.
Other titles: Slavery and freedom on the Gulf Coast, 1822–1895 | Prairie
    View A & M University series.
Description: First edition. | College Station: Texas A&M University Press,
    [2024] | Series: Prairie View A & M University series | Includes
    bibliographical references and index.
Identifiers: LCCN 2023050807 (print) | LCCN 2023050808 (ebook) | ISBN
    9781648431753 (cloth) | ISBN 9781648431760 (ebook)
Subjects: LCSH: Slavery—Texas—Gulf Coast—History—19th century. | Freed
    persons—Texas—Gulf Coast—Social conditions—19th century. | Brazoria
    County (Tex.)—Race relations—History—19th century. | Fort Bend County
    (Tex.)—Race relations—History—19th century. | Matagorda County
    (Tex.)—Race relations—History—19th century. | Wharton County
    (Tex.)—Race relations—History—19th century. | BISAC: HISTORY / United
    States / State & Local / Southwest (AZ, NM, OK, TX) | HISTORY / United
    States / General
Classification: LCC E445.T47 L86 2024 (print) | LCC E445.T47 (ebook) |
    DDC 305.800976409/034—dc23/eng/20231103
LC record available at https://lccn.loc.gov/2023050807
LC ebook record available at https://lccn.loc.gov/2023050808

Book Design by Kristie Lee

To all the souls who came before
Who cry out for justice from the grave

Contents

PART 3
Reconstruction, 1865–1895

A gallery of illustrations follows page 117.

Acknowledgments

THE SEEDS OF the first idea for this book took root with me on a research trip to Brazoria County in December 2011. While in graduate school at TCU from 2004 to 2007, seminars with Greg Cantrell and Juan Floyd-Thomas first spurred my interest in the history of slavery and the differences in that institution over space and time. In maps of the concentration of enslaved people in antebellum Texas, Brazoria and surrounding counties stood out both for the density of the enslaved population and the separation of the region from the piney woods of east Texas, an area that previously, in my mind, had centered and defined the history of slavery in Texas. On the night after my visits to the Brazoria County Historical Museum, the Varner-Hogg State Historic Site, and the Brazoria County Clerk's office on the first day of research, I fell asleep wondering how I could possibly characterize this area. Upon waking the next morning, I suddenly realized that this area, unlike most other parts of Texas, had taken on many of the characteristics of the Louisiana sugar parishes mixed with the cotton culture of the South Carolina lowcountry: The Texas lowcountry.

At the annual Texas State Historical Association meeting in Houston the following March, I presented a paper titled "The Texas Low Country: Slavery in Brazoria County 1840–1860," and I received a great deal of helpful feedback from fellow panelists and the audience. In the fall of 2015, I published an article in the *East Texas Historical Journal* in which I first suggested many of the themes that made their way into the final version of this book. As I reviewed the ever-increasing literature on the history of slavery and Reconstruction in Texas, I debated the different characterizations of the history of the state, until finally stumbling upon the idea of changes in regions of Texas over time. In December 2017, in light of the increasingly public attacks on academic history and on African American history in particular, I finally decided that I would write this book as a way of adding my voice to the efforts to move Texas history forward in a more inclusive, complete direction. At the 2018 meeting of the

Texas State Historical Association, I pitched the idea of this book to Jay Dew, then the editor in chief of Texas A&M University Press, and he enthusiastically accepted, offering me an advance contract. I might have finished this volume sooner but for the COVID-19 pandemic. I was deep in the Perry papers at the Dolph Briscoe Center for American History on Thursday March 12, 2020, with plans to come back the next day and finish that part of my research. Early the next morning the University of Texas announced its closure due to the pandemic, and my research and writing temporarily came to a halt as I scrambled to put all of my course materials online for my students when Tarrant County College decided to go fully remote for the next 18 months.

Throughout this work, I have attempted to center the experiences and voices of African Americans, while placing the presence and impact of enslaved and then freed people in Texas into greater context. Most of the sources I have used to re-create the lives and experiences of the enslaved come from court or other legal records, advertisements placed in newspapers describing escapees, or various other accounts by outside observers such as enslavers, abolitionists, or diplomats. I have also consulted archaeological studies for a sense of the material culture and living conditions of the enslaved. For these records, I, like scholars before me, had to put together the puzzle pieces and look between the lines, so to speak, in an attempt to understand and explain the actions and voices of the enslaved. I have made extensive use of all types of sources—dozens of court cases, hundreds of advertisements, and thousands of pages of deeds, wills, probates, and other legal documents. After emancipation, sources documenting African American voices became much more abundant, notably testimony in lawsuits along with the voluminous number of complaints filed with the Freedmen's Bureau, and finally the histories of churches and freedom colonies established during Reconstruction.

This work would not have been possible without the assistance and advice of a small army of fellow academics, archivists, librarians, and local museum curators. First and foremost I would like to thank Sara Frear and Jessica Wranosky, two excellent historians who took time to read the drafts of the chapters of this book as I completed them and offer their feedback and advice. In addition, I often consulted fellow historians Katherine Walters, Greg Kosc, Rachel Gunter, and Scott Sosebee with a multitude of questions about historical issues and interpretations. Daniel Sample at the George Memorial Library in Richmond, Texas, helped me find a crucial court case in the midst of the pandemic when I could not access the library myself, and Katherine Walters graciously put me in touch with the Wharton County

Historical Museum during the same time. Michael Bailey of the Brazoria County Historical Museum greatly aided me in my research in that county in the spring of 2022, and Mike Reddell of the *Bay City Sentinel* made many helpful introductions to ranchers and scholars in Matagorda County on my research trip there in the summer of 2019. I owe Chuck Grear a debt of gratitude for the maps included in this volume, as well as the archivists at the Dolph Briscoe Center for American History and the Texas State Archives who gladly helped me with all of my research requests, no matter how obscure the information I sought. I also owe Light Cummins a special thanks for his comments on the manuscript, which made it stronger.

I owe my greatest debt of gratitude to Jay Dew, who always believed in this project. If I have left out any names of people who helped me along the way, it is inadvertent, and I hope they will accept my humble thanks nonetheless.

THE TEXAS LOWCOUNTRY

Introduction

In early 1820, three brothers outfitted several small boats at the mouth of the Calcasieu River in southern Louisiana and sailed west, toward the Spanish province of Texas. Making their way along the coast for roughly ninety miles, the men put ashore on Galveston Island and made their way to Campeche, the encampment of the pirate Jean Lafitte, who had relocated to the Spanish borderlands to continue his illicit activities away from the authority of US law enforcement. Among his other enterprises, Lafitte began raiding Spanish slave ships, taking their cargo of enslaved Africans and selling them to the highest bidder. The outlawing of the international slave trade in the United States made smuggling enslaved Africans into the country a lucrative business, so much so that more than a few Americans, including the three aforementioned brothers, sold their land and other possessions and crossed international boundaries to engage in human trafficking. In the years before the invention of the famous knife that would later bear their family name, not much distinguished Rezin, James, and John Bowie as they negotiated with Lafitte, who agreed to sell them forty enslaved people for a dollar per pound; an average of $140 per person.

Departing Galveston with their human contraband, the brothers drove their captives overland through the woods and swamps of southeast Texas until they reached Louisiana. At one point at least thirty Africans escaped, and Jim Bowie attempted to track them down before giving up. At that time, Louisiana law dictated that the customs official and US marshal seize any smuggled Africans and sell them at auction to the highest bidder, awarding half of the prospective purchase price to those who alerted the authorities to the smuggling. The Bowies, after bribing the customs officer, informed on themselves, using the reward money to purchase the Africans at the subsequent auction, gaining legal title while laundering them into the United States. In all, the brothers made at least two more trips back to Galveston and cleared a total profit of $65,000. These Africans became some of the first of tens of thousands of enslaved people like them brought to Texas in the nineteenth century, people whose labor and value would build the modern foundations of the region.[1]

$\sim$

Historians of slavery and Reconstruction have more often than not attempted to portray the culture of enslaving and the experiences of African Americans in Texas as a whole, but culture and experiences in an area as vast as Texas often defy easy patterns. Rather, scholars should seek to identify and explore the different regions of Texas, focusing on commonalities and differences across different pieces of the state. This work then seeks to identify, define, and explore the origins and history of just such a region. This area, which some have labeled the Texas "Sugar Bowl," contains the lower reaches of the Brazos and Colorado rivers and their tributaries as they wend their way toward the Gulf of Mexico through what is today Brazoria, Fort Bend, Matagorda, and Wharton counties. For millions of years, these rivers have deposited rich alluvial soil along their banks, making the area some of the best farmland in Texas. Huge oak trees festooned with Spanish moss and wild peach trees dot the prairies, forests, and banks of the creeks and rivers where only the occasional gulf breezes lift the oppressive humidity and temporarily drive away the hordes of mosquitoes. It rains often, and the occasional hurricane sweeps in from the coast, flattening everything in its path. In this region, with its black soil and easy access to the sea, Stephen F. Austin chose to plant his colony in northern Mexico, and in doing so he laid the foundation for what would become the most southwestern outpost of the Deep South. Austin's Anglo colonists brought with them large numbers of enslaved African Americans, and smugglers like Jim Bowie added to the population of the enslaved with smuggled Africans. The region came to resemble the Louisiana sugar parishes in many ways, but it also took on many characteristics of the more famous South Carolina lowcountry. In a mix between the two, this land became a unique region: the Texas lowcountry. Although geographically limited, this region played an outsized role in determining the direction of Texas throughout the nineteenth century.

The area made up of Brazoria and Fort Bend counties, together with the eastern portions of Matagorda and Wharton counties, became a distinct region by design of the enslavers in Austin's colony who drove out the Karankawas and then used enslaved labor to cultivate the land. By the time of the American Civil War, enslaved people constituted more than 70 percent of the population of the four counties, the heaviest such concentration west of the Mississippi. In a signal to people who might interfere with the peculiar institution, Matagorda County officials at one time took the extraordinary step of expelling all Mexicans from the county, deeming them a threat to slavery.[2]

In the last two antebellum decades European immigrants, particularly Germans, poured into Texas sometimes bringing with them attitudes and cultures that complicated the story of slavery throughout large swaths of the state. By 1860, a little over 10 percent of the free population of Texas hailed from other countries, but less than 5.5 percent of the free population of the lowcountry arrived as foreign immigrants. The only substantive grouping of Europeans living in the region resided in the town of Matagorda, southwest of the heart of the plantation belt along Caney Creek. Although immigrants by and large did not call the region home, the lowcountry found itself surrounded by heavily immigrant communities. To the south and east, foreigners made up substantial portions of the populations of Galveston and Harris counties at 28 percent and 40 percent, respectively. Similarly, to the north and west, immigrants heavily populated Austin and Colorado counties, at 19 percent and 27 percent of the free population each. Ninety-five percent of the white population of the lowcountry came from other parts of the United States, predominantly the slave states of the American South. These demographics all established the Texas lowcountry as a region adjacent to, but largely separate, in its population and social structure.[3]

The other major purpose of this work lies in seeking a path forward across the sometimes contentious historiography of Texas identity, seeking not to align with a particular identity, but rather suggesting a unifying thesis. In attempting to make sense of Texas, historians over at least the last half century have examined and debated the basic questions of whether or not Texas was more Southern or Western, and to what degree Texas functioned as a borderlands, while incorporating the stories of women, minorities, and other traditionally underrepresented groups in reshaping the traditional narrative. Scholars have approached the history of slavery and Reconstruction along similar lines, examining the way in which the institution of slavery itself and the actions of enslaved persons shaped the history of Texas, and the lives and experiences of freed people following emancipation. Texas was not always a borderlands, nor was it always Western or Southern, but these identities ebb and flow across time and geographical spaces. Similarly, the Texas lowcountry did not permanently remain a borderlands, nor did it remain the Deep South society that evolved over time. The conclusion that then follows is that Texas, and the regions of Texas, underwent tipping points; transitional inflections at particular points in time that altered the fundamental relationships and characteristics of populations within a given geographic space.[4]

From the dual thesis of regional identity and tipping points, the following questions then guided the construction of this work. Which events caused this region to transition from a borderlands to a more traditional Deep South society and finally to Reconstruction? What events ended each time period? In terms of the institution of slavery, what impact did the peculiar institution have on Austin's original colony? How did enslavers transport enslaved people to the region? How did enslaved people react to this geographic space? In what ways did the influence of so many recently arrived Africans impact the story of slavery in the region? In what ways did the institution of slavery complicate the structures of class and gender? How did the labor of enslaved people develop the economy of Texas, and in what ways did this contribute to building the structures of modern Texas capitalism? During Reconstruction, how did freed people adjust in terms of land ownership, labor, and political participation? How did convict leasing and the birth of the Texas carcereal complex on the old sugar plantations of the region create "slavery by another name"? Finally, in what ways did whites employ the mechanisms of power and white supremacy to diminish or eliminate African American land ownership, political participation, and freedom in the overthrow of Reconstruction?

To answer these crucial questions, we must cover a considerable time frame and range of sources. The first part of the story of the Texas lowcountry involves the development of the region as a borderlands, an area of competing cultures and peoples, between 1822 and 1840. Chapter 1 details the ways in which American enslavers, led by Stephen F. Austin, established the foundation for an enslaving society in the face of opposition from the Mexican central government, often illegally importing or bringing with them thousands of enslaved African Americans. Chapter 2 delineates the history of the Texas revolution, a conflict that amounted to an enslaver's rebellion against Mexico that began at Anahuac, and the subsequent battle of Velasco in 1832. After the bloodshed at the mouth of the Brazos and the formation of the War Party, further conflict proved almost inevitable. The institution of slavery certainly was not the only cause for the secession of 1836, but for the enslavers of the lowcountry, the heart of Austin's original colony and home of many leaders of the insurrection, anxiety over the status of slavery was *the* central cause of the rebellion. Chapter 3 details the ways in which the lowcountry reached a tipping point through the opening of trade with Europe, the beginning of sugar cultivation, and the birth of the cities of Galveston and Houston. These developments all accelerated the birth of a Deep South plantation society. This does not suggest that all elements of the borderlands vanished, but simply that after 1840 the culture of the Deep South became the dominant influence in the region.[5]

The topic of slavery in this region over the course of two and a half decades does not lend itself well to a linear recounting of events. For this reason, the second part of the story is arranged topically, and chronicles the history of the enslaved and enslavers in the region between 1840 and 1865. Chapter 4 discusses the ways in which enslavers transported enslaved people to the region, through the illegal smuggling of Africans and the vast interstate slave trade, by water or land, in what amounted to a second Middle Passage.

The basic unit of community in the rural antebellum South became the neighborhood, which was often composed of adjoining plantations. Chapter 5 details the class structure of white antebellum society in the region and lays out the geography of the region by documenting and describing the plantation neighborhoods and the details of each individual slave labor camp. In addition to giving the reader a sense of place, part of the purpose of the detail in chapter 5 is also basic historical recovery that will hopefully complement preservation efforts in the region. Climate change and urbanization threaten many, if not all, of the sites described, and unless historians, archaeologists, and preservationists work quickly, they will disappear completely.

The labor of enslaved people and the profits from slavery and attendant industries produced the material foundation of the United States, and Texas was no exception. Chapter 6 delves into the intensification of Texas capitalism by examining the labor of enslaved people in the production of cotton and sugar, as well as the monetary values enslavers assigned to the enslaved people. The economic potential these values represented undergirded the regional financial system and helped attract investment. Enslaved people not only produced the wealth of the region, but also built the first internal improvements in the state in the form of railroads, canals, and port facilities. The wealth generated by the lowcountry plantation system also led to the founding of Houston and Galveston and provided the Republic of Texas enough international clout to merit diplomatic recognition and annexation.[6]

The final two chapters in part 2 engage with the topics of gender and resistance to slavery in the region. Chapter 7 examines the ways in which slavery complicated family structures in the region by focusing on the cases of two enslaved women whose relationships with their enslavers led to lengthy court battles, giving the reader unique insights into the intimate aspects of slavery, family, power, and law in the lowcountry. Chapter 8 examines the various methods of resistance to slavery employed by enslaved people, including the formation of families and religious practices, carving out their own spaces in the quarters of the plantations until their struggle resulted in a tenuous freedom in 1865.

The third and final part of this story revolves around the experiences of freed people during Reconstruction. The era of Reconstruction following the American Civil War was characterized first by military rule by the Freedmen's Bureau and the US Army, and then by political participation of freed people, who helped organize the Texas Republican Party, and the subsequent control of the Republican Party over state politics. Reconstruction ended as Congress restored the rebel states to full status under the Constitution, followed by the fall of the Republican governments to white ex-Confederates and former enslavers. In Texas, this process occurred between 1865 and 1873, but in the lowcountry the last African Americans did not leave office until 1895, meaning that Reconstruction did not fully end in the region until this latter date. Reconstruction lasted longer in the Texas lowcountry than in other parts of the state for the simple reason that three quarters of the voters in the region were African American in 1867, ensuring that a biracial Republican coalition could thrive there for two decades following the conclusion of Reconstruction in the rest of Texas. Chapter 9 examines the experiences of freed people in the region between 1865 and 1873, the traditional period thought of as statewide Reconstruction. During this time period, the Freedmen's Bureau played a large role in negotiating labor contracts, levying fines against those who abused freed people, and helped register all eligible males to vote in 1867.[7]

Although the period ended with the Clark–Giddings election controversy of 1871 and the fall of the statewide Republican government in 1873, because African Americans constituted 75 percent of voters in the lowcountry, Republicans continued to dominate county politics and send African Americans to the state legislature. Chapter 10 examines the extent to which freed people managed to become landowners as the Panic of 1873 forced white landowners to sell small parcels of land between 1873 and 1885. African Americans also established numerous freedom colonies and churches throughout the lowcountry, and the detail in chapter 10 in documenting and describing the freedom colonies and churches is also aimed at complementing historical preservation efforts before these sites disappear completely. During this time period, the state of Texas began the convict leasing regime, which has accurately been characterized as "slavery by another name." Realizing the profit from sugar production, the state began buying up old sugar plantations in the region, which remain part of the Texas Department of Corrections to this day.[8]

Finally, chapter 11 deals with the last 10 years of Reconstruction, 1885–1895. During this decade, a series of violent attacks against African American communities and equally violent coups ended Reconstruction in the region with the formation of white man's union associations. These shadow county governments, which were exclusively for whites, wrested control of county politics from African Americans at a time when the national Republican Party abandoned African American voters in the South, leading to the onset of the Jim Crow era.

The Texas lowcountry no longer exists as a cohesive region. Between the 1890s and the 1920s, most African Americans in the region relocated to Houston, creating the largest African American community in the South. The 1920 census revealed that whites constituted a majority in all four counties for the first time. Today oil and natural gas exploration, cattle raising, and prisons dominate the rural parts of the region, while the urban sprawl of the Houston metro area has swallowed up most of Fort Bend and eastern Brazoria counties. Driving through the lowcountry today, we see that the landscape appears different than it did in the nineteenth century, but the scars of slavery and the struggles of Reconstruction remain, just under the surface, in a history that, if not acknowledged, will continue to haunt the Lone Star State far beyond the twenty-first century.[9]

PART 1

A Borderlands,
1822–1840

Chapter 1

Carving Out a Plantation Society

1822–1831

ON A COLD DAY in January 1822, a massive wagon train moving south down the Coushatta Trace halted on the east bank of the Brazos River. At the head of the procession rode Jared Groce, a 39-year-old native of Virginia, and behind him in more than fifty wagons rode ninety enslaved African Americans, his white overseer Alfred Gee, the Groce family, and enough supplies and seed to start a cotton plantation. This mass of moving people must have startled the residents of Mexican Texas, but Groce was on a journey to join Stephen F. Austin's newly forming colony and extend plantation slavery into Mexico. After briefly scouting the area, Groce ferried his cotton plantation on wheels across the river, but he ultimately decided to go back and set up his residence on the east bank of the Brazos. That winter the enslaved people on the plantation that Groce dubbed "Bernardo" began erecting a house, along with slave cabins, and cultivating the soil for corn and cotton. Jared Groce had more than enough reason to leave the United States. He had run into financial trouble, and in the winter of 1818 while residing in Alabama, he took possession of forty-seven imported Africans in violation of US law, an act that could land him in legal trouble. Stephen Austin received word of Groce's troubles and lawbreaking, but that did not matter to the *empresario* (i.e., land agent), who granted Groce 10 leagues of land in what is now Austin and Brazoria counties. Austin wrote that he had granted the Virginian these 44,284 acres because "he has near one hundred slaves and may be useful on account of the property he has brought with him."[1]

Groce proved the wealthiest, but certainly not the only, enslaver among Austin's "Old Three Hundred" (a name deriving from Austin's permission to settle 300 families). Bernardo represented cotton and plantation life in the

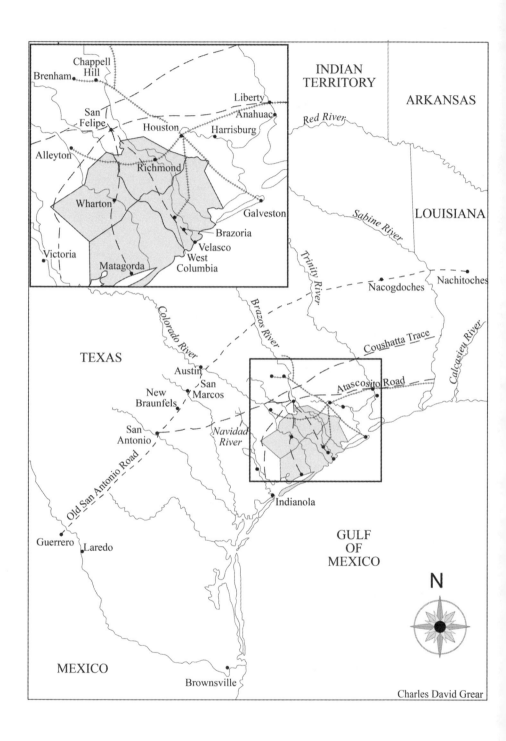

INDIAN
TERRITORY

ARKANSAS

Red River

Sabine River LOUISIANA

Nacogdoches Nachitoches

Trinity River

Brazos River

Coushatta Trace

TEXAS

Colorado River

Austin

San
Marcos

New
Braunfels

Atascosito Road

San
Antonio

*Navidad
River*

Old San Antonio Road

Indianola

Guerrero Laredo

Calcasieu River

GULF
OF
MEXICO

N

MEXICO

Brownsville

Charles David Grear

Inset (upper left):

Chappell
Hill
Brenham

Liberty

San
Felipe

Anahuac

Houston

Harrisburg

Alleyton

Richmond

Wharton

Galveston

Brazoria

Velasco
West
Columbia

Victoria

Matagorda

upcountry of Austin's colony. The most extensive enslaving and the most developed plantation culture would take hold in the lowcountry, an area that today consists of Brazoria, Fort Bend, Wharton, and Matagorda counties. Unlike Groce, most of Austin's settlers came by boat from New Orleans, landing near the mouths of the Brazos and Colorado rivers, and here they began laying the foundation for the society that would dominate the destiny of Texas.

Mexico was hostile to the institution of slavery, and certainly it took a bold breed of American enslaver to transport their human property to this foreign country, but in the person of Stephen F. Austin they had reason for their audacity. It was solely Austin's determined efforts to protect slavery that made the establishment of the lowcountry plantation society possible. In January 1821, when the government of New Spain officially accepted Moses Austin's plan for colonization, neither side mentioned slavery. Austin, however, an enslaver himself, knew that he would draw the members for the new colony from the southern part of the United States and that they would want to bring their human chattels with them. When Moses Austin died in June of 1821 in Missouri, his son Stephen, who shared his father's sentiments about slavery, took over the colonization project. Mexico declared independence from Spain on August 24, 1821, and the plan for a colony that Stephen Austin presented to the Mexican government included a grant of 80 acres for every enslaved African brought over by the settlers. Although Austin never granted any acreage under this original plan, it shows the incentives he planned to offer for those who brought their bondsmen into the frontier.[2]

The Spanish governor of Texas, Joseph de Azlor, caught in the confusion of Mexican independence, refused to allow Austin to grant any land, and so the *empresario* decided to travel to Mexico City himself to lobby for his colony and, most importantly, for slavery. Austin arrived in the capital city in April 1822, with the Mexican Congress already in its first session. The young entrepreneur immediately began to write petitions to the Congress, begging that they confirm his land grant in the form of a new colonization law. It is almost impossible to overemphasize the abolitionist sentiment present in the first Mexican Congress. A wave of antislavery sentiment pervaded the delegates, and only Austin's constant intercessions made the legalization of slavery of any kind possible in Texas. The Congress decided to consider colonization and slavery in two separate laws, but Austin continued to lobby for an expression on slavery in the laws concerning colonization. On August

20, 1822, the Congress took up debate of the colonization law and authored a bill affirming that all bondsmen already in Mexico would remain enslaved for life, but that their children would obtain freedom at the age of fourteen, which meant the gradual phasing out of the institution.[3]

The Congress did not have a chance to pass this bill, for in October 1822 Emperor Agustín Iturbide dissolved the assembly by force, replacing the Congress with a *junta* of thirty-five members. Not to be deterred, Austin began to lobby this much smaller body on the topic of slavery. On November 14, the *junta* took up the colonization bill with the objective of complete emancipation, but Austin helped convince them to honor the property rights of enslavers under previous law. After a little more than a week, the junta passed the law with an absolute prohibition of slave trading in Mexico, and with the provision from the previous draft of the law that mandated continued enslavement for those already held in bondage but freedom for their children at age fourteen.[4]

The codification in law of the colonization law appears deceptively simple. Although the contents of the debate are unknown, Austin wrote to his friend, Josiah Bell: "As the law now is, all slaves are to be free in ten years, but I am trying to have it amended . . . but I do not think I shall succeed in this point, and that the law will pass as it now is, that is, that the slaves introduced by the settlers shall be free after ten years." The fact that Austin was this discouraged just days before the debate began indicates the force of his lobbying on behalf of the peculiar institution. On January 8, 1823, Austin wrote Governor José Felix Trespalacios of Texas that he had "talked to every member of the Junta upon the necessity which existed in Texas, Santander, and all the other uninhabited provinces, that the colonists should be permitted to bring their slaves, and in this manner I procured the article." Iturbide declared the law to be in effect on January 4, 1823, and even though the new government declared the law void after the overthrow of Iturbide, the Congress issued a special proclamation reinstating the law as it previously stood. In this way the Republic of Mexico, through the agency of Stephen F. Austin, allowed American enslavers a toehold, a wedge they would begin exploiting to turn Texas into the only slaveholding province in the new republic.[5]

In August 1823, Austin returned to Texas and began organizing his colony. He sent out an announcement that he would expel disreputable characters and that he would only take payment for land in "money or negroes." In October, Austin hired three enslaved persons from Leonard Groce: two men and a woman; named Jack, Kelly, and Sally, respectively, and a younger boy named Fields to take care of Sally's child. Austin hired them for a year at a rate of $8.00 for Sally and $15.00 for each of the men. His proclamation and this personal transaction indicated that whatever legal impediments Mexico might raise to slavery, Austin intended to run his settlement just like any slave society of the American South. The criminal codes Austin laid out for the colony furthered the impression of a southern slave society. In violation of existing Mexican law, Austin prescribed whippings for enslaved people who asserted their freedom or stole. The *empresario* also dictated strict punishments for whites who harbored escapees or traded with enslaved persons without the permission of their enslavers. Even though the whippings violated the law, the political chief in San Antonio approved these regulations without comment.[6]

After Austin's return to Texas, in the summer of 1824, the Anglo colonists turned their attention to driving out the Karankawas, who had begun small raids on the settlers as early as 1822. In June 1824, the colonists fought their first engagement with these natives after several members of the tribe arrived at Brit Bailey's general store and demanded ammunition. Austin appointed Randall Jones head of a company of men that pursued the Native Americans, driving them west, but not before three of the colonists lost their lives. In August 1824, Austin decided to launch a campaign that would rid his colony of these indigenous people. Jared Groce armed thirty of the enslaved African Americans on his plantation and equipped them with horses to join in this campaign, and Austin recruited sixty Anglos. These ninety men pursued the Karankawas as far as Presidio La Bahia, whereupon a truce was called and the Karankawas were ordered to leave the colony. Ridding the land of Native Americans proved a standard part of building every plantation society in the American South, but the participation of the enslaved men from Bernardo showed that they felt they had something to gain, a stake, in clearing out the natives, perhaps in self-defense. In any event, by 1825, Austin could report that the Anglo settlers' problems with the Karankawas had begun to lessen, clearing the way for the arrival of more settlers.[7]

In early 1824, the Mexican Congress began working on a permanent constitution for their new country, and these deliberations provided the next threat to the institution of slavery in Texas. Rumors began to swirl that the Mexican Congress would outlaw slavery in this new constitution. On June 5, 1824, at the village of San Felipe, Austin, Jared Groce, John P. Coles, and James Cummings led a mass meeting in which the Anglo settlers drafted a petition expressing alarm at the rumors that the Congress planned to pass a law emancipating the enslaved. They emphasized that these enslaved people were not "Africans," but the personal servants of the settlers, and that the settlers needed this type of "property" to establish their farms and ranches. They also appealed to Article 30 of the colonization law under which they brought the enslaved to Texas. They concluded: "These Inhabitants therefore respectfully pray that your sovereignty may take their Case into Consideration and declare that the slaves and their descendants of the 300 families who emigrate to the Establishment formed by the Emprasario [sic] Stephen F Austin in this province shall be slaves for Life and that the emancipation Law which we have been informed has lately passed shall not apply to the slaves of the said 300 families." As it happened, the Congress was not considering an emancipation bill, but the panic induced by even the mention of abolition revealed the uneasiness with which the enslavers of Texas would view the Mexican government throughout the remainder of the colonial period.[8]

Although the Congress did not consider emancipation, they did pass other laws regulating slavery in the empire. On July 13, the Congress prohibited the slave trade, allowing freedom to any person the moment they touched Mexican soil. The proclamation, though, suspended all penalties for 6 months and applied only to the slave trade. As construed by the Mexican authorities in Texas, this proclamation did not prohibit settlers from bringing their human property with them. When the Constitution of 1824 went into effect on October 4 of that year, it contained no further antislavery provisions. The new governing document did, however, combine Texas with Coahuila, establishing the capital of the new state at Saltillo.[9]

As suspiciously as enslavers viewed the Republic of Mexico, from all over the South Austin received letters inquiring about the status of slavery in Texas. James Phelps wrote from Missouri: "Nothing appears at present to prevent a portion of our wealthy planters from emigrating immediately to the province of Texas but the uncertainty now pervading with regard to the subject of slavery. There has been a paragraph that has the round of newspaper publication in the United States, purporting to be an extract from a Mexican paper; which precludes the introduction of Negro property in the Mexican Republic." Although Phelps predicted that this regulation would inhibit emigration, he himself arrived in Texas in 1825 with a number of enslaved persons, as did numerous others. Austin received dozens of letters from other enslavers expressing concerns like those voiced by Phelps, and he did his best to assuage their fears. In fact, other than the status of land grants, the subject of slavery preoccupied prospective settlers more than any other subject.[10]

Some of the Anglo settlers brought the enslaved with them to Texas after they broke up their plantations or sold land and enslaved people elsewhere to finance their journey, but others went out of their way to purchase people whom they could then either take with them or ship to Texas. Once in Texas, enslavers also had ample opportunity to purchase enslaved persons from other settlers, despite legal prohibitions to the contrary. Guy Bryan, Stephen Austin's nephew, took advantage of a trip to Baltimore to purchase more enslaved people before coming to Texas. In 1823, John Botts helped the widow of Joseph Hawkins auction off the people she enslaved in the colony to other enslavers anxious to purchase them.[11]

In 1824, after Austin returned from Mexico City and began distributing official titles to lands in Texas, the legislature of the State of Coahuila and Texas began to create its own constitution, which added further layers to the question of Mexican law and slavery. The legislature approved its own colonization law on March 24, 1825, which offered a *sitio* (league) of land to every stock raiser and a labor of land (150 acres) to every farmer. *Sitios* consisted of 4,428.4 acres, and labors of land, 177 acres. The legislature also dodged the issue of slavery by stating: "In respect to the introduction of slaves, the new settlers shall subject themselves to the laws that are now and shall hereafter be established on the subject." The colonization law and the refusal of the legislature to adopt an abolitionist stance encouraged many more enslavers to immigrate to Texas in 1825 and 1826, bringing their property with them.[12]

Austin's first census of the colony, taken in late 1825, revealed the extent to which his colony was quickly becoming an extension of the American South. Of the nearly 300 family units, 69, or 23 percent, counted themselves as enslavers, with five holding more than twenty bondsmen, and another seven holding more than ten. Of the 1,800 "souls" Austin listed as living in his colony, enslaved African Americans constituted 443, or nearly 25 percent of the population. Austin noted that several settlers had begun building cotton gins and that some had started to experiment with sugar cane. Jared Groce cultivated the first cotton crop in Texas, at Bernardo, in 1823, and several of the large enslavers followed his lead. By 1826, the plantation owners were already sending cotton bales on flat boats down the Brazos to sell in New Orleans. With an average holding of 6.4 bondsmen per enslaver, a quarter of the white population enslavers and a quarter of the whole population consisting of enslaved people, the Texas lowcountry, just four years into Anglo colonization, already appeared to exhibit the hallmarks of a nascent plantation society.[13]

When the legislature of Coahuila and Texas labored to complete a constitution for their new state, more threats to slavery emerged. As word spread through Austin's colony that the legislature was hostile to slavery, rumors again began swirling that they would abolish the institution. On August 11, 1826, Anglo settler Jesse Thompson penned a letter expressing alarm over imminent abolition in Texas, stating that he now planned to return to the United States with the people he had enslaved. Evidently, Austin also took these rumors to heart and wrote a petition to the legislature, begging them to preserve slavery in the constitution. The members of the *ayuntamiento* (the city council) of Bexar also intervened to help the enslavers in Texas. After Austin learned that the Bexar government had narrowly convinced the legislature not to abolish slavery, the *empresario* decided he needed a personal envoy to plead his case. In this role, he chose his brother, James Brown Austin, who reached Saltillo in September 1826. On September 13, James Brown wrote his brother: "the most that can be obtained is permission for the three hundred families to hold their slaves."[14]

In addition to Brown Austin's efforts, Philip Hendrik Nering Bögel, known under his invented title "Baron de Bastrop" and serving as the only representative to the legislature from the Anglo Texas settlements, labored to defend slavery. Bastrop and Brown Austin together convinced the legislature to stop short of total abolition; Bastrop threatened to withhold his signature from the final document if it included abolition. On March 11, 1827, the legislature approved the final constitution, which included the following provision: "From and after the promulgation of the Constitution in the capital of each district, no one shall be born a slave in the state, and after six months the introduction of slaves under any pretext shall not be permitted." In addition, enslavers had to emancipate 10 percent of any enslaved persons when transferring title to another enslaver by way of inheritance. Each of the *ayuntimientos* had to compile a list of all enslaved persons in their jurisdiction, and they also had to submit lists of all births and deaths every ninety days. The legislature also required the local governments to provide emancipated children with the best education possible. It appeared that African slavery would die out in Texas, but the Mexican government apparently underestimated the determination of the Americans to create an enslaving society.[15]

In May 1828, representatives to the legislature of Coahuila and Texas again raised the topic of enslaved African Americans but in language that described them merely as laborers. Under this guise, the body passed a decree that read: "The Congress of the State of Coahuila and Texas, attending to the deficiency of workingmen to give activity to agriculture. . . . All contracts, not in opposition to the laws of the State, that have been entered into in foreign countries . . . are hereby guaranteed to be valid in said State." With this tacit approval, Anglos devised a scheme to introduce enslaved people while at the same time complying with the letter of the law. Before leaving the United States, enslavers would appear before a notary public and draw up a contract between themselves and the enslaved. This contract stipulated that the owner would agree to transfer their ownership of the enslaved to the contract of an indentured servant, in which the enslaved agreed to indemnify their former owner with their labor for the price at which the notary valued them. The contracts also provided that any offspring of these now "indentured servants" would begin working on the same terms as their parents at age 18. Enslavers intended the contract to guarantee that the bondsmen could never repay the amount owed, and in this way, they would become indentured servants for life. Bearing these new contracts, Anglos continued pouring into Texas, bringing with them "indentured servants."[16]

As the Americans fought with the Mexican government over the status of slavery in Texas, Anglo settlers continued to transform Texas into a plantation society. In January 1822, when the Anglo settlers aboard the *Lively* set out from New Orleans to meet Stephen Austin at the mouth of the Colorado River, they instead mistakenly entered the mouth of the Brazos River and continued upstream until they reached a point where the woods on the west bank gave way to a meadow. There they put ashore and built a small "fort," about 25 feet square. They occupied this structure for several weeks before spreading out from the "Fort Settlement." It was from this fort that the Anglo colonization of Texas began. In 1824, with Bastrop serving as his land agent, Austin began officially giving title to lands in his colony, and by 1827 the enslaved at Bernardo had constructed the first cotton gin in the upcountry. In 1824, Josiah Bell opened Marion, or "Bell's Landing," on the Brazos River, which was destined to become an important location to load cotton and sugar for the trip to New Orleans. Austin established San Felipe in late 1824, and Josiah Bell established the town of Columbia in 1826, two miles west of Bell's Landing. In 1824, Stephen Austin also entered into a contract with George

Huff of Mississippi, a mechanic, to construct a cotton gin in what would become Brazoria County. After several delays, the gin owned by Stephen and his brother, Brown, opened for business in time to refine cotton, which averaged two bales of cotton per acre in 1826.[17]

The year 1827 saw the arrival of William H. Wharton in Texas. Before he came to Texas, Jared Groce sent his daughter, Ann, to school at the University of Nashville. In Tennessee she met Wharton, scion of a prominent Tennessee family, and the two decided to settle in Texas. In December 1827, Wharton married Ann Groce at Bernardo, and Jared Groce gifted some of his land in Brazoria to his new son-in-law. That year, William Wharton established the second large plantation in Texas, and the first in the lowcountry: "Eagle Island." Wharton had the enslaved construct the first frame house in Texas with wood brought from Tennessee, and the plantation grew even larger than Bernardo. That same year, the enslaved persons Wharton brought with him from Tennessee also began to cultivate cotton.[18]

In 1828, Josiah Bell built wharves, warehouses, and sheds at Bell's Landing as business increased, and that same year Brown Austin and John Austin (no relation) established a mercantile business 15 miles from the mouth of the Brazos River, with their cotton gin, store, and outbuildings, which Stephen F. Austin named Brazoria. That year, the enslaved in Austin's colony produced 500 bales of cotton. By the middle of summer 1829, the people enslaved by Martin Varner had cultivated the first sugar cane in the colony on his plantation on Varner's Creek, and Varner had produced the first bottle of rum in Texas.[19]

Anglos also began establishing settlements in other parts of the lowcountry. In August 1826, Anglo settlers petitioned Austin to establish a town at the mouth of the Colorado River, and in 1827 Elias Wightman laid out the streets of Matagorda. As early as 1825, settlers began operating a cotton gin where the town would stand, and by 1832 Matagorda, as the first port city established in the lowcountry, had 1,400 residents.[20]

Despite the Anglos' efforts in the lowcountry to create a slave society, the aftermath of the Fredonian Rebellion again threatened the legal status of slavery in Texas. As early as the promulgation of the Adams-Onís Treaty in 1819, Spanish and then Mexican officials raised the idea of a boundary commission to survey the border between Louisiana and Texas, but the Fredonian episode provided the catalyst that prompted the Mexican government to dispatch a boundary commission to Texas, not just to survey the border, but also to keep an eye on the Anglo settlers. Suspicions had begun to grow in Mexico City that some of the Americans intended to undermine the Mexican government and deliver the province to the United States. The rebellion in east Texas merely hardened these suspicions, so President Guadalupe Victoria appointed General Manuel de Mier y Terán as head of the boundary commission. On November 10, 1827, Mier y Terán and several staff members departed Mexico City, arriving in Laredo on February 1, 1828. Throughout the rest of 1828, Mier y Terán traveled throughout Texas, observing the conditions of the countryside and the Anglo settlers. The general did not return to the Mexican state of Taumalipas until August 1829, having spent nineteen months in what is now Texas and eastern Louisiana. Even before Mier y Terán departed San Antonio for points east in March 1828, he wrote a letter to President Victoria in which he recommended that

> settlement by North Americans should be suspended in the territory of Tejas, but the established colonies should remain and be granted as much freedom as possible in the cultivation of the land, the sale of their products, and the importation of those [products] of prime necessity to them, according to their uses. If [the North Americans] are allowed to introduce slaves, the Mexicans of Tejas should also be permitted to do so, but if [slavery] is denied to some it should be denied to all.

Mier y Terán proved hostile to slavery throughout the rest of his tour, but like Stephen Austin with whom he became friends, he maintained a pragmatic view of the institution. Not until after Mier y Terán returned to Mexico City in late 1829 would the Congress act on the recommendations of the boundary commission.[21]

Even as Mier y Terán was completing his recommendations for Texas, a new threat to slavery arose. José Tornel, an abolitionist member of the Mexican Congress, introduced a bill to free all enslaved persons in the Republic, declaring: "In the abolition of slavery is involved an important political object of establishing a barrier between Mexico and the United States." The Mexican Senate was slow to pass the measure, so Tornel approached President Vicente Guerrero, who issued a proclamation freeing all of the enslaved at a time that would coincide with Mexican Independence Day. When on September 15, 1829, Guerroro issued the decree, the Anglo enslavers of Texas began to panic. John Durst of Nacogdoches wrote Stephen Austin: "We are ruined forever should this measure be adopted." Austin urged caution but added: "I am the owner of one slave only, an old decriped [sic] woman, not worth much, but in this matter I should feel that my constitutional rights as a Mexican were just as much infringed, as they would be if I had a thousand, it is the principle, not the amount, the latter makes the violation more aggravated, but, not more *illegal* or unconstitutional." Austin approached Don Ramón Músquiz, the political chief of Texas, and Músquiz agreed that he would not publish the decree until he had interceded with President Guerrero. Músquiz reminded the president that the Anglo settlers had only come to Mexico under a guarantee of their property and that the decree represented a breach of faith. "Philanthropy and the natural sentiments of humanity, cry out immediately, in favor of liberty, but the positive laws which regulate society array themselves in favor of property and declare it a sacred and individual right." Músquiz went on to warn that the decree could bring about rebellion among the Anglo settlers or even a wholesale exodus back to the United States. The governor of Coahuila and Texas added his voice to the cries of Austin and Músquiz, and on December 2, 1829, President Guerrero issued an amended proclamation, exempting Texas from the decree. Presumably, Guerrero amended his proclamation because of the inconvenience and deprivation of property it would bring to the enslavers in Texas, but without doubt the dark warnings by both Músquiz and Governor José Viesca of a possible Anglo revolt also played a part in the president's decision making. Robert Williamson, editor of the *Texas Gazette* at San Felipe, published the new decree in January 1830, assuaging the fears of the enslavers in Texas.[22]

Before Austin and the Mexican officials in Coahuila and Texas could intervene to stop the full abolition of slavery in Texas, the proclamation of 1829 inspired a number of African Americans to slip the chains of bondage by fleeing into the interior of Mexico. In December 1829, three African Americans, John, Robert, and a woman whose name has been lost to history, arrived in the village of Guerrero, Coahuila, 280 miles west of the Brazos, having escaped their enslavers in Texas. They told the interpreter that they received the news of the proclamation granting them freedom with great enthusiasm, but when their enslaver began talking of selling them in New Orleans, they took a chance on freedom, fleeing west. Luis Lombrano, the Mexican official in Guerrero who took their testimony, granted their wish and declared them free citizens of the Republic. Likewise, in one of the first runaway slave ads placed in a Texas newspaper, John Randon, one of Austin's original settlers who began a plantation on a *sitio* of land fronting the Brazos River north of the Fort Settlement, offered a $200 reward for the return of two men, Will and Adam, aged thirty-one and thirty-two, respectively. The timing of the ad indicates that Will and Adam may also have escaped in response to the freedom declaration of 1829. For Anglo enslavers in Texas, the status of slavery appeared to grow ever more tenuous as time wore on.[23]

As Stephen Austin worked to make his colony safe for enslavers, his attention turned to his sister and her family in Missouri. As early as 1824, he had urged his widowed sister, Emily, to move to Texas, and he had even dispatched his brother, Brown, to relocate them, but instead Emily Austin (Bryan) married James F. Perry in the fall of 1824, and she and her new husband opted to remain in Missouri. In August 1829, Brown Austin died of yellow fever in New Orleans, and the grief over the death of his brother prompted Stephen Austin to begin peppering his sister and brother-in-law with encouragements to move to Texas. By late 1829, Austin had arranged for Perry to settle on several leagues of land west of Galveston Bay. The *empresario* wrote his brother-in-law: "All of the difficulties as to Slaves about which I wrote you are removed, by a new law exempting Texas from the Gen. emancipation law of 15 Sep this applies to slaves brought in before the time expired for introducing them— this shows that the principle of Slavery is admitted as to Texas, and I have no doubt that in a few years this will be a Slave State." As a large enslaver, Austin planned to have Perry begin a plantation near the Gulf of Mexico along with other planters already in the colony, further laying the groundwork for this plantation society. For the moment, Perry remained reticent to leave Missouri, but Austin continued to encourage him to move to Texas.[24]

The month of April 1830 brought another challenge to slavery from the Mexican government. Alarmed by the finding of the Boundary Commission, the Mexican Congress passed the Law of April 6, 1830, cutting off further immigration from the United States. The law contained eighteen articles dealing with issues from customs duties to military garrisons in the northern provinces. Despite the wide-ranging law, it was Article 11, forbidding any further immigration from the United States, that most alarmed enslavers in Texas. Article 11 applied not only to Anglo settlers but also to enslaved African Americans. Stephen Austin protested the immigration portion of the law, and finally, the Mexican authorities agreed that Austin could continue to fulfill his colonization contracts, essentially nullifying the effects of the law concerning the lowcountry. Although Americans continued to arrive in other parts of Texas illegally with their "indentured servants," the loophole Austin exploited gave these arrivals the imprimatur of legality in the lowcountry.[25]

A traveler who boarded the sloop *Majesty* in New Orleans bound for Texas in March 1831 described the attitudes of the enslavers on board:

> There was . . . a very intelligent man from Alabama, who had several negroes with him, going to take up his abode in Texas. . . . On reaching New Orleans he had learnt for the first time that slaves cannot be held in Mexican territory, and had taken measures which had been recommended to him, to evade the general law of abolition. . . . He had obtained their attested signatures to articles of indenture, by which they bound themselves to serve him for ninety-nine years. He counseled another man, who was on board with his wife and several slaves, to do the same."

In this way, whether in wagons, coffles, or in the hold of ships from New Orleans, enslaved people continued to pour into Texas regardless of any legal prohibitions.[26]

The Law of April 6, 1830, also precipitated other changes to the lowcountry. Since part of the law required the collection of customs duties, the Mexican government dispatched soldiers to establish garrisons and customs houses. In October 1830, Colonel Juan Davis Bradburn arrived to establish a garrison near the mouth of the Trinity River, on Galveston Bay, northeast of the lowcountry. There, on a 30-foot bluff, he laid out a fort with his small garrison, and by March 1831 he had laid out the military village of Anahuac. At the mouth of the Brazos River, where the *Lively* first put ashore in 1822, Colonel Domingo de Ugartechea also arrived in the fall of 1830 with a small garrison and began construction on a fortification on the east bank of the Brazos, 150 yards from the mouth of the river. Using driftwood set into the ground upright in two concentric circles, the Mexican troops built Fort Velasco. Mexican officials also established a customs house, but not a garrison, at Matagorda. The presence of these garrisons further complicated the position of Anglo enslavers as their bondsmen began escaping to the garrisons seeking freedom.[27]

Despite the increasing dangers to slavery from the Mexican Republic, enslavers continued to pour into the lowcountry. Four miles southwest of Wharton's "Eagle Island" plantation, the first large plantation neighborhood in the lowcountry took shape in what became known as Gulf Prairie, perhaps the richest farmland in the colony. In 1824, Austin granted John McNeel a league of land on the east bank of the San Bernard River, below the town of Brazoria. He listed McNeel in his first census as a farmer and stock raiser, with his wife, four sons, a daughter, and twenty-five enslaved persons.

McNeel called the plantation he established there "Ellerslie," and soon the enslaved began raising cotton. McNeel arrived in Texas short on cash, and he wrote to Austin on October 9, 1826, "I regret exceedingly that money is not at my command at this moment as it has taken the whole of my last year's Crop to procure the articles indispensably necessary in making my establishment here." McNeel concluded that he was owed some money that he hoped to collect soon and that he had valuable property which might be of use. Despite this rough beginning, within just a few years he established Ellerslie as a prosperous plantation. In 1827, Noah Smithwick, an early settler who left a first-hand account, reported that the enslaved at Ellerslie had raised a crop of cotton and commenced building a gin. They also had a shop with iron tools that they supplemented by recycling iron from an old shipwreck in the San Bernard, evidently driven ashore by a hurricane some years before. In March 1831 a traveler described Ellerslie as "a fine estate . . . spread on an almost boundless meadow. . . . It contains a garden, with a noble cotton field, which, the year before, had yielded a crop of five thousand dollars." The dwelling was "a good log house, just on the verge of a fine grove, partly shaded by China trees, newly planted." The Texans feted their guest with a meal of venison, turkey, and coffee. The establishment of Ellerslie began to give shape to the Gulf Prairie neighborhood, the heart of the lowcountry plantation society.[28]

Austin continued to urge his brother-in-law and sister to move to Texas, and so at length James Perry finally agreed to take his pregnant wife and children and leave Potosi, Missouri, for Mexican Texas. A caravan of nearly twenty people, including nine enslaved African Americans, departed Potosi in June 1831. In August, Emily Perry and her family reached San Felipe, while James Perry went forward to establish a plantation on Chocolate Bayou, to the southeast, in what is now Brazoria County. Perry liked the Chocolate Bayou location and commenced raising cattle, but by the time the Perrys arrived, Austin had picked out a new location that he felt would suit them better, on Gulf Prairie. Austin thought that living in a more populated area would suit his sister better than the isolated location on Chocolate Bayou. He also made it clear that the plantation he wanted his brother-in-law to establish would also be his home, and by November 1831 Austin had begun sending his sister detailed plans for a plantation that would be named Peach Point. Emily liked the plans and convinced her husband to abandon the Chocolate Bayou homestead and begin anew at Peach Point. In mid-1832, the enslaved began construction of buildings on the land Austin selected on land fronting on the west bank of the Brazos River, on the Gulf Prairie.[29]

By the summer of 1832, enslavers in Texas had started to carve out the lowcountry plantation society even as they clashed with the Mexican government over slavery. Most historians agree that Stephen Austin held complex views on slavery, opposing it in principle but embracing the institution in a pragmatic attempt to establish his colony in Texas. But regardless of any misgivings he may have had, he worked to establish a slaveholding society along the Texas coast that would come to dominate the destiny of the Mexican province. Just as he served as the architect of Peach Point plantation, Austin served as the architect of the lowcountry that remained a borderland during his lifetime.[30]

Chapter 2

An Enslaver's Rebellion

1832–1836

IN THE EARLY morning darkness of June 26, 1832, two enslaved men at Ellerslie, Willis Stark and Jerry Smith, awakened Pleasant, brother of the plantation owner John McNeel, to warn him that Jim had returned. Some 10 days earlier, Jim, known as "Big Jim," an enslaved man who had learned Spanish, escaped to the Mexican garrison at Velasco, some sixteen miles to the southeast, at the mouth of the Brazos River. The circumstantial evidence convinced the McNeels that Jim intended to start an insurrection at the behest of Mexican officials. Willis and Jerry, accompanied by Pleasant, approached the cabin occupied by Jim's wife and called him to come outside. Jim tried to run, but Willis and Jerry tackled and tied him up inside the McNeel house. Some ten hours later, when Pleasant relaxed his guard for a moment, Jim's wife cut him loose, and Willis spotted him jumping from the window. Pleasant McNeel grabbed his rifle and rushed outside, confronting Jim on the edge of the woods. McNeel called out to him, ordering him to halt, but Jim turned and defiantly said, "shoot, God damn you." A report rang out, and Jim fell, mortally wounded. As he lay dying, Jim allegedly confessed his plot "to massacre . . . and burn every dwelling. The younger women were to be taken as captives to the Mexican camp."[1]

Jim's death raised considerable alarm among all the enslavers on Gulf Prairie and beyond and increased the feeling that the presence of Mexican troops, and perhaps the Mexican government itself, posed an unacceptable threat to slavery. Noah Smithwick recalled: "The negroes soon became aware of the legal status of slavery in Mexican territory, and it was probably owing to their ignorance of the language and country that more of them did not leave."[2]

Even if Jim's death was not quite as dramatic as it was later remembered, the account of his death and Smithwick's description of it spoke to the very real circumstances of African Americans, and to the anxiety of Anglos over their continued battle with the Mexican government regarding the status of the peculiar institution in Texas. This anxiety would ultimately lead to the secession of Texas from Mexico, sparked by the armed rebellion that began in the lowcountry just hours after Jim's death.

Traditionally, historians of the Texas Revolution have downplayed or dismissed slavery as a central cause of the armed rebellion that severed Texas from the rest of Mexico. According to the most traditional interpretation, "American freedom and democracy versus Mexican oppression" has been accepted as the overriding cause of the revolution, but in the last 30 years, Texas historians have begun to come to grips with the centrality of slavery to the struggle for independence. An examination of the Texas revolution in the lowcountry, extending from the outbreak of fighting at Velasco in June 1832 to the formation of the War Party, demonstrates that for both those enslaved

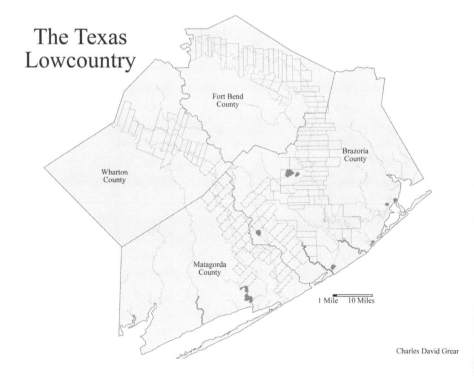

The Texas Lowcountry

Fort Bend County

Wharton County

Brazoria County

Matagorda County

1 Mile   10 Miles

Charles David Grear

in the lowcountry and the enslavers who initiated the fighting against the abolitionist Mexican government, the Texas revolution was very much an enslaver's rebellion.[3]

The trouble that ignited the rebellion against Mexico began in August 1831 at Anahuac. That month, two formerly enslaved men who escaped from their enslaver in Louisiana presented themselves to Colonel Juan Bradburn, seeking asylum. (Bradburn was from Kentucky but had immigrated to Mexico, changed his first name to Juan, and joined the Mexican army.) Bradburn added them to his garrison, putting them to work building fortifications. In November, William M. Logan, an attorney from Liberty, Texas, arrived to claim the men, but General Mier y Terán, who was then visiting Anahuac, informed Logan that he would have to apply for custody of the men through diplomatic channels in Mexico City. When Bradburn demanded that Logan provide proof of ownership, Logan traveled back to Louisiana and returned with the requisite papers. The matter took months to adjudicate, and Logan hired a local attorney, William Barrett Travis, to help him gain custody of the two men. Both Travis, an enslaver himself from Alabama, and his law partner, Patrick Jack, also an enslaver, had arrived in Texas in the spring of 1831 and had established their law practice at Anahuac. In the second week of May 1832, Travis resorted to subterfuge: Disguising himself as a man called "Ballou," he approached a Mexican sentry at night, giving him a note for Bradburn. The note reported that more than one hundred armed men from Louisiana intended to take the garrison and free the two fugitives. The Mexican commander reacted by sending out patrols, but he soon realized the note was a hoax. Suspecting Travis as the instigator, he ordered that he be arrested and brought to the fort for questioning. When Travis's law partner, Patrick Jack, stormed into Bradburn's office, seething with threats, Bradburn immediately arrested him as well. On May 24, after only six days of trying to isolate Travis and Jack in their jail cell, Bradburn stopped Harriet, a woman enslaved by local merchant James Morgan, because he suspected her of carrying notes to and from the prisoners. A note that she carried outlined an escape attempt scheduled for May 26. Bradburn suspected that Monroe Edwards, a man working as a clerk in Morgan's store, was the mastermind behind the escape attempt, and so he ordered Edwards arrested as well. To increase the security of his prisoners, Bradburn moved them to an unoccupied brick kiln, trained two cannons at the kiln, and increased the guard. After Edwards was arrested, Bradburn threw Edwards in the kiln with his co-conspirators.[4]

Back in the lowcountry at Brazoria, William H. Jack got word of his brother's arrest, and he and Frank Johnson led a group of men toward Anahuac; the group grew to a small company by the time they reached Turtle Bayou, six miles north of the Mexican outpost. The leaders of the militia, including John Austin, called on Bradburn to release the prisoners, but Bradburn had his adjutant explain that under the military laws governing Anahuac, Bradburn had the authority to detain the men for fomenting a rebellion against the military authority. The rebels captured some of the Mexican cavalry in an ambush, and after an exchange attempt where Bradburn reneged on his pledge to trade the prisoners for his men, the Anglos retreated to Turtle Bayou and issued the Turtle Bayou Resolutions on June 13. The resolutions called on General Antonio López de Santa Anna (who at that time was executing a military coup to seize power in Mexico City) to restore the protections of the Constitution of 1824 and release the prisoners. The resolutions also called on the other Anglos in Texas to take up arms against Bradburn and the Mexican soldiers at Anahuac. John Austin returned to Brazoria, reaching the village on June 20, and rallied the settlers to take the three cannons stored there and lay siege to Anahuac. On June 21, Austin commandeered the schooner *Brazoria*, lined the sides with bales of cotton for protection, and loaded the cannon on board. The ring leaders of the rebels, anticipating that Colonel Domingo de Ugartechea and his garrison of seventy-three men would not let them pass Fort Velasco in peace, now gathered a company to attack the fort. With forty men on board the *Brazoria* and the rest marching down the road on foot, the enslavers of the lowcountry prepared to attack the Mexican garrison.[5]

The rebels camped at Wharton's Landing, near Ellerslie, on the night of June 22 and for the next two days made preparations to attack the fort. On June 25, the insurgents finalized their plans: William J. Russell, commanding the *Brazoria*, would attack the fort from the river; a "division" of men under Henry S. Brown would proceed east of the fort to the beach beyond and utilize the driftwood there as barricades; and finally companies under Henry Smith and John Austin would advance from the north, using movable barricades to shield themselves while they dug trenches.[6]

After dark on June 26, the attack began. The Anglos moved in behind their barricades and fired the first shots near midnight. Both sides exchanged fire through the morning hours of June 27, and Colonel Ugartechea raised the white flag around 10 a.m., but not before seven Mexican soldiers lay dead, along with nineteen wounded. The Anglos lost seven dead and twenty-three wounded. The next day John Austin accepted Ugartechea's terms of surrender, and the Mexican soldiers departed overland for the interior.

John Austin, William Wharton, and others planned to travel overland to Anahuac to continue the fight, but by the time the battle ended, word reached Fort Velasco that the situation at Anahuac had turned in favor of the enslavers. Colonel José de las Piedras, Bradburn's immediate superior, arrived from Nacogdoches, relieved Bradburn from command, and released Travis, Jack, and Edwards on July 3.

Later that month, Brigadier General José Antonio Mexia arrived at Velasco with several warships and four hundred men, but William Wharton and the other Anglos at Brazoria convinced Mexia that they did not intend to rebel and that the Turtle Bayou Resolutions and the fight at Velasco served merely as a symbol of their support for Santa Anna. Satisfied, Mexia departed with his troops back into the interior.[7]

Most Texas historians have viewed the Anahuac disturbances and the Battle of Velasco as isolated incidents, but this interpretation ignores the context of the unrest. Enslaved men who had asserted their own freedom and enslavers initiated the problems at Anahuac. Making matters worse for the enslavers, the very presence of the Mexican garrisons at Anahuac and Velasco wreaked havoc with the institution of slavery in the lowcountry, leading the plantation owners to realize that slavery would never be secure in Texas as long as it remained part of Mexico. These threats to slavery caused the Anglos to march on Velasco and attack the Mexican garrison there in the first such clash with the central government. Finally, in the wake of the battle, the lowcountry enslavers formed the War Party and would continue to agitate for conflict against the central government until they achieved their goal in 1835. The formation of the War Party guaranteed that peace would never return to Texas until the enslavers either won the conflict or the Mexican government drove them out of the country entirely.[8]

The War and Peace parties began to take shape in the Consultation of 1832 at which fifty-five delegates, all of them Anglo, met at San Felipe from October 1 to October 6, with Stephen F. Austin presiding as president and Francis W. Johnson, as vice president. William Wharton became one of the most influential delegates. Austin belonged to the budding Peace Party, but Johnson and Wharton belonged to the War Party. Due to Austin's moderating presence, the consultation merely called for alterations to the Law of April 6, 1830, which included allowing renewed immigration from the United States. The Anglos also called for the formation of committees of vigilance, safety, and correspondence, and the separation of Texas from Coahuila. The other delegates chose Wharton to carry the petitions to Mexico City. However, Ramón Músquiz, the political chief of Texas in San Antonio, ruled the gathering illegal. For the moment, the rebellious enslavers had to regroup.[9]

Impatient for change, the enslavers of the lowcountry organized a second convention that met on April 1, 1833, again at San Felipe, but this time, members of the War Party predominated, with William Wharton serving as president. Like the attack on Fort Velasco, the membership of the convention consisted primarily of the enslavers of the lowcountry. The convention made many of the same demands as the 1832 consultation had, but this time they went further in drawing up a constitution for the proposed Mexican state of Texas. Just as the convention began, news reached them that some of the more unscrupulous enslavers had landed a cargo of Africans at Edward's Point, on Galveston Bay. This alarmed and antagonized many members of the convention, including Stephen F. Austin, because they feared this traffic would endanger their bargaining position with an abolitionist Mexican government. Before adjourning, they passed a resolution stating:

> We do hold in utter abhorrence all participation, whether direct or indirect, in the African Slave Trade; that we do concur in the general indignation which has been manifested throughout the civilized world against that inhuman and unprincipled traffic; and we do therefore earnestly recommend to our constituents, the good people of Texas, that they will not only abstain from all concern in that abominable traffic, but that they will unite their efforts to prevent the evil from polluting our shores; and will aid and sustain the civil authorities in detecting and punishing any similar attempt for the future.

The members of the convention stated that this cargo was landed by some "foreign adventurer," and just to prove how much they opposed this traffic, they ordered the resolution published in the *Texas Advocate* and various other newspapers "throughout the Mexican Republic." The adoption of this last resolution and the zealousness of the convention to disseminate it revealed that the members of the convention understood slavery as the main issue that separated them from the rest of Mexico. It also obscures the fact that it was not foreign adventurers, but rather two men already deeply involved in slavery and the slave trade in the lowcountry who had begun trafficking Africans from Cuba: Benjamin Fort Smith, a plantation owner, and his partner, Monroe Edwards. The illegal importation of enslaved Africans would remain a feature of the lowcountry until the American Civil War. As one of their last actions, the Convention of 1833 designated Stephen F. Austin to carry their petitions to Mexico City.[10]

On his way to Mexico City, Austin confided his attitudes on slavery to an early colonist, Wiley Martin. For some time in 1832, Austin toyed with the idea of pushing for the abolition of slavery in Texas, but apparently the events of 1832 and 1833 had converted even Austin to a defense of the peculiar institution. "I have been adverse to the principle of slavery in Texas," the *empresario* wrote Martin. "I have now, for the last six months, changed my view of the matter. . . . Texas must be a slave country. Circumstances and unavoidable necessity compels it. It is the wish of the people there, and it is my duty to do all I can, prudently, in favor of it. I will do so." Although Austin did not yet advocate separation from Mexico, his change of heart on slavery foreshadowed the break.[11]

The fighting at Anahuac and Velasco, together with the Conventions of 1832 and 1833, convinced the Mexican government that the Americans in Texas intended to break the province away from the rest of the country. At this point, they dispatched Colonel Juan Almonte to report on the actions of the Anglos and the condition of Texas in general. The secret instructions given to Almonte on his mission expressed in the most explicit terms Mexico's abolitionist intentions for Texas. The instructions read in part: "Sr. Almonte will seek by every possible and prudent means to make it known to the slaves who have been brought into the Republic in circumvention of the law, that [the law] gives them freedom by the mere act of stepping on territory of the Republic . . ." regardless of any contracts of indenture they signed. His orders also included instructions to inform people of color in Texas that "the government does not rate men by their color, by their origin, or by their nationality, but rather by their works." Whether Almonte ever acted on this part of his orders is not clear, but their very existence demonstrated the abolitionist sentiment of the Mexican government.[12]

In March 1834, Almonte arrived in New Orleans, and from there he traveled to Natchitoches and then into Texas at Nacogdoches. He spent most of the rest of the year traveling through Texas; in his final, secret report, he found no signs of "revolution," but clearly he saw trouble brewing, especially in the "Brazos" district. His report also demonstrated the significant role of cotton and slavery in Texas and the ongoing illicit importation of Africans from Cuba.

Almonte's reports to Mexico City surveyed the attitudes of the people of Texas, the geography, the economy, and almost every other conceivable category. From Nacogdoches in June 1834, he wrote that the citizens of the Bexar and Nacogdoches districts did not favor separate statehood, but "the ones from Brazos (and they are few) are the ones who constantly promote the aforesaid idea." Even though the colonel concluded that the citizens of Texas did not favor revolution or separate statehood, it is instructive that the only trouble he found consistently centered on the areas with the largest number of slaves.[13]

Almonte also noted the growing financial relationship between enslavers in the Brazos Valley and New Orleans merchants. In 1833, he observed that the Brazos district exported 2,000 bales of cotton, but in 1834, he expected that number to increase by 150 percent. He reported that in 1834 the cotton growers of the Brazos district planned to grow and export 5,000 bales of cotton. At 450 pounds of cotton lint each, even after paying US customs duties, the enslavers still realized a 10-cent profit per pound, for a total of 225,000 pesos, a huge and rapidly growing number.[14]

Finally, in commenting on slavery, Almonte continued to complain about the flagrant importation of Africans by Benjamin Fort Smith. In April 1834, Smith landed a cargo of fifty Africans from Cuba at Edwards's point on Galveston Bay. The Mexican colonel also observed that "other individuals are preparing to follow his example, and for this purpose they have sailed from New Orleans" for Cuba. This second illicit cargo of Africans clarified the idea that enslavers of the lower Brazos Valley would continue to take advantage of the perceived chaos in Texas to violate Mexican law and expand slavery.[15]

Juan Almonte's reports on Texas are the most complete picture of the state in 1834, but the colonel clearly missed signs of unrest. Although he traveled throughout Texas, he spent most of his time in Nacogdoches, far from the seat of unrest and secession in the lowcountry. If Almonte had spent more time in Brazoria, he might have detected the growing unrest among the large enslavers that exploded in full-scale war the next year.

Lowcountry planters took advantage of the confusion caused by the outbreak of war with the central government to continue smuggling enslaved Africans from Cuba. In February 1836, Monroe Edwards returned from Havana with his schooner *Shenandoah* with 170 Africans. William Fisher, the customs commissioner, reported to Governor Smith: "We overhauled the vessel that night, and found that the negroes had been landed—the negroes were, however, found during the night. The negroes I have given up to Mr. Edwards (the owner) on his giving bond and security to the amount of their value, to be held subject to the decision of the government." In the same letter, Fisher noted that Sterling McNeel, another brother of Ellerslie owner John McNeel, had also landed a cargo of Africans on the coast. Fisher tried to seize the vessel but with no success. The presence of this large and growing number of Africans would give the enslaved community of the lowcountry a character found nowhere else in Texas.[16]

After war with the central government began in the fall of 1835, Anglos painted the conflict as a race war they were fighting to preserve their "property" from Mexican abolitionists and to protect the sexual purity of white women. John W. Hall asked his fellow Texians: "Will you now, suffer the *colored* hirelings of a cruel and faithless despot, to feast and revel in your dearly purchased and cherished homes?" James Fannin wrote: "Not the least doubt should be any longer entertained, by any friend of Texas, of the design of Santa Anna to overrun the country, and expel or exterminate every white man within its borders. . . . What can be expected for the *Fair* daughters of *chaste white women*, when their own country women are prostituted by a licensed soldiery."[17]

Enslavers also emphasized the abolitionist nature of the threat from Santa Anna and the Mexican army. William Wharton, dispatched as an emissary to advocate for Texas in the United States, wrote: "With a sickly philanthropy worthy of the abolitionists of these United States, they have, contrary to justice, and to law, intermeddled with our slave population, and have impotently threatened in the war now pending, to emancipate them, and induce them to turn their arms against their masters." Benjamin Milam wrote to Francis Johnson: "The plan for the dissolution and destruction is laid, and every preparation is making for its execution. . . . Their intention is to gain the friendship of the different tribes of Indians; and, if possible to get the slaves to revolt. These plans of barbarity and injustice will make a wilderness of Texas, and beggars of its inhabitants."[18]

Despite Anglo Texan fears, Mexico had no definite plan of abolition. In 1836, as his army marched toward Bexar, Santa Anna wrote: "There is a considerable number of slaves in Texas also, who have been introduced by their masters under cover of certain questionable contracts, but who according to our laws should be free. Shall we permit those wretches to moan in chains any longer in a country whose kind laws protect the liberty of man without distinction of cast or color?"[19] The Mexican government never crafted a formal abolitionist policy, but Mexican soldiers certainly shielded runaways and welcomed their help in fighting the rebels.

In this atmosphere, Anglos in the lowcountry often evinced anxiety regarding insurrections. The Columbia Committee of Safety resolved: "Information having come before this committee clearly proving that much danger is to be apprehended from the slave population . . . we therefore recommend that each town and neighborhood hold immediate meetings and elect a vigilant patrol whose duty it shall be to adopt some prompt measures to keep the slave population in due subjection." Writing to Stephen F. Austin about an unfounded rumor regarding the imminent approach of thousands of Mexican soldiers, Thomas Pilgrim of Columbia asked: "would it not be prudent that a portion of our forces should stay to defend it in case of necessity? Would there not be great danger from the Negroes should a large Mexican force come so near?" R. R. Royall, chairman of the Matagorda Committee of Safety, also submitted the conclusions of his committee: "being advised that danger is apprehended from the slave population on the Brazos, that Committee recommends to their fellow citizens great caution in this particular, and the adoption of prompt measures to prevent in our section both alarm and danger." Apparently, however, these patrols did not assuage Anglo fears because in the upcountry, the San Felipe *Telegraph and Texas Register* reported that the people "have been alarmed at shadows."[20]

Enslaved African Americans took full opportunity of the fighting in the Texas revolution to assert their freedom in a variety of ways. Despite the patrols, B. J. White wrote to Stephen F. Austin on October 17, 1835, that "the negroes on Brazos made an attempt to rise." A messenger from Brazoria informed White "that near 100 had been taken up and many whiped [sic] nearly to death some hung etc. R. H. Williams had nearly Kild [sic] one of his." White related that the enslaved around Brazoria had a plot to divide the cotton farms among themselves, ship the cotton to New Orleans, and enslave white men. The veracity of this plot remains a matter of speculation, but the Anglo response to the threat and others like it—whether real or perceived—revealed their anxieties and motives in rebelling against the central government. At the same time, other enslaved African Americans took the opportunity to run away.[21]

Following the fall of Bexar, Anglo fears about rebellions reached their peak and resulted in the panic of the Runaway Scrape. (The Runaway Scrape involved Anglo colonists fleeing ahead of the arrival of the Mexican army after Goliad and the Alamo.) In anticipation of the further advance of the Mexican army, on March 5 from Brazoria, Henry Austin wrote James Perry at Peach Point that "it would be judicious for you to send Emily and the younger children" away due to "the anxiety which Emily would feel at having the enemy so

near, the apprehension of a possible rising of the negroes." Following the fall of
the Alamo, on March 17, 1836, the citizens of Brazoria chaired by Robert Mills
resolved to secure "in a proper manner all negroes," to have all able-bodied
men report to Houston's army, and to build a fortification at the mouth of the
Brazos. They adopted these resolutions because of the "alarming character"
of the information they had received of the fall of the Alamo and the "rapid"
advance of the Mexican army, "with the avowed purpose of a general extermi-
nation of ourselves, our wives, our children and all who inhabit this country.
And we have moreover been appraised of the horrid purpose" of the enemy
"to unite in his ranks, and as instruments of his unholy and savage work, the
negroes, whether slave or free, thus lighting the torch of war, in the bosoms
of our domestic circles." Echoing these sentiments, James Morgan wrote: "the
negroes . . . have manifested a disposition to become troublesome & in some
instances *daring*[. O]ne has been killed and another punished by whipping—a
third was pursued but not overtaken, when last heard from."[22]

Although the Mexican government and Santa Anna had no clear plan of
emancipation, the generals and soldiers of the Mexican army did facilitate
the emancipation of enslaved African Americans. On April 3, 1836, fourteen
enslaved men and their families presented themselves to General José Urrea,
who sent them south toward Victoria. On the same day, Sam Houston wrote
to his friend S. P. Carson through Willis, a man Houston held in bondage. In
the letter the Texas commander noted: "as for Willis, I wish you to keep him
strictly, and make him wait upon you . . . Another thing, he speaks Mexican,
and I wish him taken care of, and good care. You will have to flog him well."
After San Jacinto, as the Mexican army retreated, they took African Americans
with them. R. R. Royall returned to Matagorda to find thirteen bondsmen
"missing" from his neighborhood, and General Vicente Filisola reported that
many of the Anglos had their homes looted by African Americans fleeing with
the Mexican troops.[23]

Following the Texan victory at San Jacinto and the capture of Santa Anna,
it became apparent that the Anglos had created an enslaving republic—the
Republic of Texas. Following the issuance of the Declaration of Independence
at the town of Washington on the Brazos on March 2, 1836, the convention
drew up a constitution for their new country. At the same time that the
convention condemned and banned the African slave trade, they specifically
allowed the introduction of enslaved persons from the United States: "All
persons of color who were slaves for life, previous to their emigration to Texas
. . . shall remain in the like state of servitude," they proclaimed. "Congress shall

pass new law to prohibit emigrants from the United States of America from bringing their slaves with them and holding them on the same terms." At the same time, the convention banned any free persons of color from residing in the Republic without the express consent of the convention. The work of this convention stood as the Constitution of the Republic of Texas until 1845, creating a legal and cultural framework that made Texas an extension of the American South.[24]

Underscoring the disruption of slavery in the lowcountry and Mexican abolitionist instincts, the treaties of Velasco explicitly demanded that the Mexican army return any enslaved person to their owner. Section 5 of the treaty, signed by Santa Anna at Velasco on May 14, 1836, stated: "That all private property including cattle, horses, negro slaves or indentured persons of whatever denomination that may have been captured by any portion of the Mexican Army or may have taken refuge in the said army since the commencement of the late invasion shall be restored to the Commander of the Texian Army or to such other persons as may be appointed by the Government of Texas to receive them." The reaction to this order varied among Mexican generals still in the field. At length, General Filisola allowed Texan commissioners into his camp where they recovered some runaways, but General Urrea refused, writing: "all the slaves within my jurisdiction continued to enjoy their liberty." Captain José de la Peña even went so far as to disguise an enslaved man as a Mexican soldier to ensure his safe passage to Matamoros.[25]

On June 27, 1836, Stephen Austin arrived at the mouth of the Brazos River, fresh from his diplomatic mission to the United States. The old *empresario* traveled up the Brazos to Columbia, the site of the newly forming government of the Republic of Texas. In Columbia on July 1, Austin met with Santa Anna in a two-room cabin owned by William Jack. Austin formulated a diplomatic plan to end the war permanently by having Santa Anna request that President Andrew Jackson mediate an end to the hostilities. Ultimately, the plan failed, but it demonstrated that Austin had already begun to act as the chief diplomat of the new republic.[26]

Austin understood that the only economic and diplomatic leverage that the new enslaving republic possessed lay in the profitability of slavery and cotton. Austin ran for the presidency of the new country, but voters passed him over for Sam Houston in early September. In the same election, voters overwhelmingly favored annexation to the United States. On October 28, Houston wrote to Austin, confirming Austin's appointment as secretary of state. Austin moved from Peach Point to Columbia into a spare room in the house of George McKinstry on the outskirts of town. From his drafty quarters, Austin began laying plans to use the economics of slavery to secure annexation to the United States.[27]

Austin and Houston selected William H. Wharton as Minister Plenipotentiary to the United States, and on November 18, 1836, Austin wrote to Wharton, transmitting his instructions as representative of the new republic. Secretary of State Austin told Wharton that if the United States evinced any reticence to annex Texas, he should attempt to gain recognition from Britain and France to place pressure on Washington. "In the event therefore of discovering any such disposition in the government or Congress of the United States," wrote Austin, "you will have full and free conversations with the British, French, and other foreign ministers, on the Texas question, explaining to them the great commercial advantages that will result to their nations from our cotton, etc. and finding a market here for their merchandise, and an outlet for their surplus population."[28]

Even as Austin went about the business of leveraging cotton and slavery to secure annexation, his physical condition worsened in the winter of 1836. The *empresario* never fully recovered his health following his long imprisonment in Mexico City, and in late December when a norther blew through the lowcountry, he developed a severe cold. By Christmas his cold had worsened into pneumonia, and just after noon on December 27, 1836, Stephen F. Austin died. On December 29, the people of Columbia loaded Austin's body onto the steamer *Yellowstone* for the trip down the Brazos to Peach Point, where he was interred in the family cemetery two miles west of Perry's landing.[29]

In 1910, the State of Texas reinterred Austin's bones in the Texas State Cemetery in Austin, but in the meantime the Texas lowcountry underwent distinct cultural shifts resulting from the change Austin had brought about with his work in Texas. It seems entirely fitting that at the time of his death, the man who served as the architect of the Texas lowcountry was hard at work fostering the economic relationships that would provide the tipping point in transforming the area into a Deep South plantation society.

The long Anglo rebellion against Mexico from 1832 to 1836 served as a distinct turning point in the history of Texas, Mexico, and the United States. The institution of African slavery that Austin worked so hard to introduce became the central point of contention between the Anglo Americans and the Mexican central government. Moreover, the actions of the enslaved seeking freedom and the enslavers attempting to control them and fight off Mexican abolitionists produced an armed conflict that led to the secession of Texas from Mexico and the formation of a new enslaving republic. Throughout this tumult, the lowcountry remained at the center of the conflict. As Texas began to gradually shed its ties to Mexico and develop new economic connections to the United States and Europe, enslaved African Americans, Anglo plantation owners, merchants, and smugglers would again take center stage as the region became the first area of Texas to develop a culture and economy based on the model of a conventional Deep South plantation society.

Chapter 3

Agents of Change

The Tipping Point

1837–1840

ON FEBRUARY 25, 1839, a 400-ton British sloop, the *Ambassador,* sailed into Galveston Bay. As the first British ship to sail to the fledgling Republic of Texas, its arrival occasioned a great deal of celebration among the citizens of Galveston and the republic at large. The ship arrived with a singular mission— to collect the cotton bales produced by the enslaved men and women of the lowcountry and to carry them back to textile mills in Liverpool. The citizens of Galveston reportedly showed as much joy "as if our independence had been acknowledged at the Court of St. James." The arrival of the *Ambassador* announced the final phase of the tipping point that transformed the Texas lowcountry from a borderland to a more traditional Deep South plantation society.[1]

Until 1836, Mexico remained the biggest influence on enslaved and en- slavers alike in the lowcountry. Mexican law, soldiers, and the presence of Mexican nationals from the interior all combined to make Texas a borderland from the first settlement of Anglo Americans in 1822 until the break from the mother country. Other areas of Texas remained predominantly a borderland, at least until the end of the US-Mexican War in 1848, but the Texas lowcountry reached this tipping point earlier as economic relationships between planters and merchants tied the region to commercial centers in New Orleans, to American ports on the Atlantic, and finally, in 1839, to the textile mills in Liverpool. By 1840, the predominant influence on the Texas lowcountry was no longer Mexico, but the trans-Atlantic commercial network that provided a market to sell cotton and the sugar that became increasingly important as a cash crop in the region after 1840. Enslavers purchased everything needed to produce a Deep South plantation society—including enslaved African Americans by the thousands. For the enslaved, Mexico still played a large role in their attempts to escape bondage, a place they increasingly saw as a beacon of freedom south of the Rio Grande, even as the trans-Atlantic market economy and the addition of sugar cultivation transformed their world along the Gulf coast.

Perhaps the most important development that facilitated the transition of the borderlands was the establishment of the cities of Houston and Galveston, which soon served as the entrances to the lowcountry from the outside world. The enslavers in the interior took advantage of the merchants, financiers, and slave traders on Galveston Island and Buffalo Bayou to finance their operations. Access to these markets meant that lowcountry enslavers could expand their cotton production, begin the commercial production of sugar, and realize wild profits in the market economy on the backs of the enslaved whom they trafficked into the lowcountry. Conversely, these two cities grew in population, stature, and wealth commensurate with the profits from cotton, sugar, and enslaved African Americans.

Two brothers from New York, John and August Allen, founded Houston in October 1836. The Allens moved to Texas in 1832 and settled in Nacogdoches, supporting themselves as land speculators. After the Republic of Texas was established in 1836, the two brothers immediately thought to found a city on Galveston Island, or, failing that, on Galveston Bay. Augustus Allen invested some of his money in the new Galveston City Company, but ultimately, he and his brother decided to found a city on Buffalo Bayou, roughly seventeen miles west of the place where the bayou empties into northern Galveston Bay. In August 1836, the Allens purchased half a league of land from the heirs of John Austin at the intersection of White Oak and Buffalo Bayous. On October 18, 1836, they placed an advertisement in the *Telegraph and Texas Register* for the sale of town lots in the city that they diplomatically named for the president of the republic. "The town of Houston," they wrote, "is located at a point on the river which must ever command the trade of the largest and richest portion of Texas. . . . and when the rich lands of this country shall be settled, a great trade will flow into it, making it, beyond all doubt, the great commercial emporium of Texas." The Allens also noted that "tide waters run to this place, and the lowest depth of water is about six feet. Vessels from New Orleans or New York can sail without obstacle to this place, and steamboats of the largest class can run down to Galveston Island in 8 or 10 hours, in all seasons of the year. . . . Galveston harbor being the only one in which vessels drawing a large draft of water can navigate, must necessarily render the Island the great naval and commercial depot of the country."[2]

Despite the claims of the founders of Houston, arrivals to the new city experienced more than a few difficulties reaching the settlement. A few days before Christmas 1836, Francis Lubbock (an early Anglo immigrant who later became governor of Texas) embarked on a steamship from New Orleans bound for Quintana, a small settlement at the mouth of the Brazos River, across from Velasco. Lubbock brought with him large amounts of supplies, intent on founding a mercantile store in the new republic. Instead, he ended up selling much of his stock to the Texas army at Velasco. Within a week of his arrival, the Allen brothers convinced Lubbock to move to Houston and establish his mercantile enterprise there. At the beginning of January 1837, Lubbock loaded what was left of his supplies onto the steamer *Laura* and set out for the new town. The ship reached Harrisburg without problems, but as Lubbock wrote: "No boat had been above this place, and we were three days making the distance to Houston, only six miles by the dirt road, but twelve by the bayou. The slow time was in consequence of the obstacles we were compelled to remove as we progressed." The settlement was so obscured by brush that the crew of the *Laura* initially passed it and proceeded up White Oak Bayou before realizing their mistake. No wharves yet existed, and when Lubbock finally made his way up the muddy bank of the bayou and through the brush, he found a few tents, one of which served as a saloon, at the new town site. Several people had begun erecting houses, and when Lubbock arrived, he also found Benjamin Fort Smith hauling logs from the woods to construct a hotel. Smith sold his plantation, Chenango, to Monroe Edwards in September 1836 and used the money to finance his new venture in Houston. From the very beginning, profits from slavery in the lowcountry financed the construction of Houston, the Bayou City. In April 1837, the Allens also convinced Gail Borden, editor of the *Telegraph and Texas Register*, to move his newspaper from Brazoria to Buffalo Bayou. The newspaper issued its first edition from the new city on May 2, 1837. Despite these inauspicious beginnings, within just a few years Houston had more than 1,500 residents and served as the capital of the Republic of Texas.[3]

As Houston took shape, so did the city of Galveston. Although Galveston began with the land speculator Michael B. Menard, the genesis and growth of the island city are attributed to the partnership of Thomas F. McKinney and

Samuel May Williams. Born in Rhode Island, Samuel May Williams served as Stephen F. Austin's chief lieutenant in organizing his colony, and in 1833 Williams formed a partnership with McKinney as commission merchants at Brazoria. That year, they decided to establish a new settlement, named Quintana, at the mouth of the Brazos, across from Velasco. By 1834, the firm of McKinney & Williams had begun operating at Quintana, making it a mercantile hub for many like Francis Lubbock who were coming in to Texas, as well as for the enslavers in the interior. In 1833, Menard hatched a plot to secure the eastern end of Galveston Island for a city that would become the premier port in Texas. Menard got 4,605 acres on the island, and Thomas McKinney purchased a half interest in the project for $400. In late 1836, McKinney and Menard formed the Galveston City Company. After difficulties regarding claims to the land, Menard finally secured clear title from the Congress of the Republic of Texas, and in April 1838, the directors of the Galveston City Company met with Menard, McKinney, and Williams, leaders of the venture. In May 1838, the company held the first public auction for lots in the new city of Galveston. That same year, McKinney and Williams moved their business from Quintana to Galveston and began building the first wharf in the new city. The Allen brothers also sold McKinney & Williams lots in Houston to establish a branch of their business at the new capital. The partners also owned two steamboats, the *Laura* and the *Yellowstone*, which linked the planters in the interior to the new settlements on the coast and Buffalo Bayou. As the best deepwater port between New Orleans and Vera Cruz, Galveston grew even faster than Houston.[4]

McKinney & Williams served as the major mercantile firm in the low-country, but it faced serious competition from the firm of A. G. & R. Mills. Andrew Mills moved to Texas in 1827 from Kentucky, and in 1831 his younger brother Robert joined him at Brazoria, where they opened a mercantile firm. Both men fought in the Battle of Velasco, and in December 1834, they dissolved the firm of A.G. & R. Mills. Robert Mills formed a partnership with another of his brothers, David Graham Mills. The new firm of Robert Mills & Co. also formed a partnership with Samuel Brigham at Matagorda in 1835, using the schooner *Julius Caesar* to ferry supplies and merchandise between Brazoria and Matagorda. Like McKinney and Williams, the Mills supplied the Texas government during the war with Mexico, and Robert Mills also formed other connections to the planters in Brazoria County. Already known as the Duke of Brazoria, Robert Mills married Elizabeth G. McNeel, daughter of John G. McNeel in a bond ceremony on January 26, 1836, with a bond of $50,000. In 1837, Elizabeth died in childbirth, and Robert Mills never remarried, instead devoting himself to his business.[5]

Unlike Williams and McKinney, Robert and David Mills decided to collateralize their business with plantations and enslaved people. On October 21, 1837, Robert and David Mills purchased Bynum plantation in Brazoria County for $39,000, with $10,000 in cash and the remainder in mortgages. For this price, they acquired 1,000 acres from Wade Bynum, along with his cotton crop, corn crop, livestock, and thirty-six enslaved persons. While Robert Mills ran the mercantile business, David Mills oversaw the operations of the plantation. Eventually, the Mills would come to own three other plantations: Lowwood, Palo Alto, and Caney Place with William Warren in Matagorda County. With this substantial collateral, Robert and David Mills would eventually become the wealthiest men in Texas, but in the early days of the Republic, Robert Mills provided the main competition to Williams and McKinney in their quest to control the cotton and mercantile trade of the lowcountry.[6]

For the enslaved in the lowcountry, the years immediately after independence brought changes to their world as well. The first, most important change came in the form of the hardening of slavery and restrictions of the enslaved. On December 14, 1837, the Congress of the Republic of Texas passed a law-making insurrection, poisoning, rape, murder, burglary, and arson against any free white person capital offenses for enslaved persons. The law also erased due process for any of the said crimes and made it a crime to help any enslaved person leave the republic against the will of their enslaver. Finally, the law provided that "if any slave or free person of color shall use insulting or abusive language to, or threaten any free white person, upon complaint thereof before any justice of the peace, such justice shall cause such negro to be arrested, and upon conviction, the slave or free person of color, shall be punished by stripes not exceeding one hundred nor less than twenty-five." Whereas such ordinances had existed in Texas under Mexican rule, now in a slaveholding republic, the enslaved faced greater peril to life and limb and essentially had no legal protections whatsoever.[7]

Another major change to the world of the enslaved became the distance to Mexico and freedom. Prior to independence, enslaved men and women merely had to escape to the nearest Mexican official or garrison to assert their freedom, but after 1836 Mexico lay hundreds of miles away, exposing them to the danger of regular patrols and the semiarid environment of south Texas. As the lowcountry transitioned to a typical Deep South plantation society, the borderland shifted southward, serving as a buffer between these plantations and Mexico. Many still reached Matamoros, across the Rio Grande, but many others failed to escape or they lived as maroons in south Texas.

Joe, the enslaved man who accompanied William Barrett Travis to the Alamo, chose to celebrate the one-year anniversary of the battle of San Jacinto by escaping toward Mexico on the night of April 21, 1837. Over a month later, John R. Jones, the executor of Travis's estate, placed an advertisement in the *Telegraph and Texas Register*, offering $50 for the return of Joe, who also took two horses with accompanying saddles. By November 1837, Jones had recaptured Joe, but in the spring of 1838, Joe made his escape for good. Unable to reach freedom, he returned to the Travis family in Alabama where he lived out the rest of his life.[8]

The fugitive slave ads placed in Texas newspapers during this time revealed that many of the Africans smuggled into Texas by Monroe Edwards, Benjamin Fort Smith, Sterling McNeel, and James Fannin continually asserted their freedom, sometimes living in the woods as maroons. Leander McNeel described two African men, Arch and Iona, who escaped his plantation and that of his brother Pleasant. Arch, according to McNeel, was "about 25 years of age, a tall slim fellow, very black, some scars on his forehead, also some small scars on each side of his cheek, and a long foot; he [h]as been taken up five or six times, since he ran off from me, and made his escape every time; he has broke irons off twice since he left me; he is a great rascal, and has as much sense as an American negro; he speaks but little English." Apparently, after his recapture, McNeel sold Arch to Leander McNutt, who posted a runaway advertisement for him on September 4, 1839. According to McNutt, Arch "had an iron on one leg when he left me; he is a notorious runaway, and has spent half of his time in the woods since I owned him; he is aiming for the *Mexicans*: he has been caught twice since he runaway, [sic] and made his escape both times, the last time he was taken at the Colorado river."[9]

An African man named "Jimbo," apparently smuggled in by Monroe Edwards in 1836, escaped in 1837 with his wife and another man and lived in the woods for thirteen years before being apprehended in November 1850. During that time, the white residents of south Texas occasionally caught a glimpse of Jimbo, the "Wild Man of the Navidad," along the Navidad River northeast of Victoria. In 1851, Jimbo escaped again after being sold at public auction. The *Texian Advocate* reported that "Jimbo did not like the idea of being confined to the narrow limits of a plantation, or to have his freedom bounded in any way; so he concluded to try his hand at living again in the woods, and left his new master after a few hours acquainttance [sic] with him. Mr. B.[icford] was very kind to Jimbo, but the ungrateful wild man would not reciprocate his master's affection, and is now running at large." Whether or not anyone ever caught the fugitive again remains unknown.[10]

In addition to the growing entrenchment of slavery and the distance to Mexico, the third change in the lives of the enslaved was the introduction of the commercial production of sugar as a cash crop. Texas's cotton production lagged during the war with Mexico, and the entire country only exported 3,335 bales of cotton in the 1835–1836 growing season. With the war over, cotton production boomed, and Texas exported 9,974 bales in 1836–1837. The Panic of 1837, however, took its toll on cotton production, as exports dropped to 3,232 bales in 1837–1838. The weather then devastated the cotton crop in the lowcountry in 1840, with exports of Texas cotton bales that year dropping 15 percent below the average for the 1830s. Storms from the Gulf of Mexico blew or washed cotton bolls off the stalk, and many more bolls mildewed in the constant rain. In the face of this calamity, cotton growers in the lowcountry turned to sugar to save their finances in 1840.[11]

Even though enslavers in the lowcountry did not begin cultivating sugar commercially until 1840, the history of sugar in Texas goes back to the founding of Austin's colony. Although many planters raised small patches of sugar cane, in 1833 Eli Mercer, with his two sons and one enslaved man, began to operate a live oak rolling mill and battery of evaporating kettles on his "Egypt" plantation, on the east side of the Colorado in what would become Wharton County. Mercer managed to produce enough crude sugar of a molasses quality to supply himself and his neighbors. The next year William Stafford erected the first permanent brick sugar mill in Texas on his plantation at Stafford's Point in northern Fort Bend County. The "sugar" Stafford produced, though proving less than the name would suggest, was "as black as tar," according to one eyewitness. In 1836, the Mexican army destroyed Stafford's mill, along with the rest of his plantation, during the Runaway Scrape. After the war and the destruction of the cotton crop, Texas planters turned to the commercial production of sugar to offset any potential losses from their cotton crops. By 1841, one plantation on Caney Creek produced forty-eight hogsheads of sugar, and another on the Colorado produced thirty. Although antebellum sugar production in the lowcountry would not peak until the 1850s, by 1840 the sugar era was well underway. In 1846, James Morgan at New Washington on Galveston Bay reported: "The Sugar making business is going to bring Texas lands into notice if nothing else will. All the South seems to be waking up to this business, and now when an emigrant with 'force' (Negroes) arrives the first Cry is for Sugar lands." Although sugar never developed to any degree outside the lowcountry, it served as the foundation for the most developed plantation society west of Louisiana.[12]

Sugar changed the lives of many enslaved people in the lowcountry for a variety of reasons. Sugar required a great deal more labor than cotton and more intensive, backbreaking, sometimes dangerous labor in the hot fires of the sugar refineries. This need for labor required enslavers to import or force procreation to create many more enslaved people than they would have otherwise needed for cotton alone. Sugar planters were therefore able to amass great fortunes that rivaled those accumulated in southern Louisiana. Slavery and sugar, even more than cotton, produced the economic foundation of the lowcountry, along with many of the unique characteristics that would come to define the region.[13]

Northern capital also helped link the lowcountry to the rest of the Atlantic economy. From his office at 5 Bowling Green in lower Manhattan, Charles Morgan, owner of the first steam packet from New York to Charleston, set his sights on the Republic of Texas. Although New Orleans controlled most of the trade in the western Gulf coast, Louisiana lacked the kind of railroads necessary to reach the new republic Morgan therefore decided to open a steam packet line between the Crescent City and Galveston. In 1837 the *Columbia*, a 131-ton steamboat under the command of John T. Wright, initiated regular service between New Orleans and Galveston, carrying passengers, cargo, and enslaved persons. The *Columbia* arrived in New Orleans on November 25, 1837, and carried out twelve round-trip voyages between late November 1837 and June 1838. On June 8, 1838, Morgan augmented the *Columbia* with the *Cuba*, a 363-ton steamship owned by the firm of Bogart and Hawthorne of New Orleans. Together, these two ships constituted the "New Orleans and Texas line," with weekly service between New Orleans, Galveston, and Velasco. Although the two firms were owned by different companies, they were able to standardize their passenger and freight rates. As trade expanded, in 1839, Morgan placed his ship the *New York* on the Texas run as well.[14]

Travel by steamboat proved much faster and cheaper than other forms of transportation. The *Cuba* could make the trip from Galveston to New Orleans in thirty-six to fifty-four hours, and the *Columbia* could make the trip in thirty-three to forty-eight hours. Cabin passage to Galveston cost $30 per person, and rates for cabin and steerage $15. The rate from New Orleans to Velasco ran as high as $35. The large steamers dared not attempt to cross the sandbar at the mouth of the Brazos, but from Velasco, passengers could charter a smaller steamer like the *Yellowstone* up the river. Mary Austin Holley, Stephen F. Austin's first cousin, described her passage on the *Columbia*: "The Captain a gentleman—always at the head of the table—set out in the best style—silver forks, or what looks like silver—large and small, with ivory knives. White waiters, neat and orderly—French cook . . . & bedding the finest & whitest linen—water closets—& lady-like chamber maid, every thing nice." In 1840, Holley described passage on the *New York* by imagining herself as Cleopatra at sea.[15]

The accommodations enjoyed by the Anglo passengers obscured the fact that the New Orleans and Texas line also trafficked thousands of enslaved African Americans into Texas from New Orleans. On February 14, 1838, a forty-two-year-old enslaved man named Joseph with an enslaver named O. S. Rees boarded the *Columbia* in New Orleans and arrived in Galveston at the latest on February 16. Fifty-five more enslaved persons followed Joseph into captivity in Texas in 1838 alone, forty aboard either the *Columbia* or the *Cuba*, the rest on private schooners. Ships from New Orleans transported twenty-nine enslaved men and women into Texas in 1839 and then ninety in 1840. From there, the traffic only increased. By 1860, US Customs records contained the names of 13,000 enslaved African Americans trafficked into the lowcountry from New Orleans.[16]

In the early Republic period, the British also began to show an interest in Texas cotton and sugar, and in 1838 Texans Thomas McKinney and Samuel May Williams launched a bold plot that would at once secure for themselves a monopoly on the Texas cotton trade and open Texas up to European trade. "Our prospects are however far the most flattering [of] all the merchants in Texas for shipping the present year's crop," McKinney wrote to Williams on July 28, 1838. "[T]he whole Country seem[s] now to look to us as the only source from which the general commercial advantages of Texas are to be developed. The European trade is runing [sic] in the head of every body here and the moment we can have an arrival direct we may confidently claim to commerce . . . a monopoly of our own. There will be a few envious spirits but they will be as harmless as the viper with his teeth Knocked out." By 1838, McKinney & Williams drew heavily on business ties and money, and effectively served as the Texas branch of Henry Williams, the brother of Samuel, in Baltimore. This provided them with enough capital and connections to realize their plan to have the *Ambassador* come to Galveston.[17]

Although McKinney & Williams had Atlantic business connections, it was Robert and David Mills at Brazoria who regularly dominated the cotton trade by serving as factors, advancing the lowcountry planters' loans on their cotton crops for the next year. Robert Mills, ever the consummate capitalist, did not intend to simply cede superiority in the cotton trade to McKinney & Williams without a fight. In January 1839 as the appointed time approached for the landing of the *Ambassador*, Mills did everything in his power to undermine his competitors. S. L. Jones, acting as a purchasing agent for the latter firm, wrote to Williams:

> Mills is doing all he can and it is really amusing to see him pass about and following in my tract endeavoring to persuade the Planters to let him have the Cotton offering to leave all their debts lay over and make advances besides and saying that the story of shipping to Liverpool was all a hoax and that the little money would not last long and in fact anything that suited his purpose but it would not do and [if] Mr. H. H. Williams forwards the means as promised we will throw him such a fall it will be some time before he recovers but you know the hold he has on the Planters . . . the whole of the Brazos Merchants are leagued against us here as they say we want to monopolise [sic] the trade—You can explain the necessity of having the means forwarded immediately to secure the low Country Cotton and get the Planters once in our hands.

Even though one of their steamers ran aground on the sandbar at the mouth of the Brazos on January 31, by February 4 McKinney wrote to Williams that he used a $10,000 line of credit from James Reed & Company in New Orleans to pay the planters for the advances that Mills required them to pay back. He added that "Mills has given up all pretentions to nearly all the cotton but of course requires them to pay him[.] this is all right and of course you will say so too . . . we have now about 1,200 Bales paid for out of which we will fill the English Ship and Send the Ballance [sic] to Baltimore as fast as we can get it to Market . . . we hope to collect 3 or 400 more Bales." The amount that McKinney and Williams had to pay the planters eventually increased another $10,000, and they had to resort to keel boats to transport the cotton over the sandbar in small increments, but by the time the *Ambassador* approached Galveston in late February, they had the cotton ready and waiting. On February 25, when the English ship arrived, the *Columbia* towed it into port at the wharf of McKinney & Williams. Samuel May Williams wrote to Anson Jones, Minister from the Republic of Texas to the United States: "I have the pleasure to announce to you the safe arrival in harbor of the English barque [sic] Ambassador, and some pride in saying that this is the vessel which has sailed from Europe direct to Texas, and without doubt will be the first to convey a cargo from Texas to Great Britain. . . . The Ambassador was towed into port on the 25th of February, by the steam packet Columbia. Gen. Houston, and all the big men of Galveston went out and escorted her in, and made quite a frolic of it." The opening of trade with Great Britain marked a major turning point in the history of the Republic of Texas. From that point forward, the biggest economic influence on the lowcountry became the cotton and sugar markets in Liverpool, New Orleans, Baltimore, and New York, fully initiating the region into the trans-Atlantic market economy.[18]

In addition to their interest in Texas cotton, the British also remained concerned about illegal smuggling operations into the lowcountry. To that end, they sent several fact-finding missions to the Galveston area to explore the feasibility of diplomatically recognizing the new republic and cutting off the illicit trade in human beings. On Sunday, December 29, 1839, Francis Sheridan, a young British diplomat, set sail from Barbados for Texas on one such mission. Sheridan first landed at Velasco and met Thomas McKinney, whom he described as "a gentleman of apparently about 40 years, attired in a frock coat made out of a scarlet blanket with a black edging, & picking his teeth with a Bowie Knife. In this unpretending employment was engaged no less a person than Mr. McKinnie [sic] of the firm of McKinnie & Williams, the Barings of Texas."[19]

From Velasco, Sheridan proceeded to Galveston, which he described as "singularly dreary. It is a low flat sandy Island about 30 miles in length & ranging in breadth from 1 to 2. There is hardly a shrub visible & in short it looks like a piece of prairie that had quarrelled [sic] with the main land & dissolved partnership." One day, after returning from a horse race, Sheridan "repaired to the only interesting spot in Galveston—The Wharf of Mess[ers] McKinnie [sic] & Williams. Here I fell in with a settler who had just landed with a gang of Slaves, one or two assistants, a Driver, several long Kentuckee [sic] rifles & some large dogs."[20]

Even though Sheridan did not comment much on these enslaved men, he expounded at length on slavery in his final report. Speaking of the state of slavery in Texas, he wrote: "The great demand for labor, the immense price it [enslaved persons] fetches, the poverty & covetousness of the proprietors, all militate against the poor nigger, and I fear his leisure moments are few & his lashes frequent. The French islands will contain the human bank on which

Texas will draw, & the wanderings of our cruisers in the suppression of the Slave trade will with advantage & profit be extended to this coast." Sheridan explained that the only way to check the introduction of enslaved Africans and African Americans into Texas would be to diplomatically recognize the Republic of Texas and encourage emigration of British citizens into the country. "The Cotton lands of Texas," he concluded "will yield 3 times as much Cotton as the Carolinas or Georgia to the acre." Speaking of the lowcountry, Sheridan wrote: "the lands on the Coast subject to intermitting fevers will I think always be a Cotton planting Country, connecting also the Sugar Cane. I will here remark that a residence of several years in the last region has convinced me that it is more healthy than Louisiana being entirely free from Swamps & Marshes."[21]

By the time Francis Sherdian departed Galveston in 1840, the Texas low-country had clearly reached a tipping point. For the enslavers, Mexico had become a distant memory, and they turned their attention to attempting to maintain control over the enslaved while reaping wild profits from cotton and, increasingly, sugar by forming economic relationships with the United States as well as Great Britain. For the enslaved, Mexico became a beacon of hope, even while many who freed themselves had to settle for maroon colonies in south Texas. The early years of the Republic of Texas closed the chapter on the lowcountry as a borderland and opened a new chapter in the history of the region—that of a Deep South plantation society.

PART 2

A Deep South Society, 1840–1865

Chapter 4

Gone to Texas in Chains

*Forced Migration into
the Lowcountry*

ON A FROSTY February morning in 1834, Dilue Rose, an eight-year-old girl living at Stafford's Point, looked off to the southeast toward Galveston Bay and spotted a group of men approaching. Dilue's mother screamed that they were "Indians" approaching, and her brother ran to the fields to get her father, Dr. P. W. Rose. When the men reached the house, Mrs. Rose suggested they hide in the woods, but Dr. Rose opined that they were probably victims of a shipwreck. As they approached the Rose house, it became apparent that the group consisted of three white men, and a large gang of Africans. One of the white men introduced himself as Benjamin Fort Smith and explained that he owned a plantation to the south, in Brazoria County, and lost his way returning from landing the Africans at Edwards Point on Galveston Bay. Smith asked Dr. Rose to slaughter some cattle for them to eat, and Rose complied. Dilue remembered that "As soon as the beeves were skinned the negroes acted like dogs, they were so hungry." Smith and the enslaved Africans remained at the Rose farm for 3 or 4 more days, until his nephew Frank Terry arrived to escort them to their plantation. Because Smith had landed the Africans almost naked, Terry also brought clothing for them to wear. Before departing, Smith paraded his captives in front of the locals, and Dilue wrote that "[a]fter they were dressed, he marched them to the house for mother and us little girls to see. He tried to teach them to make a bow. . . . They did not understand a word of English. All the men and boys in the neighborhood came to see the wild Africans."[1]

The scene that Dilue Rose Harris recounted hinted at a small part of the series of forced mass migrations that brought enslaved Africans and African Americans to the Texas lowcountry. The interstate slave trade played a central role in the story of slavery in the United States in the decades before the American Civil War. For millions of African Americans, it amounted to a second middle passage, tearing families asunder and inflicting increased misery on the enslaved. Situated at the southwestern edge of the slaveholding states, Texas played an outsized role in this interstate slave trade, with almost 200,000 enslaved African Americans transported into the Lone Star State in the twenty-five years prior to the Civil War. Although the United States outlawed the African slave trade effective January 1, 1808, smugglers continued to illegally transport Africans, mainly by way of Cuba, into the country. Texas also served as the primary locus of these ventures, with smugglers taking advantage of the rebellion against Mexico to secret their human cargoes to the coast. Although the illicit traffic peaked during the rebellion, it continued periodically until 1860. Within Texas, the plantation society in the Texas lowcountry played a central role in these human tragedies, with the enslaved population growing dramatically through the Civil War. These enslaved people in turn served as the foundation of the lowcountry society. Indeed, by 1865 they constituted seven in every ten residents of the region, producing the cotton and sugar that made the lowcountry one of the primary seats of wealth and power in the "empire state of the south."

Of the multiple ways in which the enslaved entered the lowcountry, the illicit African slave trade remains the most difficult to quantify and document. One fact that is irrefutable, however, is that in the era of Anglo colonization, the African slave trade to Texas began with a young Kentuckian, Monroe Edwards. Born in Danville, Texas, in 1809, Monroe accompanied his father Moses to New Orleans following the Panic of 1819 and began working with a family friend, James Morgan, in his mercantile business. In the late 1820s, following the failed Fredonian Rebellion (the effort of Haden Edwards to form the republic of Fredonia) instigated by Monroe Edwards's uncle, both Moses Edwards and James Morgan immigrated to Texas, Moses settling at Edwards Point on the east side of Galveston Bay and Morgan establishing a mercantile business at Anahuac. Even after Moses's death in 1832, Monroe Edwards worked as a clerk in Morgan's store. In his capacity as a clerk, Monroe befriended Patrick Jack and William Barrett Travis in Anahuac and was arrested along with them during the Anahuac disturbances of 1832.

In the summer of 1832, after his release from the brick kiln in Anahuac, Edwards traveled back to New Orleans while working for Morgan and ran into an old friend, a man named Holcroft, who told Edwards about an opportunity to smuggle enslaved Africans to Brazil. Edwards agreed to join him in this venture and later that summer met Holcroft in Rio de Janeiro. There an enslaver named Signor Saleria paid Holcroft $20,000 to travel to Africa and acquire Africans for his clients, plantation owners in Brazil. Holcroft purchased a new ship, the *Teresa*, and hired Edwards for $5,000. Although a British cutter intercepted them in the Atlantic, they let them pass, and the *Teresa* successfully reached Cape Palmas on the coast of Liberia in August 1832. From Cape Palmas, the enslavers sailed northwest, arriving at Lomboko, the infamous slave-trading station at the mouth of the Gallinas River in what is now Sierra Leone. In five days at Lomboko, Holcroft and Edwards chose 198 enslaved men and women, paying $25 each in muskets, black powder, rum, cutlasses, bar iron, and tobacco. On their voyage back to Brazil, eleven of the enslaved perished, including one young man who committed suicide by jumping overboard into the Atlantic with his arms crossed and a look of "manly sadness" on his face. In Brazil, Holcroft and Edwards sold the remaining 187 captives for an average of $600 each. With the profits from his Lomboko venture in hand, Edwards returned to Texas.[2]

In early 1833, Edwards engaged a new slave-trading partner in Texas, Benjamin Fort Smith, who owned a plantation in Brazoria County. Smith and Edwards sailed to Havana, Cuba, in the spring of 1833 where they purchased a group of enslaved Africans; they landed at Edwards Point on the east side of Galveston Bay in the last days of March. Even though condemned by the Convention of 1833, Smith and Edwards made another trip to Havana, again returning to Edwards Point in early 1834. Smith, as recounted at the beginning of this chapter, became lost on the way back to his Point Pleasant plantation in Brazoria County and stopped at Stafford's Point in February, where Dilue Rose saw the men and women Smith and Edwards had trafficked from Cuba.

These ventures merely emboldened Monroe Edwards, who decided to go into business with Christopher Dart, a merchant he met in Natchez, Mississippi. Edwards convinced Dart that they could purchase enslaved Africans in Cuba, smuggle them into Texas, and realize a huge profit. Edwards got $35,410 from George Knight & Co. of Havana, a subsidiary of the mercantile firm Baring Brothers of London, to finance the enterprise. In December 1835,

Edwards and Dart arrived in Havana with $50,000 in cash and purchased 188 Africans for an average of $357 per person. Edwards finalized the transaction with mortgages, and purchased a "Brass cannon, Gun Powder, Cannon Balls, a Jolly boat, fuel, Peas, Beans, Grain, Bananas [and] Oranges" on credit. The total came to $67,116. On December 17, Edwards started back to Texas aboard the *Shenandoah*. Eighteen Africans died on the voyage from Cuba to Texas, and on February 28, Samuel Fisher, the customs collector at Velasco, observed the *Shenandoah* crossing the sandbar at the mouth of the Brazos. Because Edwards failed to check in with customs, Fisher pursued him and found that the smuggler had already landed his human cargo. That night the commissioner finally located the 170 Africans but had no choice but to release them into Edwards's custody "on his giving bond and security to the amount of their value, to be held subject to the decision of the government." Later, in March, Christopher Dart's schooner *Dart* sailed into Galveston Bay with ninety additional Africans, whom he landed with Ritson Morris at Edward's Point.[3]

During the Runaway Scrape, more than one hundred Africans smuggled in by Edwards became scattered over the Texas countryside, and during this time William Fairfax Gray described two separate encounters with different groups of these enslaved people. Near Galveston Bay on March 25, Gray recounted that a Mr. Earle had

> four young African negroes, two males, two females. They were brought here from the West Indies by a Mr. Monroe Edwards. They are evidently native Africans, for they can speak not a word of English, French or Spanish. They look mild, gentle, docile, and have never been used to labor. They are delicately formed; the females in particular have straight, slender figures, and delicate arms and hands. They have the thick lips and negro features, and although understanding not a word of English, are quick of apprehension; have good ears, and repeat words that are spoken to them with remarkable accuracy. I wrote down the names by which they called some things to which I drew their attention.[4]

On April 10, at the home of an early Anglo colonist, Ritson Morris, on Galveston Bay, Gray again encountered a group of Africans. According to Gray,

> about fifty of those poor wretches are now here, living out of doors, like cattle. They are all young, the oldest not 25, the youngest, perhaps, not more than 10; boys and girls huddled together. They are diminutive, feeble,

spare, squalid, nasty, and beastly in their habits. Very few exhibit traits of intellect. None seem ever to have been accustomed to work. Some of them gave the same names to common things that those I had seen at Edward's did; others gave different names; of course, from different tribes. . . . They are mostly cheerful, sing and dance of nights; wear caps and blankets; will not wear close clothes willingly; some go stark naked. A beef was killed at Morris' home, 100 yards from Edwards', and the Africans wrangled and fought for the garbage like dogs or vultures; they saved all the blood they could get, in gourds, and feed on it. An old American negro stood over the beef with a whip, and lashed them off like so many dogs to prevent their pulling the raw meat to pieces.[5]

These encounters speak to the common sight of the enslaved Africans smuggled into Texas during the tumultuous period of the rebellion against Mexico, but Monroe Edwards, though the most prominent, was not the only Anglo busy smuggling enslaved people into the lowcountry.

James Walker Fannin arrived in Texas in early 1833 intent on engaging in the illicit African slave trade. A twenty-nine-year-old West Point dropout from Georgia, Fannin persuaded Alabama merchant Edward Henrick to write a letter of introduction to Samuel May Williams. "I have given a letter of Introduction to a Col. Fannin," wrote Henrick. "This is one of the persons that was to be engaged in the Negroe [sic] Speculation. [Asa] Hoxey and myself has declined it for the present, and not at least until we heard from you but Fannin Would not wait for that, but is goin[g] on emideately [sic] to Cuba. . . . I believe he is an enterprising man and from what I can learn he is Worth nothing and perhaps as we say wuse [worse] than nothing, and his case is desperate, for he has nothing to loose [sic] and all to gain."[6]

As early as May 23, 1833, Fannin wrote a letter to Pedro Fernandez of Mariategui, Knight & Company (later George Knight & Co.) in Havana, asking about the price and terms of purchasing a cargo of enslaved persons for Texas. After a year of planning, Fannin arrived in Cuba with his business partner, Harvey Kendrick, preparing to send sixteen enslaved persons to Texas aboard the US schooner *Crawford*, which they purchased on credit in New Orleans for $3,500 from some of Fannin's investors, Samuel Thompson and A. B. Henshaw. On May 26, 1834, Fannin dispatched the *Crawford* from Havana to Texas for $800 and the sixteen enslaved persons. Despite the profitable nature of this smuggling, Fannin did not receive enough profit from this initial voyage to satisfy his debt for purchasing the *Crawford*. On August

22, 1834, from Mobile, Fannin wrote to Thompson, requesting more time to pay his debt and informing him that Edward Henrick of Mobile would join Fannin as a partner in his next slaving venture to Cuba.[7]

In April 1835, Fannin's creditors had him arrested in New Orleans for an unpaid debt of $3,000, but one of his partners, Michael J. Kenan of Alabama, who had already advanced Fannin $1,500 earlier in the month, posted a bond of another $1,500 to secure his release. The month after his arrest, Fannin again arrived in Havana, this time with enough credit to purchase 152 enslaved Africans. Fannin gave Mariategui Knight & Company a note for $4,258, endorsed by John W. Foster, and a letter of credit from St. John & Leavens of Mobile for $5,000 guaranteed by Michael J. Kenan. In addition to these sources of funds, it appears that Fannin's other partners, John Duncan, Abram Sheppard, and William Kingston, all of Matagorda County, each put up over $9,000 to purchase the 152 Africans.[8]

In Texas, Fannin had two different bases of operation. In several letters, he refers to being situated on Caney Creek in eastern Matagorda County, but by 1835 he had also formed a partnership with Joseph Mims, a member of Stephen F. Austin's Old Three Hundred. An enslaver himself, Mims received a league of land along the San Bernard River in Brazoria County in 1824, where he established a cotton plantation, along with a ferry across the San Bernard River. Fannin may have smuggled his initial cargo up the Brazos River or Caney Creek, but he landed his second cargo at a spot on the west bank of the San Bernard River, less than a mile south of the Mims plantation. There, the trunk of a large live oak lay parallel with the bank, forming a natural wharf, a place the local residents referred to as "African Landing." Once at the landing, the Africans, completely naked and starving, struggled up the muddy riverbank to waiting campfires, where they received clothes for the first time before being purchased, or marched in chains to the Mims plantation. When Fannin reached African Landing with his human cargo, his three investors, Duncan, Sheppard, and Kingston, all gathered, and the four men split the 152 captives into roughly four equal lots of 38 each.[9]

By August 1835, Fannin had begun selling his human cargo to the local planters on credit, before joining the rebellion against Mexico. The next month he wrote another letter to Thompson, begging more time to pay his debts. "I have since made a good trip," Fannin wrote to his creditor, "having brought for myself and others 152 negroes in May last [1835], but can not realize any cash from them until March or April, when you shall be fully paid every cent I owe you." Fannin never did satisfy his debts, and after his death at Goliad in March 1836, his estate included tens of thousands of dollars in debts and thirty-nine enslaved Africans.[10]

The illegal importation of enslaved Africans in Texas slowed following the establishment of the Republic of Texas, but over the next twenty-five years, the practice continued sporadically. Although records are sparse, it appears that nine different vessels landed on the Texas coast with cargoes of Africans between 1837 and 1860. Many of these vessels disembarked their cargo in the lowcountry, but the illicit traffic extended up the coast as far as the Sabine River. It appears that as many as 1,800 Africans might have entered Texas between 1817 and 1836, and as many as 11,500 between 1837 and 1860, for a total of over 13,000. Although most of the plantations in the lowcountry evidenced signs of enslaved Africans in different ways, it remains unclear how many Africans remained in the lowcountry, or other parts of Texas, and how many were transported to other parts of the South.[11]

The stories of people like Ned and Julia Thompson spoke to the presence of Africans in the lowcountry long into the twentieth century. In 1913, J. P. Underwood, a resident of East Columbia, interviewed Ned Thompson, who lived near West Columbia. Born in West Africa, Thompson became a victim of the slave trade when he was captured in battle by a rival tribe and sold to slave traders. He recounted to Underwood his voyage first to Cuba and then to the San Bernard River in 1840. "He remembers the customs and habits of the wild people of his native land," wrote Underwood. "Speaks the language or dialect of his people fluently. He is an interesting man, dignified, polite, well preserved and happy." When freedom came, Thompson married Julia Ann Jackson in 1868, and the couple had twelve children. Although Julia reported her birthplace as Texas, both of her parents also originated in Africa.[12]

While the African slave trade included hundreds of people forced into slavery in the lowcountry, the interstate slave trade introduced thousands in the years before the Civil War. In 1837, at the close of the conflict with Mexico, about 5,000 enslaved persons lived in Texas; roughly 1,250, or 25 percent, of whom were in the lowcountry. By 1840, the statewide number of those enslaved had risen to an estimated 14,744, while the number held in the lowcountry had increased to 3,409. By the time of annexation to the United States in December 1845, the enslaved population had increased to 27,555, while the total number in the lowcountry had increased to 5,537. At the

Table 4.1. Increase in Enslaved Population of the Texas Lowcountry, 1837–1864*

	1837	1840	Increase (I)	1845	I	1850	I	1855	I	1860	I	1864	I
Lowcountry	1,250 (est.)	3,409 (est.)	273%	5,537 (est.)	162%	7,511	136%	10,512 (est.)	140%	14,087	134%	17,053 (est.)	121%
State total	5,000 (est.)	14,744 (est.)	295%	27,555 (est.)	187%	58,161	211%	123,383 (est.)	212%	182,566	148%	240,098 (est.)	131%
Lowcountry as a percentage of state total	25%	23%		17%		13%		8.5%		7.7%		6.3%	

* See note 14.

time of the first US census of Texas in 1850, the number of enslaved persons statewide had increased to 58,161, while the number in the lowcountry had reached 7,511. In 1855, records indicated that enslaved African Americans in Texas numbered 123,383, while the counties of the lowcountry showed 10,512. The 1860 Census recorded that 182,566 enslaved African Americans resided in Texas, 14,087 of whom were in the lowcountry. By 1864, the last year for which records are available, an estimated 240,098 enslaved persons lived in Texas and 17,053 lived in the lowcountry.[13]

These numbers indicate several facts about the enslaved in the lowcountry, beginning with birth rates and infant mortality. The 1850 Census first recorded the mortality rates for the state of Texas. While Texas reported 1,429 births among the enslaved population that year compared to 877 deaths, the Texas lowcountry had 197 deaths compared to just 151 births. This means that, assuming all the infants born that year survived, the enslaved population of Texas increased by 2.45 percent, while the population of the lowcountry decreased by 0.62 percent. If 1850 proved a typical year, that would mean that there was a natural decrease of at least 6.2 percent in the enslaved population of the lowcountry in the 1850s. Brazoria County alone reported 110 deaths among the enslaved compared to just 54 births. Only in Fort Bend County did births outnumber deaths that year. Although the number of enslaved in the lowcountry accounted for 13 percent of all the enslaved in Texas in 1850, they only accounted for 10.5 percent of all births, but an astounding 22 percent of all deaths that year.[14]

In 1860, at the national level, for every 1,000 enslaved women aged fifteen–forty-nine (childbearing years), there were 1,320 children aged zero–nine. Texas was counted as an "importing" state, that is, a region that imported enslaved people in large numbers rather than "exporting" them as did the states of the Upper South. In "importing" states, the ratio of women of child-bearing years and children was substantially lower: there were at 1,104 children for every 1,000 women, as enslavers in those areas imported large numbers of "prime-age" men and women for difficult manual labor. At the low end of the spectrum, the notoriously deadly sugar-producing parishes of Louisiana had only 922 children for every 1,000 women. Texas, instead of mirroring other importing states, reflected the national average; for every 1,000 women of childbearing years, there were 1,330 children. By contrast, in the Texas lowcountry, for every 1,000 women of childbearing years, there were only 1,000 children. This rate was 10.4 percent lower than importing states, 7.8 percent higher than the Louisiana sugar-growing region, but an astonishing

Table 4.2. Rate of Survival and Increase of Prime-Age Enslaved Persons, 1850–1860*

1850	Lowcountry	Lowcountry %	Texas	Texas %	1860	Lowcountry	Lowcountry %	Texas	Texas %	Lowcountry "Survival Rates"	Texas "Survival Rates"
Men 5–39	2,752	36.6	20,339	34.9	Men 15–49	3,958	28	44,343	24	144%	218%
Men 40+	561	7.47	3,179	5.46	Men 50+	556	3.9	4,605	2.52	–0.89%	145%
Women 5–39	2,579	34	21,169	36	Women 15–49	3,599	25.5	44,627	24.4	139%	211%
Women 40+	497	6.6	3,188	5.67	Women 50+	445	3.16	4,744	2.59	–10.4%	148%

*1850 and 1860 US Censuses; "Survival Rate" indicate the rate at which an enslaved person living in 1850 could be expected to live to 1860. A 100%+ survival rate indicates an "importing" area. See Tadman, *Speculators and Slaves*, 43–44.

33 percent lower than the rest of Texas. As was the case in 1850, this indicates a low birth rate and a high infant mortality rate, and shows that most, if not all, of the increase in the enslaved population came from importation through the interstate slave trade.[15]

The population numbers indicate that most enslaved persons imported into the lowcountry consisted of prime-age men and women. The enslaved population of the lowcountry increased by 153 percent in the 1850s, but state-wide that number was double, at 314 percent. This means that the enslaved of the lowcountry increased at a rate half that of Texas as a whole. However, proportionally, the number of prime-age men and women increased in the lowcountry at a rate 18 percent higher than the rest of the state. This trend explains why the mean age of the enslaved of the lowcountry was 24.5, with a median of 22. In addition, the average increase of enslaved persons over forty years of age in the lowcountry showed a net decrease during the decade, while the state experienced a gain in the same population of just under 150 percent. These numbers indicate a higher mortality rate in this area than elsewhere in Texas, as well as a lack of nuclear family movement into the area.[16]

The sex ratio of enslaved persons in the lowcountry also demonstrated the selective nature of the population. In 1860, prime-age men composed 54 percent of all males in the lowcountry but just 48 percent statewide, while prime-age women in the lowcountry consisted of 53 percent of the population but only 49 percent statewide. Finally, the enslaved men of the lowcountry outnumbered women 52 percent to 48 percent. These numbers fit with the other indicators that the demographics of the lowcountry closely resembled that of the Louisiana sugar parishes. With very little natural increase, it appears that at least 8.3 percent of all enslaved persons destined for Texas between 1840 and 1860, almost one in ten, ended up in the lowcountry.[17]

The selective nature of the enslaved population of the lowcountry also fits with the US Customs records of enslaved African Americans imported into Texas by ship to Galveston and other points along the coast. Of the 13,430 people carried into Texas by water between 1838 and 1860, all but 95 of them (99.7 percent) came through New Orleans. These individuals accounted for 10.5 percent of all enslaved persons brought to Texas in the two decades before the Civil War, and their demographics closely resemble those of the lowcountry. The years 1838–1845 saw only 598 enslaved persons taken by boat to Texas, but statehood in late 1845 caused a huge uptick in intercoastal trade. In the four years between 1846 and 1850, enslavers carried 3,751 souls, 28 percent of the total, to the Texas coast, and the 5 years after that saw another

5,498 "importations." Finally, the last five years of records show another 3,488 people forced into slavery along the coast. Men outnumbered women 51 percent to 49 percent, and prime-age men and women (ages fifteen–forty-five) accounted for 58 percent of all those imported. Children and adolescents ages zero–fourteen accounted for another 38 percent, while those forty-six years of age and older constituted only 4 percent of the total. It seems reasonable to conclude, based on the selective nature of those imported through New Orleans, that the vast majority of the enslaved in the lowcountry after 1845 came from this source.[18]

The enslaved Africans and African Americans taken to the lowcountry came in one of three ways; either enslavers themselves traveled to purchase them in person; they sent agents to select and purchase them; or slave traders shipped them to the markets in Galveston and Houston. Elizabeth Ramsey fell into the first category. In 1841, Albert C. Horton traveled from his Sycamore Grove plantation in what would become Wharton County to Mobile, Alabama, to purchase enslaved African Americans. On the auction block, adjacent to the Mobile River, he purchased twenty-eight-year-old Elizabeth Ramsey and her infant son. Elizabeth possessed such light skin that she could almost pass for white, and her previous enslavers had used her primarily for sexual exploitation. Louisa, Elizabeth's thirteen-year-old daughter, found herself on the auction block after her mother, and although Horton attempted to purchase her as well, other enslavers outbid him, even as they inspected the child for signs of venereal disease. Instead, a man from New Orleans purchased Louisa, where she became a victim of his sexual whims for the next two decades. Horton departed Mobile with Elizabeth, her son, and several other men, and carried them back to Sycamore Grove.[19]

In July 1860, Albert Horton again departed his home, this time for Charleston, South Carolina, where he purchased fifty-eight enslaved African Americans from the estate of Mrs. Sarah Brown for the sum of $46,400. Horton paid her son, Josiah Brown, $13,700 in cash, with the rest in mortgages due on July 1, 1861, January 1, 1862, and July 25, 1862. Horton departed for Sycamore Grove later in the month with the fifty-eight individuals, only to default on his debt after emancipation in 1865.[20]

Among those who sent agents abroad to purchase enslaved African Americans, Sallie McNeill, the granddaughter of Brazoria County plantation owner Levi Jordan, wrote that her grandfather entrusted a John Evans with $10,000 in January 1859 to "purchase negroes." Evans returned in September 1860, with a dozen enslaved people. "Grandpa will take ten or eleven," wrote Sallie, "one, half-indian."[21]

If enslavers did not wish to travel to New Orleans, Mobile, Charleston, or elsewhere, or send agents to the east, no fewer than twenty-three slave dealers, auctioneers, and commission merchants kept large numbers of men, women, and children on hand for sale in Houston and Galveston. For more than a decade, John S. Sydnor, former mayor of Galveston, reputedly maintained the largest slave market west of the Mississippi on the Strand in Galveston between 22nd and 23rd Streets. Every Tuesday and Thursday at 10 a.m. he held auctions, where his booming voice called out the bids on the human beings he kept constantly on hand. In December 1838, two men named Hedenberg and Vedder, presenting themselves as auctioneers and commission merchants, advertised a 3,000-acre plantation at private sale in Houston complete with four enslaved men and women. The next year G. Everett, auctioneer and general agent, offered Houstonians the "Houston Tattersals and Auction Yard" for the sale of horses, mules, carriages, and enslaved African Americans. Immediately after annexation, H. J. Manning and S. A. Hemmett became partners in the auction and commission business in Houston. In 1847, two more men, White and Shattuck, took the "Store in Long Row next to Riordan's" to engage in the auction and commission business. By 1848, Frederick Scranton also began advertising his commission business in Long Row. Scranton's storefront was located at the "sign of the 'Old Texian.'" He offered to conduct business in Houston, Galveston, or New Orleans, and charged a 2.5 percent commission for buying and selling enslaved persons. J. Morris, on Main Street in Houston, and H. S. and L. G. Bachelder on Congress Street also advertised for the sale of real estate and African Americans. In 1849, Shaben and Brother opened their auction business in Houston, holding auctions every day, and sales by candlelight every night. For more than a decade, Henry Sampson also operated a sales and commission business in the Bayou City. By the 1850s, other merchants, such as J. Castanie, A. R. Ruthven, J. W. Wynne and R. B. Armfeld, Thomas S. Gresham, R. A. Lyton, and R. Riordan, all advertised their services in Houston with regard to buying and selling human beings. Ruthven was an Englishman and licensed auctioneer; in 1853 Gresham advertised for the sale of fifty enslaved African Americans, ten to twenty-five years old, from Virginia and Maryland; Layton advertised for the sale of fifty "young, likely Negroes" on Market Square, and R. Riordan maintained his "slave depot" near the offices of the *Telegraph and Texas Register*.[22]

In Galveston, in addition to Sydnor's store on the Strand, several other merchants also advertised their services in buying and selling the enslaved. A. F. James, who established his business in 1842, Ira M. Freeman on Tremont Street, George H. Trabue on the Strand, David Ayers, Webb and Company, J. O. and H. M. Truehart, auctioneers, and C. L. McCarty "at the sign of the Red Flag on Market Street" stand out as such merchants. McCarty, at his "Galveston slave mart," and the Trueharts, like Sydnor, kept African Americans "constantly" on hand for sale on commission. Finally, the firm of McMurry and Winstead, in the Leonard Building, behind the Tremont Hotel, advertised thirty young African Americans from North Carolina and Virginia for sale in 1860.[23]

Over the course of more than two decades, enslaved African Americans and Africans poured into the Texas lowcountry through various means: the illicit African slave trade by way of Cuba, the interstate slave trade from New Orleans, and the interstate slave trade overland. These forced migrations populated the lowcountry with more than 70 percent of the people who lived there before the Civil War and gave the region much of its unique character. Once they arrived, these people, who arrived in chains, lived on one of roughly 200 plantations, small farms, or towns, spread out over a 1,500-square-mile area divided up into distinct neighborhoods, and carved out communities for themselves in the face of an unforgiving environment of cotton, sugar, hard labor, disease, and death.

Chapter 5

Neighboring Plantations

The White Society and Geography of the Texas Lowcountry

ON WEDNESDAY, December 27, 1848, Rutherford B. Hayes, at that time a recent graduate of Harvard Law School with a law practice at Lower Sandusky Ohio, left Galveston on a steamer for the mouth of the Brazos River on his way to Peach Point to visit his college classmate and friend, Guy M. Bryan. "Wild prairie," he observed upon entering the mouth of the Brazos, "low grassy banks, chocolate-colored water, cattle, and buzzards, the striking features of the scenery of this part of the river." He reached Aycock's Landing after dark and could not observe the landscape until the next day. The home is delightfully situated," he wrote of the plantation, "in the edge of the timber, looking out upon a plain on the south extending five or eight miles to the Gulf. A large and beautiful flower-garden in front, trimmed and cultivated under the guardian eye of Mrs. Perry. . . . Within two miles there are perhaps four families, the nearest a mile off." Hayes's description of the Perry plantation and the Gulf Prairie neighborhood could have substituted for that of most of white society in the Texas lowcountry in the late 1840s. The demographics, wealth distribution, and geography of the plantation neighborhoods, and finally the design of the plantations together made up the framework that enslaved African Americans had to navigate in the years before the Civil War.[1]

The demographics and wealth distribution of the white families who inhabited the Texas lowcountry are instructive in understanding the structure of white society in the region. These statistics make it clear that the planters, along with the rest of the white families who counted themselves as enslavers, dominated almost every aspect of this society in the antebellum Texas low-country. In 1850, 3,726 whites, in 784 families, called the lowcountry home. They constituted around 2.5 percent of the white population of Texas but included 5.4 percent of all enslavers. Fifty-seven percent of white families in the Texas lowcountry were enslavers compared to 27 percent statewide. White society consisted of four groups; those at the bottom included nonenslavers, a minority of the population at 43 percent, and enslavers who possessed fewer than five enslaved persons, who constituted 18 percent of white families. In the middle was a third group, which consisted of enslavers who controlled anywhere from five to nineteen enslaved African Americans, and finally, at the top stood the planters, who possessed twenty or more enslaved persons. The last two groups, although they only made up 37 percent of white families, controlled 95 percent of all enslaved persons, with the planters alone possessing 70 percent. These numbers stood in sharp contrast to statewide numbers, where only 2 percent of white families counted themselves as planters. The decade of the 1850s only accelerated these patterns.[2]

The wealth distribution in the region also revealed the highly stratified nature of wealth holding among the white population and the dominance of the planter class. The 1860 tax rolls for Brazoria County showed that 90 percent of the wealth in the county was tied up in land, enslaved African Americans, or town lots. Land and enslaved African Americans each accounted for 43.6 percent of the total, and town lots 2.8 percent. Assorted horses and livestock accounted for 10 percent of the county's wealth. The planters possessed 75 percent of the total property, including 73 percent of the land, and 80 percent of enslaved African Americans. The middle class of enslavers owned 15 percent of the wealth in the county, and the smallest class of enslavers owned 5 percent of the total property. Among the 42 percent of the white population who were not counted as enslavers in Brazoria County, 30 percent owned some land or town lots, and 12 percent possessed only personal property. The 30 percent of white families who owned some land accounted for more than 4 percent of the wealth in the county, while the bottom 12 percent of white families owned only a few scattered horses and livestock, valued at less than 1 percent of all property. The poor white population of the lowcountry served the larger enslavers and the planter class. Most of these men worked as overseers, clerks, teachers, carpenters, blacksmiths, and slave catchers, all revolving around the plantations and the plantation system.[3]

Enslavers and enslaved alike viewed neighborhoods as the basic community unit, and the enslaved simply defined neighborhoods as plantations

Table 5.1. Structure of Enslaving by White Families in the Texas Lowcountry, 1850

	Non-enslavers	Enslavers with 1–4	Number Enslaved	Enslavers with 5–19	Number Enslaved	Planters	Number Enslaved
Texas lowcountry	43%	18%	5%	26%	25%	13%	70%
State totals	73%	15%	15%	10%	49%	2%	36%

Table 5.2. Structure of Enslaving by White Families in the Texas Lowcountry, 1860

	Non-Enslavers	Enslavers with 1–4	Number Enslaved	Enslavers with 5–19	Number Enslaved	Planters	Number Enslaved
Texas lowcountry	38%	20%	4%	25%	24%	17%	72%
State totals	72%	15%	12%	11%	43%	2%	45%

Table 5.3 Wealth Distribution among White Families of Brazoria County, 1860

	White Families	Land	Town Lots	Value of Enslaved African Americans	Total Wealth
Planters	17%	73%	23%	80%	75%
Enslavers with 5–19	18%	15%	13%	16%	15%
Enslavers with 1–4	23%	4%	50%	4%	5%
Nonenslavers with Real Property	30%	8%	14%	0%	>4%
Nonenslavers without Real Property	12%	0%	0%	0%	<1%

that shared boundaries. Geography defined the lives of the enslaved and often formed the basis for establishing freedmen's communities after emancipation. For these reasons a description of the geography, plantations, and neighborhoods they formed are necessary to an understanding of Texas lowcountry society. From the plantations that lined both banks of Caney Creek in Matagorda County, the boundaries of the lowcountry extended twenty-five miles northeast up the coast to the mouth of Oyster Creek in Brazoria County. From the coast inland, primarily along the banks of various rivers and creeks, the plantations that formed the region extended roughly sixty miles inland, to the neighborhood of Egypt on the Colorado in Wharton County, and the Pittsville neighborhood in Fort Bend County. By 1860, almost 200 separate plantations dotted the countryside, with the enslaved in the region producing nearly all the sugar and 15 percent of the cotton grown in Texas.[4]

The geography of the plantation neighborhoods in the lowcountry began with the Gulf Prairie neighborhood of Brazoria County, the neighborhood closest to the Gulf of Mexico with some of the oldest plantations in the lowcountry. Located on the west side of the Brazos, the Gulf Prairie extended roughly 9 miles from the heavy timber around the town of Brazoria down to the Gulf of Mexico. Enslavers founded nine plantations in this area, including Peach Point, the home of James and Emily (Austin) Perry, and, during his lifetime, Stephen F. Austin.

Much of the architecture and layout of Peach Point typified the homes constructed on these Gulf Prairie plantations. The Perrys located their house at Peach Point on a slight ridge 2½ miles west of the Brazos, and just on the northern edge of Gulf Prairie. The house, which had been constructed facing south to take advantage of the breezes from the Gulf, consisted of a simple one-story, twelve-room farmhouse with wooden pillars supporting a large covered porch in the front of the house. Initially constructed with raw logs, in the early 1850s the Perrys replaced the logs with milled lumber. Even by the standards of many of the other plantation houses on the Gulf Prairie, the big house at Peach Point had an unassuming appearance. Despite the rather modest appearance of the house, Emily Perry planted and maintained an impressive series of flower gardens in the front of the house.

The slave cabins at Peach Point resembled those at nearby Durazno plantation, the home of William Joel Bryan, Emily Perry's son from a prior marriage. These cabins, typically constructed of wooden planks framed around posts made of oak or bois de arc driven into the ground at the four corners of the cabin, also had brick chimneys and fireplaces, taken from bricks handmade by the enslaved. These cabins had wooden floors that were typically at least twelve inches off the ground. Although the numbers of cabins differed by plantation, on the Gulf Prairie each cabin measured roughly twenty by twenty feet, with four to five enslaved persons living in each cabin. By the middle of the 1840s, Stephen Perry ordered his enslaved to begin to cultivate sugar instead of cotton, and in the early 1850s, they constructed a sugar mill on the plantation made of brick.[5]

The architecture of the other plantations on the Gulf Prairie mostly resembled that at Peach Point, except for the three McNeel plantations, which presented a much more imposing appearance. The McNeel clan, headed by John McNeel, arrived as one of Austin's Original Three Hundred in 1825 and established a plantation on the league of land on the San Bernard River, the western edge of Gulf Prairie, granted to him by Austin. The *empresario* also granted leagues of land to four of John McNeel's sons: Pleasant, Sterling, J. Greenville, and Leander. In 1831, a visitor to Texas described the John McNeel residence as a "good log house, just on the verge of a fine grove, partly shaded by China trees, newly planted."

John McNeel had begun with merely a log cabin and built just one plantation. After his death from cholera in 1833, his sons established three plantations that far exceeded their father's plantation in elegance. J. Greenville McNeel designed the first of the large mansions at his Ellerslie plantation. When completed around 1850, the two-story brick mansion constituted one of the finest residences in antebellum Texas. Constructed of brick and containing twenty-two rooms, the mansion faced south to catch the breezes from the Gulf. The stairs, banisters, and furniture consisted of mahogany or heavy walnut. The fireplaces had marble hearths and mantels, and from the cupola, one could see far beyond the San Bernard to the Gulf of Mexico. The bottom floor contained a library, dining room, parlor, three bedrooms, a kitchen, and two pantries. Double doors opened onto the south and west galleries, which ran the length of the house, supported by brick columns. A curving driveway also approached the house from the two nearby roads. In addition to the big house, Ellerslie also had a sugar mill, hospital, blacksmith's shop, slave cabins, and an overseer's house, all constructed of bricks made on the grounds. The overseer's house and slave cabins all had two rooms, with a double fireplace, each large enough to house one family. The sugar house also contained a double set of kettles. Two roads passed several hundred feet east and south of the mansion, and at both roads, large oak posts carved with a heart, spade, club, and diamond flanked the gates to the property.[6]

West of Ellerslie, Leander H. McNeel established his Pleasant Grove plantation, with its western boundary on the San Bernard. The house at Pleasant Grove resembled Ellerslie but on a smaller scale. It also had marble mantles and hearths, and all buildings, including the slave cabins, were made of brick. According to an early observer, Pleasant Grove was also "elegantly furnished." Apparently because of the Civil War, Leander McNeel never completed the construction of the big house at Pleasant Grove. Finally, the Magnolia plantation of Leander D. McNeel, also a sugar plantation, did not contain the refinements of the houses of his brothers, but served the same purposes.[7]

On the east side of the Brazos, across from the Gulf Prairie neighborhood, extending east to Oyster Creek, stood the Jackson-Wharton neighborhood with six cotton and sugar plantations. Two of the plantations, Retrieve and Lake Jackson, belonged to Abner Jackson, and a third, Eagle Island, belonged to John A. Wharton. The other three plantations belonged to John H. Herndon (Evergreen), Patrick C. Jack, and Moses Austin Bryan.

Although Wharton established Eagle Island at an earlier date, the two Jackson properties stood at the heart of the neighborhood. Lake Jackson, the name of the lake on the banks of which the enslaved built the plantation, is an old oxbow lake, created at some time in the distant past when Oyster Creek changed course. Abner Jackson located his plantation at the southeastern bank of the lake. In the mid-1840s, Jackson had the enslaved on the plantation begin construction of the mansion. Made of bricks hand molded and fired in a brick kiln on the plantation and stuccoed with cement "fully an inch thick," the mansion consisted of two stories with twelve rooms in the shape on an "I," facing south. The main gallery was 1,160 square feet in area, with fireplaces at both ends. The back end of the house measured 1,400 square feet, with enormous porches on the east and west sides, each supported by two brick pillars. Fronting on the south side of the house, off the main gallery, was a 420-square-foot front porch with rounded edges and steps, supported by four large brick columns. The wooden floors of the house stood 3 feet off the ground. Brick walks lined the orchards and gardens that surrounded the house, in which the enslaved cultivated peaches, pears, plums, grapes, and strawberries. Abner Jackson even had the enslaved construct an artificial island in the middle of the lake for parties. The plantation contained a sugar mill, which was also made of brick, 250 yards northeast of the main house, and an overseer's house of brick some 250 yards east of the sugar mill, on the banks of Oyster Creek. Jackson also had the enslaved construct their own cabins of brick, like those at Ellerslie.[8]

Even though Lake Jackson may have become the wealthiest plantation in the Jackson-Wharton neighborhood, it could not claim distinction as the oldest. That title belonged to the Eagle Island plantation of William H. Wharton, a little more than three and a half miles southeast of Lake Jackson. Wharton established the plantation, named after nearby Eagle Lake, in 1827. The initial house, constructed by the enslaved that Wharton brought with him from Tennessee, was a simple log house with a dirt floor. In the 1830s, Wharton directed the construction of a wood frame house, one and a half stories tall, with brick fireplaces and chimneys. William Wharton sent to Europe for a landscape gardener to direct the beautification of the grounds and the small Eagle Lake. The plantation also had a sugar mill with a double set of kettles, overseer's house, and slave quarters, all constructed of brick. William Wharton had the machinery for the sugar mill made in Philadelphia with a duplicate set of equipment in case of a breakdown. Mrs. Wharton became famous for entertaining guests, and Wharton detailed one enslaved man to supply game for the family dinner table.[9]

Northwest of the Peach Point and the Gulf Prairie neighborhood, a cluster of five plantations on the west bank of the San Bernard River made up a third neighborhood in Brazoria County. Unlike Gulf Prairie, four of the white families in this San Bernard neighborhood possessed wood frame houses, but the slave cabins and sugar mills consisted of handmade brick, like the others in the county. The Christopher Bell plantation alone possessed a brick residence for the white family. The two most prominent plantations in this neighborhood became the Fannin-Mims plantation and the Levi Jordan plantation.[10]

The Mims plantation, owned in part by James Fannin prior to his death at Goliad in 1836, became the destination for most of the Africans smuggled into Brazoria County. African Landing, on the west bank of the San Bernard, stood less than two miles south of the plantation. After Fannin's death, Joseph Mims inherited Fannin's property and debts. In 1844, Mims passed away, leaving the plantation to his widow, Sarah, who ran the operation until after the Civil War. The residence of the Mims family faced south and possessed 2,400 square feet, a high-gabled roof, and a long galley running along the south side of the house.[11]

Three and a half miles southwest of the Mims house, Levi Jordan established a cotton and sugar plantation in 1848. The enslaved at the Jordan plantation built the plantation house from boards of long leaf pine brought from Florida. They also handmade the studs and sills of the house from oak, and bricks were used to construct the fireplaces and chimneys of the two-story mansion, as well as the slave quarters and sugar mill. The slave cabins sat 450 feet north of the main house and consisted of eight brick buildings, divided into four groups of two each, facing each other. Each brick building, measuring sixty feet long and twenty feet across, was subdivided into three or four cabins each, with individual fireplaces in each cabin. At one time, each building shared a common "hallway" and may also have shared a common roof. Smaller wood structures close to the Jordan residence housed the overseer and enslaved persons who worked in the big house.[12]

North of the San Bernard neighborhood, enslavers led by John Sweeney established a neighborhood on Chance's Prairie consisting of nine slave labor camps between Linneville Bayou and the San Bernard. North of the Jordan place, Thomas Winston maintained a plantation on the John Cummings League, and north of Winston John McGrew and Thomas Sweeney established labor camps on the Imla Keep League. Northwest of Thomas Sweeney, on the David McCormick League, James and Sarah Black maintained a sugar and cotton plantation and operated Black's Ferry over the San Bernard. West of the Black plantation, George Armstrong and John Sweeney operated large labor camps along Little Linneville Bayou and the center of the neighborhood. At the northern end of the neighborhood, Alexander T. Morris owned a plantation on the Zeno Phillips League, and Elias Stephens operated a labor camp called Cedar Grove on the McNeel League. Finally, Joseph Dance and his brothers owned a plantation called Cedar Brake on the McNeel League near the Cedar Grove plantation.[13]

The fifth neighborhood in the county was located near West Columbia, with seven plantations on the west side of the Brazos, from the Josiah Bell plantation north to Orozimbo, the plantations of Dr. James Phelps. The two best-developed plantations in the West Columbia neighborhood were the Patton and Osceola plantations, owned by Columbus Patton and James G. Hill throughout most of the antebellum period. Although Martin Varner established the plantation in 1824, it was Columbus Patton who purchased 13,500 acres from him in 1834. Patton then had the enslaved on the plantation construct a two-story brick house, facing northeast, on the west bank of Varner's Creek, a small tributary of the Brazos with steep banks. Completed by the 1850s, the house stood as one of the sturdiest brick houses in the county. The enslaved also constructed the sugar mill, with a double set of kettles, and slave cabins of brick made from the mud of the creek. The sugar mill stood 125 yards northeast of the house, across Varner's Creek, and some of the slave cabins were 120 yards north of the sugar mill.[14]

Osceola, the plantation built by William G. Hill after 1836, stood on the land originally owned by his wife, Eliza, the widow of J. E. B. Austin, brother of Stephen F. Austin, on the west side of the Brazos. Before the Civil War and his death in 1860, Hill operated Osceola as a cotton plantation. Osceola became the only Brazoria County plantation to begin growing sugar after the Civil War.[15]

East of the Brazos, across the river from East Columbia, a plantation neighborhood developed on Bailey's Prairie consisting of six slave labor camps. James Briton Bailey had moved to the area in 1818 and allegedly purchased land from the Spanish government, but his land was formally recognized by Stephen F. Austin in the form of a league and a labor in 1824. Bailey's home served as a center of Anglo operations in the area, and although he never owned enough people to constitute a plantation, after his death in 1832, other enslavers purchased the land. In 1837, Robert and David Mills bought 1,000 acres from the Carter League, just south of the Bailey League, and established a large sugar and cotton slave labor camp known as Bynum, which also included the old Bailey homestead. Other plantations in the neighborhood included Ridgley, home of the Munsons, and Willow Glen, established by enslaver Charles D. Sayer on the east bank of the Brazos in the Bailey League. Frank Titman, William Ward, and R. M. Collins owned the other labor camps in the Bailey's Prairie neighborhood.[16]

The final plantation neighborhood of Brazoria County stretched for twelve miles along the east bank of the Brazos River and included fourteen plantations, with Oyster Creek running through most of them. Plantations in this region that stood out included Chenango, China Grove, and Darrington. Chenango belonged to Benjamin Fort Smith and then Monroe Edwards at the time of their partnership in the illicit smuggling of enslaved Africans from Cuba in the 1830s. In this capacity, it became the final stop for many of the native Africans enslaved in Brazoria County. In the 1850s, William Sharp turned Chenango into a sugar plantation, with a brick sugar mill and brick slave quarters. Chenango lacked a grandiose mansion; instead, it featured a simple, white, one-story frame house for Sharp and his family. In 1859, Frank Terry and his business partner, William J. Kyle, purchased the plantation, which Sharp continued to manage. Chenango became one of only three plantations in the neighborhood lying east of Oyster Creek. The western boundaries of the other plantations in the neighborhood lay on the Brazos, with Oyster Creek running through them.[17]

Warren D. C. Hall founded China Grove plantation north of Chenango in 1828. He named the plantation for the China Berry trees he planted to shade his residence. In 1843, Albert Sidney Johnston purchased the property and planted hedges of Cherokee Roses, working a great deal to improve the residence. William Preston Johnson, son of the general, described the plantation in his visit in 1847:

> A double log cabin, covered with clapboard, and fronted with a wide porch, gave a rude shelter; and the pine tables, hickory chairs, and other household effects, might have suited a camp better than a permanent establishment. . . . From the front porch the view extended as far as the eye could reach over a grassy plain, unbroken except by an occasional fringe or mot of distant timber. . . . In early spring an emerald sward, embroidered with the blue lupin, the crimson phlox, the fragrant, and flossy mimosa, and a thousand flowers of varied perfume and hue, invited great herds of deer to browse on the tender grass. . . . His house was shaded by a grove of the fragrant pride of China, and the spacious yard contained towering live oaks, pecans, and other beautiful native forest trees. A hedge of Cherokee rose with its snowy bloom protected the inclosure; and an ample orchard of figs and peaches furnished its fruits for the table."[18]

Albert Sidney Johnston went into great debt to run China Grove, but he succeeded in turning it into a sugar plantation, with a brick sugar house, although, unlike other plantations in Brazoria County, he instructed the enslaved to use pine to build both their quarters and his house. About to default on his debts, Johnston left China Grove in 1849 and sold the property in 1852 to his son, William Preston Johnston. In 1860, the plantation was sold to the wealthy Houston merchant, William J. Hutchins.[19]

John Darrington, an attorney from Clark County, Alabama, acquired part of the David Talley League in northern Brazoria County and established a cotton and sugar plantation that appropriately came to be called Darrington. John Darrington never actually came to Texas; he served as an absentee landlord for six years before selling the plantation in 1847. Two years later, Sterling McNeel sold his plantation in the southern part of the county and acquired Darrington, turning it into a sugar plantation. In 1857, Abner Jackson purchased Darrington from the estate of Sterling McNeel, and Jackson ran the plantation as a sugar plantation until his death. Darrington had a sugar mill of brick and a large frame house. The slave cabins on the property also consisted of wood frame buildings.[20]

As the northernmost neighborhood of Brazoria County crossed the county line past Francis Bingham's brick sugar mill and residence, the neighborhood continued into Fort Bend County. Just north of the county line, Lewis Strobel owned a plantation between the Brazos and Oyster Creek, and north of him John C. Tomlinson maintained a cotton plantation. Finally, at the northern terminus of the neighborhood stood the Jonathan Waters plantation, Arcola.[21]

Jonathan D. Waters arrived in Texas from South Carolina in 1840 and purchased the Fitzgerald League in Fort Bend County where he founded a massive cotton and sugar plantation named Arcola. Waters had the more than 200 enslaved persons on the plantation construct a brick yard on the east bank of the Brazos, where bricks would be produced to build his residence and a sugar mill. By 1849, the enslaved had completed the residence, a sugar mill, and a cotton gin. The Waters residence, which sat near the bank of the Brazos River, consisted of a brick mansion and a family cemetery 200 yards east of the veranda of the house. The mansion commanded a view of the Brazos for several miles above and below, and the enslaved built a wharf to carry the cotton and sugar produced on the plantation to market. The house also had gardens enclosed by hedgerows of Bois d'Arc. The enslaved constructed the sugar mill on the east bank of Oyster Creek, a little more than 3 miles east of the residence, just south of Sugar Mill Lake. In 1848, Sarah Elizabeth, wife of Jonathan Waters, passed away, and three months later he married Clara Byne, but Clara too passed away—in May 1860. In her honor, Waters erected a shaft of Italian marble over her grave in the family cemetery where he had also buried his first wife as well as his brother, Philemon. In 1863, Waters purchased a large brick mansion in Galveston from Thomas League and operated it as a hotel.[22]

Seven miles northwest of Arcola, as the Brazos River and Oyster Creek wound around parallel to each other, the Stafford-Oakland neighborhood consisted of thirteen plantations on the east side of the Brazos. The Stafford's Point plantation, opened by William Stafford in the 1820s, stood at the northeast end of the neighborhood, while Smada, the plantation of Andrew Jackson Adams, sat on the south bank of Oyster Creek a little more than two and a half miles to the southeast.[23]

Four miles northwest of Smada, the Oakland plantation, later renamed Sugar Land, dominated all other sugar and cotton plantations in Fort Bend County except perhaps Arcola. Situated on the Samuel May Williams League, Williams himself established and named Oakland for the large number of live oaks on the land. As Samuel May Williams's business interests increased, he sold Oakland to his brother Nathaniel, who enlisted a third Williams brother, Matthew, to manage the plantation. In 1843, Matthew Williams instructed the enslaved to construct a brick sugar mill "a stone's throw" from the ford on the south bank of Oyster Creek. In 1852, Matthew Williams died, and Nathaniel decided to sell Oakland to the business partners William J. Kyle and Benjamin Franklin "Frank" Terry, who had just returned from the California Gold Rush. Frank Terry established his residence about a mile north of the ford on Oyster Creek, where the enslaved constructed a two-story brick mansion with large, airy rooms and fireplaces for use during cooler weather. The second floor contained verandas on three sides, with a circular staircase connecting the two floors. The mansion, lavishly furnished, became a central point for social gatherings in the Oyster Creek area for the other planter families. The semidetached large kitchen stood on the side of the south-facing mansion, and on the north side of the residence, numerous buildings such as a carriage house, stables, a smokehouse, and a storehouse all spoke to the wealth the sugar planters had accumulated. William Kyle, a bachelor, constructed a smaller house nearby, and Terry established a racetrack for horse racing halfway between his residence and Oyster Creek. The cotton gin and more than one hundred slave cabins, with one to five rooms each, stood north of the sugar mill, with Oyster Creek surrounding the residences of the enslaved on three sides. The small village occupied by the enslaved also had its own food preparation facility. Near the slave quarters stood a sawmill, and a cotton press. The sugar and cotton fields stood south of the slave quarters and the sugar mill, while Terry and Kyle kept a large herd of cattle on the land northwest of the Terry residence.[24]

The other notable plantation in the Stafford-Oakland neighborhood became the Walnut Grove plantation, a sugar and cotton plantation established by Thomas Nibbs of Alabama, 3½ miles west of Oakland on the north bank of Oyster Creek. After he passed away in the early 1840s, his widow, Ann, continued to operate the plantation and had the enslaved construct a mansion on the north bank of Oyster Creek, along with a sugar mill and cotton gin on the south bank of the creek. Ann remarried Constantine W. Buckley in 1852, six years after completion of the mansion at Walnut Grove. The mansion, constructed of bricks handmade by the enslaved from the mud of Oyster Creek, consisted of two stories and ten rooms, with a wide hall running through the middle of the house. In 1932, Mrs. Lula Roberts described her grandmother's house:

> The stairs ran up at one side of the hall. There was a large room at the head of the stairs looking down on the back yard. The rooms were spacious,

the ceilings high, the walls white plastered, and the fire-places with brass andirons were wide. Brass candelabra with crystal pendants, were on each end of the parlor mantel and the floor was covered with Brussels carpet. The parlor suite was mahogany, upholstered in black horse-hair. An oval shaped white marble table stood in the center of the room. A beautiful pier-glass in a gilt frame hung on one wall, a portrait in oil of Grandmother and her second husband hung from another. The house was colonial style with fluted columns. The Veranda railing was white. Down the broad steps a brick wall led to the gate. The flower garden was enclosed with a picket fence. No fowls were allowed in the garden but peacocks. They strutted up and down the brick walk in the sun, and their strident cries could be heard a mile away. In front of the gate ran the road, and straight on down the embankment was Oyster Creek. . . . On one side of the house were the old slave quarters, and the overseer's house. On the other were the new quarters. At the rear of the house were the quarters for the house servants, the barns, stables, poultry house and pigeon house. Farther on, quite a distance from the house, was the family burying ground.[25]

Further upstream from the Stafford-Oakland neighborhood, past the big bend in the Brazos River along Oyster Creek, the Pittsville neighborhood on the east side of the river stood as the plantation neighborhood the farthest northeast in Fort Bend County and the lowcountry. J. R. Miller owned a plantation on the Knight and White League, on the east bank of the Brazos, at the apex of the bend in the river. West of the Miller plantation, Thomas B. Burton established a plantation in the 1850s on Oyster Creek in the Samuel Isaacs League. Five and a half miles northwest of Richmond, in a bend of Oyster Creek, Samuel Mason, along with Randolph Foster established plantations on the John Foster League, 4½ miles northwest of the Mason and Foster plantations, Joseph A. Huggins owned a plantation on the Joseph San Pierre League. South of the Huggins plantation, John and David Randon, some of Austin's Old Three Hundred, established plantations on their leagues along Oyster Creek in the middle of the neighborhood. Two and a half miles southeast of the Huggins plantation, Churchill Fulshear Sr. established a large cotton plantation in the 1820s, which his son took over upon his father's death in 1831. Churchill Fulshear Jr. had the enslaved on his plantation construct a four-story Greek Revival brick mansion named Lake Hill on the plantation and a horse racing track named Churchill Downs. In the 1840s, Fulshear and the other plantation owners established the town of Pittsville, 2 miles north of the Fulshear plantation, as an escape for the white families from the unhealthy

Brazos River bottoms. Pittsville served as the home of Churchill Downs and by the time of the Civil War had become a major commercial center. At the west end of the neighborhood, James and J. C. Simonton established plantations on the Thomas Westall League.[26]

On the west side of the Brazos River in Fort Bend County, two plantation neighborhoods developed before the Civil War: the Big Creek neighborhood, and the Richmond neighborhood. Big Creek rises in south-central Fort Bend County, and from there flows twenty-five miles southeast until it empties into the Brazos River. In between the creek and the Brazos seven different enslavers established a plantation neighborhood south and east of Richmond. At the center of the neighborhood stood the Henry Jones plantation, located on one of the main roads leading to Richmond. Visitors often stopped at the Jones plantation, and although Henry Jones maintained a modest homestead during his life, at the time of his death in June 1861, his estate included more than fifty enslaved African Americans on his large cotton plantation and more than $200,000 in property. Three and a half miles northwest of the Jones plantation, Joseph Kuykendall, Jonathan Vail, and John R. Pettus established plantations on Rabb's Bayou and the Brazos River on the Joseph Kuykendall League, and Robert E. Bohannon established a plantation $3\frac{1}{4}$ miles east of the Jones plantation in the 1830s. Though important, the Big Creek plantation neighborhood was one of the smaller neighborhoods in Fort Bend County.[27]

In the very center of Fort Bend County stood the final plantation neighborhood around the city of Richmond, the old Fort Settlement, carved out of the Jane Long League, where the original Anglo colonists disembarked on the west bank of the Brazos in 1822. On the Jane Long League, at the southeast edge of the town of Richmond, James Winston, William D. Mitchell, and Everett Jovert all established plantations before the Civil War. Several large enslavers also lived in Richmond itself, along with Jane Long and Mirabeau Lamar who lived on the Jane Long League, although the number of enslaved persons Long and Lamar owned did not rise to the planter's level. Even though the Richmond neighborhood served as the county seat of Fort Bend County, it had the smallest number of plantations in the county.[28]

West of the San Bernard neighborhood, in Matagorda County, the next plantation neighborhood, the Lower Caney neighborhood, developed along Caney Creek. At some point in the distant past, the Colorado River changed course, shifting its mouth almost twenty-five miles to the southwest. Along the vacated riverbed a creek developed known as Caney Creek, or Cane Brake

Creek, which empties into Matagorda Bay almost exactly halfway between the mouths of the Brazos and Colorado rivers. Before Anglo colonization, on both sides of the creek a cane brake consisting of bamboo-like cane grew in dense clusters, five to seven miles in width on both banks of the stream. Growing as high as thirty-five feet, this cane brake proved almost impassable for human or horse. Early Anglo colonists in the area ordered their enslaved workers to clear-cut and burn the cane to make way for the planting of corn, cotton, and sugar. The Colorado River tended to overflow its banks on a regular basis, endangering crops and infrastructure, but the steep banks of Caney Creek provided shelter from such floods. In addition, the soil along Caney Creek, enriched by the sediment flowing downstream and the thousands of years of the annual death and renewal of the cane, proved to be some of the most fertile in the region. This geography encouraged the building of the cotton and sugar plantations in Matagorda County along the creek rather than the Colorado River. Referred to as "the most aristocratic creek in the South," one historian of the region wrote: "The plantations were strung along the creek; every mile or so one might find a cluster of trees and come upon another spacious . . . house." In Matagorda County, there were twenty-three plantations in two large neighborhoods: the Lower Caney neighborhood which stretched from the mouth of the creek fifteen miles inland and the Upper Caney neighborhood, six miles to the north, which extended ten miles to the Wharton County line.[29]

In the early 1840s, A. P. McCormick, Thomas Ewing, and John S. Sanborn established cotton plantations on the east bank of Caney Creek in Matagorda County. The McCormick residence stood less than a mile north of the home of George Sargent, and just 5 ¾ miles north of the Gulf of Mexico. Located on the Thomas McCoy and Daniel Deckro League, the McCormick plantation became the plantation closest to the mouth of Caney Creek. Just to the north of the McCormick place, Thomas Ewing established a cotton plantation named Cedar Lake on the southern edge of the Thomas Williams League. The Ewings owned 915 acres in Matagorda County and another 838 acres in Brazoria County, which were worked by the almost seventy enslaved African Americans on the plantation. In 1855, John S. Sanborn moved to Texas from Louisiana and established a cotton plantation on the east side of Caney Creek adjacent to and north of the Ewing plantation. Also located on the Thomas Williams League, by 1860 Sanborn had enslaved seventy-six people on the plantation.[30]

On the east bank of Caney Creek, north of Cedar Lake on the Thomas Williams League, James B. Hawkins established one of the largest sugar plantations in the Texas lowcountry. In 1845, two brothers, James B. Hawkins and John D. Hawkins Jr. of North Carolina, agreed to purchase land along Caney Creek and cultivate crops in an equal partnership. Whereas John remained an absent partner, James traveled with his family from North Carolina, arriving in Texas in 1846. The brothers contracted with a man named McNeel (probably a member of the McNeel family from Brazoria County) as an overseer and purchased 2,100 acres, 1,500 of which were on the western part of the Thomas Williams League. A part of their land, including the plantation house they bought from the Quick family, sat on the east bank of Caney Creek, but most of the land they planned to cultivate with sugarcane lay on the west side of the creek. The two-story plantation house on the banks of Caney Creek built by the Quicks in the early 1840s consisted of Cypress boards, hand-hewn foundation timbers, and wooden pegs with square nails. Constructed with a slight crawl space between the floorboard planks and the ground supported by brick pillars, the two-story house had brick chimneys at either end to service the fireplaces, a spacious front porch that faced northwest toward the creek, and a second story gallery with white pillars on the front of the house. The house consisted of 2,488 square feet of living space, and 920 square feet of porch space.[31]

The cabins of the enslaved that Hawkins had constructed in 1846 and 1847 proved decidedly less commodious than the plantation house. By 1847, the enslaved had constructed ten wooden houses with wood plank floors, along with a smoke house and a blacksmith shop with brick cisterns on the banks of Caney Creek.[32]

James Hawkins determined to go into sugar planting and toured the sugar mills in Brazoria County before beginning construction of his own sugar mill, which would become the largest in Matagorda County, in 1848. Hawkins investigated the other sugar mills in the San Bernard neighborhood and reported to his family that it took between 500,000 and 600,000 bricks to build Pleasant McNeel's sugar mill. "Their whole expense," he wrote, "including building, sugar engines, and 2 sets of kettles, everything to make 18 or 20 hogsheads of sugar a day will cost them ten thousand dollars. They will more than pay for it the first crop." Hawkins planned to have forty enslaved men harvesting the crop and producing the sugar and planned on having 300 acres of sugar in cultivation the next year with an expected yield of two hogsheads per acre.[33]

Hawkins had his cousin, George Nuttal, oversee the making of the bricks themselves. The enslaved would dig out clay from the banks of Caney Creek and press it into rectangular brick molds made of sawed wood. These molds consisted of three hollow rectangles set end to end in a 3-foot wooden rack. Two narrow slots along the bottom of the racks served to drain the water from the clay. Once the bricks were allowed to dry in the sun, they were fired in a brick kiln made of similar bricks. In this way, over the course of 1849, Nuttal and the plantation slaves produced 900,000 bricks for the sugar mill. Hawkins described the sugar mill, completed in April 1850, as "the main building for the kettles and coolers 45 feet wide and 160 feet long with a wing each side in the shape of a 'T' of the same width, and 80 feet long each. The main building to be 22 feet high and the balance to be 12 feet." When completed, a steam engine powered the sugar mill, and the building contained a smokestack 40 feet high. The enslaved on the plantation produced the first sugar crop using the mill in the fall of 1850.[34]

James Hawkins and his family also had to deal with the sickly environment along Caney Creek, and so they regularly took trips to the town of Matagorda on the coast to take advantage of the Gulf breezes. In 1854, Hawkins completed a "Lake House" for his family on Lake Austin, 8 ½ miles southwest of the plantation house on Caney Creek. With this new house on the banks of the lake, the family could regularly retreat to take advantage of the Gulf breezes that crossed Matagorda Bay. The house was two and a half stories high with nine rooms, with "cross passages and galleries all around with a large closet to every room." Hawkins had the floorboards of the house constructed of ash, and when completed the house had 6,428 square feet, with 2,232 square feet of porch space. Greek Revival in style, the dwelling had a widow's walk and a double gallery extending across the front of the house. A carpenter used walnut for the interior stairway, and wall pockets sat along the stairway for the placement of lamps. Large fireplaces and overhanging mirrors and mantles presented themselves in every room. Leading to the front of the house, oak trees, planted by Mrs. Hawkins in 1854, gave the house a most impressive appearance.[35]

Above the Hawkinsville plantation, thirteen additional plantations accounted for the remainder of the Lower Caney neighborhood up Caney Creek. Two miles north of the Hawkins plantation, Peter W. and Mary Hebert arrived in Matagorda County from Alabama with enslaved African Americans and established a cotton plantation on the Moses Morrison and William Cooper League. Peter Hebert passed away in 1848, leaving management of the plantation to his wife. By 1860, Peter W. Hebert Jr. owned the plantation along with thirty-eight enslaved African Americans. North of the Hebert plantation, on the east bank of the creek, John Henry Jones Sr. established a cotton and sugar plantation in 1848. The Jones residence consisted of a large log cabin with a wide porch and brick chimneys at each end. In addition to the Jones family, two white Southern Baptist missionaries who ministered to the enslaved African Americans, Noah Hill and J. J. Loudermilk, founded one of the first African American Southern Baptist churches on the Jones plantation. The last plantation on the Morrison and Cooper League was that of Nancy Thompson with thirty enslaved African Americans.[36]

North of the Nancy Thompson plantation, Felix and Margaret Gibson, along with Elbert and Ann Thompson, arrived from Georgia and Alabama in the 1830s and 1840s to establish cotton plantations on the Aylett C. Buckner League. In 1857, Felix Gibson passed away, leaving the plantation to his wife, Margaret M. Gibson. By 1860, she had thirty-six enslaved African Americans on her plantation. In 1838, when Elbert and Ann Thompson arrived from Alabama, they established a cotton and sugar plantation on the west side of Caney Creek at the northern edge of the Buckner League. In 1852, Thompson passed away, and in his will, he instructed his wife and children to cease sugar production and instead concentrate on cotton to avoid costly machinery repairs. In 1856, Ann Thompson married Dr. R. H. Chinn, who ordered his enslaved to build a sawmill, cotton gin, and brick kiln. Under Chinn, the enslaved constructed their quarters from bricks and lumber. During the Civil War, the Chinns also gave refuge to several whites and enslaved African Americans, including Ann's sister, fleeing Alabama ahead of United States troops. The Chinn plantation also served as a center of social activity for the plantation families on Lower Caney.[37]

Across Caney Creek from the Chinn plantation, George J. Bowie arrived with several enslaved African Americans and established a cotton plantation on the east bank of Caney Creek on the Thomas Tone and Thomas Jamison League. By 1850, the enslaved on the Bowie plantation had constructed "a respectable log house about 20 feet square, a good story and a half high, with a piazza in the front, a plaza, and a shed room in the rear (comfortable fireplaces above and below); then we have a smokehouse, a storeroom kitchen and two Negro houses and a first rate hen house in the yard and another Negro house a short distance off . . . all located within fifty yards of Caney Creek." Just south of the Bowie plantation, the village of Sugar Land grew up, where Thomas Jamison served as an early postmaster.[38]

North of the Bowie plantation, also on the Tone and Jamison League, Henry Gibson, the patriarch of the Gibson clan that arrived in Texas in 1842 from Georgia, established a cotton and sugar plantation on 553 acres. In the 1850s, Gibson raised sugar, and in 1860 thirty-seven enslaved African Americans lived on the plantation. Gibson passed away in 1862, leaving his property to his sons, one of whom, John H. Gibson, owned a plantation in the Upper Caney neighborhood.[39]

Upstream of the Gibson plantation, Robert H. Williams, William G. Warren, and James W. Stewart established plantations near a major crossroads in the lowcountry. Robert H. Williams, one of Stephen F. Austin's Old Three Hundred, arrived in Texas as early as 1823, and established a cotton plantation on the east bank of Caney Creek, which he named Rotherwood. The Williams plantation, also referred to as Caney Crossing, existed along the road from Matagorda to Brazoria, on the Robert H. Williams and Morrison and Cooper Leagues. Williams also had a two-story brick, colonial-style house in the town of Matagorda that he used as a vacation home. West of Caney Crossing, William G. Warren established a cotton and sugar plantation in partnership with Robert and David G. Mills. Named "Caney Place" on the William Rabb League, Warren established his residence on the west side of the creek, while the slave cabins and slave cemetery stood across the creek. Near Caney Place, James W. Stewart founded a cotton plantation in the 1840s on the west side of Caney Creek, which was also on the Rabb League. In 1846, Stewart purchased and shipped fifty-eight enslaved persons aboard the schooner *St. Paul* from New Orleans to Matagorda. Steward died in 1850, leaving management of the plantation to his widow, Mary E. Stewart, and his sister Elizabeth (Stewart) Thorp, wife of John L. Thorp.[40]

Near Caney Crossing and Caney Place, John L. Thorp, established a cotton plantation on the Rabb and Bostwick and Brotherton League, while Abram Sheppard founded the cotton and sugar plantation that sat the farthest west of Caney Creek in Matagorda County. Thorp arrived in Texas from Virginia in the 1840s and established a cotton plantation on Caney Creek just south of Caney Crossing. Thorp's two younger brothers worked as attorneys in the town of Matagorda, and by 1860, thirty-six enslaved African Americans worked the Thorp plantation. Almost four miles west of Caney Creek, on the Farnham Fry and Daniel McCarty Leagues, near Live Oak Bayou, Abram Sheppard founded a cotton and sugar plantation. By 1860, eighty-six enslaved African Americans cultivated sugar and cotton on the Sheppard plantation as one of the largest such establishments in Matagorda County.[41]

The Upper Caney neighborhood in Matagorda County consisted of fourteen plantations that began three miles north of the village of Caney Crossing. John

H. Gibson, son of Henry Gibson, maintained a cotton plantation along Caney Creek at the southern end of the neighborhood on the Thomas M. Duke League worked by forty-five enslaved African Americans. Near the John Gibson place, Matthew Talbot also purchased a cotton plantation in 1837 when he moved his family to Texas from Mobile, Alabama. Translating his experience as a merchant in Alabama to economic exploitation in Texas, Talbot had fifty enslaved African Americans on the plantation by 1860 and owned a home in Matagorda. Talbot also served as the Chief Justice of Matagorda County for twenty years. Just northwest of the Talbot and Gibson plantations, Roland Rugeley, another member of the Rugeley clan, maintained a cotton plantation worked by twenty enslaved African Americans on the Freeman George League.[42]

Upstream of the Gibson and Talbot plantations, five separate plantations sat on the Pumphrey A. Burnet and A. S. Sojourner League—three on the west and two on the east side of the creek. On the southwestern portion of the league, Edward A. Pearson established a cotton plantation worked by twenty-two enslaved African Americans. North of the Pearson place, William H. Wiggins also established a cotton plantation with fifty-one enslaved African Americans. Samuel W. Hardeman arrived in 1834 and planted a sugar and cotton plantation on the northwestern portion of the league. In 1836, Hardeman died, leaving the plantation to his widow, Rebecca, and sixteen-year-old son, Samuel W. Hardeman Jr. By the 1840s, the son had taken over managing the plantation, and by 1860, the younger Hardeman reported thirty-one enslaved African Americans on the plantation. On the southern part of the league, east of the creek, Edward S. "Ned" Rugeley established a cotton and sugar plantation worked by thirty-two enslaved African Americans. The enslaved on the Rugeley plantation constructed a two-story house with two bedrooms downstairs across a wide hall from the parlor, with a family sitting room behind the front hall. Upstairs, the house had two large bedrooms with wide dormer windows. Rugeley also had the enslaved on the plantation construct their own hogsheads for shipping the sugar to market. A little over a mile north of the Ned Rugeley plantation, his brother, Alexander Irvin Rugeley, established a cotton plantation worked by twenty-nine enslaved African Americans. The enslaved on the Irvin Rugeley plantation constructed a two-story colonial-style house with a wide porch and upstairs gallery in the front supported by five columns more than twenty feet tall.[43]

Northeast of the Hardeman place, on the west bank of Caney Creek, John Rugeley and John Duncan founded cotton and sugar plantations on the Amos Rawls, Benjamin Rawls, and Owen H. Stout Leagues. John Rugeley Sr., the first of his family to emigrate to Texas from Alabama, arrived on Caney Creek and purchased 2,500 acres on the Amos Rawls League in 1840, establishing a large sugar and cotton plantation. Rugeley had the enslaved on the plantation construct a spacious house on the west bank of the creek, with roses and jasmines in the gardens, surrounded by cottonwood trees. The slave cabins stood nearby, and the slave cemetery was located on the same side of the creek as the Rugeley residence. Rugeley also carefully located his family's cemetery on a slight rise on the opposite bank of Caney Creek. He passed away in 1878 and is buried in the family cemetery.[44]

John Duncan abandoned his steamship business and plantation near Mobile, Alabama, to come to Texas in 1835, founding a large cotton and sugar plantation on the Rawls and Stout, and Daniel Rawls Leagues after fighting in the rebellion against Mexico. Duncan brought with him several enslaved African Americans, and by 1860, ninety-four enslaved African Americans worked his plantation and sugar mill. One of the men Duncan enslaved, an African man named Podo, served as Duncan's overseer. The enslaved on the Duncan plantation built a three-story plantation house on the west bank of Caney Creek, with two crepe myrtle bushes in front. Duncan also used his mechanical knowledge to install a steam engine in the sugar mill. The slave quarters on the Duncan plantation, half a mile south of the Duncan residence, known as "Slave Row," consisted of log cabins with dirt floors and brick chimneys with mud and grass from the creek to fill in the gaps between the logs. In the winter the enslaved made their cooking fires in the cabins, and in the summers, they moved the fires outdoors. The enslaved also built a brick cistern at slave row. The slave cemetery on the plantation stood near the slave quarters. The enslaved produced the bricks on the plantation for the brick sugar mill and gin house. John Duncan passed away in 1878, and his family buried him in the family cemetery on the plantation.[45]

North of the Duncan land, four more plantations made up the northernmost such establishments in Matagorda County. Upstream from the Duncan place, Jesse Gordon founded a large cotton plantation on the west side of Caney Creek. By 1860, fifty enslaved African Americans labored on the land. Two and a half miles north of the Gordon plantation, Thomas P. Matthews established a cotton plantation along Caney Creek on the Zadock Woods League. In 1860, Matthews commanded the labor of seventy-nine enslaved men and women. Less than a mile and a half north of the Matthews plantation, John W. Brown owned a cotton plantation on the east bank of Caney Creek on the Woods and Charles DeMos Leagues named Grove Hill just 1,120 yards south of the Wharton County line. Finally, Eliza Pledger, sister-in-law of John W. Brown, operated a cotton plantation toiled over by twenty-four enslaved persons on the Lawrence Ramsey League, northeast of Grove Hill.[46]

Past the end of Matagorda County, the Upper Caney neighborhood continued into Wharton County. The State of Texas created Wharton County out of parts of Matagorda, Colorado, and Jackson counties in 1846 and named the county for the brothers William H. and John A. Wharton. The Colorado River flowed through the middle of the county from north to south, while Caney Creek, which originated in the central part of the county, flowed from that point southeast before entering Matagorda County 9 miles east of the Colorado. Most of the antebellum plantations and towns in Wharton County existed east of the Colorado River.[47]

At the southeast corner of Wharton County, on the east bank of Caney Creek, two enslavers established plantations on the Seth Ingram League. The James Cardwell cotton plantation, with forty enslaved African Americans, was situated closest to the county line, while Erasmus D. Galbraith established a 1,100-acre cotton plantation nine-tenths of a mile to the northeast worked by twenty-six enslaved persons.[48]

Three miles northwest of the Galbraith place, William F. S. Alexander and Maclin Stith established cotton plantations on the banks of Caney Creek in the Stephen F. Austin League. Eight years before the creation of Wharton County, Daniel Baker, John Huff, and Charles DeMorse decided to found a town (named Preston) on the east bank of Caney Creek in what was then Matagorda County. The promoters sold the first lots at public auction in April 1838. The town lasted two decades and became the center of trade for Anglo settlers along Caney Creek. Just south of Preston, Stith and Alexander located their plantations. A little less than 1.5 miles southeast of Preston, Alexander located his 1,900-acre cotton plantation, Bear Camp, on the east bank of Caney Creek, with eighty-one enslaved persons laboring in the cotton fields. The Alexander residence included a library, billiard hall, and spacious quarters for entertaining guests. Closer to Preston, Maclin Stith founded his almost 1,600-acre plantation and home, Lolla Rookh, on the east bank of the creek. Lolla Rookh became the first of three large cotton plantations established by Maclin Stith.[49]

North of Preston, in the John Huff League, Maclin Stith, Mary Bradshaw, and Charles F. Whittington all founded plantations along Caney Creek. The second Stith plantation of 1,800 acres, Hidalgo, was sited on the east bank of the creek just north of Preston. Northeast of Hidalgo, Bradshaw commanded the forced labor of twenty-seven enslaved persons, and Whittington had twenty-two enslaved African Americans on his cotton plantation in the Huff League.[50]

Northwest of the Huff League, three large enslavers established cotton plantations along Caney Creek on the Joshua and William Parker League. On the northern portion of the league, Shadrach Cayce and David Stevens founded cotton plantations on the east side of the creek. Cayce enslaved twenty-eight African Americans on his plantation, and David Stevens enslaved one hundred and seven persons on his plantation. At the northern end of the Parker League, Mrs. S. D. Calloway placed her cotton plantation along the northern boundary of the league.[51]

Upstream of the S. D. Calloway plantation, six planters established cotton and sugar plantations on the Eli Hunter and Bartlett Sims League at the northern terminus of the Upper Caney neighborhood. On the southern end of the league, Lemuel Calloway located his plantation on the east bank of Caney Creek. Northwest of the Calloway place, Maclin Stith established his third plantation, Oakland, along with James W. Day, who also ran a cotton plantation along the creek. Above Oakland, Burr Albert Harrison worked a cotton and sugar plantation with eighty-three enslaved African Americans. North of the Harrison place, John Lawson and Isaac Handy established large cotton plantations on the Hunter and Sims Leagues. At the corner of the Lawson and Harrison plantations, Dick Lawson had the enslaved on the family plantation build a general store called Lawson's Corner, and local plantation owners also contributed to a church at the small settlement that grew up around the store.[52]

In 1846, with the creation of Wharton County, William Kincheloe donated land on the east bank of the Colorado River to establish a county seat, also named Wharton. Situated between Caney Creek and the Colorado River, the town became the largest settlement in the county, and near Wharton, six large enslavers established plantations in the second neighborhood in Wharton County. A. A. McWillie established a cotton plantation on 2,281 acres in the Kincheloe League, with his residence located near the Wharton city cemetery in the heart of town, while twenty-nine enslaved African Americans labored in his cotton fields. Northeast of Wharton, also on the Kincheloe League, Edward Carson and Alexander Miller established cotton plantations bordering each other with a combined fifty-five enslaved persons. Benjamin Lee also maintained a cotton plantation on the Kincheloe League, while east of town on Caney Creek Joseph Anderson enslaved twenty African Americans on his plantation in the Martin Allen League.[53]

The five preceding plantations paled in comparison to the size of Sycamore Grove, the home of Albert Clinton Horton, and the 170 enslaved African Americans he exploited there. Through the work of his slaves, Horton cultivated both cotton and sugar on the 2,214 acres of Sycamore Grove in the Randall Jones League, and his big two-story home became one of the principal residences on the road from Wharton to Matagorda, nicknamed "Alabama Road." The Greek Revival-style house, constructed of brick and "scantlings" from trees on the plantation in 1846, had two rooms upstairs and two downstairs, with each room featuring three large windows. An attached kitchen stood perpendicular to the rear of the house, and a large, extended porch protruded from the middle of the front of the house. The Horton family cemetery stood a couple of hundred yards from the house.[54]

The third plantation neighborhood in Wharton County took shape along Peach Creek, four miles north of Wharton, where seven enslavers established large cotton plantations. On the Kincheloe League along Peach Creek Alexander Moore, James O. Myers, and George Quinan established cotton plantations with a combined 185 enslaved African Americans. Residents in the area founded the village of Peach Creek on the creek in the early 1840s. East of the Quinan plantation, Henry Crisp established a cotton plantation along Peach Creek on the Isham B. Phillips League, and to the west William P. and Joel Hudgins established plantations along the creek on the Alexander Jackson League. At the western end of the neighborhood, Richard H. P. Sorrell founded a huge cotton plantation along Peach Creek in the Stephen F. Austin League worked by 123 enslaved African Americans. Joel Hudgins, who moved to the area in 1840, instructed the enslaved on his plantation to construct a seventeen-room, two-story house with a detached kitchen. Also distinguished by heavy cypress doors and handmade bricks, the house stood as one of the central landmarks of the neighborhood.[55]

The fourth plantation neighborhood in Wharton County, the Glen Flora neighborhood, took shape west of Wharton, on the east side of the Colorado River, with eleven large cotton plantations. Immediately west of Wharton, on the Abner Jackson League, Thomas Thatcher, Jackson Alexander, and Charles Bolton maintained large cotton plantations. The Thatcher plantation was closest to Wharton with the 1,600-acre Charles Bolton plantation, Valhalla, in the middle of the league and the Jackson Alexander plantation, Fleetwood, farthest to the west, roughly two miles northwest of Wharton. On the three plantations combined, 181 enslaved African Americans toiled away in the cotton fields. Most of the plantation owners along the Colorado placed their own residences two to three miles from the river with their cotton fields between the residences and the river. Valhalla, for instance, lay 2.46 miles north of the Colorado.[56]

West of Fleetwood, John W. Gordon and Edwin M. Sanford established massive cotton plantations on the Stephen F. Austin League. On the east side of the league, Gordon owned a massive, 2,500-acre cotton plantation on the east bank of the Colorado on the Austin League, and west bank of the Colorado on the Robert Kuykendall League. Fifty-three enslaved African Americans worked the Gordon plantation, the only such place in Wharton County to have land on the west side of the Colorado.[57]

On the other side of the Stephen F. Austin League, Eugene M. Sanford established the Glen Flora plantation in the middle of the neighborhood. Sanford arrived in Wharton County in the 1850s and named the plantation after his old place in Virginia. The forty-one enslaved African Americans on the plantation molded the bricks for the house by hand, building the first story entirely of brick. The walls of the bottom floor consisted of four rows of brick a total of eighteen inches thick covered on the outside with a thin layer of stucco. For the top floor, Sanford purchased lumber in Alabama, had it shipped to Matagorda, and then transported overland by ox-drawn wagons. The colonial-style house, when completed, had wide verandas on the front and back of the house. Sanford designated the bottom floor, with two large rooms, as slave quarters, with nothing but dirt floors. The top floor featured a wide hall down the middle of the house, with four spacious rooms, two on each side of the hall.[58]

Past Glen Flora, the fifth and final neighborhood in Wharton County took shape around the Texas settlement of Egypt. The final plantations in the Glen Flora neighborhood were located in the Robert Kuykendall League, where enslavers established four large cotton plantations at the west end of the neighborhood. Thomas Sanford, Isham Thompson, John B. Walker, and George G. Williams all maintained cotton plantations on the Kuykendall League worked by a combined 146 enslaved African Americans. West of the Kuykendall League, the Egypt neighborhood took shape on the John C. Clark, James W. Jones, John P. Borden, Joseph Newman, and Andrew Rabb Leagues.[59]

Although the Egypt community was located at the northwest end of Wharton County, it was the oldest settlement in the county. A member of Stephen F. Austin's Old Three Hundred, John C. Clark established a residence in this neighborhood in the early 1820s. During the drought of 1827, other Anglos desperate for food traveled to the fertile neighborhood for corn "like going down to Egypt for grain." Clark arrived in Texas as early as 1823 and sustained injuries in a fight with Karankawas that same year. As one of the original Anglo settlers, he received a league of 4,428.4 acres on the east bank of the Colorado, where he established a cotton plantation. By the time of Clark's death in 1862, 138 enslaved African Americans labored on Clark's two plantations, which he referred to as the Upper plantation and Lower plantation.[60]

In 1829, in the town of Liberty in Amite County, Mississippi, Gail Borden Jr. married Penelope Mercer and later that year moved to Texas. By 1832, Borden had convinced his father-in-law, Eli Mercer, to move to Texas, and Mercer purchased 500 acres in the John W. Jones League from Thomas Borden. Mercer established a plantation there, known as Mercer's Crossing because of the ferry that Mercer operated on the Colorado. In 1833, Mercer and the enslaved on his plantation produced the first sugar in Texas. By 1860, thirty enslaved African Americans labored in the cotton and sugar fields of the Mercer plantation.[61]

In 1830, John C. Clark sold the western half of his league to William J. E. Heard, who established a plantation on his 2,222 acres. The settlement of Egypt developed around the Heard residence, at the northwest corner of his plantation, 3 miles north of the Colorado River, at one of the highest points in Wharton County, 140 feet above sea level and 37 feet above the Colorado River. Completed in the 1840s, the enslaved on the Heard plantation constructed a two-story red-brick house at the highest point on the land. The house had a wide front porch with seven columns in the front. By 1860, forty enslaved African Americans labored away in the sugar and cotton fields on the Heard place. The slave cabins on the plantation were made of wood, with wooden floors about a foot off the ground, and brick chimneys. The cabins measured roughly ten feet square, with two small steps leading up to a covered porch six feet wide supported by four wooden posts. The slave cemetery stood 235 yards west of the Heard residence.[62]

In addition to Clark, Mercer, and Heard, four other enslavers established cotton plantations in the Egypt neighborhood. On the Clark League, Isaac Heard established a cotton plantation with twenty-three enslaved African

Americans. West of Egypt, on the Newman League, Dr. Bartley Stanchfield established a cotton plantation with twenty-two enslaved African Americans, and at the west end of the neighborhood R. J. Battle maintained a cotton plantation with eighty-five enslaved African Americans on the Rabb League.[63]

The nearly 200 large slave labor camps in the four counties of the Texas lowcountry before the Civil War produced the neighborhoods of the region, shaping the geography, lives, and communities of the enslaved African Americans who gave their blood, sweat, tears, and lives laboring in the coastal heat and humidity. Cultivating cotton and sugar cane in the most fertile soil in Texas, the enslaved in the region managed to amass huge amounts of wealth for the enslavers, particularly the planter class, who took advantage of every part of their bodies, labor, and reproductive capacities to establish the foundation for capitalism in Texas.

Chapter 6

Extracting Every Ounce of Profit

Slavery's Capitalism in the Texas Lowcountry

ON FEBRUARY 26, 1840, Edwin Waller approached William P. Scott, the chief justice of Brazoria County, to take out a mortgage on five enslaved men. Using Christopher Dart and E. J. Townes as witnesses, Waller accepted $4,034.99 in cash from Robert Mills in exchange for mortgages on Isaac, Abraham, Tow, Olilla, and Alado, aged twenty-one to thirty-four. Waller mortgaged these men on the understanding that they would remain in his possession until and unless it became necessary to seize them in repayment of the debt. The use of these men as collateral in securing a loan revealed one small transaction in the larger system of valuation, debt, and credit in which enslavers endeavored to extract every ounce of profit from the bodies and labor of the enslaved men, women, and children of the Texas lowcountry.[1]

At its core, the system of African slavery in the antebellum United States was an economic institution predicated on forced labor. As such, it bridged the gap between mercantilism and modern capitalism, laying the foundation for the material wealth of the United States. The profits from slavery in the Texas lowcountry served the same function for a large portion of Texas. Enslavers relentlessly commodified every aspect of the bodies of the enslaved throughout their lifespan, from fetal development to the grave. In their efforts to create a system of credit and debit, a nascent kind of capitalism, enslavers kept meticulous track of every expense.[2]

The vast majority of the capital in the Texas lowcountry flowed through the merchants of Galveston, who provided banking services and financed the purchasing of land and enslaved individuals, while also serving as cotton and sugar factors, taking crops on consignment, and furnishing enslavers with the cash they needed to run their operations. The most successful of these merchants collateralized their own firms with large plantations and hundreds of enslaved individuals, bringing the cycle of slavery's capitalism full circle.

Cotton, sugar, and cattle constituted the crops and livestock that enslavers marketed to the outside world. The fertile soil allowed enslavers to extract double the average number of cotton bales per acre than the rest of the state, and the available evidence suggests that cotton bales in the lowcountry contained more lint on average than the typical cotton bale. The introduction of sugar gave the largest enslavers in the region not only more profitability, but also more stability in their wealth, as the failure of a sugar crop could be covered by the cotton crop in any given year. Adding a third layer of diversification, many enslavers, especially in Wharton and Matagorda counties, ran large herds of cattle, further stabilizing their operations.

As chattels under Texas law, enslaved African Americans provided both labor and capital, making them extraordinarily liquid assets. Enslavers used enslaved persons as collateral in several ways; they would take out mortgages and deeds of trust on them as a way of purchasing them or raising quick cash, or as endowments in trusts for their children or grandchildren. Enslavers also perfected coercive methods of maximizing productivity among the enslaved, freely utilizing the whip to incentivize cotton production. As cotton reached its maximum profitability in the two decades before the Civil War, the price of enslaved persons spiked, reaching their height in the late 1850s. The lowcountry became the epitome of this trend, as average prices of enslaved persons rose steadily, outpacing even national trends. In their zeal to increase the number of enslaved persons and decrease prices, enslavers in the lowcountry advocated a reopening of the African slave trade and engaged in widespread forced procreation.

The profits from the lowcountry allowed the merchants and wealthiest planters to leverage their fortunes into building internal improvements, creating the infrastructure of the region that would far outlast the institution of slavery. The money from slavery built the cities of Houston and Galveston and financed the building of canals and the first railroads in Texas, all to ease the transportation of crops to market. These cities and the railroads that linked them to the rest of the South laid the foundation for the economy that would propel the state of Texas into the modern era.

The commission merchants of Galveston and Houston provided the financial backing that allowed capital to circulate through the Texas lowcountry. A number of merchants in Houston and Galveston accepted crops on consignment to keep capital flowing to the interior, but in the two decades before the Civil War, two firms also offered banking services to enslavers in the lowcountry: the Commercial and Agricultural Bank, successor to the firm of McKinney & Williams, and the firm of R. & D. G. Mills. These two firms circulated millions of dollars in currency around the Gulf, giving the profits from slavery in the lowcountry a national importance in promoting slavery and agriculture.[3]

Samuel May Williams acquired a charter for the Commercial and Agricultural Bank in 1835, under Mexican law, but it took the entrepreneurial Williams twelve years to open the bank. The firm of McKinney & Williams operated the bank as an appendage of their firm, but by the late 1840s, Williams turned all his attention to converting his business solely to banking. Even though the constitution of the Republic of Texas outlawed banking, the First Congress of the Republic of Texas confirmed the Mexican charter for the Banco de Comercio y Agricultura dated April 30, 1835, in legislation passed on December 10, 1836. Therefore, despite the constitutional prohibition on banking that also made its way into the 1845 constitution of the state of Texas, Williams assumed that the law would allow him to operate his bank unhindered. From investors Williams finally obtained the necessary specie to capitalize the bank, and on December 30, 1847, Niles Smith, representing the state of Texas, certified that the bank vault had $100,000 in specie as required by the original charter, and on January 1, 1848, the bank, located at the corner of Market and 23rd Street in Galveston, opened for business. For the next five years, the Commercial and Agricultural Bank operated unimpeded, printing bank notes that circulated on par with specie around the Gulf coast, giving planters in the Texas lowcountry the flexibility to expand their operations. The main criticism of the bank became the amount of interest charged for loans. In Texas, lenders could charge up to 12 percent interest, but New York merchants could not charge more than 7 percent and New Orleans merchants not more than 8 percent. However, neither New York nor New Orleans merchants would lend capital to planters in Texas without substantial collateral; the Commercial and Agricultural Bank, although it charged more in interest, did not require nearly as much collateral, taking on greater risk than merchants in other cities. At its height, Williams's bank circulated perhaps $300,000 in paper around the Gulf.[4]

The firm of R. & D. G. Mills became the primary competitor to the Commercial and Agricultural Bank, as well as the stronger bank in Galveston. Robert Mills ran his mercantile business out of Brazoria until 1848. The original firm, named A. G. & R. Mills, dissolved in 1834 and changed its name to Robert Mills & Co. On January 20, 1848, Robert Mills and his brother, David Graham Mills, founded the firm of R. & D. G. Mills. In 1849, Robert Mills moved to Galveston where he opened his commission business and bank, while David Mills made his home at Lowwood plantation in Brazoria County. The brothers also owned two other cotton and sugar plantations in Brazoria County, Bynum and Palo Alto, and held half-interest in Caney Place, the William Warren plantation in Matagorda County. Robert Mills purchased five acres in Galveston, and he had the enslaved build a large plantation-style house for himself there. Mills opened his commission business and bank a few blocks away on the Strand. The Mills approached their banking business differently than the Commercial and Agricultural Bank. Instead of issuing their own paper money, Robert Mills acquired tens of thousands of dollars in notes from the defunct Northern Bank of Mississippi at Holly Springs and the Alabama Railroad Company of Brandon, Mississippi. Mills endorsed these notes, placing his initials "R.M." on the reverse of the notes. These bills, called "Mills money," circulated throughout Texas and the Gulf on par with specie.[5]

Litigation over these banks began in 1853. That year Samuel May Williams and the Commercial and Agricultural Bank stood trial in the Galveston District Court before Judge Peter W. Gray for violating the Texas antibanking statute of March 20, 1848. Gray ruled against the Commercial and Agricultural Bank, and Williams appealed the decision to the Texas Supreme Court. In 1857, Gray also handed down a decision against R. & D. G. Mills under the same statute. Samuel May Williams died on September 13, 1858, in Galveston, and the Texas Supreme Court upheld the decision against his bank. Meanwhile, Robert Mills remained very much alive and the wealthiest man in Texas. In 1859, the Texas Supreme Court ruled in favor of Mills based on the rationale that he had not issued his own currency, but rather merely circulated the Northern Bank of Mississippi notes as Mills money, technically remaining within the bounds of the law.[6]

The institution of slavery provided the stability and political clout that allowed R. & D. G. Mills to survive the litigation while the Commercial and Agricultural Bank failed. By 1860, the Mills considered themselves the wealthiest men in Texas and the largest enslavers. In Brazoria County, David Mills reported 313 enslaved African Americans, along with 2,500 acres of improved land for real property valued at $364,234, and personal property valued at $250,000. That year, the enslaved African Americans produced 25,000 bushels of corn, 712 hogsheads of sugar, and an unknown amount of cotton. In Galveston County, Robert Mills reported $700,000 in real estate and $9,000 in personal property. These figures do not include the separate property of the firm of R. & D. G. Mills that was worth tens of thousands of additional dollars in property including five sloops and eighteen steamships. Some sources placed Robert Mills's total wealth as high as $5 million. Mills leveraged this enormous wealth into partnerships in firms located in New Orleans and New York. Previous studies have pointed to Robert Mills's partnerships in these various firms as the reason for the superior stability of R. & D. G. Mills, but the census and tax rolls make it apparent that Mills's actual stability and worth derived primarily from collateralizing the firm with the more than 300 enslaved African Americans who produced prodigious amounts of sugar, cotton, and corn.[7]

The Panic of 1857 allowed Robert Mills to display the superior stability of his operation. The Commercial and Agricultural Bank and R. & D. G. Mills had close to a million dollars in paper spread throughout Texas and the South when news of the panic reached Galveston. The panic resulted in runs on the two banks on October 19–20, 1857. Samuel May Williams had some trouble in meeting the demand, and he closed the bank for a few hours on October 20. As a result, some investors sold the bank notes at a 25 percent discount that night, only to have the Commercial and Agricultural Bank resume payments the next day. Meanwhile, although Robert Mills also had some trouble meeting demand, he did not close his bank on October 20, and instead managed to pay his investors with bars of Mexican silver he kept on hand. By the time the litigation against the two banks reached the Texas Supreme Court, the panic had allowed the Mills to prove the stability of their bank.[8]

The merchants and bankers allowed enslavers in the Texas lowcountry to cultivate cash crops and maintain large herds of cattle. Cotton and sugar were the main crops cultivated by the enslaved in the lowcountry. In the antebellum era, cotton became the most widely raised cash crop in the lowcountry. By 1844, enslavers in Brazoria County had dedicated fully half of all cultivated acres to cotton. In 1850, the fertility of the soil allowed the enslaved to produce 10,501 bales of cotton that year: 18 percent of the state total. In 1860, the enslaved harvested 45,766 cotton bales worth of cotton, a 435 percent increase over 1850, but only 11 percent of the state total.[9]

The soil of the region allowed enslavers to realize as much as 2,000 pounds of lint per acre, compared to 1,200 or 1,400 pounds per acre in the rest of the state. Most bales in the lowcountry averaged 500 pounds of lint; much larger than the 400 pounds indicated on the census forms or the estimated 450 pounds per bale common in the rest of Texas. Cotton sold for roughly 10.8 cents per pound in both 1850 and 1860. After shipping costs, the enslaver could count on 8 or 9 cents per pound in profit. At 9 cents per pound, an enslaver in the lowcountry could make $45 per bale and $180 per acre of cotton planted. According to one large enslaver, the average enslaved person could produce ten bales of cotton per year, or 5,000 pounds of lint: a profit of $450. These numbers indicate that the enslaved in the lowcountry produced well in excess of $2 million in cotton in 1860 alone.[10]

The cultivation of sugar presented more hardships and dangers for the enslaved and greater financial risks for enslavers. As a result, sugar dominated the lowcountry from the early 1840s through the mid-1850s, but its production had begun to decline by 1860. Sugar producers in the lowcountry could count on extracting 1,500 to 1,600 pounds of granulated sugar per acre, and by 1844 Brazoria County, the largest sugar-producing county, had 2,600 acres planted in sugar, producing 3,900,000 pounds of sugar. In addition, enslavers could count on producing as a by-product roughly 80 gallons of cane molasses for each 1,000 pounds of sugar produced. With each hogshead weighing roughly 1,000 pounds, the enslaved in Brazoria County produced 3,900 hogsheads of sugar and 312,000 gallons of molasses. The sugar era in the lowcountry peaked in 1852 when the enslaved cultivated 10,924 hogsheads of sugar and 873,920 gallons of molasses. Except for a slight rebound in 1858 when the enslaved produced 81 percent of the 1852 high, sugar declined in production until reaching just 4,336 hogsheads in 1860. The average enslaved "hand" could cultivate 10,000 pounds of sugar per year, or about 6.25 acres of cane. Texas sugar sold for anywhere from 4 to 6 cents per pound in the antebellum years, making each hogshead worth at its highest $60. In the 1850s, molasses sold for 8 cents a gallon, with 100 gallons constituting each barrel. At these prices, each enslaved "hand" could produce up to $600 of sugar and $64 of molasses per year. At the height of sugar cultivation in 1852, the enslaved of the lowcountry produced $655,400 worth of sugar cane and $69,913 of molasses, for a total of over $700,000 for the year. If the enslaved cultivated the maximum amount of cotton and sugar possible, each "hand" could produce as much as $1,114 in profits per year.[11]

Enslavers also maintained large herds of cattle which they both slaughtered for food and drove overland to market. In 1850, there were 129,992 head of cattle in the lowcountry, including 50,192 in Brazoria County alone. By 1860, the number of cattle had increased to 187,776, or 6.8 percent of the total for the entire state. Although cattle in the lowcountry remained below cotton and sugar as a cash crop, the valuation of these bovine averaged $5.89 a head, from a high of $6.23 in Fort Bend County to a low of $5.36 in Matagorda County. These cattle represented an investment of over $1.1 million in 1860, or just under 5.5 percent of all property in the region. Early Anglo settlers in the lowcountry often used cattle for payment of debts, and the practice continued through the antebellum years. James Perry maintained a large herd of cattle on Chocolate Bayou in Brazoria County, and every year Perry would drive cattle from Chocolate Bayou to Dollar Point on Galveston Bay for shipment to market, making them some of the first cattle drives in Texas history. John Duncan maintained a large herd of cattle on his plantation in Matagorda County, and other enslavers also trained the enslaved as cowboys. Sam Jones Washington, an enslaved man born c.1848 in Wharton County, recalled that his enslaver, Sam Young, ran a small farm on the west bank of the Colorado River and raised just a little cotton, along with vegetables. Washington began by running errands for Young, before the enslaver taught the young man to ride a horse. After learning to ride, Washington herded cattle most of the time. Washington continued to work as a cowboy for three years after emancipation before becoming a farmer. Although the role and profitability of cattle in the lowcountry paled in comparison to cotton and sugar, the tax records and contemporary accounts make it clear that it played a part in the capitalism of slavery in the region.[12]

The profitability of slavery in the lowcountry also depended on the outlay of capital necessary to realize the incredible profits from cotton and sugar. In terms of capital investments, enslavers had to consider the costs of land, cotton gins, sugar mills, overseers, the cost of food and medical care for the enslaved, and the purchase prices of the enslaved themselves. The value of land varied depending on its desirability for agriculture. In 1850, land in the Texas lowcountry ranged from a low in Matagorda County of $1.38 an acre to a high of $2.90 in Wharton County. By 1860, those values had dramatically increased from a low in Matagorda County of $3.30 an acre to a high of $13.98 an acre in Wharton County, the most valuable land in Texas. Likewise, "improved acres," or land under cultivation, jumped as well. In 1850, the region had a total of 48,860 improved acres, or 7.6 percent of the state total. By 1860, that total had jumped to 110,741 but had fallen to just 4.27 percent of all improved acres in Texas. In 1860, Matagorda County had a total of $70,257 in cultivated acres, Fort Bend County $362,212, Brazoria County $299,720, and Wharton County $324,881, for a total of just over $1.5 million in improved land.[13]

Sugar mills, cotton gins, and other farm implements constituted the second largest outlay of capital for most enslavers. By 1860, Brazoria County had $531,717 in agricultural implements and infrastructure, Fort Bend County $129,175, Matagorda County $89,745, and Wharton County $97,965, for a total of $848,602. However, a healthy percentage of the dollar amount of this infrastructure included the more than forty sugar mills in the region. Sugar mills used horse or steam power. The numbers made it abundantly clear that the steam-powered mills far outpaced their more primitive counterparts, making them more valuable. In 1852, the fifteen mills still using horsepower to process sugar cane ground 2,166 hogsheads of sugar, while the twenty-nine steam-powered mills processed 8,837 hogsheads. Brazoria County alone had twenty-nine of the forty-four mills, and they varied widely in value. At the top end, Morgan L. Smith at Waldeck owned a brick sugar mill valued at $50,000. Eight mills counted their value at $20,000 each, six at $15,000 apiece, two at $12,000, one at $10,000, one at $8,000, and ten at $5,000, for a total of $392,000 in sugar mills. The *Texas Planter* noted that in 1856 the value of the sugar mills, land, and enslaved persons represented a total investment of $1,134,000 for these twenty-nine sugar planters against a gross profit of $464,080 in sugar for the year.[14]

The third, and largest outlay of capital for enslavers involved the purchase of enslaved individuals themselves. In assigning dollar values to human beings, enslavers had to factor in a return on investment that included sex, age, health, and a multitude of other factors. Broadly speaking, enslaved persons can be grouped into four age categories for the purpose of determining monetary values. Children, from birth to age eleven constituted the first category. At this age, enslavers attempted to value the enslaved mainly on potential for future return on investment. For both boys and girls this calculation included the potential for work in the fields, and for girls it also included future reproductive potential. The second category, adolescence and early adulthood, included those aged twelve to twenty-two. During this stage of life, prices rose dramatically as both boys and girls began work in the fields at age twelve and began to realize their reproductive capacities. Enslaved men and women who brought the highest prices became those adults ages twenty-three to thirty-nine. During this phase of life, both men and women reached their highest potential for both manual labor and reproduction. Finally, the last category of enslaved persons became those aged forty and older. Those in this final category saw their prices drop dramatically as the hideously brutal toll that slavery took on the body began to manifest itself.[15]

During the 1830s, not enough enslaved children lived in the Texas low-country to acquire a representative sample, but in the last 25 years of slavery the prices of enslaved children in the lowcountry outpaced even the national average. In the 1840s, the average appraised price of boys adjusted for the 1860 Consumer Price Index averaged $260.83. In the 1850s, the average peaked at $341.74, a 31 percent increase. Finally, during the Civil War, the mean dipped to $249.78, with the overall average for the region at $248.12 compared to a national average of $212. Girls brought a slightly lower price, in the 1840s, averaging $230.62 but also peaking in the 1850s at $291.08. Again, prices dropped during the Civil War to $209.48, for a regional average of $243.73, a statistically insignificant difference for boys of the same age. The price of girls in the Texas lowcountry also remained significantly above the national average of $190.[16]

Prices rose dramatically during adolescence and early adulthood. For males of this age, the mean valuation became $739.83 in the 1830s, before dropping to $572.64 in the 1840s. Prices appear to have dipped in the 1840s as enslaved persons spilled into the lowcountry, producing a glut in the market. Prices spiked in the 1850s to $781.58 before again dropping to $722 during the Civil War. For this age category, males in the lowcountry brought a considerably higher price at $704 than the national average of $610. Women in this age group averaged $736 in the 1830s, before also dipping to $578.62 in the 1840s, and then rising to $746.74 before finally dropping to $626.93 during the Civil War. The average prices for women of this age group in the lowcountry showed an even greater difference than those for men at $672.07 compared to the national mean of $517.[17]

Enslavers consistently assigned those enslaved men and women in the prime of adulthood the highest dollar values. In the 1830s, men averaged $728.33 before dropping to $634.94 in the 1840s. Values rose in the 1850s to a high of $822.93, before dropping slightly to $812.94 in the 1860s. The average of $749.78 for men in the lowcountry mirrored almost exactly the national average of $747 for the larger United States. For women in the 1830s, prices stood at $747.50, before also dipping to $614.09 in the 1840s. Values for women also realized their highest point in the 1850s at $713.53 before also dropping to $605.54 in the war years. The average for adult women in the Texas lowcountry of $670.16 stood remarkably above the national average of $528.[18]

Not enough enslaved individuals aged 40 and older lived in the Texas lowcountry to obtain adequate data in the 1830s, but by the 1840s, the average value for men stood at $337.45, even lower than the mean of $464.50 for women in this age group. In the 1850s, appraisals rose to $605.14 for men, with the exact same figure for women. Finally, during the war, the price dropped to $407.76 for men and $258.69 for women. Still, the average valuations for both men and women in this oldest group remained above the national average at $450.12 for men and $439.10 for women compared to the national average of $433 for men and $268 for women.[19]

A variety of factors could also affect the valuation of enslaved men and women. Abe, a thirty-nine-year-old blacksmith enslaved on the Oakland plantation in Fort Bend County brought a hefty sum of $1,258.80, while an appraiser valued Andrew, a forty-nine-year-old carpenter at the Lake Jackson plantation in Brazoria County at $1,328. Conversely, Jimmy, a thirty-year-old man with only one arm, was appraised for $249. Milor, a 35-year-old man in the estate of Roberta Ewing of Matagorda County listed as having "a sore leg, crippled," came in at $207.50. Repeatedly escaping could also decrease the price asked. Edmund, a forty-five-year-old "notorious runaway" also listed in the Ewing estate came in valued at only $332.[20]

As prices rose, enslavers tried desperately to increase the enslaved population, including forced procreation. This type of sexual exploitation of the bodies of enslaved women and men was vividly remembered by those affected for the rest of their lives. Sam Jones Washington, enslaved in Wharton County, recalled that he did not know his father, that his enslaver would call his father for "service," to impregnate women, and that most of the young women on his enslaver's farm were not married to allow for this sort of breeding arrangement. Similarly, Sarah Ford, enslaved on the Patton plantation in Brazoria County, recounted decades later that her mother told her that the white people would not let those who worked in the fields marry and that they would just put a man and a "breedin'" woman together "like mules." The lack of affection between the two chosen individuals did not matter; if women refused, they would receive a whipping. Pinkie Kelly, a child enslaved by Greenville McNeel, told an interviewer that her father drove oxen but that she did not know for sure whether he was her father because children at that time did not necessarily know their fathers. These accounts indicate that this type of sexual violence remained ubiquitous in the Texas lowcountry in the decades before emancipation.[21]

Enslavers in the Texas lowcountry also freely used the whip to incentivize cotton and sugar production. Christopher Anthony, enslaved on the Patton plantation in Brazoria County, recalled that the overseer "sho' use to whip" those who worked in the fields. Sarah Ford remembered that the "bullwhip

Table 6.1. Prices of Enslaved Males (Adjusted for 1860 Consumer Price Index)

	1830s	1840s	Percentage Increase/Decrease	1850s	Percentage Increase/Decrease	1860s	Percentage Increase/Decrease	Texas Lowcountry Average	National Average	Percentage Higher/Lower
Childhood (Ages 0–10)	N/A	$260.83	N/A	$341.74	+31%	$249.78	–27%	$248.12	$212	–15%
Adolescence and Early Adulthood (Ages 11–22)	$739.83	$572.64	–22.6%	$781.58	+37%	$722	–8%	$704	$610	–13%
Adulthood (Ages 23–39)	$728.33	$634.94	–12.8%	$822.93	+30%	$812.94	–1.3%	$749.78	$747	–0.4%
Superannuated (Ages 40+)	N/A	$337.45	N/A	$605.14	+79%	$407.76	–33%	$450.12	$433	–4%
Average	$734.08	$451.59	–38.5%	$637.84	+41%	$548.12	–14%	$538	$501	–7%

Table 6.2. Prices of Enslaved Females (Adjusted for 1860 Consumer Price Index)

	1830s	1840s	Percentage Increase/ Decrease	1850s	Percentage Increase/ Decrease	1860s	Percentage Increase/ Decrease	Texas Lowcountry Average	National Average	Percentage Higher/ Lower
Childhood (Ages 0–10)	N/A	$230.62	N/A	$291.08	+26%	$209.48	–28%	$243.73	$190	–22%
Adolescence and Early Adulthood (Ages 11–22)	$736	$578.62	–23.4%	$746.74	+29%	$626.93	–16%	$672.07	$517	–23%
Adulthood (Ages 23–39)	$747.50	$614.09	–18%	$713.53	+16%	$605.54	–16%	$670.16	$528	–22%
Superannuated (Ages 40+)	N/A	$464.50	N/A	$605.14	+30%	$258.69	–57%	$439.10	$268	–39%
Average	$741.75	$471.96	–36.4%	$589.12	+25%	$425.16	–28%	$506.27	$375.75	–26%

Table 6.3. Prices of Enslaved Males (adjusted for 2020 Consumer Price Index)

	1830s	1840s	1850s	1860s	Texas Lowcountry Average
Childhood (Ages 0–10)	N/A	$8,404.98	$11,012.23	$8,048.91	$9,155.38
Adolescence and Early Adulthood (Ages 11–22)	$23,840.28	$18,452.76	$25,185.63	$23,265.73	$22,686.10
Adulthood (Ages 23–39)	$24,087.44	$20,460.31	$26,518.09	$26,196.18	$24,315.51
Superannuated (Ages 40+)	N/A	$10,873.99	$19,500.04	$13,139.65	$14,504.56
Average	$23,963.87	$14,548	$20,554	$17,662.62	$17,665.39

Table 6.4. Prices of Enslaved Females (adjusted for 2020 Consumer Price Index)

	1830s	1840s	1850s	1860s	Texas Lowcountry Average
Childhood (Ages 0–10)	N/A	$7,431.50	$9,739.76	$6,750.28	$7,853.85
Adolescence and Early Adulthood (Ages 11–22)	$23,716.86	$18,645.45	$24,062.95	$20,202.19	$21,565.86
Adulthood (Ages 23–39)	$24,087.44	$19,788.44	$22,992.79	$19,512.93	$21,595.38
Superannuated (Ages 40+)	N/A	$14,968.05	$14,341.29	$8,336.03	$12,548.45
Average	$23,902.15	$15,208.36	$17,694.20	$13,700.36	$15,913.63

on your bare hide" made her forget anything "good" about her life at that time. Typically, during cotton harvesting season, enslavers expected male field "hands" to pick an average of at least 200 pounds of cotton per day. The enslaved man or woman who picked less than their "quota" for the day would receive a whipping at the end of the day. The records of overseers from the lowcountry reflected these practices. The ledger of the overseer for Valhalla, the Bolton plantation in Wharton County, revealed the desperate nature of harvest season for the enslaved as they struggled to pick more cotton than they had the day before to avoid the dreaded bullwhip. The twenty-two men at work in the fields averaged 185 pounds of cotton per day during the week of August 9–14, 1858. Only four had two consecutive days where they picked less cotton than the day before. Two unfortunate men, Patrick and Ted, suffered three consecutive negative days. The overseer listed both men as out "sick" on the fourth day, possibly from the whippings he imparted. The women in the fields averaged less than the men: 153 pounds per day. Of the twenty-eight women working in the cotton fields the same week, only five suffered through two consecutive negative days, while only one suffered three consecutive negative days. Emphasizing the fear of punishment, the average increase in cotton harvest was an astonishing 118 percent increase over the day before after two or more negative days. In sum, the enslaved on the Bolton place harvested 44,450 pounds of cotton in six days, enough to create nearly ninety bales. The zig-zag patterns of cotton production point to the desperation to avoid the physical punishment inflicted by the overseer's whip.[22]

In the county records, other than mortgages, deeds of trust served as the primary financial instrument used in collateralizing debt through the enslaved. In a deed of trust, an individual could mortgage the enslaved through a third party, a trustee. Generally, the trustee would take possession of the title to the enslaved and maintain the prerogative to sell in case the grantee failed to repay the debt owed the grantor. In an example of this type of transaction, on April 1, 1843, Levi Jones transferred two town lots in the city of Galveston along with Ben, aged forty-five, Tom aged forty-six, Nancy, aged nineteen, and Richard, aged seven, to Gail Borden in exchange for $1,060 in specie. Richard Jones served as the trustee in this arrangement and retained the right to sell the lots and four people with five days' notice. In this case, Richard Jones also served as the middleman in another way; he lent the specie to Gail Borden to give to Levi Jones to secure the property. In the case of a default, Jones would sell the property to recoup his losses, and any profit over and above the original loan would accrue to him.[23]

Table 6.5. Record of Cotton Picked by the Enslaved on the Bolton Plantation, August 9–14, 1858

	August 9	August 10	August 11	August 12	August 13	August 14
Mose	255	305	300	315	300	290
Ralph	240	300	295	300	305	295
Lemon	240	230	250	300	310	300
T. Bill	140	250	245	225	235	200
Oliver	180	220	230	225		
Tom	155	210	195	220	230	225
Butler	145	215	225	230	200	
Isah	150	200	230	210		
M. Henry	150	200	195	210	220	180
Charles	125	215	190	210	200	190
Patrick	170	200	195	185	180	"sick"
Harrison	160	200	190		180	
Ted	115	195	190	180	155	"sick"
Mon	121	150	190	180	155	190
G. Bill	130	165	145	160	180	
George	100	150	165	175	145	155
Jeff	120	140	130	155	130	135
W. Henry	100	125	135	140	155	120
Y. Henry	110	120	130	125	120	
Howell	95			120	125	130
Ruben	110	120				
Liza	150	300	250	240	310	
Tilda	200	298	300	310	320	315
Hannah	145	225	190	200	200	190
Loueza	100			110	120	130

Table 6.5. Continued

	August 9	August 10	August 11	August 12	August 13	August 14
Sarah	100	180	160	190	160	150
Lucinda	138	200	190	200	190	200
Monty	95	100	125	180	100	
Sally	95	100	128	160	140	130
Gracy	125	190	200	200	205	205
Rebecca	115	170	180	190	180	170
Francis	140	190	200	200	205	195
Phany	130	185	200	190	200	185
Betsey	120	185	155	190	200	185
Judy	110	130	120	180	200	
Mary	125	130	140	155	145	165
Martha	120					
Margaret	95					
Polly	90	100	110	120	125	100
Clara	100	95	100	110	105	115
Laura	85	90	95	100	100	95
Martha Ann	100	140	150	160	130	170
Jenny	100	95	80	75	90	95
Lucy	50	60	65	40	45	
Franry	300	450	445	475	560	480
Marsha	75	95	105	100	95	100
Sela	80	85	90	85	85	80
Charity		100	95	195	190	180
Rena	80	95	85	105	100	100

The Borden–Jones transaction also reveals several other aspects that became common in these transactions. Jones placed no stipulations in the transaction regarding interest on the loan. This was not uncommon because both parties understood that the profit from the labor of the enslaved would serve as interest. The time limit on repayment also remained unstated in the deed books, but generally, from the available records, it appears that twelve months evolved as the standard timeframe for repayment. When grantors did specify interest in the contract, generally 10 percent per year stood as the standard rate. In the deed books, deeds of trust outnumbered outright mortgages at least two to one, if not more, and most of these instruments involved not only enslaved people, but also land, crops, and every other conceivable form of property, from horses to sugar houses.

The business of turning enslaved people into instruments of collateralized debt obligations gave the financing of slavery as an economic institution its life blood in the Texas lowcountry. The capital raised through neighbors or large firms allowed individuals to purchase enslaved persons on credit or raise money to purchase land and other commodities by borrowing against their human property. The thousands of transactions recorded in county deed books probably do not even begin to scratch the surface of this neo-capitalism because many similar transactions doubtlessly occurred "off the books" between neighbors, friends and family without the need to record the transaction with the county. The millions of dollars involved provided the capital to expand slavery beyond anything possible without a similar system of debt and credit.

Mortgages on types of property other than enslaved men and women certainly took up much more space in the county deed books but raised far less capital. In 1849, a mortgage on a town lot in Galveston could raise $100, with another $137.50 for a house on that lot. In contrast, an enslaved man between the ages of twenty-five and thirty could bring at least $400 as collateral during this time period, nearly 170 percent of the capital that could be raised on the lot and house. It remains difficult to tell just how much money mortgages and deeds of trust generated on enslaved people as opposed to other types of property, but other studies have found that at least two-thirds of all money raised from collateralized debt in the slave states came from the value placed on enslaved individuals.[24]

Litigation involving enslaved men and women constantly filled the courts of the lowcountry as well. On July 6, 1853, George W. Tilley of Wharton County purchased an enslaved sixteen-year-old man named Friday from

F. Scranton and Company in Houston. Standard practice in selling enslaved individuals at that time dictated that the seller had to issue a warranty on the enslaved person, swearing to their soundness of mind and body. Scranton provided such a warranty in the sale, but not long after Tilley returned to Wharton County, Friday began showing signs of epilepsy. That fall, just months after the sale, Friday died of convulsions despite the medical care provided, and Tilley sued Scranton for a breach of warranty. At the trial, held on December 29, 1855, Tilley claimed Friday's value at $1,500, and asked for that amount plus $500 in interest, damages, and the cost of medical care. Witnesses at trial testified to Friday's fits, but split on whether the young man was ill when purchased, or whether he died of heatstroke. The jury found for Tilley in the amount of $1,100, along with interest dating back to the sale, and $30 in damages. Scranton appealed to the Texas Supreme Court for a new trial, but the high court, in the case of *Tilley v. Scranton* (1856), affirmed the judgment of the jury and the lower court.[25]

Other lawsuits, although they involved less money, also filled the county courts. In April 1851 at Quintana, Pleasant McNeel and Reuben Brown of Brazoria County placed a wager on a one-mile horse race. Both men bet one enslaved man each or the monetary equivalent to the winner of the race. Brown staked a man named Jeff, and McNeel bet a 45-year-old man named Gabriel. In lieu of actually surrendering the enslaved man "on demand," to the winner, the loser could pay the monetary equivalent of $1,000 in cash. Brown's horse won the race, and McNeel allegedly refused to surrender either Gabriel or the cash. On November 22, 1851, Brown filed suit in Texas district court to collect the wager. Cases like this one, ranging from suits over medical services rendered, to monetary compensation for various types of labor from enslaved persons filled the county and state courts in the Texas lowcountry, adding yet another layer to the capitalism of slavery.[26]

Enslavers leveraged the wealth created by slavery to create the first internal improvements in Texas in the form of canals and railroads. The shifting sandbar at the mouth of the Brazos endangered the marketing of the cotton and sugar down that river. Although the Republic of Texas chartered a railroad company to serve the lowcountry as early as 1838, these initial plans fell apart due to a lack of investors, and in 1842 the Congress of the Republic of Texas instead chartered the "Brazos Canal Company." Plans for the first canal began in 1843, but the German engineer hired by the company drowned in 1844, and in 1845 Abner Jackson took over its construction. Jackson entered into an agreement with William G. Hill and James Perry to formally take the project forward. Jackson and the others planned to construct the first part of the canal from Oyster Creek to Bastrop Bayou, and the second section from Oyster Creek to the Brazos. Jackson selected a place for the first part of the canal at the edge of his Lake Jackson plantation where Oyster Creek and Bastrop Bayou only stood about one mile apart. Although there is no corroborating evidence, it appears that enslaved men from Abner Jackson, William Hill and James Perry, dug the canal, a waterway roughly fifty feet wide and three feet deep. In April 1848, the first steamboat, the *Pioneer*, traversed the canal, although it remains unclear how many boats used the waterway. The enslaved under Jackson never constructed the second half of the planned canal, and by 1850 the Brazos Canal Company exhausted its funds and dissolved. The residents nicknamed the Brazos Canal the "slave ditch."[27]

The second major canal initiative began in Galveston in 1848. Backed by Robert and David Mills, the legislature chartered the "Galveston and Brazos Navigation Company" in 1850. Taking a route to the south of the Brazos Canal, the designers intended the new canal to connect the Brazos, San Bernard, Peach Creek, and the Colorado River to west Galveston Bay. By June 1854, the enslaved had constructed fifty miles of waterway, fifty feet wide and 3.5 feet deep connecting the Brazos River with Oyster Creek and San Luis Bay. Although enslavers established a regular steamboat service on this new canal, the company, deeply in debt, folded in 1856.[28]

By the middle of the 1850s, to ease the transportation of cotton and sugar to market in Houston and Harrisburg, enslavers had abandoned the idea of canals in favor of railroads. In 1841, the Republic of Texas granted a charter to the Harrisburg Railroad and Trading Company, but nothing ever came of this original venture. The company, later renamed the Harrisburg Town Company, transferred all their town lots to Sidney Sherman, veteran of the rebellion against Mexico, and Sherman succeeded in attracting northern capital to construct a railroad. The Third Legislature of the State of Texas granted a charter to the Buffalo Bayou, Brazos, and Colorado Railroad on February 11, 1850. The company fathers included Sidney Sherman, W. J. Hutchins, William Marsh Rice, and others. Late in 1852, a Boston engineer, John A. Williams, began laying out the route on the west bank of Buffalo Bayou at Harrisburg, and by August 1, 1853, the company had laid the first twenty miles of track, from Harrisburg to Stafford's Point for the first locomotive, the "General Sherman." From Stafford's Point, the company intended to make a straight line of track to Richmond, but the owners of Oakland Plantation, William J. Kyle and Frank Terry, intervened. They convinced the railroad to insert a slight curve in the route of the tracks, so that the railroad would pass directly by their sugar mill at Oakland on Oyster Creek. The railroad agreed, and by December 1855 the company had completed track to the east bank of the Brazos River opposite the town of Richmond. Constructing a bridge over the Brazos proved a difficult proposition, but the company succeeded in building a rudimentary "pile" bridge instead of a proper railroad trestle. This bridge, although it was sometimes dangerous in times of high water, remained in service until well after the Civil War. By the fall of 1860, the railroad reached all the way to Alleyton, on the east bank of the Colorado River across from Columbus.[29]

Other railroads followed quickly on the heels of the Buffalo Bayou, Brazos, and Colorado Railroad. In 1856, the city of Houston constructed the Houston Tap Railroad to connect the city's 6.5 miles to the BBB&C Railroad. The Houston Tap opened on October 21, 1856. Taking advantage of the railroad route, William J. Kyle and Frank Terry helped charter the Houston Tap and Brazoria Railroad to connect Houston to Brazoria County. Many of the enslavers in Brazoria County paid for their stock in the company by having the enslaved men and women construct the railroad grade. By 1859, the enslavers had extended the railroad to Sandy Point, and by 1860 it reached East Columbia, connecting the heart of the lowcountry by rail to Houston. Locals nicknamed this second railroad the "sugar road" for the service it provided to the large sugar plantations in Brazoria County. By 1860, enslavers had also constructed the Galveston and Houston Railroad to connect the two cities with an impressive railroad bridge built between Virginia Point and Galveston Island completed in 1860, and the Texas Central Railroad, beginning the connection between Houston and New Orleans. Although the golden age of railroads did not arrive in Texas until after the Civil War, the foundations of that mode of transportation began with the prompting of merchants and enslavers in the lowcountry anxious to connect the fertile bottomlands with the commercial centers of Houston, Galveston, and beyond. This rail network laid the foundation for the larger network of railroads that would connect Texas by land with the larger world after the Civil War.[30]

In extracting every ounce of profit from the bodies of the enslaved and the land in the Texas lowcountry, enslavers created a kind of nascent capitalism and enough wealth to command the construction of the first canals and railroads in Texas. However, the amount of cotton and sugar produced, the dollars generated, and the infrastructure built through this hideous form of human exploitation sometimes masked the true human toll exacted on the lives of the enslaved, their day-to-day lives, and their intimate relationships.

Ellerslie (Brazoria County Historical Museum)

Sycamore Grove (Wharton County Historical Museum)

Sycamore Grove (Wharton County Historical Museum)

Washington Edwards, born in Africa and smuggled into Texas by Monroe Edwards. Brazoria County, 1889. (Texas State Library and Archives 1905/11–1)

Ned and Julia Ann (Jackson) Thompson. Freed people. Ned Thompson was born in Africa and smuggled into Texas up the San Bernard River c. 1840. Photograph by J. P. Underwood, Brazoria County, 1913. (Brazoria County Historical Museum)

John S. Sydnor's Auction and Commission House on The Strand in Galveston. (*Texas Almanac*, 1857)

'Cinto (San Jacinto) and Lucy Lewis, freed people living in the brick slave cabins at Ellerslie, 1934. (Brazoria County Historical Museum)

Sarah (Mitchell) Ford (1854–1945), freedwoman formerly enslaved on the Patton plantation. Photograph taken in Houston, July 9, 1937. (Library of Congress Manuscript Division WPA Slave Narrative Project: Container, A931, vol. 16, part 2)

Sam Jones Washington (eighty-eight years old), freedman formerly enslaved by Samuel Young in Wharton County. Photograph taken in Fort Worth, July 30, 1937. (Library of Congress Manuscript Division WPA Slave Narrative Project: Container, A932, vol. 16, part 4)

Philles Thomas (c. 1863–1938), freedwoman formerly enslaved by David G. Mills at Lowwood, Brazoria County. Photograph taken at Fort Worth, 1936. (Library of Congress Manuscript Division WPA Slave Narrative Project: Container, A932, vol. 16, part 4)

Patsy Moses (seventy-four years old), freedwoman, formerly enslaved in Fort Bend County. Photograph taken November 15, 1937, at Mart, Texas. (Library of Congress Manuscript Division WPA Slave Narrative Project: Container, A931, vol. 16, part 3)

Collar fastened by a blacksmith around the neck of Lewis, a man enslaved on the Mims plantation in Brazoria County in an attempt to keep him from seeking his freedom. This device became known as "Lew's Horns" and remained on Lewis's neck until after emancipation. The collar measured 12″ tall and 25″ from tip to tip of the upward-facing prongs. The oval collar itself measured 10″ by 7.75.″ The original artifact remains in private hands in Brazoria County. Pictured here is a full-size replica in the Brazoria County Historical Museum. (Photograph by the author, 2022)

Ammon Underwood House, East Columbia, Brazoria County. (Photograph by the author, 2022)

From left to right Sam Simon, Jobe Clemons, and Hiram Clemons ringing the dinner bell on the side of the Chenango sugar mill, constructed of handmade bricks, Brazoria County. Photograph taken in 1947. (Brazoria County Historical Museum)

Chenango sugar mill c. 1936 (Brazoria County Historical Museum)

Lake Jackson (Brazoria County Historical Museum)

Levi Jordan plantation house (Brazoria County Historical Museum)

Arcola sugar mill adjacent to Oyster Creek, Fort Bend County, the only intact antebellum sugar mill in the United States. The tin roof was added in the twentieth century. (Photograph by the author, 2022)

Waldeck (Brazoria County Historical Museum)

Waldeck sugar mill (Brazoria County Historical Museum)

Slave cabin at Egypt, Wharton County. The tin roof was added in the twentieth century. (Photograph by Jessica Lundberg, 2019)

Slave cabins at Durazno (Brazoria County Historical Museum)

Sweeney-Waddy slave cabin, East Columbia, Brazoria County. The cabin was originally located on the Sweeney plantation where Old Ocean, Texas, is today. It was the home of the enslaved family of Mark and Larkin Waddy. The cabin was moved to East Columbia before 1983. (Photograph by the author, 2022)

Ethiopia Baptist Church, Waldeck. Constructed in the 1850s. Here, white ministers preached to the enslaved and sometimes to whites as well. (Brazoria County Historical Museum)

Patton Plantation House (now the Varner-Hogg State Historic Site), pre-1927. (Texas Historical Commission)

Patton Plantation House (now the Varner-Hogg State Historic Site), as it appears today. (Photograph by the author, 2022)

Freedom Tree, Palmer Plantation, Fort Bend County. It was under this tree that those enslaved on the Palmer Place learned of emancipation in 1865. (Photograph by the author, 2022)

Freed people Charlie and Isabella Brown, Brazoria County c. 1880s. (Brazoria County Historical Museum)

Convicts working in the sugar fields at Arcola c. 1908

Walter Moses Burton (1829–1913). Born into slavery in North Carolina and brought to Fort Bend County, Texas, by his enslaver in 1850, Republican voters elected Burton sheriff and president of the Union League of Fort Bend County in 1869—the first elected African American sheriff in Texas and the United States. In 1874, he won election to the Texas State Senate, representing the 13th Senate District consisting of Austin, Fort Bend, and Wharton Counties in the 14th Legislature. He subsequently won election to the 15th, 16th, and 17th Legislatures from the 17th Senate District consisting of Fort Bend, Waller, and Wharton Counties, representing that district from 1876 to 1883. He died on June 4, 1913, and was buried in Morton Cemetery, Richmond, Texas. (The State Preservation Board)

JACOB FREEMAN

Jacob Freeman (1841–1900). Born into slavery in Alabama, he arrived in Texas in 1852 with his enslaver. He won election to the Colored Men's Convention at Brenham and won election to the Texas House of Representatives for the 14th Legislature from the 13th House District in 1874, representing Austin, Fort Bend, and Waller Counties. He was subsequently elected to the 16th Legislature in 1879, representing the 37th House District, consisting of Fort Bend, Waller, and Wharton Counties. Although a Republican, he ran unsuccessfully for the Texas House as a Populist candidate in 1886. (The State Preservation Board)

W. H. HOLLAND.

William H. Holland (1841–1907). Born into slavery in Marshall, Texas, he was freed by his white enslaver and father, Bird Holland, in the late 1850s before William moved to Ohio. He enlisted in the 16th United States Colored Troops in 1864 and fought at the battles of Nashville and Overton Hill. After the war, Holland attended Oberlin College for two years beginning in 1867 before moving back to Texas, and in 1876 he won election to the Texas House in the 15th Legislature, representing the 37th House District, which consisted of Fort Bend, Waller, and Wharton Counties. He died in Mineral Wells on May 27, 1907. (The State Preservation Board)

Benjamin Franklin Williams (1819–1886). Born into slavery in Virginia in 1819, Williams lived in South Carolina and Tennessee before his enslaver removed him to Texas in 1859. After emancipation he became a Methodist minister and helped establish Wesley Methodist Chapel in Austin in 1865. By 1868, Williams had become vice president of the Union League and a staunch Republican. He served as a delegate to the Constitutional Convention of 1868–1869, and in 1870 he won election to the Texas House in the 12th Legislature, representing Lavaca and Colorado Counties, where he was the tallest member of the House at 6'2". In the 12th Legislature he also came in third in the race for Speaker of the House. He subsequently moved to Fort Bend County, where he helped establish Kendleton, and he won election to the Texas House in the 16th Legislature in 1879, representing Waller, Fort Bend, and Wharton Counties. In 1885, he won election to the 19th Legislature, representing Waller and Fort Bend Counties. He returned home to Kendleton and died there in January 1887 while still in office. (The State Preservation Board)

Nathan H. Haller (1845–1917). Born into slavery in Charleston, South Carolina, on July 8, 1845, Haller was brought by his enslaver to Walker County, Texas, before 1860. After emancipation, he became active in Republican politics in Walker County and moved to Brazoria County before 1892. That year he won election to the Texas House in the 23rd Legislature, representing the 40th District, which consisted of Brazoria and Matagorda Counties. In 1894, he won a contested election to again represent the 40th District in the 24th Legislature. His term of office ended in 1895, and he left office as the last Republican to represent the Texas lowcountry during Reconstruction. He moved to Houston, where he died on February 27, 1917. (The State Preservation Board)

Chapter 7

Complex Households

*Gender, Sex, and Slavery in the
Texas Lowcountry*

IN 1855, Sarah Black of Brazoria County filed for divorce. According to her petition, on August 15, 1854, Sarah caught her husband, James E. Black, in the act of "illicit sexual intercourse" with an enslaved "mulatto" woman named Susan. The next month, she caught her husband with another enslaved woman named Ann. When she confronted him, Black told his wife that "a damn good whipping or cowhiding would do her good, and that he would give it to her unless she minded her own business." Furthermore, Mrs. Black alleged that for the "past two or three years" every time she spoke to her husband, he "would reply 'go to hell you god damned old bitch,'" along with other threatening language. Despite these indignities, it appears that the heart of Sarah Black's complaint consisted of the allegation that in the recent past, her husband ordered the overseer and the enslaved to disregard her orders and that at one point an enslaved woman raised a stick to her and threatened to whip her. James Black stood by and laughed, refusing to have the woman whipped for her behavior. In the end, the court dismissed Sarah Black's petition.[1]

Sexual contact between enslavers and their enslaved "property," especially enslaved females, was ubiquitous. Sexual relations that crossed the color line became more noticeable in cities of the lower South like New Orleans or Charleston, and these arrangements included a full range of sexual relationships, from chance encounters to romance, from pedophilia to voyeurism, both heterosexual and homosexual. The most common relationship revolved around "concubinange—sustained sexual contact" between an enslaved woman and her enslaver, both in the more visible situations in large cities as witnessed in the exploitation of Louisa Picquet and her mother, as well as in less visible locales. In fact, according to one prominent scholar, "the practice of concubinage in these smaller Southern locales has been woefully underestimated largely because rural isolation permitted an invisibility on isolated farms and plantations where these women toiled." Such was the case in the Texas lowcountry, where only extended legal proceedings and court testimony revealed the truly complex nature of these relationships. Although several examples from the region exist, the two that provide the most insight into this aspect of enslaving are the stories of Rachel Patton, or Bartlett, of Brazoria County and Sobrina Clark and her children of Wharton County.[2]

On Wednesday November 1, 1854, Charles Patton and David Murphee filed a petition in Brazoria County Court asking that the court find Columbus "Kit" Patton, the brother of Charles Patton and a wealthy enslaver, mentally incompetent to manage his own affairs. This petition set off a titanic legal battle centering on the dynamics of the Patton family and an enslaved woman named Rachel.

The Pattons, some of Austin's earliest Anglo settlers, arrived in Texas in the early 1830s, setting in motion the drama that would ultimately play out in the late antebellum years. On July 12, 1831, sixteen-year-old Columbus R. Patton wrote a letter to Stephen F. Austin from his home in Hopkinsville, Kentucky. "I intend in emigrating [sic] to Texas this fall," wrote the young Patton, "and you will confer a favour [sic] that I hope I shall be able to reciprocate by answering my enquiries and giving me any general information you may deem expedient relative to that country. My intent is to take with me a stock of goods and some negroes for farming." Whatever information Austin returned to Patton, it appears that Columbus Patton arrived in San Felipe in the fall of 1831, the first of his large family that would follow. Columbus was one of nine Patton siblings, seven sons and two daughters, the children of John D. and Hester Patton of Hopkinsville. By 1832, Columbus's older brothers William and St. Clair had joined him in Texas, and within a short time so had his brothers Matthew and Charles, his younger sisters America and Margaretta, along with his parents, who maintained residences in Hopkinsville and Texas. The Pattons also brought several enslaved African Americans with them from Kentucky, and although the initial number remains unclear, by 1840 the family enslaved at least forty men, women, and children.[3]

The Pattons enjoyed a close relationship with the family of Austin Tyler, another enslaver from Hickman County Kentucky, ninety miles southwest of Hopkinsville. On July 23, 1830, Mathew C. Patton, one of the older sons of the family, married Matilda Tyler, sister of Austin Tyler, in Hickman County. Three years later Austin Tyler "left" an eighteen-year-old enslaved woman named Rachel with the Pattons in Texas.[4]

On April 4, 1834, Columbus Patton purchased a league and a labor of land from Martin Varner at San Felipe for $13,000, the first of several land purchases he would make in the name of his father. The land, located along Varner's Creek north of West Columbia, became the focal point for the Patton plantation and business activities. Even as their landholdings and purchases of enslaved African Americans continued, the unhealthy environment of Brazoria County took a toll on the family. Both Matilda Tyler Patton and Matthew C. Patton died by 1838, leaving their four-year-old son, Matthew T. C. Patton, in the custody of his uncle Columbus. Two years later, on August 25, 1840, the seventy-one-year-old patriarch of the family, John D. Patton, died, leaving his sons Columbus and St. Clair to probate his will. By the time of his death, John D. Patton owned forty enslaved African Americans, over 5,500 acres in Brazoria County, and a total estate worth $26,795.[5]

With the death of his father, Columbus took over the role of family patriarch. In this capacity he enlarged his landholdings, instructed the enslaved on his plantation to begin constructing a brick Greek Revival mansion on the bank of Varner's Creek, provided for his mother and sisters, and began grooming his nephew Matt, now next in line to head the family. Columbus maintained a friendly relationship with his brother St. Clair, but he did not care for his brother Charles. Ironically, however, Columbus and Charles had something in common: both men took concubines for themselves from among the enslaved women left to them by their father. Charles lived with a young woman named Ardenia, a year his junior, and Columbus cohabitated with Rachel. Although both relationships became well known, Rachel began to function as the woman in charge of the plantation on Varner's Creek, much to the embarrassment and chagrin of the rest of the family, and the white community of West Columbia.[6]

As the decade progressed, tensions between Columbus, Rachel, and the rest of the family increased. While Charles maintained a separate household on the east side of the Brazos River, St. Clair, America, Margaretta, Matt, and Hester continued to live with Columbus, even as Rachel took greater control of the household. In 1843, Hester complained to Columbus that when she commanded Rachel to churn butter, the enslaved woman refused. Columbus responded to his mother that she "was bringing up that old thing again." Hester also complained that once when she was speaking to Rachel, "she wheeled off and put her arm a kimbo [sic] and paid no attention to her at all." Hester M. Patton died on September 14, 1843, at the age of seventy-two, and her children buried her in the family cemetery on the plantation. After her death, America, who married David Aldridge in December 1842, and Margaretta, who married David Murphee on January 8, 1845, both moved away from the plantation on Varner's Creek.[7]

Meanwhile Columbus's relationship with Rachel continued to rankle the white community. Rachel regularly attended the Methodist Church in East Columbia, and one Sunday in 1845, she sat near the women of the Tinsley family. Although she normally sat on pews reserved for whites, on this particular Sunday her actions somehow upset the women of the Tinsley family. Isaac Tinsley complained to the pastor of the church and asked the reverend to "speak to her and let her know which seats were intended for slaves." The pastor apparently did speak to Rachel, and after that, Columbus and Isaac Tinsely had a "falling out that lasted about three months."[8]

St. Clair Patton continued to live with Columbus until he, too, had a quarrel with his brother over Rachel in 1847. E. S. Jackson worked for Columbus Patton as an overseer, and at some point, in the spring of 1846 Rachel came to dislike him intensely. As Jackson recalled: "At the time I was at work for him she seemed to take a dislike to me and would not pour out my coffee for several mornings! And one morning I got up from the table and threatened to break a chair over her. Patton was sitting at the table. She flew around behind Mr. Patton & he walked out after me and said she should not do so again that he would have it all fixed." Jackson quit shortly thereafter, and Charles Grimm replaced him as overseer. Grimm noted that in 1847 Columbus and St. Clair had a falling out and did not speak to each other again before the death of the latter on December 2, 1849.[9]

By the early 1850s, at the age of thirty-six, Columbus Patton began showing signs of mental degeneration. According to witnesses, his vision began declining in 1851, and both his plans for his plantation and his behavior became increasingly eccentric. Although he experienced periods of lucidity, many of his neighbors and friends noticed a marked change in his demeanor. The decline in both his mental and physical health led the other members of the family, particularly his siblings Charles and Margaretta and his nephew Matt, to fear for the future of the family estate.[10]

As Columbus's health declined, his relationship with his nephew Matt became increasingly strained. In 1850, Columbus decided to send Matt away to school in Danville, Kentucky, in hopes that after his education he could carry on the family business. Matt made it as far as his Uncle Austin Tyler's plantation near Hickman before he stopped and refused to continue east. Fearing that Columbus would be displeased with his decision, Matt convinced Tyler to write and explain the situation. In April 1851, Tyler wrote to Columbus, informing him of Matt's decision and stating that there "was a good school in the neighborhood" which the younger Patton could attend. After remaining a short time in Kentucky, Matt Patton returned to Brazoria County to work for Columbus as an overseer.[11]

Sometime in 1853 Matt and Columbus experienced a serious falling out that disrupted the entire Patton plantation and business empire. While working for his uncle, Matt got into an argument with Rachel and whipped her. Columbus immediately banished his nephew from the plantation, threatening the younger man's position as heir to the family estate. The family rift grew more pronounced until David Murphee and Charles Patton filed their petition in Brazoria County Court asking Chief Justice Samuel W. Perkins to find Columbus mentally incompetent.[12]

Judge Perkins found enough merit in the petition to order the county sheriff, Robert J. W. Reel, to produce Columbus Patton in court at noon the next day, November 2. Perkins also ordered Reel to assemble a jury to hear the case. The next day at noon, Columbus Patton appeared in court and after hearing the evidence against him, a jury of twelve men found "that said C. R. Patton is not of sound mind." Perkins appointed John Adriance and Charles Patton guardians of the estate, with Charles Patton charged to "engage some competent medical gentleman to accompany him on his way . . ." to an asylum.[13]

Following the finding of *non compos mentis*, Charles Patton and John Adriance determined to commit Columbus Patton to the South Carolina Lunatic Asylum in Columbia. The Brazoria County sheriff accompanied Columbus to South Carolina. The asylum, housed in a Greek Revival building designed by the Charleston architect Robert Mills, admitted Columbus Patton as a patient on November 18, 1854, at the rate of $250 per year, plus an initial charge of $175 on account of the "advanced nature" of his disease. There, under the care of Dr. J. W. Parker, Columbus Patton began his long convalescence.[14]

Back on the banks of Varner's Creek, Charles Patton took charge of the plantation and immediately put Rachel to work in the cotton fields. During this time, Charles continued to run his brother's affairs and would travel to visit him. This new state of affairs suddenly came to an end in the fall of 1856.[15]

On September 29, 1856, Columbus Patton died after a "short illness." That day, the attendants of the asylum carried his body to Ebenezer Lutheran Church Cemetery, some 350 yards southwest of the hospital, and buried him near the "east" edge of the churchyard. His death set in motion a hotly contested legal battle over his estate in Brazoria County.[16]

Charles Patton and John Adriance learned of the death of Columbus Patton in late 1856, but Adriance did not begin assembling a record of the assets and liabilities of the estate until early 1857. In late January of that year, Adriance ventured out to Varner's Creek with Ammon Underwood to collect any papers left behind in the house. After a search of the mansion, Adriance and Underwood discovered a cache of papers in a desk. Adriance recalled that "there was some little order among the papers in the desk and there were other papers in an old trunk in the South Room. . . . The upper part of the desk that contained the papers had been broken open." Among the papers, Underwood discovered Columbus Patton's last will and testament, dated and signed June 1, 1853. Adriance informed Charles Patton that he had discovered a will, and on Tuesday, January 27, 1857, he notified the Brazoria County Court of Columbus Patton's death and presented the will to the court over the objections of Charles Patton, Matt Patton, America (Patton) Ragland, Margaretta (Patton) Murphee and David Murphee.[17]

The contents of the will revealed the reason for the objections. Sometime in the 1840s, Columbus Patton became the guardian or custodian of a Henry Patton, reportedly born in Germany in about 1843 and began his will by providing for the child. "I give to my 'Dutch Boy' Henry Patton five thousand dollars to be put at interest so soon as it can be taken from my estate without making forced sale of property," Columbus Patton wrote. He then named four enslaved individuals, Jacob Steel, or "Big Jake," Solomon, Rachel, and Maria, stating that he wanted them to "remain the property of his estate," and "let to live with whom they wish without hire and one hundred dollars per year given to each of the women out of my estate so long as they live." He also bequeathed to Mary Brown Phelps three enslaved individuals, John, Lucinda and her child, and then left the balance of his estate, valued at over $161,000, to his nine-year-old niece, Mary Hester Aldridge. If anything happened to Mary before she married or turned twenty-one, Columbus wanted his estate divided equally between the children of his sisters America and Margaretta. He also invited his sister America to live on his plantation until her daughter Mary came of age. Patton named John W. Brooks, John W. Harris, and Elisha M. Pease executors of his estate and disinherited his brother and nephew by stating bluntly: "I have no other heirs and desire no others under any pretext or excuses."[18]

With the estate at stake, Charles and Matt began working furiously throughout February building a court case that would invalidate the will on the grounds that Columbus was already mentally incompetent at the time he wrote the will and that Rachel manipulated him into cutting them out of their inheritance. Charles gathered affidavits or convinced the court to issue subpoenas to more than a dozen individuals, and in March Chief Justice Perkins began reviewing and hearing their testimony.

The first witnesses concentrated on Columbus Patton's alleged insanity. Mary Roberts of Harris County testified that Patton appeared deranged to her during a conversation she had with him on July 4, 1853, in the company of other young women. Other witnesses also testified to his derangement and to his lack of mindfulness regarding the state of his plantation. In summarizing the testimony of the witnesses, the attorney for the heirs wrote of a fence Patton commanded his overseer to construct "which when finished would not hold anything which stood on four legs if it desire to escape, which fence was to enclose a pasture for his brood mares some forty or fifty in number which pasture when so enclosed contained neither water shade or grass and in which pasture he placed his stock of horses which not regarding said fence immediately escaped to the surrounding prairie and forest." The witness also described an "impractical" machine Patton had designed which he termed a "Gyascutus." He testified that Patton had him build a fence around part of the plantation by simply piling logs in a heap and requesting that he "insert upon the top rails of his fence sharp instruments to impale and destroy the squirrels as they attempted to get into the field."[19]

Charles Grimm testified that Columbus Patton tried to construct a series of canals through the plantation. The overseer testified "that the principle [sic] and main canal to be made when there was seldom any water, and the branches leading from said canal being upon lower ground than the said main canal and to be tributaries to the main canal the slough which was to furnish the water to these canals being dry except in the most rainy seasons of the year."[20]

One of Patton's neighbors also testified to his religious beliefs. Evidently, Patton began claiming a belief in deism. He also claimed that Andrew Jackson Davis had discovered the "true path to heaven" through spiritualism, and he "advocated the directions contained in the works of . . . Davis and constantly earnestly and believingly conversed about them."[21]

After the testimony regarding his insanity, the witnesses also attested to his relationship with Rachel and claimed that she manipulated him into disinheriting his nephew and brother. The court summarized the position of the heirs as follows:

> that during the entire year of 1853 the said C. R. Patton was of unsound mind and incapable of making a valid will and testament. And by way of further amendment they say that the said instrument offered for probate is not the last will of the said C. R. Patton, but that it was extorted from him by the threats, fraudulent conduct, and artful advices of a certain Negro woman slave named Rachel with whom the said C. R. Patton lived in disgraceful intimacy and who had undue influence and control over the said C. R. Patton, and who is one of the legatees named in said will, being allowed one hundred dollars per annum and in effect set free. And they further say that of the fraudulent conduct, and cunning advices of the said Negro woman Rachel, the said C. R. Patton was prejudiced against them, and that said instrument is not the last will of the said C. R. Patton, but was extorted and forced from him by the undue influence of his slave.[22]

Ten of the witnesses testified about the relationship between Columbus and Rachel. Charles Grimm recalled: "The negro woman Rachel occupied the position of a white woman as much as any I ever knew. From the time I went there [in] 1847 to the time he was taken away. I should say she was the mistress of the plantation. I never saw her do anything more than pour out coffee and wait on the table. . . . I thought they lived more like man and wife and that she had more control over him than I ever saw a lady have over her husband or as much so . . . Rachel had a knowledge of the contents of that will. After Mr. Adriance and Mr. Underwood left[,] she came into my room and asked me if they had found a will. I told her there was a paper found which I supposed was his will. She knew [knew] what was in it as well as I did after reading it and told me all about it[;] who the property was left to and who was set free and all about it. She talked about the will and observed that Master Mat did not get anything. . . . She said the reason that Mat did not get anything [was] that he was always pursuing her and beating her and that was the reason he did not get anything."[23]

E. S. Jackson testified: "I couldn't say the woman Rachel occupied the position of a servant[.] If she wanted warm cakes or coffee, she had servants to bring it & seemed to have charge of the house and because, she . . . appeared to have a great deal of influence over Mr. Patton. I have seen them in conversation together though I never heard it. . . . I have known Mr. Patton to whip house negroes when she[,] Rachel[,] would tell him & have known her to whip them herself. . . . She had a horse she used to use & she claimed it. I never saw anyone else use it." George O. Jarivs, a resident of Brazoria County, added: "Whenever there was any new goods brought to town & the young ladies would purchase dresses, Rachel was sure to go and purchase some just like them. She wore those dresses on the plantation where the young ladies were. I have seen Rachel sit down in the rooms with Mr. Patton & converse with him often. I have heard him & her have little spats frequently. And once when he threatened to whip [her] she replied come on."[24]

John Adriance, in his capacity as a merchant, testified to Rachel's spending habits. "I know the woman Rachel," he stated,

> and always thought she had great influence over Mr. Patton. She has been in the habit of coming into my store from the time I went into business until I went out, and buying more fine dresses than any lady in the community. Up to 1852 when I went out of business. . . . I can hardly tell how much the woman Rachel spent annually with me when I was doing business. We kept an account with her individually. She frequently paid cash & sent in meal and meat from the plantation. This meal and meat & butter was sent in, in payment of her account & she frequently purchased family supplies which were charged to Col. Patton. She has paid me in cash at one time as high as twenty five or thirty dollars and had some charged to her master's account besides. She was in the habit of trading with other stores. She bought dry goods for herself to a larger amount than my wife bought. Judging from her bills with me her accounts were at least one hundred and fifty dollars a year. Mostly fine drapes. She dealt also in Columbia at other stores.[25]

Horace Cone, another neighbor of Columbus Patton, summarized the witnesses' position regarding Rachel when he testified: "I have heard her [Rachel] talking about the affairs of people in the community that would generally engross the attention of white people. So far as my knowledge extends I regard her as being shrewd."[26]

In the face of this testimony, on April 4, 1857, Justice Perkins set aside the will of Columbus Patton, invalidating the document. Almost immediately, John W. Brooks, named as an executor in the will, filed an appeal of the court's decision. Concerned that the decision of the court might be overturned, the Pattons began working on a compromise proposal to settle the estate ahead of the appeal.[27]

On April 17, 1857, the heirs presented their compromise to the Brazoria County Court. Remaining anxious "to terminate all controversy touching [the estate] now devise weighty and soluble considerations . . . that said Brooks should not prosecute his appeal," the Pattons agreed to honor all of the special bequests named in the will and to divide the remainder of the estate into five equal parts between Mary, Matt, Charles, America, and Margaretta. They also agreed to entrust the $5,000 for Henry Patton to the care of Charles Brooks and allocate $2,000 to Elisha Pease to pay the attorneys involved in the case. Finally, although they noted that Maria had "departed this life," they agreed to honor the provisions regarding Rachel. The court accepted the compromise, and although the probate of the estate would continue until 1883, in the end Rachel received a modicum of freedom and the money just as provided in the will.[28]

Following the settlement of the estate, Charles Patton continued to administer the plantation and allowed Rachel to live in her own house on the property. Columbus Patton wanted Rachel to live "free of hire," but Charles did not honor that part of the will and hired Rachel out at the rate of $70 or $75 per year, although he did not specify to the estate the nature of her work. Beginning in 1858, John Adriance also began filing lists of the goods Rachel purchased from the firms of Ammon Underwood and Nash & Barstow in West Columbia. In January 1859, Adriance reported to the court: "your petitioner has suffered the negro woman Rachel to choose for herself the place where or family in which she should live and has engaged to pay her the sum of one hundred dollars a year, the most of which years allowance to said woman Rachel up to the present time has been paid & a part of the same appears in account of Nash & Barstow."[29]

Despite this arrangement, Rachel apparently irritated Charles Patton so much that in late 1859 or 1860, he acted to get rid of her. In March 1860 Adriance reported to the court "The negro woman Rachel has been induced to remove to Cincinnati, Ohio. Petitioner has and will continue to pay the annual allowance provided for her. But her presence near the plantation and slaves belonging to said estate was believed to have become exceedingly injurious to the interest of said estate and perhaps dangerous. That it was deemed not only best but necessary to procure her removal and she was therefore induced to remove to Cincinnati." Once in Ohio, Rachel, who began using the last name Bartlett and petitioned an Ohio court, which granted her freedom and naturalization as a citizen of the United States. When John Adriance learned of her actions, he seized her free papers and brought her back to Texas, forcing her back to work in the fields of the Patton plantation throughout the rest of the Civil War.[30]

⁓

As the drama of the Patton household played out, the saga of another complex household began taking shape on the banks of the Colorado in Wharton County. The story of this family reached an inflection point during the Civil War with the largest auction of enslaved persons in the history of the lowcountry. On Tuesday, February 3, 1863, the auction began at 10 A.M. sharp at the door of the Wharton County courthouse. The shouted bids and the sharp rap of the auctioneer's gavel created a macabre rhythm as the tragedy continued for a sustained 6 hours. The dreaded beat began again the next day, and by 4 p.m., more than twenty enslavers had purchased 139 souls for an astonishing $207,367, tearing families and friends asunder and whisking them away to new places with unknown fates.[31]

The sale at the door of the Wharton County courthouse marked the turning point of a saga that began with the arrival of twenty-four-year-old John C. Clark to Texas in 1822. Born in South Carolina in 1798, Clark joined Austin's newly forming colony in 1822, and in the winter of 1822–1623, Clark and two other men traveling up the Colorado River in a canoe came under attack by a band of Karankawas. The attackers wounded Clark, who almost died and only gradually recovered. In 1824, Austin granted Clark (nicknamed the "Indian fighter") a league of land on the east side of the Colorado in what would become Wharton County. There on Peach Creek, Clark established one of the first plantations in Texas, and in 1830 he sold the western half of his league to William J. E. Heard, who established Egypt. John Clark never attempted to replicate the finery of other enslavers like the Pattons; he was instead content to live in a humble one-room log cabin measuring eighteen by twenty feet with a wooden floor. Regardless of how much wealth he accumulated, Clark lived in this cabin for the rest of his life.[32]

Clark purchased his first enslaved individual, Clarissa, in 1830, and from there the number of people he enslaved only increased. After he purchased Clarissa, he bought a girl named Hannah to help with the housework. Like many in the Colorado bottoms, Hannah died shortly after her arrival, and in 1833 or 1834 John Clark purchased a woman named Sobrina, about 5 years his junior, from Wilson Gilbert. Clarissa later recalled "after Clark came home he put Sobrina in the house and stated he wanted her for his own woman. . . . Mr. Clark ate with her, slept with her and drank with her and always made much of her. John Clark told me at the time he got her he had taken Sobrina for a wife and he would forsake all others for her—Sobrina was after that the mistress of the plantation and I had to wait on her the same as if she was white. She gave the orders on the place she carried the keys and had management of everything." Clark "called Sobrina sometimes his old woman. Sobrina called him her old man." Within a year of her arrival, Sobrina became pregnant with her first child by John.[33]

By the time John Clark and his family fled east during the Runaway Scrape in the spring of 1836, they had two small children with them: Lourinda, who was "about three feet high," and Nancy, a "suckling child." The young family retreated as far as the Trinity and returned to the plantation in 1836 "before cropping." After the rebellion against Mexico ended, John and Sobrina welcomed a third child, a son, named Bishop, in about 1841.[34]

Throughout the 1840s and 1850s, John continued to develop his business, eventually possessing at least two cotton plantations, all while attending to his family. "He always made a difference between his children and the colored children & slaves on the place," recalled Clarissa. The Clarks also led a somewhat secluded existence. They did not have any close neighbors, and according to Clarissa, "Clark had but little to do with white people he was mostly with and placed himself on an equal footing with the blacks." Albert Horton testified that "Bishop, Nancy and Lourinda were his children. They were all treated different than slaves." According to Horton "Bishop was always in Mr. Clark's company & often in his lap and called him papa."

Although Clark clearly loved Sobrina and his children, he acted as a typical enslaver in most other ways, demonstrating his sense of white supremacy. An example is seen in his attitudes toward what men his daughters should marry. Pleasant, a man enslaved by Clark, expressed a romantic interest in Lourinda, and Clark responded unequivocally. "Pleasant Ballard, a negro wanted to mary [sic] Lourinda," Albert Horton testified, "and Mr. Clark objected because he was a negro and he wanted her to marry a Gentleman." Pleasant Ballard himself recalled: "[Clark] said he should kill me before I marry her. . . . I told him I was as good as Lourinda was and he got his gun to shoot me and I ran away."[35]

As for his son, David Prophet, Clark's one-time overseer, remembered that "Bishop was not compelled to work. He attended to the stock." Dan Owens recalled that when another man hit Bishop in a fight, Clark yelled: "who of you boys struck Bishop . . . God damn the man or boy that struck Bishop. When they strike him they strike my blood and if they set foot on my place I will blow a light hole through him."[36]

Unlike Columbus Patton, John Clark evidently felt that living with an enslaved woman as his wife meant that he had to place a distance between himself and his white neighbors. Reason Byrne testified that Clark "was visited very little by his neighbors if any[.] I have heard his neighbors say that the reason they did not visit him was on account of him . . . keeping a negro woman. . . . Clark said his relations had treated him with silent contempt." David Prophet remembered "The people around him [Clark] did not visit him on account of his having a negro wife."[37]

In 1861, Clark fell ill, and despite Sobrina and Lourinda tending to him, died, leaving no will and no white heirs. William J. Phillips, chief justice of Wharton County, appointed Isaac N. Dennis and James D. Whitten administrators of Clark's estate. For the next year Dennis and Whitten attempted to find any white heirs to John Clark's property without success, and at the January 1863 term of the county court, Phillips ordered the administrators to auction off all of the property of the estate, which now included Sobrina, Bishop, Lourinda, and Nancy. Although many in the county knew that Clark regarded Sobrina as his wife and that her children were also his children, people like Isaac Dennis regarded the arrangement simply as that of Clark sexually exploiting Sobrina "as men did in those days." From there, the laws of slavery and the dictates of white supremacy took hold, making John's wife and children the property of his estate.[38]

Builders completed the Wharton County courthouse, the site of the sale, in 1857. A block east of the Colorado, facing away from the river on Monterey Square, the courthouse consisted of a two-story brick building 40 feet square, with a fireplace in every room. In February 1857 the county replaced the wire fence around the building with a plank fence framed on one hundred mulberry posts set 8 feet apart. Chinaberry trees ringed the courthouse square. Enslavers crowded into the fenced lawn on that fateful Wednesday morning to begin placing bids on the land, implements, and enslaved persons of the Clark estate. John W. Gordon won the bid to purchase Sobrina for $100, as well as Bishop and seven other individuals in a lot for a total of $10,200. Maclin Stith purchased Lourinda, and Uriah C. Coolgrove of Brazoria County bought Nancy. By the end of the second day of the sale, the people, land, and farming implements of the estate brought a total of $450,147.55. As he administered the sale of Bishop, Isaac N. Dennis overheard bystanders remark "that it was hard that a man's own son should be sold with his property."[39]

The stories of the Pattons and Clarks stand out because of the lengthy legal battles that ensued over the estates of Columbus and John, but it remains unclear how many other households in the Texas lowcountry could have told similar stories, which are now lost to time. In all likelihood, Sarah Black's divorce petition represented the most common form of exploitation found in the households of the region but keeping an African American woman as a wife or concubine was commonplace in large plantation societies throughout the South. The institution of slavery that created the Texas lowcountry's social structure formally ended in June 1865, but the legacy of slavery and the stories of the families themselves would continue through the Reconstruction era and beyond. The intimate spheres of the lives of the enslaved and enslavers alike illuminated the family structures of the region and the systems of concubinage inveterate to the institution of slavery, giving us insight into the inner lives of those who navigated these complex households.

Chapter 8

The Long Struggle

Resistance and Emancipation in the Texas Lowcountry

ONE DAY just before Christmas 1865, Charley Burns ran, breathless, into the yard of the Patton place on Varner's Creek. As he ran, he began shouting: "everybody free, everybody free." Incredulously, the other enslaved people on Varner's Creek began to gather in the yard, along with Charles Patton. Shortly thereafter, a squad of soldiers arrived, led by a captain who immediately told Patton not to say a word. The captain stood in the yard and announced freedom aloud to the astonished onlookers, and then said: "I came to tell you de slaves are free and you don't have to call nobody master no more." For a few minutes, the stunned audience "milled around like cattle." The long dark night of slavery in the Texas lowcountry had finally ended.[1]

Emancipation marked the end of the striving for freedom that characterized the lives of the enslaved. Resistance carried out by the people of the lowcountry involved not only escaping and sometimes taking up arms against their enslavers, but also practicing their own forms of religion, engaging in letter-writing campaigns, forming families, and in some cases suicide. These acts of defiance constituted the heart of the long struggle between enslavers and the enslaved until the day freedom arrived.

Among the acts of resistance against slavery, escaping and asserting their freedom was the most common form of rebellion. Most enslaved African Americans attempted to escape multiple times during their lives, and their respective success depended on a variety of factors. Slave patrols operated constantly on the edges of each neighborhood, with most, if not all, white men expected to take part in capturing anyone away from their enslaver without permission. Sam Jones Washington related to an interviewer how, at the age of twelve, a slave patrol almost caught him in a sugar cane field, breaking the stalks and sucking out the syrupy marrow. A passerby, hearing the popping stalks, yelled at the children to identify themselves. Without answering, Sam and his companions ran at breakneck speed through the fields and woods, outsmarting and outrunning the "patte roller."[2]

If an enslaved person did manage to make it past the slave patrols and the packs of dogs that often accompanied them, they generally had three destinations in mind. The first and most common form of escape involved making their way to the woods, swamps, or river bottoms nearby and simply staying there for a few days or a few weeks to escape an anticipated whipping, difficult labor in the fields, or simply to live free in the Texas wilderness. As was generally the case with most of these escapes, family ties or lack of food drove enslaved people back to their enslavers within a few days. Their second major escape plan involved making their way back to their family, friends, or acquaintances at the home of a previous enslaver. The third destination of those who managed to get past the dogs and patrols involved the ultimate escape to Mexico—the land of freedom south of the Rio Grande.

Enslavers well understood these motivations and destinations. In most cases, word of mouth around the neighborhood, local slave catchers, packs of dogs, and the passage of time generally brought most of the enslaved back, but for those who stayed away long enough, enslavers placed advertisements in local newspapers to capture them. Between the 1830s and the 1860s, more than 1,000 advertisements seeking enslaved African Americans appeared in Texas newspapers; more than 250 of which were from enslavers who lived in the lowcountry. Ninety-six percent of the advertisements from the lowcountry sought men who averaged twenty-seven years of age, often in groups of two or three. The newspapers often also identified the property the escapees took with them, such as horses, clothing, or firearms. The enslaved also took advantage of the calendar, as many of them would attempt escape around the Christmas and New Year's holidays when enslavers halted work and relaxed their vigilance. Many more escaped in the summer at the height of cotton- and sugar-planting seasons.[3]

J. D. Waters of Fort Bend County exemplified those who attempted to reunite with their families. On July 28, 1858, Waters placed an advertisement in the Houston *Weekly Telegraph* offering a $50 reward for the return of two men, Peter and George, each about 23 years old, Peter, a very active likely fellow, weighs about 140 lbs. rather low, George, very stout and heavy, not tall, weighs about 175 lbs. both black. They will make for Cedar Bayou, and Old river, as Peter was raise[d] there by a Mr. Algins, where his mother now lives. I will pay the above reward to any one delivering said negroes to me in the city of Houston. It is supposed they rode off two white horses, as such are missing from the neighborhood, a reward of 25 dollars is offered by the owner of said horses delivered to him in Fort Bend county."[4]

In typical fashion for those who might be headed for Mexico, Joel Hudgins of Egypt in Wharton County placed an advertisement in the *Texas Monument* in July 1852 looking for an enslaved man named

Abraham, copper colored, about 5 feet 5 inches high, rather heavy built, full eyes, with small patches of beard about his throat. Said boy is 23 or 24 years old, and very talkative when alarmed. Do not know what kind of clothes or hat he had on, but he carried with him a fine large Mackinaw blanket, nearly new. The boy was brought to this country last winter by a man named LITTLE, and sold to me. I believe he was brought from the State of Tennessee. He also rode off a large sorrel American horse, with new brands on him. He is what would be called a red sorrel, with a small stain on his face, some white on his neck, from the use of the collar; one or the other of his hips a little short, 15 or 16 hands high, walks, trots and paces well, about 8 years old, has on shoes before, and is a fine saddle horse. Said boy had on one of his legs a clog of iron, when he left. He will, I have no doubt, aim for the West, as he was caught a few weeks since at Seguin, on his way to Mexico. I will give $25 reward for the safe delivery to me of said boy and horse, or for his safe security in some jail where I can recover him again.[5]

Enslaved African Americans of the Texas lowcountry frequently attempted escape, but certainly not without forethought, because enslavers imposed severe whippings, beatings, or worse if they recaptured the fugitives. Often, simply the threat of a whipping induced the enslaved to head for the woods in the first place. Sarah Ford recalled that her father would run away and hide after Jake Steel, an enslaved man and the overseer on the Patton place, threatened to whip him. Once he stayed away for an entire year, wading through the creeks and rivers to throw the dogs off his scent. Sarah remembered that when her father returned he looked wild, with the "hair standin' straight on he head and he [sic] face." Big Jake, or Uncle Jake as they called him, dealt with those who escaped harshly. As punishment for escaping, Sarah recalled seeing Jake stake her father to the ground, spread eagle, lying on his stomach. The overseer then took a piece of hot iron called a "slut," and a block of wood with holes in it, filling the holes with tallow and putting the iron in the fire until the grease sizzled before slowly dripping the liquid onto the man's bare back. After that, Jake took the bullwhip, using it liberally, before chaining his victim in the stock house for several days with nothing to eat. Sarah recalled that her father carried the grease scars on his back until the day he died.[6]

Similarly, Ann Thomas of Brazoria County remembered that her husband purchased Adeline, a six-year-old girl, as a nursemaid for their son, but Adeline often ran away following threats of a whipping. "Sometimes she was disobedient," remembered Ann, "and did not mind what I said to her. When I would threaten to whip her, presently afterwards she was missing, and I would have to nurse myself. That day in the evening she would be brought home by some of the field hands having found her hiding in some weeds in the field. She got a whipping from my husband on the first sight of her." Ann's husband, John Thomas, later put Adeline to work in the cotton fields, and the girl often received whippings after escaping from that work, too. One day Adeline broke the handle of a water pitcher at the well and hid to avoid another beating. The next day "one of the men went to look for something he wanted under the dwelling house when he found Adeline in a hole fast asleep. He caught her and brought her to the house and my husband gave her a remembrance that time she did not soon forget. . . . when she asked me to beg her off from getting whipped, I replied, 'no, Adeline I have begged you off for the last time.'"[7]

On October 12, 1861, Sallie McNeil, then living at the plantation of her grandfather Levi Jordan, wrote in her diary:

> The Hounds caught "Mose the Runaway" who was fettered with a stiff leg iron, so that he could neither outrun the dogs or climb out of the way, consequently was bitten in several places. Poor negro! he is idle at work & runs to escape it and the lash. And is treated with severity when he is caught, besides half-starving in the woods. . . . The tears rose indignantly to my eyes, when Mose was led up that evening ragged and bleeding. I could say or do nothing, for he brought the trouble & pain on himself. Words of abuse & ridicule only were given him . . . I learned the next day that he was severely whipped to make him tell the truth . . . —moaning and confined in the stocks without food or water.[8]

On the Mims plantation in Brazoria County, a man named Lew escaped so often that an enslaver had a blacksmith fasten a seven-pound iron collar around his neck with two sharp, upward protrusions that some thought resembled horns. The enslaver intended the collar, which people began referring to as "Lew's Horns," to discourage the man from running, but it only made him more determined. During the years that Lew wore the collar around his neck he had to wrap rags around it to cushion his neck so he could sleep at night, and during the Civil War he managed to swim across the San Bernard River and remain in hiding until emancipation.[9]

Resistance also extended to violence against enslavers. Although the lowcountry never saw large, organized revolts like those in other parts of the South, individual acts of retribution occurred frequently. On March 11, 1855, an enslaved man killed his enslaver, Charles Moscer of Tres Palacios in Matagorda County. According to the *Columbia Democrat*, the man "was caught a few days afterwards, but found hanging in a tree." In March 1844, the *Houston Telegraph* reported that "[t]he overseer on the plantation of Mr. Burdit near Richmond was killed by one of the slaves, who attacked him while at work. The slave after committing the fatal deed fled and has not yet been taken." In the same article, the paper reported that two enslaved men on the plantation of Frank Terry in Brazoria County "attacked" Terry "with knives and axes," but Terry "defended himself with a large heavy whip until he drew a pistol and shot one so as to disable him. With a well-directed blow of his whip, he broke the arm of the other and forced him to submit." These and other acts of violence pervaded the stories of slavery in the lowcountry.[10]

Overcome by the brutality of slavery, some of the enslaved escaped by committing suicide. In the 1930s, an interviewer located Adeline Marshall, a freedwoman formerly enslaved by Ephraim J. Brevard along Oyster Creek. Now over seventy years of age, living in Houston, Adeline recounted that "Captain" as she called Brevard, brought her from South Carolina as an infant and that she never knew her parents. "Cap'n he a bad man," she continued, with he and his overseers whipping and beating enslaved people constantly to make them work. Brevard evidently did not take age into consideration, and Adeline recalled that he sent her and others into the fields to work as soon as they could walk, using a switch instead of a bullwhip on the younger children, delivering a stinging pain. The woman recalled that sometimes Brevard and his henchmen put people in stocks for days at a time without water until they were almost dead. When enslaved people did die from this treatment, Brevard simply had them dig a hole behind the horse lot, place the body in a simple wooden box, dump them in and cover it up without any preaching or prayer. Adeline told her interviewer that sometimes people committed suicide to escape such treatment. At one point they whipped a man she referred to as "Beans" so badly he could not work anymore, and the next morning they found him hanging from a tree behind the slave quarters, having killed himself to escape the misery.[11]

Other acts of resistance resulted in more positive outcomes. After enslavers separated Elizabeth Ramsey and her daughter Louisa on the auction block in Mobile in 1841, Louisa's enslaver, a John Williams, kept her locked in his house in New Orleans for the next two decades, where she gave birth to four children, only two of whom survived. Williams would not even allow Louisa to attend church as she had with her mother in Georgia, and so Louisa "'begin . . . to pray that he might die, so that I might get religion; and then I promise the Lord one night, faithful, in prayer, if he would just take him out of the way, I'd get religion and be true to Him as long as I lived." Williams did eventually become sick and die, but before he did, he promised to free Louisa and her children if they would travel to New York. She promised him that she would, and Williams freed them in his will. Louisa did not leave New Orleans right away, but when Williams's brother threatened to reenslave her for debts owed by his brother, she fled in the night and made it as far as Cincinnati before she ran out of money. In 1847, when Louisa reached Cincinnati, she met and married a Henry Picquet, a free man whose mother Louisa had known in Georgia. Meanwhile, Louisa's mother, Elizabeth Ramsey, wrote a letter to her daughter when she still lived in New Orleans, and Louisa, upon reaching Cincinnati, began writing letters to her mother in Texas in hopes of finding her. One day in 1858, Henry Picquet met a man from Texas who knew Elizabeth's enslaver, Albert Horton. Louisa devised a way to send her mother a letter, and on March 8, 1859, she finally received a letter from her mother in return. Throughout the spring and summer of 1859, the two exchanged epistles as Horton demanded $1,000 to purchase Elizabeth. Louisa began crisscrossing Ohio and New York, soliciting donations to raise the money. After almost giving up hope, finally in October 1860 Louisa managed to raise $900 cash with which she ransomed her mother.[12]

The communities that formed in the slave quarters of the Texas low-country provided the strongest bulwark for resistance against slavery. These communities rested on the twin pillars of family and religion and carried the enslaved through emancipation. The formation of families and intimate bonds served as the bedrock of the enslaved communities of the region, but these families and relationships faced obstacles like those in the Louisiana sugar cane country. As enslaved individuals fought to form familial bonds, the slave trade, an uneven sex ratio, and the high mortality rate created impediments difficult to overcome. The slave trade created psychological and emotional barriers to creating new intimate bonds or bearing children. Torn away from their families elsewhere, any new relationships represented a second family for many, with all the accompanying emotional strain attached to those first separations. Furthermore, men outnumbered women in the region, giving women increased power to choose a mate but leaving many men without companionship. Finally, as death stalked the enslaved of the lowcountry, at least 25 percent of live births ended in the deaths of the children before the age of twelve, adding to the emotional burdens of the survivors. As a result of these hardships, the enslaved of the lowcountry cared for each other by forming communities not only of blood relations but also of fictive kin.[13]

Despite the hardships, many of the enslaved did manage to form intimate relationships. Some chose casual relationships, others opted for long-term commitments, while still others chose marriage. Many of the romances began around the holidays when they enjoyed more time to socialize. On March 30, 1861, Sally McNeill wrote in her diary: "Tonight Sam & Irene—a girl of hardly fifteen, are to be married. This is the fourth marriage since Christmas. The ice once broken & the others follow in rapid succession! Several of the lately married have already had matrimonial quarrels."[14]

James Perry kept meticulous records of the relationships and children of the enslaved at Peach Point in Brazoria County. Of the seventeen enslaved women who gave birth between 1836 and 1864, Perry noted marriages for just seven couples. These seventeen women gave birth to a total of fifty-nine children in twenty-eight years, for an average of almost 3.5 children per woman, an average of 2.1 births per year. However, fifteen of the fifty-nine children, fully one quarter of them, died before reaching their twelfth birthday. The union of Sam and Chany represented the typical family at Peach Point. Chany gave birth to Sarah Ann in 1843 and Flurry in August 1845. A preacher christened Flurry on July 22, 1849, but she died of whooping cough the next year. Chany also gave birth to Texana on December 18, 1846, and to Manuel on February 14, 1849, but both died of whooping cough in 1857, leaving the couple with just one child who reached adulthood. The next generation, Sarah Ann, married a man named Pernes in September 1859, at age sixteen, and gave birth to Wigfall on December 25, 1860, and Chany on December 4, 1864. These relationships created the basis of the communities that formed within the slave quarters, allowing many to psychologically escape the most dehumanizing aspects of their plight.[15]

Religious practices also proved key to the formation of these communities and a primary form of resistance. Every enslaver maintained different standards as to which religious practices were to be allowed, but most of the enslaved appear to have occupied a religious borderland where Christianity and Conjure traditions intersected. At Waldeck in Brazoria County in 1856, John Adriance ordered the enslaved to construct a brick church called the "Ethiopia Baptist Church," where white ministers preached to them. Sallie McNeil noted in her diary in 1861 that one Sunday the white minister came back to their plantation to preach a sermon to the enslaved there. Sarah Ford remembered that Charles Patton had an arbor where they had "preaching" on Sundays, the only place she ever heard singing while enslaved. One day, an older man named "Uncle Lew" preached the Sunday sermon, according to Sarah, and said that the Lord made everyone equal, including white and Black people. When Charles Patton learned of Lew's theology, he ordered his overseer to put the old man to work in the cotton fields as punishment.[16]

Enslavers intended religion to aid in their efforts to enslave, but the blending of Conjure and Christianity allowed the enslaved to use religion and magic to help sustain them. Although some religious services took place under the eye of the enslaver, or under the supervision of a white preacher, the vast majority of religious ceremonies took place in secret, where the enslaved did not need to fear repercussions for their expressions of spirituality. In most of the neighborhoods, the enslaved held religious services either in a central cabin in the quarters or under the branches of a large tree situated near the middle of the neighborhood. In the quarters and in these secret locations, religious ceremonies emerged in an amalgamation of Christian and Conjure practices. Unlike Christianity, Conjure is not an organized religion; it is "African American occultism" and includes "magic, practices, and lore . . . healing, spells, and supernatural objects." Conjure is part of a larger religious tradition referred to as "Voo Doo," "Hoo Doo," or "Root work," which combines Christian beliefs and West African spiritual practices. Traditionally, scholars have regarded Christianity and Conjure as opposed to each other, but many of the enslaved appear to have blended the different traditions and practices seamlessly into a "usable" religion adapted to their circumstances.[17]

Patsy Moses, born into enslavement, detailed what she learned regarding what she termed "conjure and voodoo and luck charms and signs." Patsy reported that they met in secret places with a voodoo kettle. People would come gather around the kettle when the moon was dark, and the Voodoo doctor would wave them to come in close. The men practicing Voodoo would strip to the waist and start to dance with a drum beat in the background. They would dance faster and faster and pray until they fell down "in a heap." She spoke of a conjure healer named Dr. Jones who walked about in a coat like a preacher with sideburns and used roots for his medicine. He did not cast spells like the Voodoo doctor, but he used roots to cure smallpox, a bacon rind to cure mumps, and sheep wool tea for whooping cough. To cure snake bites and whooping cough, Dr. Jones used alura and saltpeter and bluestone mixed with brandy or whiskey. This healer could break conjure spells with broth. Charms, tokens, and visions also played an important part in protection or luck. Dreaming of clear water let you know you were on the right side of God, while a good charm bag made of red flannel with frog bones and a piece of snakeskin and some horse hairs and a spoonful of ashes would protect you from the enemy. According to Patsy, a man working in the field always had three charms hanging around his neck; one to make him lucky in love, one to protect him, and one for luck in dice games. If you suffered from indigestion, Patsy related that you should wear a penny around your neck. The woman told her interviewer that if you nailed a horseshoe over your door for luck, it should be from the left hind foot of a white horse. However, of all the charms Patsy recommended, the rabbit's foot possessed the greatest power. One man even used a rabbit's foot to successfully escape. He "conjured" himself by taking a good, soapy bath to keep the dogs off his scent, and then he said "hoodoo" over the rabbit's foot before wading through a creek. Patsy opined that a graveyard's rabbit foot from a rabbit killed by a cross-eyed person was the best, and that you should pour some whiskey on it from time to time to keep it effective.[18]

The secession of Texas from the United States and the subsequent Civil War provided the third inflection point in the history of the Texas lowcountry, resulting in emancipation for the enslaved and the end of the Deep South plantation society. Just as they had nearly three decades earlier, the enslavers of the region took a lead role in consummating the secession movement and the subsequent war that irrevocably changed the region, bringing the long struggle of resistance to fruition.[19]

Although enslavers rushed to war, life for most of the enslaved remained unchanged. Even so, the Texas Troubles (a series of fires blamed on abolitionists that set off a panic among the white Texas population in 1860) and later the presence of US troops on the Texas coast gave new life to the struggle for freedom. On July 8, 1860, when mysterious fires broke out in north Texas, enslavers and newspaper editors quickly stoked the flames of fear about abolitionists and insurrection by the enslaved throughout the state and the entire South. On July 25, a group of enslavers at Matagorda met to "take into consideration the late outrages committed by fiends in human form at Dallas and other places." The committee decided to raise a company led by Dr. E. A. Pearson to ready themselves to march to the assistance of their fellow enslavers in the northern part of the state and to appoint a police force to ensure that none of the enslaved possessed firearms or any incendiary devices. On August 10, 1860, Sallie McNeil wrote in her diary: "Mond. was election day; the time appointed for a general uprising of the Negroes against the Whites. Urged on by Abolitionists they burnt towns & houses in the northern part of the state. Patrols & vigilance committees are being appointed." After the November elections, the young woman noted: "Our worst foes are in our midst. Negro insurrections will be constant and bloody, under the guidance of the Abolitionists." Ultimately, enslavers uncovered no major plots of insurrection in the lowcountry, but the *Matagorda Gazette* reported that a vigilance committee in Richmond arrested two mapmakers named Parker and Hughes, on suspicion of abolitionism. Finding no evidence, the vigilantes nevertheless horsewhipped one of the men and ordered them both to leave the state.[20]

The lives of the enslaved continued mostly as they had been before the war, but there were some notable exceptions. For example, the rebel authorities conscripted some enslaved men to build fortifications, and enslavers coerced others into accompanying them to the front as personal attendants, even as the enslaved took advantage of these situations to make their escape to freedom. Philles Thomas, a woman born into bondage at David Mills's Lowwood place, recalled that the Confederates conscripted her father to build breastworks in Galveston and that one day, while he watched the cannon balls from the US ships falling all around, a train car loaded with rocks careened down the line and killed him. The rebels also dispatched some of the enslaved of the lowcountry to work on fortifications elsewhere on the Gulf coast. For instance, the Confederate government paid James Tankersley of Brazoria County $276 on January 31, 1864, for the labor of six men named Griffin, John, Robert, Richard, Hiram, and Judge on the fortifications at Mobile, Alabama. At the battle of Arkansas Post in January 1863, US troops captured the rebel garrison and liberated the enslaved men accompanying rebel soldiers from Fort Bend and Matagorda in the 24th Texas (Dismounted) Cavalry and the

6th Texas Infantry. Daniel Connor, Quartermaster of the 24th Texas, gave a pass to an enslaved man named Jeff to return to Fort Bend County before the surrender, but Jeff evidently had other plans, and slipped the chains of bondage while Connor sat in a prisoner-of-war camp in Ohio. After his release, Connor began search for Jeff, to no avail. As the war progressed and US troops continued to make their presence felt along the Texas coast, not a few individuals made their escape to the "Yankees" and freedom.[21]

The end of the Civil War came to the Texas lowcountry at the start of June 1865. On June 2, rebel General Edmund Kirby Smith boarded the USS *Fort Jackson*, anchored off the sandbar at the entrance to Galveston harbor to sign the surrender terms for the last rebel troops in the field. Three days later, Captain Benjamin Sands docked at Galveston aboard the USS *Cornubia* and proceeded to the US Customs House at the corner of Avenue E and 20th Street, where he raised the Stars and Stripes over the city for half an hour. On Sunday, June 18, Major General Gordon Granger arrived in Galveston at the head of US troops to occupy Texas and established his headquarters in the Ostermann building at the southwest corner of 22nd Street and The Strand. From his headquarters, on the morning of Monday June 19, Granger issued General Orders No. 3, which read: "The people of Texas are informed that, in accordance with a proclamation from the Executive of the United States, all slaves are free. This involves an absolute equality of personal rights and rights of property between former masters and slaves, and the connection heretofore existing between them becomes that between employer and hired labor. The freedmen are advised to remain quietly at their present homes and work for wages. They are informed that they will not be allowed to collect at military posts and that they will not be supported in idleness either there or elsewhere." Granger directed his order published in the local papers, and on June 21, the *Galveston Weekly News* published the statement for the first time. Even with this proclamation, the future for African Americans in the lowcountry remained unclear.[22]

Despite the symbolic significance of Juneteenth, word of freedom did not immediately reach the people of the lowcountry. On March 3, 1865, the Congress of the United States established the Bureau of Refugees, Freedmen and Abandoned Lands, more commonly referred to as the Freedmen's Bureau. Abraham Lincoln appointed Major General Oliver Otis Howard to head the agency, and he was tasked with "the supervision and management of all abandoned lands, and the control of all subjects relating to refugees and freedmen from rebel states." Howard appointed twelve assistant commissioners, including Brigadier General Edgar M. Gregory, whom he appointed to govern the bureau's Texas branch. Gregory finally stepped ashore in Galveston on September 5, 1865, a total of 78 days after Juneteenth. Gregory established his headquarters at the US Customs House and began the process of Reconstruction in Texas. In assisting Gregory, Brigadier General William E. Strong traveled north as far as Huntsville. He reported that cruelty continued unabated and that freedom had not yet reached the interior of the state. Not until Gregory himself started out on December 10 for the "Lower Brazos Oyster Creek, Old Caney and Colorado Districts" did the people of the lowcountry learn of their own freedom. Gregory and his staff made a point of stopping at many of the plantations and towns to announce the end of slavery, so that finally, by Christmas 1865, more than 6 months after Juneteenth, slavery in practice began coming to an end.[23]

The formal announcements of freedom in the Texas lowcountry developed into a predictable event, US officials or others would call a meeting, often in front of a plantation residence or under a tree in the quarters, and give a brief speech to the gathered crowd. On the Palmer Plantation in Fort Bend County under a huge spreading live oak tree near the quarters, Ed Gibbs, born into slavery in Georgia, accompanied by the white overseer, gathered the twenty-four African Americans who labored on the land and announced that they now enjoyed freedom, and could stay and continue to work for wages, or go as they pleased. Thirty-six miles to the southwest in Brazoria County, Freedmen's Bureau officials gathered a huge crowd of people from as many as fourteen plantations under the bows of two huge Bois d'Arc trees in front of the John Sweeney house on Chance's Prairie and told them of their freedom in one of the largest such ceremonies in the lowcountry, and so it went throughout the region as the people whose sweat, toil, blood. and tears had watered the ground for generations pondered their futures.[24]

PART 3

~

Reconstruction,
1865–1895

Chapter 9

The Struggle for Equality

1865–1873

ON THURSDAY, October 5, 1865, Miles, a freedman working on the land of his former enslaver, Henry Dunleavy, in Fort Bend County, complained that he could no longer pick cotton that day due to illness. Dunleavy took his heavy walking stick and beat Miles on the head and shoulders, cutting him deeply. That same month in Brazoria County a white man named James Lankesly got into a heated dispute over wages with an "old" freedman named Robert Jones and struck him in the mouth with the butt end of his revolver "and also beat him over the head with his fists," knocking out a tooth and leaving extensive bruising. These and countless other acts of violence marked the beginning of the war of Reconstruction in the Texas lowcountry.[1]

Reconstruction in the Texas lowcountry marked the period of adjustment from legalized slavery to the kind of quasi-freedom for the African American community that continued for a majority of the twentieth century. Generally, historians have defined Reconstruction in Texas as Presidential Reconstruction from 1865 to 1867 and Radical Reconstruction from 1867 to 1873. During the first period, although the Texas branch of the Freedmen's Bureau attempted to impose order, former enslavers carried on generally as they had before the Civil War, dominating the state and local governments and carrying out hundreds, if not thousands, of acts of brutality against freed people. During the second period, Congress took control of the Reconstruction process, sidelining President Andrew Johnson and forcing white Texans to allow the full benefits of freedom to the African American community. This period ultimately ended after the readmission of Texas to the United States in 1870 and the reestablishment of state government by ex-Confederates in 1873.[2]

The Texas lowcountry experienced Reconstruction in much the same way as the rest of the state but with important differences, mainly the fact that Reconstruction, which ended for most of Texas in 1873, continued for another twenty years along the Gulf coast. The years 1865–1868 brought extreme violence against freed people, and only with the establishment of the Texas Republican Party in Houston in 1867 and the registration of all male citizens to vote that same year did things begin to change as newly enfranchised African Americans began voting and holding office, dominating the local governments. Because African Americans constituted roughly 75 percent of the population of the region, they and their white allies continued to dominate the county-level governments long after 1873.

The first eight years following the end of legalized slavery in the Texas lowcountry brought not peace, but a sustained period of contention, as whites attempted to maintain their dominance over the region by force and African Americans used the law, the courts, the Freedmen's Bureau, and political organizing to pursue their goal of full equality.

The first steps toward freedom in the lowcountry involved the Freedmen's Bureau. From Galveston, Edgar Gregory began establishing subdistricts presided over by subassistant commissioners (SACs) to oversee the duties of the bureau in various parts of Texas. From the first subdistrict at Houston that oversaw Harris and Montgomery counties, Gregory established three subdistricts in the lowcountry, first at West Columbia where Captain James Hutchison took command of the "Columbia" subdistrict in January 1866 with a jurisdiction that included all of Brazoria County and Matagorda County "east of the Colorado." At the same time, Gregory appointed Captain Sam C. Sloan to command the Richmond subdistrict, which included all of Fort Bend County, and finally Captain J. W. McConaughy took over the Wharton subdistrict, which encompassed Wharton County. All three of these subdistricts existed, under various subassistant commissioners, from January 1866 to December 1868. The Bureau designated Columbia Subdistrict 4, Richmond Subdistrict 12 and Wharton Subdistrict 5.[3]

Perhaps the most outsized role of the Freedmen's Bureau for African Americans in the first 3 years after emancipation involved the negotiation and enforcement of labor arrangements. Although land ownership remained one of the primary aspirations of African Americans, the bureau did not provide any assistance in that arena and instead served as a "labor clearinghouse." Of the three subdistricts in the lowcountry, extensive records of contracts have survived only for the Columbia office. The head of this subdistrict, Captain

James Hutchison, was a US officer of the Veteran Reserve Corps. He and his three successors, working out of Leander McNeel's old Pleasant Grove house on Gulf Prairie, oversaw enforcement of these contracts. In 1866, landowners negotiated 126 contracts with freed men and women, 54 of them for wages, 18 for a quarter share of the crop produced that year, 43 for a third of the crop, 2 for a half-share of the crop, and the remaining 9 for a mixture of wages and share of the crops. The wages negotiated ranged from $15 down to $2, with William H. Sharp at Chenango paying the highest average wages. Sharp negotiated contracts with fifty-one workers that year, for an average of $10.80 per person. In 1867, landowners negotiated sixty-eight contracts, this time with only fourteen of them for wages and the remainder for a share of the crop. Although the Columbia office maintained a register containing the substance of the contracts, they did not preserve the text of the actual contracts. Only in the Richmond subdistrict did an actual contract survive, with a freedman named J. C. Mitchell. The contract specified that Mitchell would receive one-third of the interest in the crop raised on the plantation in question, and that a day's labor would consist of no more than ten hours. Any more than that would result in extra pay. Furthermore, the contract specified that the freedman would work on Sundays and at nights only if necessary, to protect the plantation from destruction by "storms, floods, fire, or frost." The contract would be null if either party broke the agreement. With these agreements in place, the people of the lowcountry began laboring with the hopes of becoming self-sufficient.[4]

The Freedmen's Bureau also attempted to curtail violence and the cheating of freed people but to little avail. From 1865 to 1868, Freedmen's Bureau sub-assistant commissioners recorded 6,794 complaints from the thirty-four field offices in Texas, most of them filed by African Americans. The three offices in the lowcountry fielded 499 of these complaints, or 6.6 percent of the total for the state. The most common complaints revolved around money—usually, the white landowners' failure to pay their employees or their withholding of pay under various pretenses. A typical complaint of this kind came from Charles Doublin, a freedman, who filed a complaint on September 20, 1868, alleging that Charles Westall, his employer, had unjustly withheld wages from him. Arthur Honer, the Freedmen's Bureau SAC for Columbia at that time, ordered Westall to appear and explain himself. Doublin's complaint did not stand alone, and the SACs did their best to mediate differences between landowners and their employees.[5]

Texas proved the most difficult posting for the Freedmen's Bureau for a variety of reasons, not the least of which became the pervasive violence that plagued the state. According to the bureau's records, white Texans murdered 900 freed people and committed another 1,325 assaults against them between 1865 and 1868. Of these crimes, the lowcountry saw thirty-one reported murders: eight in Brazoria County, two in Matagorda, seven in Wharton, and fourteen in Fort Bend, along with another sixty-two assaults. Wharton County led the way in the last category, with twenty-three reported assaults, more than a third of the total for the region. In a typical example, Christiana, a freedwoman, complained that her employer, an R. Turner, assaulted her with a stick after she exchanged heated words with Mrs. Turner. The Freedmen's Bureau SAC fined Turner $25 for the crime. In one of the most harrowing accounts of murder recorded in Texas, F. G. Franks, the Freedmen's Bureau SAC at Wharton in 1868 wrote a letter describing the murder of a young African American man named Jim Jackson. On July 17, 1868, Jackson took up the task of tending to the horses of his employer, Alex Jackson, on the West San Bernard. Without provocation, three white men, led by John T. Copeland and Charles Brooks, rode up. Copeland shot Jackson in cold blood and left his body there for an hour before returning to put a rope around his neck. The men dragged the body to a nearby watering hole, mutilated it "in a manner in which decency forbids further description," and then threw the body in the water.[6]

Rachel Bartlett (Patton) also became the victim of an assault in 1868. On April 16, 1868, S. C. Roberts, an ex-Confederate soldier, assaulted Rachel near Columbia. The details are unknown, but the parties settled the case for $5 out of court. Following the death of Charles Patton in 1870, Rachel filed suit against John Adriance for his failure to follow the agreement of the heirs in the case of the estate of Columbus Patton. She alleged that after being taken to Cincinnati by Adriance against her will, she petitioned a court in Ohio, which granted her letters of freedom and naturalization, but Adriance withheld them from her and forced her back to the Patton plantation to work "as a common field hand." Adriance also failed to pay her the $100 per year stipulated in Columbus Patton's will or to provide her with a place to live after emancipation. For her rent of $5 per month beginning in June 1865, the injury done her by forcing her to work as a field hand, the labor itself and interest, in her lawsuit Rachel demanded $3,325 from Adriance. The Brazoria County court found enough merit in the case that Adriance settled with Rachel Bartlett out of court in October 1871, and the court ordered Adriance to pay all court costs, amounting to $26.72. The terms of the settlement are unknown, but in all likelihood Adriance provided Rachel a house in which to live and money with which to survive. Rachel Bartlett, who gave her name as Patton to the census taker in the 1880 census, lived alone in a house in East Columbia, not far from John Adriance. This is the last glimpse we have of the life of one of the most remarkable women in the history of the Texas lowcountry.[7]

Although the violence would continue unabated, politics began to change when the US Congress took control of Reconstruction policy. After overriding President Andrew Johnson's veto of the Reconstruction Act of 1867 on March 2 of that year, the Congress placed Texas and the rest of the rebel states under military rule. Under this act, Texas and Louisiana became the Fifth Military District under the command of Major General Phillip H. Sheridan, who took command of the district on March 19, 1867. Sheridan placed General Charles C. Griffin in command of Texas, with his headquarters at Galveston. After removing Governor James Throckmorton from power as "an impediment to reconstruction" in April, Griffin went about registering all eligible men to vote. The military appointed a three-man board of voter registrars for each county, and these men began the registration process in June and July 1867. When the boards completed their work, the rolls showed 59,633 whites and 49,479 African Americans eligible to vote in Texas. The military ruled 7,500 to 12,000 white men in the state ineligible to vote, or they voluntarily absented themselves from the process.[8]

This meant that African Americans became overrepresented among voters statewide, but the numbers in the Texas lowcountry showed even more startling differences. A total of 5,005 men in the four counties registered to vote in the summer of 1867: 1,249 whites and 3,756 African Americans, making African Americans 75 percent of registered voters, with a little over 300 white men not registered in the region. Even if all the white men had registered, whites would still have constituted only 32 percent of voters. These numeric disparities guaranteed that African American voters would control politics in the lowcountry for the next two decades.[9]

A group of Texas Unionists traveled to the National Union Convention in Philadelphia in August of 1866 and came away Republicans, determined to form a Republican Party in Texas. In April 1867 prominent Unionists met in Austin and called for a convention to form a Texas Republican Party, and in Galveston George T. Ruby helped form the Galveston National Republican Association. These new Republicans also took the opportunity of these first meetings to introduce the Union Loyal League to African Americans. The Union League, which maintained a strict veil of secrecy, first organized in 1863 to advance the policies of Abraham Lincoln, and it served as the shadow arm of the Republican Party. In Texas, the league helped the new Republicans form party machines among African Americans in the state. The secrecy of the organization gave freedmen and white Unionists the ability to participate in the political process without fearing open violence. George Ruby began attempting to organize chapters of the league in the counties of the lowcountry, and while he experienced success especially in Fort Bend and Wharton, he ran into conflict in Brazoria County. In late March 1867, Ruby dispatched Reverend Houston Reedy, an African American preacher and organizer for the African Methodist Episcopal Church, to the Columbia district to organize a chapter of the league. When Reedy arrived, he found Reverend Joseph Welch, a white missionary, attempting to convince the African Americans there to join his church. Welch convinced the locals that Reedy had come as an "emissary" of the former Confederates, and only the intervention of James Hutchison, the SAC at Columbia, convinced the freedmen that Reedy had their best interests in mind. Eventually, the league managed to organize in Brazoria under the leadership of Judge James H. Bell, son of Josiah Bell, but this early conflict guaranteed that not many African Americans from Brazoria County attended the first Texas Republican Party State Convention in Houston in July 1867.[10]

On July 4, 1867, at the Harris County courthouse at 301 Fannin Street in Houston almost 600 delegates representing thirty-one counties, the vast majority of them African Americans, gathered to organize the Texas Republican Party. The courthouse, which the designers intended to be an expensive, colonnaded Greek Revival structure, possessed only walls, floors, and a roof before the Civil War halted construction. At this half-finished building, James Bell opened the convention by reading the Declaration of Independence to the delegates. Former Governor Elisha Pease served as the president of the convention, and George Ruby as the second vice president. Other men from the lowcountry who served on the Committee on Platform and Resolutions included W. E. Horn of Wharton County, along with Henry Curtis and Daniel Gregory of Fort Bend. Despite the cries of the local white papers about the "Radical Negro convention," the platform adopted by the Republicans proved anything but radical. They began by stating that "we recognize the National Republican party as the means under Providence of saving our country and government from the calamity of successful rebellion" and "[t]hat we do not hesitate to declare ourselves unconditional Union men." As for demands, they advocated for the creation of "a system of free common schools for the equal benefit of all children and youths of the scholastic age, without distinction of race or color, to be supported by equal and uniform taxation." They also called for the creation of homesteads "out of our vacant, unappropriated public domain." The convention continued until July 7 before the new Texas Republican Party adjourned its first gathering.[11]

The first political test for the newly enfranchised voters of the lowcountry came with the election of delegates to write a new Texas state constitution in 1868. General Winfield Hancock, who took command of the Fifth Military District after the death of General William Reynolds from yellow fever in 1867, ordered elections held on February 10 and 14, 1868, to determine whether or not to hold a convention to write a new state constitution that could readmit Texas to the Union. Lowcountry voters overwhelmingly voted in favor of the convention and elected four white radical Republicans to represent the region: Erwin Wilson of Brazoria, W. E. Horne of Fort Bend, W. J. Phillips of Matagorda, and A. P. McCormick of Brazoria. The convention assembled on June 1, 1868, and consisted of ninety delegates, ten of whom were African American. During the convention, the lowcountry delegates supported Edmund J. Davis and the agenda of his faction. After two months of debate, the convention still had not settled on a new constitution, and they adjourned to ask for a special tax to continue their work.[12]

Even as the new constitutional convention continued its work, the Texas Republican Party assembled for its second annual meeting in Austin on August 12, 1868, to consider the party's agenda. W. J. Phillips, Irvin Wilson, Walter Warmly, A. P. McCormick, George P. Douglass, Edward Creery, and Murray Cole represented the lowcountry at this Republican gathering. At this meeting, which lasted two days, the Republicans urged the constitutional committee to reject all laws and decisions of the Texas legislature from 1861 to 1866, to develop a system of public schools for the state, and to provide for internal improvements and a system of "Foreign Immigration" (encouragement for the immigration of foreigners into Texas) as these items remained "of vital interest to the state." After these resolutions, on August 13, they adjourned as the president of the convention, Judge James Bell, called for "three rousing cheers for Grant and Colfax."[13]

The constitutional convention resumed its work on December 7 after a special tax to pay for the gathering was levied. Finally, on February 8, 1869, the convention adjourned and submitted a constitution for ratification by the people of Texas. Although confusion reigned toward the end of the convention, and only forty-five delegates signed the final document, Wilson, McCormick, and Phillips did sign the constitution, with Horn having returned early to

Wharton County. The new constitution outlawed slavery, recognized equality before the law of all persons, allowed African American men to sit on juries, and made public school attendance compulsory, among other progressive measures. In the general election held from November 30 to December 3, 1869, lowcountry voters turned out to approve of the new document in over-whelming numbers.[14]

In addition to the ratification of a new state constitution granting African Americans full rights of citizenship, 1869 became a banner year for African American voters in the lowcountry in other ways as well. In the election for sheriff that year in Fort Bend County, Walter Moses Burton, destined to be-come perhaps the most distinguished African American politician to emerge from slavery in the lowcountry, won the race, becoming one of the first African American sheriffs in Texas and the South. Born into slavery in North Carolina in 1840, Walter Burton arrived in Fort Bend County with his enslaver, Thomas Burke Burton, who established a plantation on the Sarah Isaacs League along Oyster Creek, northwest of Richmond, in 1850. While enslaved, his enslaver taught Walter to read and write, and when emancipation came, Walter began working to become a prominent member of the community. He served as the president of the Fort Bend County Union League before winning the election for sheriff, and in his new job he became even more active in politics, serving as a delegate to the 1869 Republican state convention.[15]

The Republican split at the constitutional convention gave shape to the 1869 gubernatorial race under the new constitution. Andrew Jackson Hamilton, who opposed African American suffrage, declared himself a candidate for governor and received backing from many white Texans and moderate Republicans. In opposition, Edmund J. Davis, president of the constitutional convention and leader of the radical Republicans, ran against him. Davis received the backing of most African American voters, and in the election, the voters of the lowcountry heavily backed Davis, giving him the victory in a very close statewide vote. Brazoria County voted for Davis by a margin of 603 to 434, Fort Bend 986 to 171, Matagorda 402 to 27, and Wharton 577 to 49, for a total of 2,568 for Davis against 681 for Hamilton. Statewide, Davis won the election with only 51 percent of the total vote, a margin of 955 votes.[16]

The 1870 Census of the Texas lowcountry revealed a great deal about the continuity and change ushered in by the previous decade. As a result of the refugeeing of enslaved people during the Civil War and the death of white men in rebel armies, the overall population in 1870 stood at 5,163 whites and

16,276 African Americans, making the freed people 76 percent of the total population. These numbers ranged from a low of 63 percent in Matagorda County to a high of 85 percent in Wharton County. The most dramatic change came in the amount of wealth wiped out by emancipation. Almost 44 percent of the wealth of enslavers was lost directly upon the freeing of enslaved people, and at the same time, land values also dropped precipitously. In Brazoria County, the tax rolls valued land at $8.13 an acre in 1860; that value dropped to $5.34 by 1866. Overall, land in the region declined from an average of $10 an acre in 1860 to $3.91 an acre in 1870, a decrease of 60 percent. These figures indicate that former enslavers of the lowcountry lost at least 70 percent of their wealth through emancipation and depreciated land values. However, in terms of *relative* wealth, not much changed. Most of the former enslavers held on to their land and their status, and only a handful of African Americans managed to scrape up enough money to purchase any real estate. Among the thousands of African American households in the region, just forty-five reported owning any amount of real estate, with an average value of $398 and a median value of $250. The amounts ranged from $10 owned by Jeremiah Nelson, a sharecropper from Fort Bend County, all the way up to $5,000 owned by Emma Jane Smith also of Fort Bend County. The vast majority of African Americans worked as sharecroppers, while a few worked as carpenters, woodcutters, or butchers. That year the region produced 9,812 bales of cotton, 2.8 percent of the total for the state, and 1,840 hogsheads of sugar, 91 percent of the state total. In a sign of a subtle economic shift, the census showed $188,268 worth of cattle in the lowcountry, 6.4 percent of the total value for the state. Over time, cattle would overtake cotton and sugar, but in 1870, the relative economics and population of the lowcountry remained largely the same as they had been in 1860.[17]

The new decade began on an ominous note for African Americans in Texas as the US government withdrew from the state, leaving the fate of the freed people to the ex-Confederate white majority in the state. After the Twelfth Legislature ratified the Fourteenth and Fifteenth Amendments, President Ulysses Grant signed an act readmitting Texas to the United States on March 30, 1870. Even though Edmund J. Davis remained governor, the retraction of protection from the federal government promised hardships for the African Americans of the lowcountry even though Republican governments remained in place at the county level.

The first real political battles after readmission took place in 1871 in the election for members of the US House of Representatives. The Texas lowcountry was part of the Third Congressional District of Texas, and in 1869 the voters sent radical Republican William T. Clark, US veteran and Galveston resident, to represent them in Congress. The Third District consisted of twenty-four counties and stretched from Hillsboro and Corsicana all the way down to Houston, the lowcountry, and Galveston. The Third District also contained the largest percentage of African Americans voters in any congressional district in Texas, making it potentially the most Republican in the state.

In 1871, Clark faced challenges to his nomination from two men, African American Texas Senator Matthew Gaines of Washington County and Louis W. Stevenson, veteran of the Freedmen's Bureau. Republican leaders in Austin rejected Gaines and Stevenson in favor of Clark, leading Gaines to believe that the Republican Party in Texas no longer served the interests of African Americans. After losing Gaines's support, Clark rushed back from Congress to shore up his support among African American voters. He solicited the help of George Ruby and began attending African American gatherings in the lowcountry and elsewhere. He also appeared at the Emancipation Day celebration in Houston on June 19 and took part in the baseball game that afternoon. After a contentious Third District convention in Houston that summer, Clark emerged with the nomination of the party and the backing of the Union League. For his part, Louis Stevenson decided to run as an independent, potentially siphoning votes away from Clark. The Democrats nominated ex-Confederate Dewitt Clinton Giddings to run against Clark and Stevenson in the general election.[18]

The elections for all four US House seats in 1871 quickly turned into a nightmare for Davis and the Republicans as returns began arriving in Austin in October. The initial balloting indicated that Democrats had handily swept three of the districts; only the Third District reported a close result, with Giddings leading Clark by just 135 votes. Clark won a majority in only eight counties in the district, with his strongest support coming in the lowcountry. In Brazoria County, the vote was 850 to 386 for Clark, with 30 voters throwing their support behind Stevenson. In Fort Bend County, voters chose Clark over Giddings 1,207 to 345 with no votes for Stevenson. Matagorda County also chose Clark 304 to 151, with three votes for Stevenson. Only in Wharton County did Giddings carry the day, with 857 votes for the Democrat compared to just 525 for the Republican and no votes for Stevenson.[19]

Intimidation and violence against African Americans and Republican voters in general plagued the elections in Texas that year, but the returns from the lowcountry do not point toward violence, but rather massive voter fraud in Wharton County. In Brazoria County, the percentage of voters who turned out to vote between the 1869 gubernatorial election and the 1871 congressional election increased slightly, from 58 percent to 69 percent, probably due to white voters once again taking part in the process. In Fort Bend, turnout also increased, from 66 percent to 89 percent, again probably due to increased white voting. In Matagorda County, voter turnout remained mostly static, only increasing from 53 percent to 57 percent, with no indication of foul play. Wharton County provided a different story. According to the 1870 Census, 811 men of voting age lived in Wharton County. In the 1869 election, the county cast 577 votes for Davis and 49 for Hamilton, a 77 percent turnout. In 1871, Wharton County reported 525 votes for Clark, a reasonable analogue to 1869, but the county then reported 857 votes for Giddings, a total of 571 votes more than the number of potential voters living there the previous year.[20]

With just 135 votes separating Clark and Giddings, Republicans in Austin began investigating potential fraud. The Texas State Election Returns Board rejected the votes from Limestone and Freestone counties because of violence reported against Republican voters. The board then rejected the returns from Bosque County on the grounds that the county submitted no official returns, and it also threw out some of the ballots cast in Brazos and Washington counties on the basis that they were improperly marked or were cast at a "white man's ballot box." These amended totals gave Clark the victory by 711 votes. The board issued Clark a certificate of election, and he proceeded back to Washington to take his seat.[21]

The US House of Representatives seated Clark on January 10, 1872, even as Giddings gathered evidence to appeal his case. On January 31, 1872, the Federal District Court for the Western District of Texas indicted Governor Davis and other Republican officials for "willfully, unlawfully, and feloniously [making] a false and untrue tabular statement of the votes cast by the legal voters of the Third Congressional District." A federal circuit court eventually acquitted the defendants of the charges, but the ruling helped Giddings convince people outside Texas that Davis was corrupt, and Clark complained that the legal action discouraged people from submitting affidavits on his behalf. Beginning on February 1, the US House gave both men 60 days to gather evidence for their respective cases, but while Giddings had amassed a great deal of evidence for the alleged fraud, Clark was limited mostly to statements from Republican officials. At the end of the 60 days, the House Committee on elections voted in favor of seating Giddings, and the full House concurred, seating Giddings on May 13, 1872. These events marked the last time that the African Americans of the lowcountry would have a Republican represent them at the national level during Reconstruction.[22]

As the political battles of the lowcountry played out at the ballot box and in Congress, a legal drama of epic proportion began to unfold in Wharton County. The wrangling over the immense unclaimed estate of John C. Clark commenced soon after his death. A woman named Mildred Ann Wygall and her brother Richard Clark became the first to file a claim to the estate in 1867, representing themselves as the long-lost siblings of John Clark. The case soon became muddied by others challenging Wygall and Clark's claims. The case, filed in Wharton County, was transferred to Fort Bend and then back to Wharton before the state legislature ordered the case tried in Travis County in 1871. Both alleged siblings died in 1870, and the court substituted a nephew named Joseph Wygall in their place. The next year a jury decided the case in favor of Joseph Wygall, but not before the children of John Clark filed their claim to their father's estate.

On Christmas Day 1869, Sobrina Clark died, and after the New Year, her children approached F. G. Franks, a local white attorney in Wharton County, about representing them in a bid to claim their father's estate. On September 15, 1870, Bishop Clark signed an agreement for Franks to represent him and his sisters, Nancy and Lourinda. On March 28, 1871, Franks filed a petition in district court in Wharton County to sue Texas State Treasurer George W. Honey on the basis that Bishop, Lourinda, and Nancy, notwithstanding the Wygall case, were the legal heirs of John Clark. Presiding over the case was Judge William Burkhart, who set the trial for August 1871.[23]

Honey's attorneys stalled for time. After Franks called Clarissa Bird as a witness, the state's attorneys asked for a continuance on August 10 on the grounds that they needed time to prepare their defense, and Judge Burkhart granted the request. On August 16, Honey's attorneys then filed a motion to determine whether Sobrina had any other children, as they would also become heirs to the Clark estate. Burkhart granted the defense a continuance, and on August 18 he set aside the Wygall verdict and ordered a new trial for December.[24]

On December 4, 1871, the term of the Twentieth Judicial District of Texas commenced with Burkhart presiding in the old Wharton courthouse. The irony of the moment could not have escaped Nancy, Lourinda, and Bishop, as they arrived to press their case for their inheritance, walking up the court-house steps from which they had been auctioned off as human chattel almost 9 years earlier. Franks began with the testimony of Clarissa Bird (who died shortly after giving her testimony in August). Witnesses agreed that Bishop, Lourinda, and Nancy were the children of John C. Clark, so that left the question of whether or not the union of Sobrina and John Clark constituted a legal marriage in a state that prohibited interracial marriage. Franks argued that John and Sobrina entered a common law marriage by living together and procreating in Mexican Texas, before the Congress of the Republic of Texas outlawed interracial marriage in 1837. The witnesses called by Franks all testified that John and Sobrina lived together and regarded each other as man and wife and that Clark treated his children differently from the other enslaved children on his plantation. Meanwhile, the attorneys for the state of Texas called witnesses, who although none of them could claim that they knew the reclusive Clark well, all testified that they never saw the man treat Sobrina or her children any differently than any other enslaved people. On December 11, the defense rested its case, and the next day Burkhart charged the jury, instructing them that "[i]n determining whether or not a marriage existed between said Clark and the said Sobrina you will take into consideration the manner in which the parties lived together . . . whether Clark recognized these Plffs [plaintiffs] as his children and treated them as such." That same day, Henry Fleming, the jury foreman, announced that the jury had reached a verdict in favor of the plaintiffs. With the jury verdict, Bishop, Lourinda, and Nancy became the inheritors of the $450,147.55 left by their father and were now some of the wealthiest people in Texas. George Honey's attorneys appealed the decision to the Texas Supreme Court, but the high court affirmed the decision of the lower court in the case of *Honey v. Clark* in 1872.[25]

The elections in the fall of 1873 marked the close of the first chapter of Reconstruction in the Texas lowcountry. Although Republicans statewide lost, the elections proved that the lowcountry remained a Republican stronghold. In 1873, the Democrats nominated former rebel captain Richard Coke to run against Governor Edmund J. Davis. Amid widespread voter intimidation and violence against African Americans, Coke soundly defeated Davis with 100,415 votes compared to 52,141 for Davis. In Brazoria County, the voters supported Davis by a margin of 1,428 to 336. Fort Bend County similarly supported Davis 1,159 to 261. Matagorda County also voted for Davis 388 to 186, and in a further sign of voter fraud, the vote totals from Wharton County did not survive in the records of the Texas secretary of state. These results made it clear that even as Democrats took back control of the state, the voters of the lowcountry showed no sign of turning from the Republican ticket.

In the December 2, 1873, election, Walter Moses Burton, the sheriff of Fort Bend County, ran for the Texas Senate from the Thirteenth District, and the election turned into a contested affair. On the ballots in the four counties of the district, the various county clerks listed and spelled Burton's name no fewer than four different ways. In Fort Bend County, Burton received 973 votes under the name "W. M. Burton," and 180 votes under the name "Wm Burton." In Austin County, Burton received 605 votes under the name "William Burton," where someone scratched out the last part of the name, leaving just the first letter, "W." In Wharton County, Burton got another 664 votes under the name "Walter M. Burton," and he received 154 under the name "William Burton." Finally, in Waller County Burton got another 664 votes under the name "William Burton." Meanwhile, Burton's Democratic opponent, Z. Hunt, received 1,938 votes to Burton's 3,240, but Hunt argued that officials should disqualify all the votes for "William Burton," giving him the victory by "72 votes." When the Legislature convened in January 1874, Burton asked the Senate to swear him in on January 19, the same day Hunt presented his protest. The Senate voted to refer the dispute to the Committee on Privileges and Elections. On February 11, 1874, the committee presented their findings, recommending that the Senate seat Hunt, and "that to adopt any other course than that we respectfully recommended, would be setting a dangerous precedent." The next day, other members of the committee presented a minority report finding that the Senate should seat Burton on the grounds that, based on sworn affidavits and the absence of any other candidate with the same last name, the voters who cast ballots for "W. Burton" and "William Burton" intended to vote for Walter M. Burton. The Texas Senate voted to approve the minority report, and seated Burton on February 20, 1874.[26]

The elections of 1873 also had important implications for Fort Bend County elected leaders. Succeeding Walter Burton was a freedman named Henry Ferguson who won the office of county sheriff, an office he would hold until 1888. Ferguson was a "tall, rawboned man with broad, stooped shoulders, and wore a slight mustache and a cutaway coat. He was a man of great dignity, never talked loud in conversation and looked one in the face when he talked." Like his predecessor, Ferguson appointed white deputies to carry out various responsibilities, including confronting any white men who ran afoul of county law. Along with his brother, Charles M. Ferguson, who would become Fort Bend County district clerk in 1882, Henry Ferguson served as the leader of African American Republicans in Fort Bend County until the end of Reconstruction there.[27]

African Americans in the Texas lowcountry made political and social progress in the 8 years after emancipation as they used every resource at their disposal to achieve some measure of equality. Still, the doors of economic opportunity, in particular land ownership, remained firmly closed to most residents of the region. The end of statewide Reconstruction in Texas and the losses of Republicans in 1871 and 1873 seemed to end any hope of further gains, but two factors forestalled a complete end to progress. In the fall of 1873, several of the largest banks in the United States failed, leading to the Panic of 1873, which forced open the door of land ownership for many African Americans. Second, Republican governments remained in place at the local level, guaranteeing the continued election of Republican candidates to the legislature, and control of almost all county offices. However, as the state of Texas began to run out of public land and revenue, state officials initiated a system of convict leasing that was overwhelmingly concentrated in the lowcountry, and they began creating new prisons by purchasing old plantations. Within ten years these policies initiated the Texas lowcountry's entry into the era of the "New South."

Chapter 10

The Places in Between

1873–1885

ON THURSDAY, September 18, 1873, Jay Cook & Company, the largest bank in the United States, closed their doors following a run on the bank. Two days later, the New York Stock Exchange suspended trading for 10 days to let the fallout from what became known as the Panic of 1873 calm. By November, dozens of the nation's largest railroads had failed, initiating an economic depression that lasted through the end of the decade.

The fallout from the Panic of 1873 brought important changes to the Texas lowcountry. The depression contracted the already flooded market for cotton, forcing white landowners to sell off parcels of land, thereby opening a brief window through which African American land ownership reached an all-time high in the region. With the door to land pried open, freedom colonies appeared and grew as African Americans created communities of their own in the places in between the old plantations. In these colonies, they acquired land, established churches and schools, and sought greater self-sufficiency. At the same time, the Panic of 1873 put increasing financial pressure on the cash-strapped state government, and the legislature responded by cementing and expanding their program of convict leasing, forcing many African Americans in the lowcountry back into a condition of virtual enslavement. Realizing the profitability of sugar grown by convicts, the state of Texas began buying up old sugar plantations and converting them into prison farms, laying the foundation for what would become the largest carceral complex in the world. Through all these changes, the biracial Republican county governments remained in place, supported by African American voters, which increasingly incensed the white minority.

Brazoria County

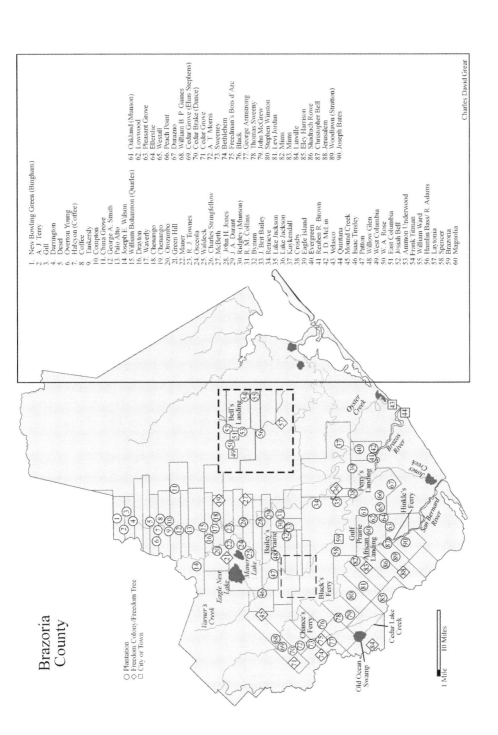

○ Plantation
◇ Freedom Colony/Freedom Tree
□ City or Town

Charles David Grear

1. New Bowling Green (Bingham)
2. A J Terry
3. Gill
4. Darrington
5. Desel
6. Overton Young
7. Halcyon (Coffee)
8. Coffee
9. Tankersly
10. Compton
11. China Grove
12. George A. Smith
13. Palo Alto
14. Joseph F. Wilson
15. William Bohannon (Quarles)
16. Draxton
17. Waverly
18. Chenango
19. Chenango
20. Orozimbo
21. Green Hill
22. Maner
23. R. J Townes
24. Osceola
25. Waldeck
26. Charles Stringfellow
27. McBeth
28. John H. Jones
29. J. A. Durant
30. Ridgley (Munson)
31. R. M. Collins
32. Bynum
33. J. Brit Bailey
34. Retrieve
35. Lake Jackson
36. Lake Jackson
37. Kuykendall
38. Crosby
39. Eagle Island
40. Evergreen
41. Reuben R. Brown
42. J D McLin
43. Velasco
44. Quintana
45. Mound Creek
46. Isaac Tinsley
47. Patton
48. Wiflow Glen
49. West Columbia
50. W. A. Rose
51. East Columbia
52. Josiah Bell
53. Ammon Underwood
54. Frank Titman
55. William Ward
56. Hamlin Bass/ R. Adams
57. Laytonia
58. Spencer
59. Brazoria
60. Magnolia
61. Oakland (Munson)
62. Lowwood
63. Pleasant Grove
64. Ellerslie
65. Westall
66. Peach Point
67. Durazno
68. William B. P. Gaines
69. Cedar Grove (Elias Stephens)
70. Cedar Brake (Dance)
71. Cedar Grove
72. A. T. Morris
73. Sweeney
74. Bethlehem
75. Freedman's Bois d' Arc
76. Black
77. George Armstrong
78. Thomas Sweeny
79. John McGrew
80. Stephen Winston
81. Levi Jordan
82. Mims
83. Mims
84. Linville
85. Eley Harrison
86. Shadrach Rowe
87. Christopher Bell
88. Jerusalem
89. Woodlawn (Stratton)
90. Joseph Bates

The seven years between 1873 and 1880 saw several hundred African Americans purchase their own land. For enslaved people, freedom had always existed in the woods and swamps in between the old plantations, where people escaped enslavement or lived in maroon colonies, and it was in these very spaces that African Americans most often purchased land. Land ownership rates differed by county in the lowcountry, from a low of 12 percent of African American farmers who owned their own land in Fort Bend County to a high of 74 percent in Brazoria County, but on average about one-third of African American farmers owned land by the end of the decade. However, African American farms still averaged far less land than their white counterparts. In Brazoria County, the average farm totaled 499 acres, while the average African American landowner owned just under 58 acres. In Fort Bend County, the average African American farm consisted of just 26 acres, while the county average remained much higher at 159 acres. Most of these African American farmers raised enough corn and or cotton for their families and the market, and they tended small herds of livestock. The market for sugar cut out these "smallholders" because of the complexity and cost of the system.[1]

Although the means by which African American landowners raised enough money to purchase land varied, familial ties appear to have assumed a strong correlation to land ownership. Ninety-five percent of African American landowners were married, making it likely that in most cases husband and wife pooled enough money between them to purchase land. Multigenerational patterns were also in evidence. In Brazoria County, three generations of the Hall family owned their own land: Henry M. Hall, a married farmer who owned 145 acres; his father Taylor Hall, who owned 9 acres; and his grandfather, African-born Joseph Hall, who, at the age of ninty, could claim 4 acres as his own. Beset by the Panic of 1873, even the firm of R. & D. G. Mills declared bankruptcy, and in February 1872, Andrew G. Mills Jr., the African American son of David G. Mills, purchased 150 acres of land for himself from his father and uncle. In Fort Bend County, 68 percent of African American farmers worked as sharecroppers, but some did manage to purchase their own land. In December 1872 Sheriff Walter M. Burton managed to procure 96 acres on the west side of the Brazos River from Thomas H. Borden in the Samuel Isaacs League for $900 in cash. The ownership of this land helped Burton cement his position as a leading member of the community and facilitated his successful run for the Texas Senate.[2]

Among the hundreds of stories of African Americans who purchased land in the years after the Civil War is the most intriguing saga of Emma Jane Smith

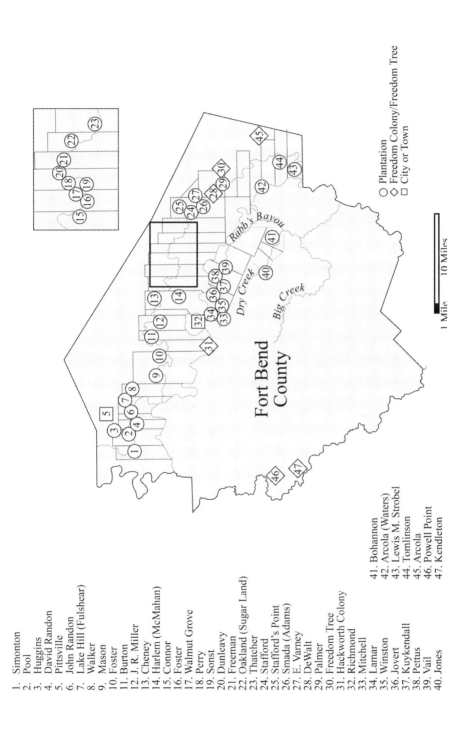

1. Simonton
2. Pool
3. Huggins
4. David Randon
5. Pittsville
6. John Randon
7. Lake Hill (Fulshear)
8. Walker
9. Mason
10. Foster
11. Burton
12. J. R. Miller
13. Cheney
14. Harlem (McMahan)
15. Connor
16. Foster
17. Walmut Grove
18. Perry
19. Sonst
20. Dunleavy
21. Freeman
22. Oakland (Sugar Land)
23. Thatcher
24. Stafford
25. Stafford's Point
26. Smada (Adams)
27. E. Varney
28. DeWalt
29. Palmer
30. Freedom Tree
31. Hackworth Colony
32. Richmond
33. Mitchell
34. Lamar
35. Winston
36. Jovert
37. Kuykendall
38. Pettus
39. Vail
40. Jones
41. Bohannon
42. Arcola (Waters)
43. Lewis M. Strobel
44. Tomlinson
45. Arcola
46. Powell Point
47. Kendleton

Plantation
Freedom Colony/Freedom Tree
City or Town

Fort Bend County

Rabb's Bayou
Dry Creek
Big Creek

1 Mile   10 Miles

and her family. In 1840, three brothers, Thomas H., George W., and William
W. McMahon, arrived in Fort Bend County from the United States. While his
brothers remained in Richmond as merchants, in 1839 William W. McMahon,
the oldest brother, purchased several hundred acres from John Morton in
the Morton League and began a sugar plantation that he named Harlem. In
1848, the *Houston Telegraph* reported: "We were shown a sample of this year's
production, from the plantation of William W. McMahan [sic], in Fort Bend
County. We have never seen a finer sample in the market. It is fully equal to
the best imported sugar. . . . Mr. McMahan [sic] we believe, is the pioneer in
the sugar culture in the county."[3]

Born into slavery in 1839 or 1840 in Virginia, Emma Jane Smith found
herself a victim of the interstate slave trade at a young age before arriving in
Fort Bend County, having been acquired by McMahon as one of the almost
seventy enslaved people at Harlem. McMahon took Emma Jane as his concubine, and in 1854 she gave birth to their first child, Cora. Emma Jane gave
birth to their second daughter, Alice, in 1856, and then two sons: Millard in
1858, and Sydney in 1862. By the time of emancipation, William and Emma
Jane had another daughter, Ada, born in 1864. The relationship continued
even after emancipation, and Emma Jane gave birth to twin girls, Jenette and
Jenola, in 1868, bringing the total number of children to seven for the twenty-
eight-year-old Emma Jane and the sixty-five-year-old William.[4]

After his fortune was destroyed by the emancipation, McMahon sold his
plantation to his brother, Thomas H. McMahon, now the principal partner in
the First National Bank of Galveston. William accepted $5,000 in gold from
his brother for the 400-acre Harlem plantation on December 1, 1868. William
evidently then gave the money to Emma Jane to provide for herself and their
children, and in December 1869 Emma Jane Smith purchased 105 acres of the
old Lum farm, adjacent to the southeast corner of Harlem plantation in the
Jane Wilkins League for $1,200 from Thomas McMahon. The 1870 Census
showed Emma Jane Smith and her seven children, plus her son-in-law, Frank
Ross, husband to Cora, with $5,000 in real estate, living adjacent to William
W. McMahon and his wife Mary in Fort Bend County. In 1870 Emma Jane
Smith gave birth to her eighth child by William, a son named Oscar. In 1873,
the couple welcomed their ninth child, another son named Horace. Mean-
while, Mary McMahon had died (sometime after 1870), and on March 3, 1874,
William W. McMahon legally married Emma Jane Smith in Fort Bend County,
with Emma Jane passing as white to avoid the state's antimiscegenation laws.
The couple homesteaded their 105 acres, and in 1876 Emma Jane, at the age of

thirty-six, gave birth to her tenth and final child, Bertha, by her now seventy-four-year-old husband. Soon after, in 1877, McMahon died, leaving Emma Jane a widow, and just a year later, in 1878, Emma Jane herself died, without leaving a will. The couple's eldest daughter, Cora, and son-in-law Frank Ross also followed in death before 1880, leaving Alice and her husband, John Felch, to head the family, and Millard to carry on farming the homestead. The 1880 Census recorded that Alice and John Felch and their children were living on the land along with Millard, Sydney, Ada, Jennete, Jenola, Oscar, Horace, and Bertha McMahon as well as Cora's two children, Emma and Neoma Ross.[5]

Meanwhile in Galveston, Thomas H. McMahon died in 1871, leaving his widow Eliza to settle his estate. McMahon had fallen into debt to the New York firm of Guion & Williams, and the firm sued Beven R. Davis, the court-appointed administrator for the McMahon estate to recoup their debt. On July 14, 1874, the US District Court for the Eastern District of Texas handed down a ruling giving the McMahon estate, including Harlem plantation and most of the Lum place, to Guion & Williams. In 1884, the state of Texas, anxious to purchase sugar plantations for their burgeoning convict leasing program, bought Harlem plantation and the part of the old Lum place not owned by the McMahons from Guion & Williams and converted it into the Harlem State Prison Farm. Agents of the state then went about surveying other good bottom land to purchase adjacent to Harlem.[6]

On July 6, 1885, Jenola McMahon married George W. Brooks in Fort Bend County, and the next month the couple initiated a civil suit in the 23rd Judicial District of Texas against her siblings for an equitable division of the land. At roughly the same time as the suit, Millard ran for and won election as Fort Bend County commissioner for Precinct 3. The trial for the land, presided over by Judge William H. Burkhart, began in September 1885. The plaintiffs valued the land at $1,050 along with thirty-five head of cattle and a mule. Because Emma Jane died intestate, the law of heirship took precedence, and the judge ordered an equal partition of the land into ten parcels of 10.5 acres each on October 2, 1885. This division, though, did not satisfy Jenola and G. W. Brooks, and they requested that the court also equitably divide the thirty-five head of cattle on the land. The court appointed a three-man commission to survey the land, and on October 10, the three commissioners appeared before the court and reported that the land could not be equitably divided because most of the improvements existed on the southern end of the land, and the cattle could not be gathered in so late in the year. Considering this report, the court ruled that the land be sold at public auction with the proceeds divided in ten ways. On December 1, 1885, Walter Andrus, the clerk of the 23rd Judicial District Court, sold the land at auction to Charles M. Ferguson, the Fort Bend County clerk, for $1,330. Shortly after the sale, the state acquired the land from the county as part of the Harlem State Prison Farm. Most of the McMahon siblings moved to Houston in the years following the loss of their land.[7]

Another remarkable story of African American land ownership in this period is that of Charles Brown of Brazoria County. Born into slavery in what is now West Virginia in approximately 1840, Brown was freed by his enslaver, who provided him with enough money to move to Texas. Precisely when he arrived in Brazoria County, however, remains unclear. Shortly after emancipation, Brown married Isabella, a woman formerly enslaved on the Dance Cedar Brake plantation. Beginning in 1869, Brown scraped up enough money to begin purchasing parcels of land from the Smelser family on the James F. Perry League in the western part of the county, and in 1873, Brown became one of the trustees who purchased two acres from the Dance family to establish St. Mary's African Methodist Episcopal Church. By 1883, Brown had amassed enough wealth to purchase the old Dance homestead of over two hundred acres. The 1887 Brazoria County tax rolls indicate that Charlie Brown owned an astounding 1,801 acres valued at $7,500, along with four horses and two hundred head of cattle. Brown began purchasing parcels of land in West Columbia, and by the end of Reconstruction he was living in the old Spencer Dance house, which he purchased in 1887. Brown moved the house, originally built in East Columbia, to his property in West Columbia, where he lived with Isabella and their eleven children. With his land acquisitions, Charlie Brown became the largest African American landholder in Brazoria County in the nineteenth century.[8]

∼

As African Americans acquired land and strove to achieve self-sufficiency, they established their own communities and churches "up in the sand hills, down in the creek and river bottoms, and along county lines," in the places in between the old plantation neighborhoods. During the long Reconstruction in the lowcountry, freed people established more than thirty freedom colonies and dozens of churches scattered across the region.[9]

Brazoria County contained the most freedom colonies, with eleven documented settlements and nineteen churches. Near the old Lake Jackson plantation, an independent freedom colony developed, and in 1867 worshippers established True Honor Baptist Church. Five years later, the residents also established Evergreen Baptist Church. These churches served as the heart of the community and provided places of worship, space for schools, and centers for political organizing.[10]

Northwest of Lake Jackson, the town of Laytonia (sometimes spelled Latonia) took shape on the west bank of the Brazos, in between Brazoria and West Columbia. In 1868, African Americans founded two churches near the settlement, Hall Chappell Baptist Church and Ministry of Reconciliation First Baptist Church, and by 1876 the town added a post office. David Blair, a forty-four-year-old Baptist minister born in Virginia, and his wife Ardena founded Hall Chappell Baptist Church. In 1881, congregants also founded White Oak Baptist Church, and in 1887, Wilhite African Methodist Episcopal Church opened its doors. The post office disappeared by 1878, but the settlement persisted well into the twentieth century.[11]

Mound Creek rises in southern Fort Bend County and meanders south past Damon Mound until it intersects with the San Bernard River roughly a mile and a half northwest of West Columbia. Just north of the intersection of the two bodies of water, African Americans formed a freedom colony known as Mound Creek near the banks of the creek. In 1884 the founding of St. Paul African Methodist Episcopal Church gave the community a focal point, and the settlement persisted well into the second half of the twentieth century. Meanwhile, in nearby West Columbia, worshippers also founded Blue Run Baptist Church in 1871, and these two churches served the African American communities in Mound Creek and West Columbia.[12]

North of West Columbia, African Americans also established freedom colonies and churches on both sides of the Brazos. On the west bank of the river, just north of Maner Lake, African American worshippers established Green Hill African Methodist Episcopal Church in 1870 to serve the people living near the old Maner, Osceola, and Orozimbo plantations in what was known as the Green Hill community. East of the Brazos River, freed people also established the community of McBeth, just across the railroad tracks from Anchor, northwest of what would become Angleton.[13]

The northernmost freedom colony in Brazoria County took shape near the old Chenango plantation, where freed people established a community and two churches. In 1864, Grant Addison organized a Baptist congregation on the Chenango plantation, and after emancipation, the congregation moved the church to its present location under the leadership of Pastor Walter Romely and Deacon Jessie Alexander as Providence Baptist Church. By

1869, Chenango had a post office, and by 1884, the town had forty residents. In 1886, Pastor M. W. Williams organized the Bethelder Missionary Baptist Church on the outskirts of the old Tankersley plantation seven miles north of Providence Baptist Church.[14]

In the land between the Chance's Prairie neighborhood and the Upper Caney neighborhood, many freedom colonies located in the lowcountry took shape on both sides of the Brazoria-Matagorda County line. On the Brazoria side, in 1867, freed people established St. Mary's African Methodist Episcopal Church, and the settlement of Cedar Grove rose up around it on the western edge of the plantation of the same name. The community enjoyed a post office for just one year, from 1886 to 1887, but the settlement persisted well into the twentieth century.[15]

Southeast of Cedar Grove, on the land of the old Sweeney plantation, African Americans established the community of Bethlehem and the Bethlehem African Methodist Episcopal Church in 1868. Southeast of Bethlehem, a sizeable freedom colony called Mims developed on the land of the old Fannin-Mims plantation near the west bank of the San Bernard River. In the Mims community, freed people established three churches in the years after emancipation: Grace United Methodist Church in 1865, Zion Temple African Methodist Episcopal Church in 1881, and Magnolia Baptist Church in 1889. Congregants also established nearby Galilee Baptist Church to the south, near Hinkle's Ferry, in 1878.[16]

The final two freedom colonies in Brazoria County took shape west and southwest of Mims at Linnville and Jerusalem. African Americans founded the settlement of Linnville on the Matagorda County line west of the Mims community near the banks of Linnville Bayou, and by the late 1880s the community had a thriving school. South of Linnville, worshippers founded two churches in the vicinity of the Jerusalem community: Jerusalem Baptist Church in 1866 and St. Paul Missionary Baptist Church in 1867. By the 1880s the settlement also included a school.[17]

North of Brazoria, in Fort Bend County, African Americans formed five freedom colonies and seven churches in the postemancipation period. On the old Arcola plantation freed people established the settlement of Arcola, which gained a post office by 1869 and served as the site of a railroad junction in 1878. By 1884, the settlement featured two general stores and a Baptist Church. Northwest of Arcola, African Americans established the settlement of Dewalt, named for Thomas Waters DeWalt, the white former enslaver who divided up his land into small plots for sale to the freed people after emancipation.

In 1869 near DeWalt, parishioners, led by Reverend David King, founded St. John Missionary Baptist Church, which would become the focal point of DeWalt.[18]

In the central and western part of Fort Bend County, African Americans founded the Hackworth Colony across the Brazos from Richmond and the communities of Powell Point and Kendleton. In Richmond, freed people founded Mount Vernon United Methodist Church in 1867, Mount Carmel Baptist Church in 1869, and Mount Vernon Missionary Baptist Church in 1882. Just across the Brazos River, freed people founded the Hackworth Colony after emancipation, and on the western edge of the county African Americans also began purchasing land around what would become Kendleton. In 1869, a former enslaver named William Kendall divided his land up into one hundred-acre tracts and sold them to freed people for anywhere from 50 cents to $1.50 per acre. As the population increased, the residents formed the town of Kendleton in the 1870s. In 1882 a railroad arrived in the town, and in 1884 the settlement acquired a post office. Worshippers established Newman Chapel United Methodist Church in 1866 and Oak Hill Baptist Church ten years later. One of the more prominent residents, Henry Green, won a seat as commissioner of Precinct 2 in 1882, and subsequently held the position of constable for Precinct 2 from 1884 to 1888. In the 1880s, some of the residents of Kendleton established the community of Powell Point, just to the north.[19]

Near Caney Creek, in Matagorda County, African Americans established nine freedom colonies and a number of churches in the Reconstruction period. Just over a mile from Jerusalem in Brazoria County, freed people founded the settlement of Cedar Lake on the Matagorda County line. In 1872, Reverend Henry Woodward founded the Bethlehem Christian Church at Cedar Lake, which became the focal point of activities in the community. Just north of Cedar Lake, the freedom colonies of Cedar Lane and Bell Bottom came into existence in the post-Civil War period. At Cedar Lane, Reverend Dennis Grey and John Alexander founded Shiloh Missionary Baptist Church in 1866. This church, along with nearby St. Mark Missionary Baptist Church, which served the Bell Bottom community, became the central spiritual, education, and political locales of these settlements during Reconstruction.[20]

Northwest of Cedar Lane, near Linnville, freed people established the settlements of Vann and Liveoak along Caney Creek. King Van (or Vann), formerly enslaved by Abram Sheppard and Samuel G. Powell, founded the settlement of Vann on 374 acres that he owned with his parents, Odo and

Matagorda
County

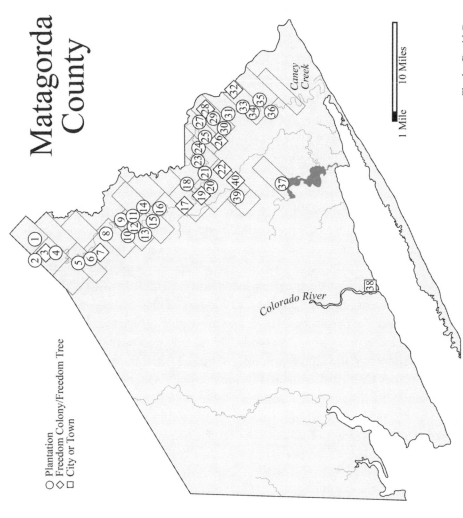

Colorado River

Caney Creek

○ Plantation
◇ Freedom Colony/Freedom Tree
□ City or Town

1 Mile
10 Miles

Charles David Grear

1. Eliza Pledger
2. Grove Hill (Brown)
3. Grove Hill
4. Thomas Matthews
5. Jesse Gordon
6. John Duncan
7. Podo
8. John Rugeley
9. Irvin Rugeley
10. Samuel Hardeman
11. Ned Rugeley
12. Wiggins
13. E.A. Pearson
14. Roland Rugeley
15. John H. Gibson
16. Matthew Talbot
17. Hudgins
18. R. H. Williams
19. Mount Pilgrim
20. William G. Warren
21. John L. Thorp
22. Vann
23. Henry Gibson
24. Bowie
25. Chinn
26. Cedar Lane
27. Gibson
28. Bell Bottom
29. Nancy Thompson
30. John H. Jones
31. Peter W. Hebert
32. Cedar Lake
33. Hawkins
34. John S. Sanborn
35. Cedar Lake (Ewing)
36. A.P. McCormick
37. Hawkins Lake House
38. Matagorda
39. Abraham Sheppard
40. Liveoak

Fatima, in partnership with Joseph Sorrell and George Washington. Odo, Fatima and Joseph Sorrell were all born in West Africa, while King Van and George Washington were born in Texas to African parents. Africans and African Americans held Christian worship services in their houses around the settlement until they could afford to build a church building. In 1896, Odo and Fatima sold half an acre of their land for $5 to Deacon Charles Gatson to establish Berean Missionary Baptist Church, which became the center of the community. Just west of Vann, African Americans organized a community named Liveoak that by 1867 centered on a church they referred to as Grapevine. The community also boasted a school by the same name. The first church building had only a dirt floor, but in 1875 the community constructed a building to house both the church and the school, which residents later renamed Vine Grove Christian Church.[21]

North of Liveoak, freed people established the communities of Mount Pilgrim and Hudgins. Along the banks of Caney Creek near the old Caney Crossing plantation, Reverend Anthony Martin and his congregants, who had gathered for worship services long before emancipation, established Mount Pilgrim Missionary Baptist Church in 1884. The small community of Mount Pilgrim grew up around the church, with many of the residents still living in the nearby brick cabins. Three and a half miles north of Mount Pilgrim, a freedman named Ino Hudgins purchased several acres of land on the east bank of Caney Creek for $25 an acre in 1874, and the community of Hudgins grew up around the area.[22]

In the Upper Caney neighborhood, freed people established the settlements of Podo and Grove Hill in the years after the Civil War. Around the quarters of the enslaved on the Duncan plantation on the banks of Caney Creek, a freedom colony arose on the land of Abel Head "Shanghai" Pierce, who purchased the property after the death of John Duncan in 1878. The most prominent resident of the settlement became Podo, an African man formerly enslaved by Duncan, and the settlement grew after the New York, Texas, and Mexican Railroad installed track through the area and a bridge over Caney Creek there known as "Podo's Bridge." North of Podo, on the opposite bank of Caney Creek, the freedom colony of Grove Hill began to grow after the establishment of Grove Hill Missionary Baptist Church in 1884. Founded by Jack Yates and London Branch near the quarters of the enslaved on the old Brown plantation, Grove Hill existed before the establishment of the nearby town of Pledger, and the church also served as a school for African American pupils. Like Podo, Grove Hill and Pledger grew with the introduction of the railroad at the turn of the century.[23]

Over the county line in Wharton County, freed people founded eight more freedom colonies and many churches during Reconstruction. Around Lawson's Corner and the old Harrison and Lawson plantations between Peach Creek and Caney Creek, African Americans formed a freedom colony that eventually became known as the town of Burr. In 1874, Reverend J. C. Crolby organized the Shiloh Baptist Church just to the south, near the community of Boling. During Reconstruction, a freedman named Isam Davenport served as justice of the peace and county commissioner at Burr, and he held court before "the big pecan tree" in the community.[24]

Northwest of Burr, between that place and the town of Wharton, E. W. Roberts established a settlement for African Americans that became known as Dinsmore. "The original plat had thirty-eight blocks, with nine avenues running east to west and six streets running north to south. One lot was designated for a school, with a park across the street. The streets and avenues had the names of local citizens. The lots were small but cheap, and gave descendants of former slaves, now working as tenant farmers, sharecroppers, or hired agricultural workers, a place to build and own their own homes."[25]

West of the town of Wharton, African Americans established freedom colonies at Sorrell, Old Jerusalem, Spanish Camp, Sand Ridge, and Elm Grove. Southeast of the old Glen Flora plantation, on land near the old Sorrell place, freed people formed a community that took the same name. Just to the north, freed people founded the community of Old Jerusalem, centered on Jerusalem Missionary Baptist Church. On the western edge of Old Jerusalem, African Americans founded the community of Spanish Camp near the old Clark place, replete with two churches: Camp Zion Baptist Church, which dated its founding to 1870, and Rising Star Baptist Church, which was established in 1888. West of Spanish Camp, near Egypt, African Americans established the community of Sand Ridge, and on the western edge of the county, freed people established the community of Elm Grove.[26]

Even as the people of the lowcountry worked to establish their own communities and churches, financial constraints also put pressure on the state of Texas to reform the state prison system. As African Americans attempted to take their place in free society amid the general chaos of Reconstruction, local sheriffs began arresting and convicting them of property crimes that mandated incarceration in the state penitentiary in Huntsville, causing the

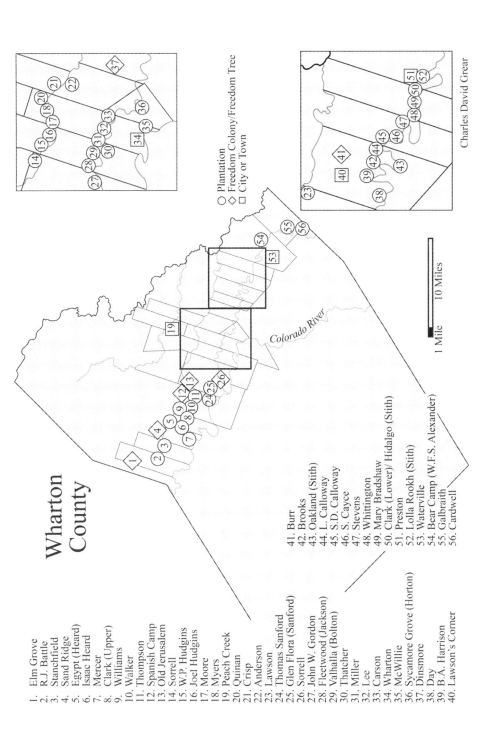

Wharton County

1. Elm Grove
2. R.J. Battle
3. Stanchfield
4. Sand Ridge
5. Egypt (Heard)
6. Isaac Heard
7. Mercer
8. Clark (Upper)
9. Williams
10. Walker
11. Thompson
12. Spanish Camp
13. Old Jerusalem
14. Sorrell
15. W.P. Hudgins
16. Joel Hudgins
17. Moore
18. Myers
19. Peach Creek
20. Quinan
21. Crisp
22. Anderson
23. Lawson
24. Thomas Sanford
25. Glen Flora (Sanford)
26. Sorrell
27. John W. Gordon
28. Fleetwood (Jackson)
29. Valhalla (Bolton)
30. Thatcher
31. Miller
32. Lee
33. Carson
34. Wharton
35. McWillie
36. Sycamore Grove (Horton)
37. Dinsmore
38. Day
39. B.A. Harrison
40. Lawson's Corner

41. Burr
42. Brooks
43. Oakland (Stith)
44. L. Calloway
45. S.D. Calloway
46. S. Cayce
47. Stevens
48. Whittington
49. Mary Bradshaw
50. Clark (Lower)/ Hidalgo (Stith)
51. Preston
52. Lolla Rookh (Stith)
53. Waterville
54. Bear Camp (W.F.S. Alexander)
55. Galbraith
56. Cardwell

○ Plantation
◇ Freedom Colony/Freedom Tree
□ City or Town

Colorado River

1 Mile   10 Miles

Charles David Grear

prison population to explode. At the close of the Civil War, the incarcerated population of Texas stood at a mere 146, but by 1896 the number of prisoners ballooned to an astonishing 4,421, increasing at an average rate of more than 200 per year. Although they never constituted much more than 30 percent of the total population of Texas, African Americans made up 48 to 57 percent of the prison population in the nineteenth century.[27]

With the rapidly increasing number of prisoners, the limited facilities in Huntsville, and the need for revenue, in 1866 the legislature began debating the terms under which the state could lease convicts for work outside the penitentiary. Under Governor James Throckmorton, the Eleventh Legislature passed a law for "Employment of Convict Labor on Works of Public Utility," opening the door for leasing convicts to private entities. The same law also designated convicts as either first or second class. First-class prisoners, almost all of them white, consisted of arsonists, horse thieves, and murderers, while second-class prisoners, the vast majority of them African American, consisted of those convicted of nonviolent crimes. Only second-class prisoners would work outside the penitentiary. From the beginning it became apparent that state officials would almost exclusively work African Americans outside the prison.[28]

Between 1866 and 1871, the Board of Public Labor allowed a limited lease of prisoners to railroads and a larger lease to James McKee of Galveston, owner of the Galveston Canal Company. Increasing reports of the brutal treatment of prisoners in railroad camps and complaints from the Board of Directors of the State Penitentiary led Governor Davis and the Republican legislature to contemplate a complete lease of the penitentiary to an outside entity, and after an investigation by the Twelfth Legislature, on March 22, 1871, the governor signed a bill into law allowing for such an arrangement. On April 29, 1871, the state of Texas negotiated a lease with the politically connected Galveston-based firm of Ward, Dewey & Company. Led by Nathan Patten, A. J. Ward, and E. C. Dewey, the company agreed to pay the state a series of flat fees per year that could have amounted to a total of $325,000 to the state. Ward and Dewey made some improvements to the penitentiary in Huntsville but began making a profit by subleasing African American prisoners to work on sugar plantations in the lowcountry.[29]

Former enslavers greeted the leasing system with enthusiasm. With freedmen understandably reluctant to work in the stifling, deadly sugar fields, production of the crop dropped off dramatically in the years after

1865. M. S. Munson of Brazoria County wrote in 1867 that "the present crops are about but half the average." A former enslaver from Fort Bend County wrote that the freedmen "have worked . . . to kill time instead of grass and weeds." Illustrating the drop in production, J. B. Hawkins of Matagorda County reported producing 150 hogsheads of sugar in 1865, and only 60 the following year.[30]

Ward, Dewey & Company put African American convicts back to work in the sugar fields, bound by chains, watched over by armed guards, in a system justifiably labeled "slavery by another name." By 1875, the company managed 1,453 prisoners statewide, with 314 of them, or 21 percent, working on the old sugar plantations. In Brazoria County 130 men labored in the sugar fields or at brickmaking at Lake Jackson, the Patton place, and China Grove. In Fort Bend County, more than 100 men labored on three plantations, including Arcola, and in Matagorda County J. B. Hawkins and John Duncan employed another eighty men in agriculture. In the heat, humidity, and dangers of the sugar fields, suffering and death pursued the prisoners just as they had in slavery.[31]

Allegations of cruelty against the prisoners and profit losses soon overshadowed the Ward, Dewey & Company lease. The matter came to a head in March 1875 when a New Orleans newspaper published a story exposing the plight of sixty-seven military prisoners transferred from Kansas to Texas. Facing public outcry, Governor Richard Coke appointed a committee to investigate the conditions of the prisoners. The committee met at Huntsville on April 15, 1875, and spent four days interviewing everyone from the owners of the company to private citizens in Huntsville.[32]

The report of the committee revealed widespread abuse of the prisoners and signaled the beginning of the end of the Ward, Dewey & Company lease. In addition to complaints of abysmal food and scanty clothing, the committee also outlined torture imparted by the guards in the form of whipping and stocking the prisoners as punishment for infractions of the rules or attempts to escape. The guards often placed inmates in the stocks with their feet almost off the ground, causing their necks to bear the full weight of their bodies. In these conditions, stocking caused the death of at least four men, two of them at Lake Jackson. The whips used on the prisoners, as described in the report, consisted of a strip of leather an inch and a half thick with holes throughout designed to cause blisters. The committee reported finding a seventeen-year-old at the Patton place who had just endured 604 lashes on his bare back. The young man was unable to lay on his back for eight weeks and could not have experienced more pain "had hot coals been heaped upon his back." In another instance, the guards administered 500 lashes to the back of a prisoner named John Henry before they took him from the camp and shot him. A prisoner named Lewis, who attempted escape from Lake Jackson received a whipping so severe he died during his transfer to another prison.[33]

The guards also employed a torture device in the camps known as "the horse." The device consisted of "a vertical post with several holes bored into it" into which the guards inserted a peg ten inches long and two inches in diameter. The guards then forced the inmates to straddle the peg with their backs against the post, their feet chained to metal rings in the ground, causing excruciating pain to the genitals. More than one of the inmates suffered permanent physical and psychological damage from "the horse."[34]

In August 1876, after publication of the committee report, the legislature terminated the Ward, Dewey & Company lease. Although public outrage played into the decision, it appears that shoddy recordkeeping, the Republican leanings of the lessees, and the fact that the company owed the state of Texas over $70,000 for mismanagement of the prisoners and the prison itself were bigger factors in the termination of the contract. Over 1,700 prisoners passed through the hands of the company between 1871 and 1876. Of these, approximately 300 escaped, and the company could not account for the whereabouts of another 182. In addition, the known death toll amounted to 137, with the guards having murdered twenty-eight men, and with diseases, mostly malaria, having claimed the lives of another 109. This brought the total of escapes, disappearances, and deaths to 619, an astonishing 36 percent of all inmates.[35]

Following the dismal failure of the Ward, Dewey & Company lease, Governor Richard Hubbard and the legislature temporarily leased the penitentiary to the firm of Burnett and Kilpatrick while they went about arranging for another long-term lease in the fall of 1877. When the fact that Hubbard previously conducted business with Burnett and Kilpatrick led to questions about his ethics, the governor insisted that the new bidders for the long-term lease deliver their bids to the secretary of state in sealed envelopes. In December 1877, Hubbard opened the envelopes from nine bidders and awarded the contract to the business partners Edward H. Cunningham and Littleberry A. Ellis. The contract provided that Cunningham and Ellis take possession of the state penitentiary and all the convicts under the supervision of Thomas J. Goree whom Hubbard appointed as superintendent of the penitentiary in

1878. The contract commenced on January 1, 1878, and would run for a term of five years, with the lessees paying the state of Texas $3.01 per prisoner per month for the life of the lease. Furthermore, the business partners had to submit a bond in the amount of $100,000 as insurance.[36]

The Cunningham and Ellis lease eventually proved much more lucrative to the state of Texas and permanently located the center of convict leasing, and the Texas carceral complex after it, on the old sugar plantations of the lowcountry. Born in Mississippi in 1827, Litlleberry Ambrose Ellis moved to Bowie County, Texas, in 1859, where he enslaved eight people in 1860. In 1862, he enlisted in Captain W. L. Scott's company of Tennessee Artillery at Lewisville, Arkansas. His company disbanded in 1863, with Ellis promoted to the rank of sergeant major. At the close of the war, he moved to Jefferson, Texas, and opened a business as a wholesale grocer, before purchasing 2.000 acres of land in the Battle and Cartwright Leagues in Fort Bend County, which included parts of four antebellum plantations, one of which was Walnut Grove. Ellis opened his own sugar plantation there, which he named Sartartia in honor of his eldest daughter. In the following years, he also purchased 3,300 additional acres in the Battle and Hodge Leagues, expanding his sugar operation. Born in Arkansas in 1834, Edward H. Cunningham moved to Bexar County, Texas, in 1856, opening a small ranch on Martinas Creek. In 1861, he became captain of an infantry company known as the Mustang Greys, Company F, 4th Texas Infantry, which was part of Hood's Texas Brigade. Cunningham received a promotion to major of the 4th Texas in November 1862, and then to lieutenant colonel and assistant adjutant general under Hood, where he probably met Littleberry Ellis, who was serving in the Army of Tennessee. After the war, Cunningham returned to Bexar County, and in 1875 he formed a partnership with his fellow ex-Confederate for the purpose of acquiring the contract for the state penitentiary, using the convicts to work in the sugar fields.[37]

By 1880, Cunningham and Ellis managed 2,157 prisoners, 1,233, or 57 percent, of whom were African American men. According to the semiannual report filed with the governor, Cunningham and Ellis worked 84 percent of the convicts outside the prison, including 1,033 on plantations. By far the largest concentration of convicts included the 407 convicts on twelve different sugar plantations in the lowcountry. Littleberry Ellis himself worked ninety-eight men on the old Coffee place in Brazoria County and at Sartartia in Fort Bend County. The other plantations in Brazoria County utilizing convict labor included Ball, Hutchings & Company, which owned Retrieve; Dodd, Brown & Company, which owned China Grove; Epperson & Company at Darrington; John Wells, who owned Osceola; and twenty-six men at Lake Jackson. In Matagorda County, J. B. Hawkins worked twenty-six men on his place, and in Fort Bend County Thomas W. House employed forty-four men at Arcola. M. B. Dunleavy, David Terry, and the partnership of Quigg & Pendall rounded out the sublessees who worked convicts in sugar on their land in Fort Bend County. This brought the total number of convicts to 221 in Brazoria County, 159 in Fort Bend County, and 27 in Matagorda County. One observer in the 1880s described Oyster Creek in Fort Bend County as "a low mosquito-infested swamp and the sluggish bayous were habitats for alligators and noisome creepers. Convicts labored bare legged in wet sugar cane fields, dying like flies in the periodic epidemic of fevers. Civilian labor could not be kept on the place. In those days, a free man who stayed more than two weeks was suspected of hiding out from the sin of commission or omission."[38]

The conclusion of the Cunningham and Ellis lease in 1883 demonstrated the financial prosperity created for the state of Texas and the lessees. Cunningham and Ellis paid the state of Texas a total of $367,339 during their five years, or an average of $73,468 per year, an amount that represented almost 3 percent of the state's revenue. The lessees also cleared a total profit of more than $500,000. With the expiration of the Cunningham and Ellis lease, the legislature began moving to purchase old plantations for itself on which to work the convicts. In 1884, the state purchased the Wynne plantation in Walker County near Huntsville, and the next year it purchased Harlem for $25,000, which became Harlem State Prison Farm. At the same time, Cunningham and Ellis extended their partnership and constructed a 600-ton sugar mill on Oyster Creek that they named the "Imperial" mill. The next year the two men dissolved their partnership; Ellis retired, leaving his operation to his sons, and Cunningham expanded his landholdings in Fort Bend County to include more than 20,000 acres, including the Sugar Land plantation which he purchased from the Terry family. Cunningham also expanded his business operations by converting old plantation buildings at Sugar Land into barracks and other elements of a company town and the beginning of the Imperial Sugar Company. At the conclusion of the long Reconstruction, convicts still worked the sugar fields throughout the lowcountry, this time not only for lessees like Cunningham and Thomas W. House, but also for the state of Texas. For those African

Americans caught in the convict leasing system slavery never ended; it just evolved.[39]

The twelve years following the end of statewide Reconstruction in Texas saw the lowcountry economically transition into the "New" South, even while the last remnants of Reconstruction held firm with a biracial Republican coalition in control of county governments as African Americans acquired land and built their own communities and churches in the places in between. In a bitter irony, even as these signs of progress emerged, the state of Texas began a new system of racial control and laid the foundation of the Texas carceral complex in the region. As these changes developed, an increasingly angry white minority plotted a permanent end to Republican rule and the last remnants of Reconstruction.

Chapter 11

The Birth of Jim Crow

1885–1895

ON SUNDAY, September 25, 1887, trouble developed between two white men in Matagorda County and a group of African American county officials. John Nuckles and Dan Kennedy from the Sargent area refused to go to work on the county roads alongside a group of African American men. Justice of the Peace A. B. Brown ordered Constable Jerry Matthews to arrest Nuckles and bring him before the court. Matthews rode to the Nuckles residence where he encountered not the wanted man, but one of his employees named Stafford. The two men exchanged words, and Matthews rode off. Stafford pursued him on horseback, murdered him in cold blood, and dragged his body into the swamp. When Matthews did not return, a number of African American men led by Oliver Sheppard and Barton Hawkins armed themselves and marched to the Nuckles residence. Intimidated by the crowd, Nuckles, under guard of some of his friends, rode toward Rainy to obtain a summons for the arrest of the armed men. Word quickly spread of an "uprising" among the African Americans in Matagorda County, and the ensuing violence made headlines throughout the United States as the Vann Massacre, marking the violent clash that initiated the birth of Jim Crow in the Texas lowcountry.[1]

In the last two decades of the nineteenth century, the national Republican Party abandoned African American voters in Texas and the South, leading to the rise of Jim Crow. White Democrats in Texas took their cues from national developments and used the support of Democrats in Austin to drive African Americans from office, often with violence. When violence and intimidation did not completely succeed, they formed white man's union associations that effectively disenfranchised African American voters at local and state levels.

Limiting their membership to white men, these white man's unions served as a shadow arm of the Democratic Party, guaranteeing that only those who belonged to the unions could vote or win nomination for office in the spring primaries. African Americans could still vote in the fall elections, but they could no longer nominate candidates or run for office, thereby breaking up the Republican Party machines. The establishment of these white man's unions permanently ended Reconstruction as they chased the last elected African Americans from office or barred them from renomination and reelection.[2]

The fall elections of 1884 marked the beginning of the end of Reconstruction in the lowcountry. That November Grover Cleveland won the presidency, the first Democrat to do so since the Civil War, and although the counties of the lowcountry voted overwhelmingly for Republican James G. Blaine, violence broke out in the lower Brazos River Valley, giving one of the first hints of what the years ahead had in store for the region. In Washington County, where Republicans had controlled politics since 1869, masked white men entered a polling place in Chappell Hill while election officials counted the ballots and opened fire, killing three African Americans, including an election judge. The election in Washington County that year swept the Republicans out of office, showing the effectiveness of violence in suppressing the African American vote. Despite the debacle further north, a freedman named Benjamin Franklin Williams, a distinguished Methodist minister, politician, head of the Union League, and resident of Kendleton, won election to the Texas House of Representatives from the Fourteenth District, representing Fort Bend and Waller counties. Frustrated by Williams's election and taking their cue from the election of Cleveland and the violence in Washington County, in 1885 P. E. Pearson and other white Democrats of Fort Bend County organized the "Rosebud Club": the forerunner of the first white man's union in the region.[3]

The fall elections of 1886 brought more chaos, and more violence in Washington County, in a case that would trigger an investigation by the US Senate. In Chappell Hill, despite initial reports of a tranquil election, multiple ballot boxes disappeared, and in early December a mob lynched three African American men to stop them from raising the alarm about the fraudulent election. Looking for help from Washington, DC, three Washington County men petitioned the Republican-controlled US Senate to investigate the election, and in January 1887, to bolster the case for the proposed voting rights bill of Senator Henry Cabot Lodge, multiple senators agreed to launch an investigation.[4]

Following the fraud and lynchings farther north, a series of violent acts against African American communities in the lowcountry began with the Vann Massacre. On Sunday September 25, 1887, as word began to spread of a group of armed men at the Nuckles home, Sheriff Ned Wadsworth of Matagorda County called on Sheriff M. J. Hickey of Brazoria County for aid, and Hickey wired Texas Governor Lawrence S. Ross, informing the governor that "there are indications of a general uprising." Ross wired Captain Frank A. Reichardt, commander of the Houston Light Guard militia company, ordering him to take his company to Columbia. Wadsworth warned African Americans to stay away from the Sargent area, but not before a group of sixty white men from Brazoria County, and an unknown number of white men from Wharton County, started toward southeast Matagorda County. Although calm temporarily returned, the groups of men pressed on, intent on killing African Americans "and ending forever the supremacy of 'the blacks.'" On their way south, the Wharton County men found a random man named Munson hiding in a corn field along the way and shot him. At the same time, the Brazoria mob terrorized a group of African American wagon drivers they met along the road. On Monday, after assembling at the Nuckles home, the mob pursued Oliver Sheppard and Barton Hawkins to Sheppard's cabin at Vann. According to one account, the mob found Sheppard standing on the porch with a Winchester and opened fire on him as he retreated into the cabin. Sheppard returned fire while the white men laid siege to the cabin long into the night. During the fighting, the mob shot and killed Barton Hawkins. The next morning the white men returned to the cabin to find Sheppard and his family gone, having fled the county. The Vann Massacre ended with two dead, and the community traumatized. According to a local history, this incident convinced African Americans "to remain in the background and leave the government of the county to the whites." Although Matagorda County would not officially have a white man's union association for another seven years, the massacre effectively removed most Republicans from power.[5]

Six months after the Vann Massacre, violence broke out in Wharton County; at the same time, the US Senate began taking testimony about the elections in Washington County. Predictably, the violence in Wharton centered on Spanish Camp, which had become the center of political organizing for both Republicans and Democrats in the county. In the redistricting after the 1870 census, the Republican legislature created the Thirteenth House District out of Fort Bend, Austin, and Wharton counties; African American Republican candidates won this district in every election up to and including the election for delegates to the Constitutional Convention of 1875. At the convention, Lloyd H. McCabe represented the district, and after the convention Wharton County became part of the Thirty-Seventh House District, which also included Waller and Fort Bend counties. African Americans continued to win every election for the Thirty-Seventh District as the 1880 census approached. In 1880, Doc C. Lewis, a Republican farmer from Spanish Camp, won election to the Texas House. In the redistricting of 1881, the Democratic legislature put Wharton County in the Sixty-Sixth House District, with Brazoria, Matagorda, and Galveston counties. Galveston contained enough white Democrats to outvote African Americans in the other three counties, ending the Republican reign. After the end of Doc Lewis's term, white Democrats, all but one of whom had a Spanish Camp post office, represented the district for the rest of the decade.

As the home of the white Democratic state representative, the continuing presence of thriving African American landowners at Spanish Camps invited the ire of white residents, and a dispute over land finally brought the issue to a head. In late 1887, a group of white men ordered some African Americans off their own land, but they refused, resulting in a lawsuit in the district court. W. H. Burkhart, the Republican district judge, ruled in favor of the defendants in January 1888, and their attorney advised his clients to occupy their land and defend it with force. At two or three o'clock on the morning of Sunday, February 26, a "posse" of a dozen or more white men armed with Winchesters and shotguns approached the cabin near the James Wygall farm with eight African American men and boys inside. The mob doused the outside of the cabin with kerosene and set the building afire. As flames leaped up the side of the building, five of the startled occupants awoke and ran outside only to have the white men gun them down in their tracks while two small boys, paralyzed with fright, burned to death in the cabin. The mob wounded an eighth victim, but he survived, riding into Wharton to tell Sheriff Jones of the murders. That night the mob also lynched another African American victim. One reporter wrote: "nothing remains but the charred logs of the cabin and the bones of the two boys. The five slain men were buried by the sheriff's posse." The district judge and district attorney called on Governor Ross for help, and the governor dispatched half a dozen Texas Rangers to keep the peace and investigate the crime. On March 15, many of the prominent white residents of Wharton County penned a letter to Ross, objecting to placing the Rangers in Wharton as a result of a "feud between parties and their friends fighting for possession of a tract of land." Despite this protest, Ross refused to immediately recall the

Rangers. The officers eventually arrested four suspects, but the Spanish Camp Massacre convinced many African Americans to abandon Wharton County, and politics in general, effectively destroying the Republican county machine.[6]

In Fort Bend County, Republicans sensed that their dominance of county politics was in danger, and in 1887, they nominated a slate of white candidates who identified as Democrats in a fusion ticket and in an effort to mollify the militantly white supremacist regular Democrats, who derisively nicknamed the white Democrats with the backing of the African American vote "Woodpeckers." The biracial coalition carried the elections that year, but the regular Democrats insisted on nothing short of complete white supremacy by removing African American influence altogether. On July 2, 1888, regular Democrats gathered in Richmond to hold the first countywide Democratic meeting since before the Civil War. At the mass meeting, the members of the Rosebud Club reconstituted themselves as the Young Men's Democratic Club, vowing to take back control of county politics.[7]

Events in the summer of 1888 exacerbated the tensions in Fort Bend County. That summer, the regular Democrats began referring to themselves as Jaybirds, a reference to a bit of doggerel depicting the Jaybird as the enemy of the Woodpecker. On August 2, 1888, someone shot and killed J. M. Shamblin, owner of the old Walnut plantation and leader of the Young Men's Democratic Club. Then on September 3, a person or persons shot and wounded the new Jaybird leader, Henry Frost, as he walked home from the bar he owned. The Jaybirds blamed African Americans for both shootings. On September 4, a mass meeting was held in Richmond, and a resolution was passed in which the Republican leaders of Fort Bend County were held to be "morally responsible" for the assassination of Shamblin and the attempted assassination of Frost. Two days later several hundred Jaybirds assembled in the district courtroom and passed a resolution demanding that certain African American community leaders, including District Clerk Charles M. Ferguson, schoolteachers J. D. Davis and H. G. Lucas, restaurateur Peter Warren, barber Charles M. Williams, county commissioner Tom Taylor from Kendleton and his brother Jack, all leave the county within ten hours. After the meeting ended, the three hundred heavily armed white men rode double file to every African American residence in Richmond, stopping to read their proclamation at each door. All five targeted residents of Richmond left the county immediately, along with Sheriff Henry Ferguson, who departed with his brother Charles. Unwilling to ride to Kendleton themselves, the mob sent messengers to inform the Taylors of the proclamation, but the men responded defiantly. When the Jaybirds learned of the resistance, they called for volunteers, and hundreds of armed white men descended on Richmond on September 8, forming themselves into a "militia" under P. E. Pearson. The new county sheriff wired Governor Ross to send Texas Rangers, but on September 10 word arrived that the Taylors had changed their minds and had fled the county, defusing the mob.[8]

Following the expulsion of the African American leaders from the county, the Jaybirds went about planning for the fall elections, even as the Woodpeckers and Republicans struck back. On September 21, the Jaybirds gathered and nominated a slate of candidates for county office under the title of Regular Democrats. At the same time, the Woodpeckers gathered and nominated their own slate of candidates, calling themselves the Independent Democrats. In the last week of September a small caucus of African American Republicans gathered in Richmond in secret and decided to back the Woodpecker slate of candidates. In the election held on November 2, 1888, the Woodpeckers defeated the Jaybirds for every county office, ensuring that African Americans continued to have a strong voice in county politics, a situation that enraged the Jaybirds and their supporters.[9]

As events in Fort Bend County played out, at the national level the Republican Benjamin Harrison narrowly defeated Grover Cleveland for the presidency in November 1888, and Republicans won control of both the House and Senate. With the presidency and Congress now in Republican hands Henry Cabot Lodge began planning to push ahead with his voting rights bill in an effort to protect the franchise for African Americans in the South.

Fallout from the elections of 1888 continued to simmer in Fort Bend County and finally came to a head in the summer of 1889. One of the more heated feuds between Jaybird and Woodpecker leaders involved Ned and Volney Gibson of the Jaybird faction, and Kyle Terry, the Woodpecker County tax assessor. The feud came to a head on June 21, 1889, in Wharton when Ned Gibson appeared to testify in a criminal trial, and Kyle Terry ambushed him, emptying both barrels of a double-barreled shotgun into his chest. The murder of Ned Gibson lit the fuse for what would become known as the Battle of Richmond. In reality, it was less of a battle than an armed coup.[10]

On the evening of Friday August 16, 1889, the Jaybirds attacked the Woodpeckers in and around the Fort Bend County Courthouse. The gunfight that followed resulted in the death and wounding of a number of men from both sides, and after twenty minutes the Woodpeckers withdrew, leaving control of Richmond to the Jaybirds. Governor Ross sent in the Houston Light Guards to establish martial law on August 17, and the governor himself traveled to

Richmond to restore the peace and conduct negotiations, which resulted in the resignation or removal of every Woodpecker from office.[11]

The Jaybird–Woodpecker War gave birth to the first white man's union association in the Texas lowcountry. On October 3, 1889, a gathering at Richmond voted to form the Jaybird Democratic Association, which formally organized and adopted a constitution on October 22, 1889. The bylaws of the association stipulated that only whites could be members of the association and that no candidate could run for county office without the support of, and membership in, the association. African Americans could still vote in the fall elections, but for all practical intents and purposes, the Jaybird Association removed the franchise from African Americans, ending Reconstruction and giving birth to the era of Jim Crow in Fort Bend County.[12]

Watching the events in Fort Bend, the whites of Wharton County rushed to organize their own white man's union association. On Monday, November 25, 1889, a committee of organizers, led by Edwin Hawes, met at the Wharton County courthouse and voted to form an organization they named "The White Man's Union Association of Wharton County." In the aftermath of the violence at Spanish Camp, the Republicans of Wharton County offered little resistance, allowing the organizers at Wharton to adopt a constitution very similar to the Jaybird constitution and so removing the franchise from African Americans in Wharton County.[13]

As Jim Crow rapidly gained ascendance, Senator Henry Cabot Lodge (R-Mass.) presented his voting rights bill to the US House of Representatives on June 14, 1890. After a fierce debate in the House, the bill passed the Republican-controlled chamber on July 2, 1890, by just seven votes. In the Senate the bill foundered, filibustered by southern Democrats. Although Republicans possessed a majority in the Senate, the bill died in February 1891 after Silver Republicans traded away their support of the bill for support of the Sherman Silver Purchase Act, and northern Republicans traded their support for votes in favor of the McKinley Tariff. The death of the Lodge bill heralded the era of Jim Crow at the national level and guaranteed that the national Republican Party would not come to the rescue of African American suffrage in the South. The Republican Party had abandoned African American voters.

Although the prospects for African Americans appeared dim, the redistricting of Texas following the 1890 Census opened a new door of opportunity. In 1891, the legislature created the Fortieth House District out of Brazoria and Matagorda counties. This created an opportunity for African American voters in the region to have representation in the legislature for the first time since the death of Benjamin F. Williams in 1886. In response to this development, Nathan H. Haller, an African American resident of the district, decided to run for the new seat. Born into slavery in Charleston, South Carolina, on July 8, 1840, Haller's enslaver brought him to Walker County, Texas, before freedom arrived. After emancipation, Haller farmed in Walker County and served as a county commissioner there before moving south.[14]

Haller ran for the legislature without serious opposition in November 1892 and took his seat as one of only two African Americans in the Twenty-Third Texas Legislature when that body convened in the pink granite State Capitol building in Austin on January 10, 1893. Haller served on the Committees for Labor, Penitentiaries, and Roads, Bridges, and Ferries, and on February 8, 1893, he introduced House Bill 469 to establish a branch of the University of Texas (UT) for "the colored youths of Texas." Haller's bill proposed to establish a branch of UT in Austin and allocated $50,000 for the purchase of a site and $25,000 a year thereafter for maintenance and funding. The bill was referred to the Committee of Education, where it ultimately died on the calendar. Meanwhile, in Brazoria County, the city of Alvin incorporated in 1893, and the white citizens there began a movement to divide the county and dilute the African American vote. In the legislature on February 25, 1893, Haller presented a protest against a division of the county from the Brazoria County commissioners. Ultimately, the movement to divide the county failed, but a simmering battle over the location of the seat of government continued.[15]

In early 1894, Haller announced his intention to run for reelection, and the white people of Matagorda County decided that the time had arrived to form a white man's union association. They circulated a petition to create such an organization, and enough of the white men of the county signed on that the Matagorda County White Man's Union Association took effect in 1894, extending the full power of Jim Crow into the county. On September 18, 1894, in one of their first moves to consolidate power, the Matagorda County White Man's Union held a vote changing the county seat from Matagorda to the newly created Bay City, a predominantly white city in the middle of the county, west of the old plantation belt and the majority of the African American population.[16]

After Nathan Haller learned of the events in Matagorda County, he changed his official residence to Brazoria County in his run for reelection. This time the white Democrats put up more of a fight in the candidacy of Robert C. Duff of Brazoria. The election took place on November 6, 1894, and A. R. Masterson, the county judge for Brazoria County and the election judge for the Fortieth

District opened the ballots and canvassed them on Friday November 30, 1894. Masterson declared Duff the winner with 1,310 votes compared to 1,166 for Nathan Haller, and the judge issued Duff a certificate of election. Haller contested the results of the election, taking his case to the Texas House of Representatives in January 1895. An investigation revealed that Masterson had awarded Duff 1,112 votes from Brazoria County and 198 votes from Matagorda County, but that the judge awarded Haller no votes from Matagorda County. In fact, the investigation determined that Matagorda gave Haller 194 votes, which gave him a total of 1,360, a 50-vote majority. Even so, a majority report of the Committee on Elections and Privileges concluded that Duff won the election because Haller did not contest the case within the thirty days required by law, while a minority report from the same committee found that Haller *had* contested the election within the allotted thirty days. On February 13, 1895, the full House of Representatives voted to adopt the minority report by a vote of 76 to 40, and the next day Nathan Haller took his oath of office as Representative of the Fortieth District.[17]

The news of Haller's victory infuriated the whites of Brazoria County, who decided to take matters into their own hands. In 1894, in a bid to keep the county seat in Brazoria, the ruling Republican faction of the county constructed a large, Victorian-style courthouse, not far from the town lot owned by Nathan Haller. In the spring of 1895, the night before the canvassing of the election returns, a small group of white men gathered at the future site of the Angleton Grammar School and planned a coup to take control of the county government. Their deliberations that night resulted in the creation of what they called the Taxpayers' Union of Brazoria County: a white man's union association. The next day they began posting notices around Brazoria that they would not allow any African Americans elected to county office to assume their duties. They then surrounded the county courthouse and stationed more armed men in the upper stories of the buildings surrounding the courthouse to stop any resistance by force. The coup proved successful, and the establishment of the Taxpayers' Union of Brazoria County marked the triumph of white supremacy in the county. In 1896, in a bid to consolidate their power, the white voters of the county held a vote on moving the county seat from Brazoria to Angleton, east of the old plantation belt. The white residents of Alvin voted for Brazoria, in protest of not having their city on the ballot. Despite this dissension, Angleton beat out Brazoria by 290 votes, physically removing the seat of county government from most of the African American residents.[18]

As the events in Brazoria County played out, Nathan Haller continued to discharge his responsibilities in the House of Representatives. On April 30, 1895, the Twenty-Fourth Legislature adjourned, only to have Governor Charles Culberson call them back into special session on October 1, 1895. Six days later, the legislature finished its business, and Nathan Haller walked out of the House chamber and down the pink granite steps of the Capitol building, taking with him the close of Reconstruction in the Texas lowcountry.[19]

Conclusion

Ain't No More 'Cane on the Brazos

ON JANUARY 16, 1925, Texas Governor Pat Neff signed a pardon for a prisoner at the Harlem State Prison Farm named Walter Boyd after the man performed a variety of songs for the governor on a visit to the prison. The prisoner, whose given name was Huddie William Ledbetter, left "Sugarland," as prisoners often called it, and carried on with his life and musical career, having acquired the nickname "Lead Belly" while incarcerated. In 1933 when John and Alan Lomax first recorded Leadbelly, they discovered the fertile ground that prisons played in giving birth to the folk music of the American South. One such song they recorded revolved around sugar cultivation in the Brazos Valley:

> Ain't no more cane on the Brazos
> It's all been ground down to molasses
> You shoulda been on the river in 1910
> They were driving the women just like they drove the men.
> Go down Old Hannah, don'cha rise no more
> Don't you rise up til Judgement Day's for sure
> Ain't no more cane on the Brazos
> It's all been ground down to molasses
> Captain don't you do me like you done poor old Shine
> Well ya drove that bully til he went stone blind
> Wake up on a lifetime, hold up your own head
> Well you may get a pardon and then you might drop dead
> Ain't no more cane on the Brazos
> It's all been ground down to molasses.

The music of Leadbelly and others like him tapped into a twentieth-century description of much of what previously constituted the Texas lowcountry; now a land of urban sprawl, prisons, oil, and cattle.[1]

Of all the changes that have taken place in the region since 1895, perhaps the most striking one has involved its demographics. In 1900, 31,541 African Americans still called the region home, compared to 22,897 whites. By that date, the "other great migration" had already begun, with hundreds and then thousands of people from the region relocating to the Third and Fourth Wards of Houston, where they began to create the largest African American community in the South. In addition, a movement by white officials to attract European immigrants to offset the African American population also began, changing the composition of the population. The 1920 Census showed that African Americans constituted a minority in all four counties for the first time, with a total population of 28,428 compared to 55,509 whites. Only in Fort Bend County did the African American population even come close to matching the white population. World War II accelerated the exodus to Houston, so that by the 2020 Census African Americans made up just 18.9 percent of the population, led by Fort Bend County with 21.3 percent. In terms of urbanization, the lowcountry today consists of two urban and two rural counties. Both Fort Bend and Brazoria counties are considered urban today, a part of the Houston metropolitan area, while Wharton and Matagorda counties are rural, although they are part of the greater Houston area.[2]

The success of the white man's union associations in keeping African Americans from the polls, coupled with the Populist movement, encouraged the Texas Legislature to follow suit, resulting in the Terrell election laws of 1903 that allowed political parties to bar anyone they chose from voting in the primaries of that party. In 1923, the legislature passed a law explicitly banning African Americans from voting in the Democratic primary, and not until 1944 did the Supreme Court of the United States rule these laws unconstitutional in the case of *Smith v. Allwright*.[3]

Even with this decision, the white man's union associations persisted until Fort Bend County African Americans, including Willie Melton, Arizona Fleming, and John Terry, with the help of attorney William J. Durham and the National Association for the Advancement of Colored People, sued the Jaybird Association for the right to vote in the county Democratic primaries. Headed by A. J. Adams, the Jaybird Association responded to the charges, and on May 1, 1950, the US District Court for the Sothern District of Texas ruled against the Jaybirds. Fleming and others organized the African American vote, and 72 percent of eligible African Americans in the county voted in the Democratic primaries in the spring of 1951. The Jaybird Association appealed the decision and won their case in the Fifth Circuit on January 11, 1952. Fleming, Melton, Adams, and the NAACP then appealed to the United States Supreme Court, which struck down the Jaybird Association as unconstitutional, both as a violation of *Smith v. Allwright* and as a shadow arm of the Democratic Party, on May 4, 1953, in the case of *Terry v. Adams*. This decision brought an end to the white man's union associations in Texas.[4]

The economy has also undergone significant changes, although the four counties still contribute 5 percent of all the cotton produced in Texas annually. Oil also played a major part in the economy of the region with the opening of the first oil field at West Columbia in 1901, with subsequent oil strikes at Damon Mound, and then on the old Patton place in 1920. Since that time, oil, natural gas, and other mineral extraction have driven much of the economy of Brazoria County. The Dow Chemical Company moved its headquarters to Freeport in 1939, giving rise to the Freeport-Brazosport industrial complex. In 1942, Dow purchased the old Lake Jackson plantation and established the city of Lake Jackson as a company town. By 1910, landowners ground most of the sugar produced in the region down to molasses. After Texas gradually outlawed convict leasing between 1910 and 1912, the sugar industry experienced a corresponding decline. The Imperial Sugar Company remained, founded the city of Sugar Land as a company town, and continued to grow domestic sugar, but between foreign competition and a lack of cheap labor, the banks of the Brazos saw the last sugar cane in 1928. Outside of the urban areas of the lowcountry today, cattle often wander over old plantation ruins, next to new pump jacks, or old cotton fields, still producing the white, fluffy crop, albeit largely through mechanization. The starkest reminder of the region's troubled past lies with the twelve major prisons still in operation today in Brazoria and Fort Bend counties. These prisons are predominantly occupied by men of color, giving living evidence that the past is never really past. The Imperial Sugar Company also maintains its corporate headquarters in Sugar Land today, testimony to the profitability of slavery and convict leasing. Imperial Sugar is the oldest continuously operating business in Texas, a Fortune Five Hundred Company seemingly so unaware of their ties to slavery that the phrase "Since 1843" appears on the outer packaging of all Imperial Sugar products.[5]

Despite all these changes, the history remains, just under the surface. Through the efforts of preservationists, visitors can still see the old Patton place (now the Varner-Hogg Plantation), along with the house and outbuildings at Egypt, the Mirabeau Lamar home in Richmond, the Levi Jordan house near the San Bernard, and the Ammon Underwood house in East Columbia, but only two cabins occupied by the enslaved remain intact. Urbanization or neglect have erased or obscured most of the history of the enslaved people and of the convicts who built the region. Only when construction crews dig up the occasional skeleton, when a school district tries to place a building over an old cemetery, or when someone taking a tour of the Varner-Hogg asks an uncomfortable question does the brutal history of the region begin to resurface.

Most of Texas history still struggles to emerge from beneath the myths fastidiously created and actively cultivated by those who want to erase truths that to them *feel* inconvenient and threaten the power they hold as shapers of the historical narrative. Of the points at which silences enter into the historical narrative, the people of the Texas lowcountry have suffered most from the moments of fact retrieval in the making of narratives and from the moments of retrospective significance in the making of history. Michel-Rolph Trouillot might have been writing about the lowcountry when he said: "We are never so steeped in history as when we pretend not to be, but if we stop pretending, we may gain in understanding what we lose in false innocence."[6]

Notes

Introduction

1. John Bowie, "Early Life in the Southwest—the Bowies," *De Bow's Review of the Southern and Western States* (New Orleans, 1852), 378–382; J. Frank Dobie, "Jim Bowie: Big Dealer," *The Southwestern Historical Quarterly*, Vol. 60, No. 3 (January 1957), 337–357.

2. Paul D. Lack, "Slavery and Vigilantism in Austin Texas 1840–1860," *The Southwestern Historical Quarterly*, Vol. 85, No. 1 (July 1981), 1–20.

3. The 1860 United States Census for Texas. For an overview of German influence in Texas, see Terry G. Jordan, *German Seed in Texas Soil: Immigrant Farmers in Nineteenth-Century Texas* (Austin: University of Texas Press, 1966). For examples of how German immigrants complicated enslaving, see James C. Kearney, *Nassau Plantation: The Evolution of a Texas German Slave Plantation* (Denton: University of North Texas Press, 2010).

4. Much of the inspiration for the historiographical questions regarding regional identity that I attempt to answer in this work comes from Walter L. Buenger, "Making Sense of Texas and Its History," *The Southwestern Historical Quarterly*, Vol. 121, No. 1 (July 2017), 1–28. For perhaps the foremost book on framing Texas as a Southern state and slavery in Texas, see Randolph B. Campbell, *Empire for Slavery: The Peculiar Institution in Texas* (Baton Rouge: Louisiana State University Press, 1989). For the view that Texas constituted a borderland, see Sean M. Kelley. *Los Brazos de Dios: A Plantation Society in the Texas Borderlands 1821–1865* (Baton Rouge: Louisiana State University Press, 2010) and Andrew Torget, *Seeds of Empire: Cotton, Slavery, and the Transformation of the Texas Borderlands 1800–1850* (Chapel Hill: University of North Carolina Press, 2015).

5. The full historiography of the Texas revolution is lengthy, but a good summary of the most traditional interpretation comes from *A School History of Texas*: "If we stop for a moment now and look back over the troubles that have been described, we shall see that most of them grew out of the failure of the Mexicans and the colonists to understand each other, and this was chiefly due to the fact that they belonged to different races." The schoolbook went on to state that Texas "belonged" to Mexico but that "[n]either can we blame the Americans, for they come of a people who have never borne oppression with patience." Eugene C. Barker, Charles S. Potts, and Charles W. Ramsdell, *A School History of Texas* (Chicago: Row, Peterson & Co., 1913), 97. Not until Paul Lack's essay "Slavery in the Texas Revolution," did modern Texas historians begin to explore slavery as a cause of the revolution. Lack followed up this article with a monograph, *The Texas*

Revolutionary Experience: A Political and Social History 1835–1836, in which he devotes a chapter to slavery in the struggle. The best treatment of slavery in the Texas revolution is Andrew Torget's *Seeds of Empire: Cotton, Slavery, and the Transformation of the Texas Borderlands, 1800–1850*. Randolph B. Campbell, *Gone to Texas: A History of the Lone Star State*, Second Edition (Oxford: Oxford University Press, 2012), 131; Paul D. Lack "Slavery in the Texas Revolution," *The Southwestern Historical Quarterly*, Vol. 89, No. 2 (October 1985), 181–202; and Paul D. Lack, *The Texas Revolutionary Experience: A Political and Social History 1835–1836* (College Station: Texas A&M University Press, 1992). For an excellent example of the transformational impact of the profits from slavery, see Calvin Schermerhorn, "Commodity Chains and Chained Commodities: The U.S. Coastwise Slave Trade and an Atlantic Business Network," in Jeff Forret and Christine E. Sears, *New Directions in Slavery Studies: Commodification, Community, and Comparison* (Baton Rouge: Louisiana State University Press, 2015), 11–29.

6. The study of capitalism and slavery has received renewed interest from historians in the last decade and is a vibrant and growing field of scholarship. The classic study is Eric Williams, *Capitalism and Slavery* (Chapel Hill: University of North Carolina Press, 1944). More recently, Edward E. Baptist in *The Half Has Never Been Told: Slavery and the Making of American Capitalism* (New York: Basic Books, 2014) makes a compelling case for slavery as the foundation of American capitalism. Joining Baptist is Calvin Schermerhorn's *The Business of Slavery and the Rise of American Capitalism, 1815–1850* (New Haven, CT: Yale University Press, 2015). Other notable contributions to this field include Sven Beckert and Seth Rockman (eds.), *Slavery's Capitalism: A New History of American Economic Development* (Philadelphia: University of Pennsylvania Press, 2016); Gavin Wright, *Slavery and American Economic Development* (Baton Rouge: Louisiana State University Press, 2006); Kathleen M. Hilliard *Masters, Slaves, and Exchange: Power's Purchase in the Old South* (New York: Cambridge University Press, 2014); Caitlin Rosenthall, *Accounting for Slavery: Masters and Management* (Cambridge, MA: Harvard University Press, 2018); Daina Ramey Berry, *The Price for Their Pound of Flesh: The Value of the Enslaved, from Womb to Grave, in the Building of a Nation* (Boston: Beacon Press, 2017), and Jeff Forret and Christine E. Sears (eds.), *New Directions in Slavery Studies: Commodification, Community, and Comparison* (Baton Rouge: Louisiana State University Press, 2015). Antebellum Texas has received little scholarly coverage in the context of this growing literature on capitalism and slavery.

7. The historiography of Reconstruction is extensive, but the first, and in some ways still the most comprehensive, treatment of this pivotal period is *Black Reconstruction in America 1860–1880* by W. E. B. Du Bois (New York: Horace, Harcourt and Brace, 1935.) The best modern synthesis of the topic remains Eric Foner's *Reconstruction: America's Unfinished Revolution, 1863–1877* (New York: Harper Collins, 1988.) The first history of Reconstruction in Texas was written by a young University of Texas (UT) professor, Charles W. Ramsdell, in 1910. Already teaching at UT, Ramsdell completed his PhD in 1910 at Columbia University under William Dunning. Ramsdell, echoing the attitudes of his mentor, published his treatise *Reconstruction in Texas* that same year. In this work, he portrayed African American voters and white Radical Republicans in Texas as "the rule of a minority, the most ignorant and incapable of her population under the domination of reckless leaders." Not until the 1960s would white scholars begin to

challenge Ramsdell and Dunning's assessment. Reconstruction in Texas has received a great deal of attention in the last six decades, with the most notable works including Alwyn Barr, *Reconstruction to Reform: Texas Politics, 1876–1906* (Dallas TX: Southern Methodist University Press, 1971); Carl Moneyhon, *Republicanism in Reconstruction Texas* (College Station: Texas A&M University Press, 1980); Randolph Campbell, *Grass-Roots Reconstruction in Texas 1865–1880* (Baton Rouge: Louisiana State University Press, 1997); Dale Baum, *The Shattering of Texas Unionism: Politics in the Lone Star State during the Reconstruction Era* (Baton Rouge: Louisiana State University Press, 1998), James M. Smallwood, *Time of Hope, Time of Despair: Black Texans during Reconstruction* (Port Washington, NY: Kennikat Press, 1981); James M. Smallwood, Barry A. Crouch, and Larry Peacock, *Murder and Mayhem: The War of Reconstruction in Texas* (College Station: Texas A&M University Press, 2003); Barry A. Crouch, *The Dance of Freedom: Texas and African Americans during Reconstruction* (Austin: University of Texas Press, 2007); and Kenneth W. Howell (ed.), *Still in the Arena of the Civil War: Violence and Turmoil in Reconstruction Texas 1865–1874* (Denton: University of North Texas Press, 2012).

8. Convict leasing in Texas has received increased scholarly interest in the recent past. The first full work to consider the topic was Donald R. Walker, *Penology for Profit: A History of the Texas Prison System 1867–1912* (College Station: Texas A&M Press, 1988). Other notable works include Robert Perkinson, *Texas Tough: The Rise of America's Prison Empire* (New York: Picador Press, 2010) and Theresa R. Jach, "'It's Hell in a Texas Pen': Life and Labor in the Texas Prison System 1840–1929" (PhD dissertation, University of Houston, 2009); Thomas Michael Parrish, "'This Species of Slave Labor': The Convict Lease System in Texas 1871–1914" (MA Thesis, Baylor University, 1976), and Theresa R. Jach, "Reform versus Reality in the Progressive Era Texas Prison," *Journal of the Gilded Age and Progressive Era* (Vol. 4, No. 1, January 2005), pp. 53–67. See also Reign Clark, Catrina Banks Whitley, Ron Ralph, Helen Graham, Theresa Jach, Abigail Eve Fisher, Valerie Tompkins, Emily van Zanten, and Karissa Basse, "Back to Bondage: Forced Labor in Post Reconstruction Era Texas. The Discovery, Exhumation, and Bio-archeological Analysis of Bullhead Convict Labor Camp Cemetery (41FB355)," James Reese Career and Technical Center Campus, 12300 University Boulevard, Sugar Land, Texas (August 2020). https://www.fortbendisd.com/Page/131568 (accessed January 24, 2021). Convict leasing, of course, was not unique to Texas. For a more national treatment, see Douglas A. Blackmon, *Slavery by Another Name: The Re-Enslavement of Black Americans from the Civil War to World War II* (New York: Doubleday Press, 2009), and Michelle Alexander, *The New Jim Crow: Mass Incarceration in the Age of Colorblindness* (New York: The New Press, 2010).

9. The language historians use to describe the subjects of their study is of paramount importance in shaping any historical narrative. The linguistic choices in this narrative reflect the historiography of slavery and gender, with the notable exception of the term *plantation*. The reader should not infer anything romantic or nostalgic from this word. Plantations were slave labor camps, replete with all the horror and degradation that phrase implies. However, despite the facts of slavery, enslaved people created distinct communities within their own quarters that elevated at least parts of these camps above the traditional connotations of that phrase. Because of the problematic history of the

term, plantation certainly is not the best word for these labor camps, but in the absence of a linguistic middle ground between slave labor camp and plantation, the latter is probably the most efficacious term.

Chapter 1

1. James V. Woodrick, *Bernardo: Crossroads, Social Center and Agricultural Showcase of Early Texas* (Austin, TX: James V. Woodrick, 2016), 24–25. For the material relating to Groce's illegal dealing in smuggled enslaved people, see *Letter from the Secretary of the Treasury, Transmitting in Obedience to a Resolution of the House of Representatives, of the 31st Ultimo. Information in Relation to the Illicit Introduction of Slaves into the United States: With a Statement of the Measures Which Have Been Taken to Prevent the Same, January 13, 1820* (Washington, DC. Gales and Seaton, 1820); Stephen F. Austin's Census of his colony, Archives of the Texas General Land Office, Austin Texas ~U+http://www.glo.texas.gov/ncu/SCANDOCS/archives_webfiles/arcmaps/webfiles/landgrants/PDFs/1/0/3/4/1034583.pdf +U~(accessed March 4, 2018).

2. Lester Bugbee, "Slavery in Early Texas I," *The Political Science Quarterly*, Vol. 13, No. 3 (September 1898), 391.

3. Ibid., 392–393.

4. Ibid., 394–395.

5. Stephen F. Austin to Josiah Bell, November 22, 1822, and Austin to Trespelacios, January 4, 1823, as quoted in Bugbee, "Slavery in Early Texas," 395.

6. Stephen F. Austin to Jared Groce, October 19, 1823, in Eugene C. Barker (ed.), *Annual Report of the American Historical Association for the Year 1919: The Austin Papers, Vol. II, pt. 1* (Washington, DC: Government Printing Office, 1924), 701; Randolph B. Campbell (ed.) and William Pugsley and Marilyn S. Duncan (comp.), *The Laws of Slavery in Texas* (Austin: University of Texas Press, 2010), 10.

7. Greg Cantrell, *Stephen F. Austin: Empresario of Texas* (New Haven, CT: Yale University Press, 1999), 136–139.

8. Barker (ed.), *The Austin Papers*, Vol. II, pt. 1, 810–811.

9. Bugbee, "Slavery in Early Texas," I, 397–399.

10. Stephen F. Austin to James A. E. Phelps, June 16, 1825, as quoted in Bugbee, "Slavery in Early Texas," 401.

11. Guy Bryan to Mrs. Emily Austin Bryan, New Haven, Connecticut, April 25, 1851, in the James Perry Papers, Dolph Briscoe Center for American History, The University of Texas at Austin; Botts to Austin, Alexandria Louisiana, September 14, 1824, in Barker (ed.), *The Austin Papers*, Vol. 1, 895.

12. Article 46 of the Constitution as quoted in Bugbee, "Slavery in Early Texas," 402.

13. Stephen F. Austin, 1825 Census, Archives of the Texas General Land Office; James A. Creighton, *A Narrative History of Brazoria County* (Waco: Texian Press, 1975), 28–29.

14. Bugbee, "Slavery in Early Texas," 403–404; "Jesse Thompson and J. C. Payton to Sprowl," August 11, 1826. Barker (ed.), *The Austin Papers*, Vol. II, pt. 1, 1405–1406.

15. Bugbee. "Slavery in Early Texas," 404–409.

16. Ibid., 409–412.

17. Clarence R. Wharton, *History of Fort Bend County* (San Antonio, TX: The Naylor Co., 1939), 6; James A. Creighton, *A Narrative History of Brazoria County* (Angleton, TX: Brazoria County Historical Commission, 1975), 27–29. Bell called "Bell's Landing" Marion, but the other settlers continued to refer to it by the former name. It is now the town of East Columbia. The town of Columbia that Bell laid out is now the city of West Columbia.

18. Merle Weir, "Wharton, William Harris," accessed February 11, 2018, http://www .tshaonline.org/handbook/online/articles/fwh08. Eagle Island Plantation is now in the city of Clute, Texas.

19. Creighton, *A Narrative History of Brazoria County*, 29. The Varner plantation was located just north of Columbia (now West Columbia), and today it is preserved as the Varner-Hogg Plantation State Historic Site. See Stephen F. Austin to Israel Waters, July 30, 1829, in Barker (ed.), *The Austin Papers*, Vol. 3, 243. Waters partnered with Varner in building a distillery on Varner's plantation, and they sent the first bottle of rum to Austin.

20. Barker (ed.), *The Austin Papers*, pt. 3, 1395–1997; *Handbook of Texas Online*, Diana J. Kleiner, "Matagorda, TX," accessed March 24, 2018, http://www.tshaonline .org/handbook/online/articles/hlm35.

21. Alleine Howern, "Causes and Origin of the Decree of April 6, 1830," *The Southwestern Historical Quarterly*, Vol. 16, No. 4 (1913), 394–398.

22. Lester Bugbee, "Slavery in Early Texas II," *Political Science Quarterly*, Vol. 13 (1898), as reprinted in Campbell (ed.), *The Laws of Slavery in Texas*, 37.

23. For the story of John, Robert, and their female companion, see Luis Lombrano to the Governor of Coahuila and Texas, December 29, 1830, *Fondo Siglo XIX, caja 12, fondo 8, expediente 11, Archivo General del Estado de Coahuila*, Ramos Arzipe, Mexico, as quoted in Torget, *Seeds of Empire*. The runaway slave ad for Will and Adam was placed in the *Texas Gazette*, San Felipe, February 5, 1830. Randon's plantation was located where the Riverwood Forest at Weston Lakes neighborhood now stands near Fulshear, Texas.

24. Cantrell, *Stephen F. Austin*, 240; Stephen F. Austin to James Perry, December 31, 1829, in Barker (ed.), *The Austin Papers, Vol. II*, 307–308.

25. Howern, "Causes and Origin of the Decree of April 6, 1830," 415–416.

26. M. Fiske, *A Visit to Texas: Being the Journal of a Traveler Through Those Parts Most Interesting to American Settlers with Descriptions of Scenery, Habits, &c &c* (New York: Goodrich & Wiley, 1834), 10–11.

27. Margaret Swett Henson, *Juan Davis Bradburn: A Reappraisal of the Mexican Commander of Anahuac* (College Station: Texas A&M Press 1982), 53–54. Mary Delanie Boddie, *Thunder on the Brazos: The Outbreak of the Texas Revolution at Fort Velasco, June 26, 1832* (Angleton, TX: Brazoria County Museum 1978), 8. The City of Surfside Beach, Texas, now stands at the location of Fort Velasco.

28. The 1826 Census of Austin's Colony; John McNeel to Stephen F. Austin, October 9, 1826, in Eugene C. Barker (ed.), *The Austin Papers*, Vol. II (Washington, DC: Government Printing Office, 1928), 1473; Noah Smithwick, *The Evolution of a State* (Austin TX: Steck-Vaugn Co., 1968), 28–29; M. Fiske, *A Visit to Texas: Being the Journal of a*

Traveler Through Those Parts Most Interesting to American Settlers with Descriptions of Scenery, Habits, &c &c (New York: Goodrich & Wiley, 1834), 38–40.

29. Light Townsend Cummins, *Emily Austin of Texas 1795–1851* (Fort Worth: Texas Christian University Press, 2009), 98–99. For the house plans, see Stephen F. Austin to Emily Perry November 30, 1831, in Barker (ed.), *The Austin Papers*, Vol. II, 719.

30. Lester Bugbee maintained that Stephen Austin "was not an advocate of slavery. . . . he fully understood that his colonists must come from the slaveholding portions of the United States." Gregg Cantrell wrote that "he [Austin] carried with him into adulthood conflicting attitudes toward slavery. . . . Thus we find a man who in his racial views was neither typically southern nor northern, neither liberal nor reactionary." Both of these analyses are correct in that Austin personally held conflicting views on slavery, but all of his actions went toward legalizing slavery and keeping it legalized in Texas, thus creating the foundation for the lowcountry plantation society. Bugbee, "Slavery in Early Texas II," 47–48; Cantrell, *Stephen F. Austin*, 9–10. Andrew Torget perhaps put it best when he wrote: "For Austin the question of slavery had always been secondary to his larger vison for the development of Texas into a thriving extension of the American cotton frontier. Yet precisely because cotton served as the foundation of that vision, slavery became the primary means for accomplishing what Austin hoped to build in his settlement. Whatever his personal convictions about enslavement, Austin recognized that white Americans hoping to make their fortune in cotton along the Mexican borderlands considered slavery to be the indispensable institution. And so he committed himself to creating a slave country in Texas." Andrew Torget, "Stephen F. Austin's Views on Slavery in Early Texas," in Richard McCaslin, Donald E. Chipman, Andrew Torget (eds.), *This Corner of Canaan: Essays on Texas in Honor of Randolph B. Campbell* (Denton: University of North Texas Press, 2013), 123.

Chapter 2

1. John G. McNeel Jr., "Early Settlement in Brazoria," n.d., John Salmon "Rip" Ford Memoirs, pp. 179–181, Box 2Q510, Dolph Briscoe Center for American History, The University of Texas at Austin. John McNeel was absent that morning, with the Anglo contingent preparing to attack the Mexican soldiers at Velasco.

2. Noah Smithwick *The Evolution of a State: Or Recollections of Old Texas Days* (Austin, TX: P. N. Gammel, 1900. Austin: University of Texas Press reprint, 1983), 24.

3. The full historiography of the Texas revolution is lengthy, but a good summary of the most traditional interpretation comes from *A School History of Texas*: "If we stop for a moment now and look back over the troubles that have been described, we shall see that most of them grew out of the failure of the Mexicans and the colonists to understand each other, and this was chiefly due to the fact that they belonged to different races." The schoolbook went on to state that Texas "belonged" to Mexico, but that "Neither can we blame the Americans, for they come of a people who have never borne oppression with patience." Eugene C. Barker, Charles S. Potts, and Charles W. Ramsdell *A School History of Texas* (Chicago: Row, Peterson & Co., 1913), 97. Not until Paul Lack's essay, "Slavery in the Texas Revolution," did modern Texas historians begin to explore slav-

ery as a cause of the revolution. Lack followed up this article with a monograph, *The Texas Revolutionary Experience: A Political and Social History 1835–1836*, in which he devotes a chapter to slavery in the struggle. The best treatment of slavery in the Texas revolution is Andrew Torget's *Seeds of Empire: Cotton, Slavery, and the Transformation of the Texas Borderlands, 1800–1850*. Even with this new focus on slavery, perhaps the leading current single volume on Texas history dismisses the argument for the centrality of slavery in the conflict with the statement that the argument is undermined "by the fact that slavery was not a major issue in any of the developments from 1830 to 1835. It played no important part in the disturbances of 1832." See Randolph B. Campbell *Gone to Texas: A History of the Lone Star State*, Second Edition (Oxford: Oxford University Press, 2012), 131; Paul D. Lack, "Slavery in the Texas Revolution," *The Southwestern Historical Quarterly*, Vol. 89, No. 2 (October 1985), 181–202; Paul D. Lack. *The Texas Revolutionary Experience: A Political and Social History 1835–1836* (College Station: Texas A&M University Press, 1992); and Andrew J. Torget. *Seeds of Empire: Cotton, Slavery, and the Transformation of the Texas Borderlands, 1800–1850* (Chapel Hill: University of North Carolina Press, 2015).

4. Henson, *Juan Davis Bradburn*, 94–98. In her biography of Bradburn, Henson acknowledged that "[m]uch of the antipathy toward Bradburn rested on his enforcement of the national law against slavery." The arrival of Travis and Jack in the spring of 1831 made them undocumented immigrants practicing law without a license. Monroe Edwards was the nephew of Haden Edwards. James Morgan initially leased some of the people he enslaved to work on the fortifications at Anahuac but recalled them when he became afraid that they would learn of Mexican law and assert their freedom.

5. The ranks of the Anglos who attacked Velasco in 1832 consisted almost entirely of enslavers from the lowcountry; they included William Wharton, John Austin, Abner Kuykendall, Edwin Waller, John G. McNeel, Pinckney McNeel, Sterling McNeel, Andrew Mills, Robert Mills, Thomas W. Moore, Martin Varner, James "Brit" Bailey, Asa Mitchell, Henry Smith, Henry Munson, Robert H. Williams, Andrew Westall, Thomas Westall, James Westall, and many others. The Texas Genealogical Society, *Stirpes*, Vol. 21, No. 3 (September 1981), 179–180.

6. Mary Delaney Boddie. *Thunder on the Brazos: The Outbreak of the Texas Revolution at Fort Velasco June 26, 1832* (Lake Jackson, TX: Brazoria Historical Museum 1977), 20–23.

7. Boddie, *Thunder on the Brazos*, 22–29.

8. For the formation of the War and Peace Parties, see Jodella Kite, "The War and Peace Parties of Pre-Revolutionary Texas," *East Texas Historical Journal*, Vol. 29, No. 1 (1991) and Jodella Kite "The War and Peace Parties of Pre-Revolutionary Texas 1832–1835," MA Thesis, Texas Tech University, 1986.

9. *Handbook of Texas Online*, Ralph W. Steen, "Convention of 1832," accessed April 8, 2018, http://www.tshaonline.org/handbook/online/articles/mjc09.

10. For the membership of the 1833 convention, see E. W. Winkler, "Membership of the 1833 Convention of Texas," *The Southwestern Historical Quarterly*, Vol. 45, No. 3 (January 1942), 255–257. For the resolution on the African slave trade, see Eugene C. Barker, "The African Slave Trade in Texas," *The Quarterly of the Texas State Historical Association*, Vol. 6

No. 2 (October 1902), 151. On May 31, 1833, Stephen F. Austin wrote to Samuel May Williams: "B. F. Smith's cursed foolish trip has done great harm and I am sorry he ever came to Texas—." See Barker (ed.), *The Austin Papers*, Vol. 3, 984. Benjamin Fort Smith came to Texas from Alabama in 1832 and purchased land that was originally granted to Jared Groce in Brazoria County. He named his plantation Point Pleasant. See Brazoria County Deed Records Volume C, pp. 207–208. Monroe Edwards would purchase the plantation from Smith in 1836 and rename it "Chenango." Edwards and Smith landed the ninety-six Africans at "Edwards Point" (now "Eagle's Point") in the city of San Leon, Texas. Chenango was located on the east bank of the Brazos River, 9 miles north of Bell's Landing (now East Columbia.) It is forty-two miles from Edward's Point to Chenango. For more on the African slave trade in the lowcountry, see chapter 4.

11. Stephen F. Austin to Wiley Martin from "Matamoros," May 30, 1833, in Barker (ed.), *The Austin Papers*, Vol. 3, 981.

12. Jack Jackson (ed.) and John Wheat (trans.), *Almonte's Texas: Juan N. Almonte's 1834 Inspection, Secret Report & Role in the 1836 Campaign* (Austin: Texas State Historical Association, 2003), 40. In addition, by 1833 Mexico stopped extraditing those who had escaped to the United States. Sarah E. Cornell, "Citizens of Nowhere: Fugitive Slaves and Free African Americans in Mexico, 1833–1857," *Journal of American History*, Vol. 100, Issue 2 (September 2013), 356.

13. Jackson and Wheat (eds.), *Almonte's Texas*, 134.

14. Ibid., 250–251.

15. Ibid., 138–139. For more on this voyage, see chapter 4. Also see "The Reminiscences of Mrs. Dilue Harris," *Quarterly of the Texas State Historical Association*, Vol. 4 (October 1900), 97–99. It is unclear if Monroe Edwards was also involved in this second voyage, although it seems likely. The other smuggling operations Almonte references are those of James W. Fannin. See chapter 4.

16. Fisher to Smith, March 2, 1836, in John H. Jenkins (ed.), *The Papers of the Texas Revolution 1835–1836*, Vol. 4, 290 (Austin: Presidial Press, 1973). Hereafter referred to as *PTR*. For more on African slave smuggling, see chapter 4.

17. *The Telegraph and Texas Register*, March 5, 1836, and James Fannin to James Robinson, February 7, 1836, in *PTR*. Vol. 4, 280.

18. William Wharton, *Texas: A Brief Account of the Origin, Progress, and Present State of the Colonial Settlements of Texas*, in Jenkins (ed.), *PTR*, Vol. 9, 240; Benjamin R. Milam to Francis Johnson, July 5, 1835, in Barker (ed.), *The Austin Papers*, Vol. 4, 82–83.

19. Santa Anna to Ministry of War and Marine Army of Operations, February 16, 1836, in Carlos E. Casteneda (ed.), *The Mexican Side of the Texas Revolution* (New York: Graphic Ideas, Inc., 1970), 65.

20. The Brazoria *Texas Republican*, September 26, 1835; Thomas Pilgrim to Stephen F. Austin, October 6, 1835, in Barker (ed.), *The Austin Papers*, Vol. 4, 162; R. R. Royall to Stephen F. Austin, September 30, 1835, in Barker (ed.), *The Austin Papers*, Vol. 4, 144; The San Felipe *Telegraph and Texas Register*, October 10, 1835.

21. B. J. White to Stephen F. Austin, October 17, 1835, in Barker (ed.), *Austin Papers*, Vol. 4, 190. R. H. Williams appears to refer to Robert H. Williams, one of Austin's Old 300, who owned a plantation, Rotherwood, on lower Caney Creek in what is now

Matagorda County. The enslaved African Americans on Rotherwood raised the first cotton on Caney Creek and built the third cotton gin in the colony in 1827. On early maps, Rotherwood was the site of an important crossing of Caney Creek, "Caney Crossing," along the road that connected Brazoria and Matagorda. Today, the site of the plantation is less than two miles north of Cedar Lane, Texas. Mary McAlister Ingram, *Canebrake Settlements: Colonists, Plantations, Churches, 1822–1870* (Bay City, TX: Mary McAlister Ingram, 2006), 40. An example of these runaways is Sterling, Joe, and Richard, who ran away from the home of William Hunter at the Fort Settlement (now Richmond). See the Brazoria *Texas Republican*, July 4, 1835.

22. Henry Austin to James Perry, March 5, 1836, in Barker (ed.), *The Austin Papers*, Vol. 4, 318; Resolutions of the meeting of the Citizens of Brazoria, March 17, 1836, in *PTR*, Vol. 5, 98–99; James Morgan letter of March 24, 1836, in *PTR*, Vol. 5, 181–182.

23. Casteneda (ed.), *The Mexican Side of the Texas Revolution*, 246; Sam Houston to S. P. Carson in *PTR*, Vol. 5, 309–310; R. R. Royall to T. J. Rusk, May 14, 1836, and Vicinte Filisola to Comandante de las fuersas de Texas, May 22, 1836, in Thomas J. Rusk Papers, Box 2G32, Dolph Briscoe Center for American History, The University of Texas at Austin.

24. For the convention's condemnation of the African slave trade, see *PTR*, Vol. 9, 340; For the section of the Constitution dealing with enslaved persons, see *PTR*, Vol. 9, 338.

25. The (Public) Treaty of Velasco at https://www.tsl.texas.gov/treasures/republic/velasco-public-2.html (accessed June 3, 2018); Diary of Jose Urrea in Castaneda (ed.), *The Mexican Side of the Texas Revolution*, 277–278. De la Pena wrote that when he was left alone with the enslaved man in question, "this poor wretch explained to me his anguished situation and the cruel tortures that awaited him. I would have committed a crime against humanity, as General Filisola did, had I not protected his freedom. . . . Other unfortunates were liberated in the same way by other army officers." Jose Enrique de la Pena, *With Santa Anna in Texas: A Personal Narrative of the Texas Revolution*, Carmen Perry (trans. and ed.) (College Station: Texas A&M University Press, 1975), 179.

26. Cantrell, *Stephen F. Austin*, 348–349. After signing the Treaties of Velasco on May 14, President David G. Burnet entrusted the safety of Santa Anna to Captain William H. Patton, whose family owned the old Varner plantation near Columbia. On June 4, Patton transferred Santa Anna to Columbia for his own safety, after several attempts on his life by angry Texans. The general stayed at the cabin of William Jack for a month and a half. Finally, after more attempts were made on his life, in mid-August Patton moved the general to the plantation of James A. E. Phelps, Orozimbo, on the west bank of the Brazos, 8 miles north of Columbia. Finally, in October 1836, newly elected president Sam Houston dispatched Santa Anna to Washington and then to Mexico aboard a US ship. See Castaneda (ed.), *The Mexican Side of the Texas Revolution*, 88–91.

27. Cantrell, *Stephen F. Austin*, 360–364; Campbell, *Gone to Texas*, 160.

28. Austin to Wharton, November 18, 1836, in George P. Garrison (ed.), *The Diplomatic Correspondence of the Republic of Texas*, Vol. 1 (Washington, DC: Government Printing Office, 1908), 135–140.

29. Cantrell, *Stephen F. Austin*, 365–368.

Chapter 3

1. *The Telegraph and Texas Register*, February 27, 1839; Torget *Seeds of Empire*, 203.

2. *The Telegraph and Texas Register*, October 18, 1836; Andrew W. Hall, *The Galveston-Houston Packet: Steamboats on Buffalo Bayou* (Charleston, SC: The History Press, 2012), 30–31.

3. Francis R. Lubbock, *Six Decades in Texas; or Memoirs of Francis Richard Lubbock, Governor of Texas in War Time, 1861–1863. A Personal Experience in Business, War and Politics* (Austin, TX: B. C. Jones & Co., 1900), 41–47; Smith sold Monroe Edwards 1,300 acres, seventeen enslaved Africans, and his cotton and corn crop on September 10, 1836, for $35,000. The Africans had names like Ado, Cuggo, Bancola, Caro, Itassi, and Juacco. See the Brazoria County Deed Records Book A, pp. 23–24; *The Telegraph and Texas Register*, May 2, 1837. The editor of the paper was the same Gail Borden who invented condensed milk. See Joe B. Frantz, *Gail Borden: Dairyman to a Nation* (Norman: Oklahoma University Press, 1951). Francis Lubbock also related an incident that happened to him in December 1836: "coming from Quintana to Brazoria on horseback, I was belated, got lost, and had to spend the night in the Brazos bottom. The darkness was made hideous by the yelping of wolves, the cries of the Mexican panther, and the never ending hum of mosquitos. Being green from the States, I almost despaired of life, while anxiously waiting the issue. The welcome morning brought me deliverance, but on my arrival at the boarding house my face appeared so disfigured by mosquito bites that my wife scarcely recognized me. This horrible night's experience in the Brazos bottom six decades ago is still distinct in my memory." Of all the changes that have occurred in the Texas lowcountry between 1836 and the present, the author can attest from personal experience that the one constant is the mosquitoes. Lubbock, *Six Decades in Texas*, 44.

4. Margaret Swett Henson, *Samuel May Williams: Early Texas Entrepreneur* (College Station: Texas A&M University Press, 1976), 50, 95–96; *Handbook of Texas Online*, Curtis Bishop, "MCKINNEY, WILLIAMS AND COMPANY," accessed July 22, 2018, http://www.tshaonline.org/handbook/online/articles/dfm01.

5. *Handbook of Texas Online*, Marie Beth Jones, "MILLS, ROBERT," accessed July 22, 2018, http://www.tshaonline.org/handbook/online/articles/fmi39; *The Texas Republican*, July 25, 1835, November 14, 1835.

6. Brazoria County Deed Records Book A, pp. 153–154; *Handbook of Texas Online*, René Harris, "MILLS, DAVID GRAHAM," accessed July 22, 2018, http://www.tshaonline.org/handbook/online/articles/fmi64.

7. *Telegraph and Texas Register*, February 24, 1838.

8. *Telegraph and Texas Register*, May 21, 1837; Ron J. Jackson Jr. and Lee Spencer White, *Joe: The Slave Who Became an Alamo Legend* (Norman: Oklahoma University Press, 2015).

9. *Telegraph and Texas Register*, August 5, 1837; September 4, 1839; Edwin Waller placed a runaway ad for two African men named Gumby and Zow. (See *The Telegraph and Texas Register*, July 22, 1837.) For more on maroons in the Old South, see Sylviane A. Diouf, *Slavery's Exiles: The Story of the American Maroons* (New York: New York University Press 2014).

10. The Victoria *Texian Advocate*, August 7, 1851. Mr. P. Bicford purchased Jimbo for $207 at auction before he escaped. The Navidad River is approximately seventy miles southeast of Chenango, the plantation of Monroe Edwards in Brazoria County, from which Jimbo likely escaped.

11. "Imports into New Orleans, from the Interior, for Ten Years—from the 1st September to the 31st August in Each Year," *DeBow's Review*, Vol. 1, No. 1 (1/1846), 50; *Telegraph and Texas Register*, February 24, 1841; Abigail Curlee, "A Study of Texas Slave Plantations, 1822–1865," PhD dissertation, The University of Texas, 1932, 175; J. Carlyle Sitterson, *Sugar Country: The Cane Industry of the South, 1753–1950* (Westport, CT: Greenwood Press, 1953), 42.

12. J. D. B. Debow, *The Industrial Resources of the Southern and Western States*, Vol. III (New Orleans, 1853), 285. Egypt plantation, founded by Mercer, got its name during the drought of 1827 when grain was in short supply. Mercer managed to grow enough for himself and his neighbors, and when the settlers ran short on grain, they went to the Mercer place "like going up to Egypt for grain." The plantation lies 3 1/2 miles east of the Colorado River, on the highest ground available in Wharton County. Today (2021), several of the original sugar kettles from the evaporating battery of 1833 are in use as flower planters in the front yard of the brick plantation house built by William Heard Northington's enslaved in 1849. It is ironic that a good portion of the Imperial Sugar Company of the late nineteenth and twentieth centuries was located on the old Stafford plantation. The plantation is now the location for the city of Stafford, Texas. Dilue Harris, "The Reminiscences of Mrs. Dilue Harris I," *The Quarterly of the Texas State Historical Association*, Vol. 4, No. 2 (October 1900), 96; *Telegraph and Texas Register*, February 9, 1842; James Morgan to William Swartwout, February 20, 1846, in Feris A. Bass Jr. and B. R. Brunson (eds.), *Fragile Empires: The Texas Correspondence of Samuel Swartwout and James Morgan 1836–1856* (Austin, TX: Shoal Creek, 1978), 292.

13. For more on the production of sugar, see chapter 9.

14. James P. Baughman *Charles Morgan and the Development of Southern Transportation* (Nashville: Vanderbilt University Press, 1968), 22–25. Morgan was the main competitor to Cornelius Vanderbilt in Southern transportation, and he also helped bankroll William Walker's Nicaragua filibuster in the 1850s; Calvin Schermerhorn, *The Business of Slavery and the Rise of American Capitalism, 1815–1860* (New Haven, CT: Yale University Press 2015), 204.

15. Baughman, *Charles Morgan*, 25–27; Mary Austin Holley to Mrs. William M. Brand, December 19, 1837 (quotation) and November 12, 1840 (trip on the *New York*), Mary Austin Holley Papers, Dolph Briscoe Center for American History, The University of Texas at Austin. Mary Austin Holley was a cousin of Stephen F. Austin.

16. RG 36 US Customs Service New Orleans Outward Slave Manifests January 1836–December 1838, HM 2007, Box 7 E.1630, National Archives, Fort Worth, Texas. In 1807, when the United States outlawed the international slave trade effective January 1, 1808, the US Customs Service was established to enforce the ban. Any ship carrying any enslaved person had to file a customs form with the name, age, and description of the person, as well as the owner/shipper, port, name, and description of the ship, as well as the intended destination. Part of the form was an oath swearing that the persons

listed had not been born outside the United States after January 1, 1808. The name of Joseph and the other roughly ten thousand enslaved African Americans brought to Texas from New Orleans are in the files of the US Customs Service, Record Group 36, in the National Archives in Fort Worth, Texas.

17. Thomas McKinney to Samuel May Williams, July 28, 1838, Samuel May Williams Papers, Rosenberg Library, Galveston, Texas.

18. S. L. Jones to Samuel May Williams, January 31, 1839, and McKinney to Williams, February 4, 1839, Samuel May Williams Papers, Rosenberg Library, Galveston, Texas; Samuel May Williams to Anson Jones, March 11, 1839, in Anson Jones Memoranda and Official Correspondence Relating to the Republic of Texas, Its History and Annexation (New York: Arno Press 1973), 145–146; see also Abigail Curlee Holbrook, "Marketing the Cotton Crop in Antebellum Texas," *The Southwestern Historical Quarterly*, Vol. 73, No. 4 (April 1970), 431–455; Andrew J. Torget, *Seeds of Empire: Cotton, Slavery and the Transformation of the Texas Borderlands, 1800–1850* (Chapel Hill: University of North Carolina Press 2015), 199–202.

19. Willis W. Pratt (ed.), *Galveston Island, Or a Few Months Off the Coast of Texas: The Journal of Francis C. Sheridan 1839–1840* (Austin: University of Texas Press 1954), 30–31. Here, Sheridan is referring to the Baring Brothers of London, one of the first large mercantile firms in the world. See Peter E. Austin, *Baring Brothers and the Birth of Modern Finance* (London: Pickering and Chatto, 2007).

20. Pratt (ed.), *Galveston Island*, 31–32 and 50–51.

21. Ibid., 89–90, 117–118, and 126.

Chapter 4

1. Dilue Harris, "The Reminiscences of Mrs. Dilue Harris I," *The Quarterly of the Texas State Historical Association*, Vol. 4, No. 2 (October 1900), 85–127. In May 1834, Ben Fort Smith sent word that one of the Africans had escaped; he remained in the Stafford Point neighborhood for several months and at one point tried to break into the Rose house. He "had a large knife he had stolen, also a flint and steel for striking fire," according to Dilue Rose. Dilue also remembered that the night he tried to break in, "He fought the dogs and ran them under the house. He talked and yelled, but we could not understand his gibberish. The dogs attacked him several times, but he would whip them, and they would run under the house, bark, howl, and whine." At one point, "A Mr. Battle made friends with the negro and fed him and tried to get him in the house, but he was too smart. Mr. Battle caught him and tried to tie him, but the negro cut Mr. Battle severely. He then left our neighborhood, crossed the Brazos and Colorado rivers, and made his way to the Navidad bottom. He was often seen by travelers and was called the Wild Man of the Navidad." This was apparently the same man mentioned in chapter 3.

2. *Life and Adventures of the Accomplished Forger and Swindler Colonel Monroe Edwards* (New York: H. Long and Brothers, 1848), 17–21; Lora-Marie Bernard, *The Counterfeit Prince of Old Texas: Swindling Slaver Monroe Edwards* (Charleston SC: The History Press, 2017), 81–84. Lomboko was also the location where the infamous slaver *La Amistad* embarked the enslaved men who had overpowered the crew in 1839. The British navy destroyed Lomboko in 1849.

3. Baring Brothers originated in the early eighteenth century, but by 1760, they began to expand their business, located in London with ties to the Baltic. By 1795, they had a branch in Philadelphia. Beginning in the 1820s, the Barings invested in the Cuban sugar market, and in the same decade they began doing business with the new firm of Mariategui, Knight & Co. of Havana. The Barings extended new lines of credit to the latter company in 1831 following George Knight's visit to London. By 1837, the reconstituted firm of George Knight & Co. became the sole Barings agent in Cuba. Despite the abolitionist triumph in Great Britain, the Barings began investing in slave smuggling, using their Havana subsidiary to disguise their dealings. Baring Brothers also helped finance the Louisiana Purchase in 1803 and did not go out of business until 1995. ING absorbed the remnants of the company. See A. B. Leonard and David Pretel (eds.), *The Caribbean and the Atlantic World Economy* (New York: Palgrave McMillan 2015), 240–250; and Peter E. Austin, *Baring Brothers and the Birth of Modern Finance* (London: Pickering and Chatto, 2007). With power of attorney from Monroe Edwards, Christopher Dart signed a mortgage made out to George Knight & Co. at New Orleans on August 29, 1836. As collateral, Edwards signed over half interest to all his land and slaves in Texas to Dart on April 18, 1837. After their failure to repay George Knight & Co., the company sued Edwards and Dart in Brazoria County. Brazoria County Deed Records, Volume A, pp. 188 (December 11, 1838); Cases 680 and 492, *George Knight & Co. vs. Monroe Edwards*, Brazoria County Deed Books, Vol. A, pp. 177–178, 183–184, 190. See Samuel Fisher to the General Council, March 2, 1836, in Jenkins (ed.). *Papers of the Texas Revolution*, Vol. 4, pp. 190; Ben C. Stuart Papers, Rosenberg Library, Galveston. For more on Monroe Edwards, see Brian P. Luskey "Chasing Capital in Hard Times: Monroe Edwards, Slavery, and Sovereignty in the Panicked Atlantic," *Journal of Early American Studies*, Vol. 14 (Winter 2016), 82–113.

4. William Fairfax Gray *From Virginia to Texas, 1835: Diary of Colonel William F. Gray Giving Details of His Journey to Texas and Return in 1835–1836* (Houston TX: Gray, Dillaye & Co. 1909), 147.

5. Ibid., 158–159. Unfortunately, the vocabulary Gray spoke of has not survived, or it was never located with his diary and papers. These Africans appear to have come from tribes belonging to the Yoruba speakers of Senegambia, the region between modern Senegal and Gambia. See Sean M. Kelley and Henry B. Lovejoy, "The Origins of the African Born Population of Antebellum Texas: A Research Note," *The Southwestern Historical Quarterly*, Vol. 120, No. 2 (October 2016), 217–233.

6. Edward Henrick to Samuel May Williams, August 28, 1833, Samuel May Williams Papers, Rosenberg Library, Galveston, Texas.

7. Ruth Cumby Smith, "James W. Fannin Jr.., In the Texas Revolution," *Southwestern Historical Quarterly*, Vol. 22 (1919), 80; Contract signed by J. W. Fannin and Harvey Kendrick, May 26, 1834, "Texas Letters and Documents," *Texana*, Vol. 1, No. 2 (1963), 170–172; James W. Fannin Probate Case 162, Brazoria County Clerk's Office, Angleton, Texas.

8. James W. Fannin Probate Case 162, Brazoria County Clerk's Office, Angleton, Texas.

9. According to a story circulated among locals in Brazoria County, at some point a smuggler landed a cargo of Africans at African Landing and then stopped to play cards

and visit with the various planters who met him there to purchase the enslaved men and women. Their card game continued late into the night, and when one of the planters decided to return home, he could not find his large Newfoundland dog. The next morning, upon more careful inspection, the enslaver discovered a pile of dog bones picked clean where the campfire for the Africans had been the previous night. See Andrew Platter "Educational, Social, and Economic Characteristics of the Plantation Culture of Brazoria County, Texas," EdD dissertation, University of Houston, 1961, 150–151. At the present date (2021), all traces of African landing have disappeared, although it was located near 28°58′20.87″N, 95°33′47.23″W. Sterling McNeel was also identified as one of the enslavers engaged in the Cuba to Texas slave trade by Samuel Fisher, the customs collector at Velasco.

10. James F. Perry was apparently one of the purchasers of Fannin's Africans because he made out a promissory note to Fannin on August 24, 1835, for "value received," in the amount of $1,973.34. James Perry Papers, Briscoe Center for American History, The University of Texas at Austin; Fannin to Thompson, September 15, 1835, James W. Fannin Probate Case 162, Brazoria County Clerk's Office.

11. In his MA thesis, Fred Thompson estimates the total number of Africans smuggled into Texas at 5,000, but the best study of this subject to date is Fred McGhee's PhD dissertation, "The Black Crop: Slavery and Slave Trading in Nineteen Century Texas." McGhee documents the trade at 13,377. See Thompson, "The Origins and Development of the African Slave Trade into Texas," MA Thesis, University of Houston (1972), 118–119; McGhee, "The Black Crop," PhD dissertation, The University of Texas at Austin (2000), 131. One of the lesser-known smuggling operations involved camels imported into Texas under Secretary of War Jefferson Davis in 1858. The camels arrived in Galveston on October 16, 1858, aboard the *Thomas Watson*, but it appears that the *Watson* engaged a smaller vessel, the *Lucerne*, to disembark smuggled Africans up the Texas coast. Along with its capabilities to haul camels from Africa, the *Thomas Watson* also possessed all the requisite facilities of a slaver. See Michael E. Woods, "The Dark Underbelly of Jefferson Davis' Camels," *Journal of the Civil War Era* (Vol. 7, No. 4), December 2017.

12. Creighton *A Narrative History of Brazoria County*, 171–174. Ned Thompson variously listed his birth year as 1825, 1826, or 1830. This would have made him between ten and fifteen years old when he was captured in Africa and between eighty-three and eighty-eight when Underwood interviewed him. Julia Ann (Jackson) Thompson variously listed her birth year as 1845, 1849, or 1850, making her roughly twenty years younger than her husband. In October 1879, Thompson purchased fifty acres of land from the estate of J. W. Dance for $250, in the upper quarter of the S. M. Williams League west of West Columbia (Abstract 039139). In May 1901, Thompson sold the mineral rights for the forty-one acres he still owned to the J. M. Guffey Company. Both Ned and Julia appear to have died prior to 1920, and both were buried in the Island Cemetery in the Mound Creek Community, which is now on private property at 29°10′32.83″N 95°41′38.82″W. The last of the Thompson children, Mamie (born January 14, 1890), passed away at Bay City, Texas, of cancer on November 12, 1969. The 1880, 1900, and 1910 US Censuses for Brazoria County; Brazoria County deed records Book D, Volume S, 200 (October 13, 1879), Book D, Vol. 56, p. 4 (May 4, 1901); Death Certificate of

Mamie Thompson, Matagorda County, Texas, November 20, 1969; 161–01–2, 020–00 (SSN 462–88–9104-T).

13. There are several sources for these numbers, beginning with the 1850 and 1860 US Censuses. Statistically, the census numbers are largely trustworthy. The second source is the tax rolls kept annually by every Texas county. However, predictably, enslavers consistently underreported the number of enslaved for tax purposes. The 1850 Census revealed that enslavers undercounted the number of enslaved by 20.8 percent in Texas as a whole and by 13.5 percent in the lowcountry. The 1860 Census revealed an undercount of 13.8 percent in Texas and an undercount of 8.97 percent in the lowcountry. Thus, it appears fair to estimate that, statewide, enslavers undercounted on tax rolls by a rate of 17.3 percent per year and 12.25 percent in the lowcountry. Therefore, for the years in which only tax rolls are available, I have added the above percentages to the total statewide and in the lowcountry. The 1864 numbers saw an obvious jump statewide from enslavers elsewhere in the South, making enslaved African Americans refugees in Texas; the lowcountry would have received relatively few of these refugees, as the vast majority came over land. See Campbell, *An Empire for Slavery*, 54–56, 264–266.

14. Mortality Schedules for the State of Texas, 1850 Census of the United States.

15. Alabama, Arkansas, Florida, Georgia, Louisiana, Mississippi, South Carolina, and Texas are counted as "importing" states, while Delaware, Washington, DC, North Carolina, and Virginia are considered "exporting" states. Michael Tadman, *Speculators and Slaves: Masters, Traders, and Slaves in the Old South* (Madison: University of Wisconsin Press, 1989), 12, 69.

16. The enslaved's *prime age*—15 to 45—marked the years when they had their highest value for both work and reproductive potential. Typically, the higher the amount of cotton, and especially sugar, that was grown, the higher the number of prime age enslaved persons desired by enslavers. The demographic information comes from the 1850 and 1860 US censuses, whereas the ages derive from a dataset of 964 enslaved individuals in the lowcountry compiled by the author from wills, probate minutes, and deeds in the four counties.

17. The 1850 and 1860 US Censuses; Tadman, *Speculators and Slaves*, 12. Tadman estimates that 28,622 enslaved African Americans entered Texas by means of the interstate slave trade in the 1840s and another 99,190 in the 1850s.

18. RG 36 US Customs Service, New Orleans Outward Slave Manifests 1838–1860, National Archives, Fort Worth, Texas.

19. Hiram Mattison, *Louisa Picquet the Octoroon, or Inside Views of Southern Domestic Life* (New York: Hiram Mattison, 1861), 16–19. Louisa reported that her original enslaver, her biological father, sold her and her mother because Louisa looked too much like his white daughter for the comfort of his wife.

20. Receipt for purchase of enslaved people, July 25, 1860, Charleston, South Carolina. Albert C. Horton Papers, Dolph Briscoe Center for American History, The University of Texas at Austin. Albert Clinton Horton was the great-great-grandfather of famous American playwright Horton Foote, who grew up in Wharton County.

21. Ginny McNeill Raska and Mary Lynne Gasaway Hill (eds.), *The Uncompromising Diary of Sallie McNeill 1858–1867* (College Station: Texas A&M University Press 2009), 45, 87, 169.

22. *The Telegraph and Texas Register*, December 12, 1838; January 1, 1846; November 16, 1846; December 7, 1846; November 11, 1847; February 10, 1848; February 10, 1849; August 7, 1850; December 5, 1851; January 5, 1852; February 24, 1854; October 1, 1856; April 8, 1857; April 29, 1857; June 9, 1858; July 14, 1858; Advertising section of the 1857 *Texas Almanac*; *Lone Star* (Washington, TX), December 20, 1851; *Washington (Texas) American*, January 13, 1856; June 16, 1857; Long Row was the first Houston commercial/shopping area. A reproduction of some of the buildings may be found across Bagby Street from Sam Houston Historical Park in downtown Houston today.

23. *The Galvestonian*, March 27, 1839; *The Civilian and Galveston Gazette*, November 21, 1854, November 18, 1856, June 11, 1858, March 6, 1860; *The Galveston News* September 16, 1857; *The Semi-Weekly Journal* (Galveston), June 16, 1853; *The Galveston Tri-Weekly News* May 7, 1863; March 31, 1865; June 11, 1865. The original Tremont Hotel was opened by McKinney & Williams in 1839 at the corner of Post Office Street and Tremont Street (23rd) in Galveston. The current hotel was opened in the 1970s at the current location.

Chapter 5

1. Rutherford Birchard Hayes, *The Diary and Letters of Rutherford B. Hayes, Nineteenth President of the United States*, Charles Richard Williams (ed.) (Columbus: Ohio State Archeological and Historical Society, 1922), Vol. 1, 246–249. Hayes and Bryan had attended Kenyon College in Gambier, Ohio, together.

2. The 1850 and 1860 Censuses of the United States.

3. Tax Rolls for Brazoria County, 1860; the 1860 US Census for Brazoria County, Texas. The town lots in Brazoria County lay in the towns of Velasco, Quintana, Liverpool, Brazoria, West Columbia, and East Columbia.

4. Much of the information about the locations of the plantations come from three sources: The Texas Historical Commission Atlas at https://atlas.thc.state.tx.us/Map (accessed May 27, 2019); the Texas General Land Office Land/Leasing Map Viewer at http://gisweb.glo.texas.gov/glomapjs/index.html (accessed May 27, 2019); and the tax rolls for Brazoria, Fort Bend, Matagorda, and Wharton counties. Except where otherwise noted, these are the sources for this chapter. For more on the neighborhoods of the Old South, see Anthony E. Kaye, *Joining Places: Slave Neighborhoods in the Old South* (Chapel Hill: University of North Carolina Press, 2007). In 1850, enslaved African Americans in the lowcountry produced 10,473 bales of cotton, 18 percent of the state total. They also produced 7,063 hogsheads of sugar, 96 percent of the total for Texas as a whole. In 1860, enslaved African Americans in the lowcountry produced 45,389 bales of cotton, 11 percent of the state's total. That same year, the enslaved in the lowcountry produced 4,487 hogsheads of sugar, 88 percent of the total for the state. See the 1850 and 1860 agricultural censuses of the United States.

5. The nine plantations on the Gulf Prairie were Peach Point, Durazno, the Hawkins, Munson, Westall, and Lowwood plantations, and the three McNeel plantations: Ellerslie, the home of J. Greenville McNeel; Pleasant Grove, the home of Leander McNeel; and Magnolia, the home of Pleasant McNeel. The Peach Point home was located at 28°58'34.87"N, 95°28'7.50"W where a Texas Historical Marker is located today in

Jones Creek, Texas. Durazno was 1.67 miles to the southeast where the Texas Historical Marker is today at 28°57′28.0″N 95°26′59.0″W. There is an unmarked slave cemetery 235 yards southeast of the Durazno house site at 28°57′21.0″N 95°26′57.0″W. The Gulf Prairie Cemetery, which contains the original resting place of Stephen F. Austin, as well as many of these plantation owners, is just a few yards west of the site of the original Peach Point big house at 28°58′34.0″N 95°28′22.0″W. Light Townsend Cummins *Emily Austin of Texas 1795–1851* (Fort Worth: Texas Christian University Press, 2009), 107–109, 242; Abner J. Strobel *The Old Plantations and Their Owners of Brazoria County, Texas* (Lake Jackson, TX: Lake Jackson Historical Association, 2006 edition), 7, 12–24; The Brazosport Archaeological Society *Durazno Plantation*, http://lifeonthebrazosriver. com/Durazno-Plantation.pdf (2009) (accessed March 14, 2019).

6. Creighton, *Narrative History of Brazoria County*, 221–224; A. A. Platter, *Educational, Social, and Economic Characteristics of the Plantation Culture of Brazoria County, Texas*, 106–107; Brazosport Archaeological Society, *John McNeel Plantation Ellerslie Plantation John Greenville McNeel James Marion Huntington Pleasant Grove Plantation Leander H. McNeel Sugar Plantation of Pleasant D. McNeel* (*Magnolia*), http://lifeon thebrazosriver.com/Ellerslie-Plantation-John-Greenville-McNeel-Kate-Huntington. pdf (2014) (accessed March 14, 2019). The mansion at Ellerslie burned to the ground in the late 1890s, and some of the other buildings were destroyed in the Hurricane of 1900. The overseer's house burned down in 1983. The machinery for the sugar mill was disassembled in 1953. A Texas historical marker along State Highway 36 just north of Jones Creek, Texas, marks the far northern end of the plantation, the ruins of which are on private land. The marker is located at 28°59′05.0″N 95°30′17.0″W.

7. Strobel, *The Old Plantations and Their Owners of Brazoria County, Texas*, 24; Brazosport Archaeological Society, *John McNeel Plantation Ellerslie Plantation John Greenville McNeel James Marion Huntington Pleasant Grove Plantation Leander H. McNeel Sugar Plantation of Pleasant D. McNeel* (*Magnolia*), http://lifeonthebrazosriver.com/Ellerslie-Plantation-John-Greenville-McNeel-Kate-Huntington.pdf (2014) (accessed March 14, 2019). The Pleasant Grove plantation house served as the headquarters of the Freedmen's Bureau for the area during Reconstruction, and today Pleasant Grove, Magnolia, and Lowwood Plantations are all part of the Clemens Prison Farm. The Pleasant Grove mansion was torn down by the state of Texas after acquiring it as part of the Clemens Farm. The McNeel family cemetery is also part of the Clemens facility today.

8. Strobel, *The Old Plantations and Their Owners of Brazoria County, Texas*, 54; Joan Few, *Sugar, Planters, Slaves, and Convicts: The History and Archaeology of the Lake Jackson Plantation Brazoria County, Texas* (Self-Published, 2006), 28, 139. The ruins of the Lake Jackson house and sugar mill have been the subject of archaeological investigation by several groups. The ruins of the main house and sugar mill on the banks of Lake Jackson are now owned by the Lake Jackson Historical Society at 95°28′5.47″W, 29° 3′6.28″N. The area where the overseer's house stood is now a plot of land owned by Dow Chemical Company. An intriguing clue as to the location of the slave quarters came to light in 2014, with the discovery of a slave cemetery at the northeastern tip of the Brazos Mall, along the south bank of Oyster Creek, about 1,145 yards east of the site of the main house. This, along with the parking lot of the mall itself was probably the location of the slave cabins, which have long since disappeared.

See https://www.houstonchronicle.com/news/houston-texas/houston/article/In-Lake-Jackson-discovery-of-slave-remains-helps-5719674.php (accessed March 15, 2019). The Retrieve plantation, 4 miles north of Lake Jackson on the east bank of Oyster Creek, was similar in almost every respect to the Lake Jackson plantation. By 1858, both sugar mills at Retrieve and Lake Jackson were using steam engines instead of mules to process sugar cane. Abner Jackson sold his half interest in Retrieve to James Hamilton, former governor of South Carolina and Republic of Texas diplomat in 1842. Retrieve was used as part of the convict lease system starting in 1911, and in 1918 the state of Texas purchased the plantation to use as a prison farm. It is now known as the Wayne Scott Unit of the Texas Department of Criminal Justice at 6999 Retrieve Rd. Angleton, TX 77515. "Retrieve Plantation" https://tshaonline.org/handbook/online/articles/acr01 (accessed March 15, 2019).

9. Strobel, *The Old Plantations and Their Owners of Brazoria County, Texas*, 48–49. The location of the big house at Eagle Island is marked with an historical marker at the entrance of the Restwood Memorial Park in Clute, Texas, at 29°01'09.0"N, 95°25'11.0"W. William Wharton and his wife Sarah Ann (Groce) Wharton are buried in this cemetery. They were originally buried in the Eagle Island Plantation Cemetery on the other side of the lake five hundred yards northeast of the marker for the house at 29°01'22.0"N, 95°25'03.0"W. The slave cemetery for Eagle Island has been discovered in a residential neighborhood 1,080 yards northwest of the marker for the house at 29°1'33.81"N, 95°25'35.54"W.

10. The five plantations in this neighborhood were the Christopher Bell, Levi Jordan, Mims, Stephen Winston, and Asa Strayton (Stratton?) plantations. See Strobel, *The Old Plantations and Their Owners*, 7.

11. The Mims house stood on the south side of the current Texas State Highway 521 on the west bank of the San Bernard River at 29°00'35.0"N, 95°35'19.0"W. The cemetery for the Mims family is on the north side of SH 521 at 29°00'33.8"N, 95°35'49.6"W, 907 yards west of the river. The slave cemetery for the plantation is located at 29°00'15.2"N, 95°35'31.5"W, 810 yards to the southeast. Brazosport Archaeological Society, "Joseph Mims-James Walker Fannin James Calvin McNeill Plantation," http://lifeonthebrazos river.com/Joseph-Mims-Plantation.pdf (accessed March 31, 2019).

12. The Levi Jordan plantation is now owned by the Texas Historical Commission and is open to the public for tours and a museum at 7234 FM 521 Brazoria, TX 77422. As a result, the Jordan plantation has been the most thoroughly studied. Kenneth L. Brown, "Material Culture and Community Structure: The Slave and Tenant Community at Levi Jordan's Plantation, 1848–1892," in Larry E. Hudson Jr. (ed.), *Working towards Freedom: Slave Society and Domestic Economy in the American South* (Rochester, NY: University of Rochester Press, 1994), 95–118. https://www.thc.texas.gov/historic-sites/levi-jordan-plantation-state-historic-site (accessed March 31, 2019).

13. The city of Old Ocean grew up around the John Sweeney plantation, and the city of Sweeney grew up around the Thomas Sweeney plantation. A historical marker in Old Ocean today marks the location of the John Sweeney plantation. Cedar Grove was located along Dance Bayou, east of what is now FM 524 and the San Bernard National Wildlife Refuge. In 1845, James E. Black purchased one thousand acres of land from David McCormick on McCormick's League on the west bank of the San Bernard River

between what is now Sweeney and Old Ocean. By 1855, Black also owned seventy enslaved African Americans and a sugar mill on his plantation. McCormick had operated a ferry at an earlier date, and Black continued to operate the ferry, named Black's Ferry, where FM 22, the Damon Black Ferry Road, crosses the San Bernard today at 29°4′42.97″N, 95°40′58.22″W. Black died intestate on March 6, 1858, and Sarah Black, along with James Black's adult children from a previous marriage inherited his estate. He was buried in Columbia Cemetery, West Columbia, Texas. Sarah Black died on May 5, 1864, and was buried in the Black family cemetery on the plantation. The Black cemetery is located on County Road 359, 1.5 miles west of FM 1459 at 29°4′44.56″N, 95°42′34.82″W. The grave has evidently been lost, as there is a memorial stone to Sarah Black in the Munson Cemetery at Bailey's Prairie, Brazoria County. For a fuller description of the Chance's Prairie neighborhood, see David Phelps McCormick, *The Scotch Irish in Ireland and America* (David P. McCormick, 1897). Charles, or Charlie Brown, a freedman, later purchased the Dance plantation in 1883, eventually making him the wealthiest African American man in Brazoria County by the time of his death in 1920. Brazosport Archaeological Society, "Cedar Brake Plantation John Spencer Dance-John Henry Dance-Charles Brown," http://lifeonthebrazosriver.com/Cedar-Brake.pdf (accessed May 25, 2021). Today, there is a historical marker commemorating Charlie Brown at the corner of Brown Street and W. Brazos Avenue in West Columbia, Texas, at 29°8′42.31″N, 95°39′1.79″W.

14. The Patton plantation is now the Varner-Hogg State Historic Site at 1702 N. 13th St. West, Columbia, TX 77486. Texas Governor James Hogg purchased the plantation as a vacation home in the early twentieth century, and drillers discovered oil on the property, making the Hogg family wealthy. The hurricane of 1900 destroyed the sugar mill and slave cabins, the ruins and foundations of which are still visible. In all likelihood, the remainder of the slave cabins, as well as the slave cemetery, existed in what is now the Columbia Lakes Subdivision of West Columbia. Ima Hogg, daughter of the governor, altered the plantation house, including connecting the detached kitchen, and stuccoing over the brick exterior of the house. The Hoggs also changed the house to face the rear, or southwest, and removed the second-floor exterior porches. https://www.thc.texas.gov/historic-sites/varner-hogg-plantation-state-historic-site/varner-hogg-plantation-history (accessed April 6, 2019).

15. Osceola now stands on private property, with no historical markers. Paul Spofford of New York purchased the plantation in 1870 and built a sugar mill on the property. The Osceola sugar mill still partially stands at 29°12′35.64″N, 95°33′32.55″W. Much of the plantation now stands beneath Manor and Eagle Nest Lakes, the former of which is owned by Haliburton. The Hill residence, along the Brazos, stood at approximately 29°12′32.32″N, 95°33′41.45″W. The other plantations in the West Columbia neighborhood included the Josiah Bell plantation, where East Columbia now stands; Waldeck, between Patton Place and Osceola; the Maner plantation north of Waldeck; and the Orozimbo plantation of Dr. James Phelps where the rebels held Santa Anna after the battle of San Jacinto. The Brazosport Archaeological Society, "Orozimbo Plantation," at http://lifeonthebrazosriver.com/OsceolaPlantation.htm (accessed April 6, 2019); Brazosport Archaeological Society, "Josiah H. Bell Thaddeus C. & James H. Bell John W. Brooks William A. Rose Plantation," at http://lifeonthebrazosriver.com/BellsL

andingBrazoriaCounty.htm (accessed April 6, 2019); *Handbook of Texas Online*, Diana J. Kleiner, "WALDECK PLANTATION," accessed April 06, 2019, http://www.tshaonline .org/handbook/online/articles/acw01.

16. James Brit Bailey insisted in his will that he be buried on his land, standing up, facing west, with his rifle and a jug of whiskey at his sides. According to local lore, his ghost still wanders the prairie, looking for more whiskey. The tree under which he was buried is known as Bailey's Tree. The tree died some years ago, but the grave remains, overlooking Flag Pond near the Bar X Ranch Subdivision. The ruins of the sugar mill for Bynum remain in a public park in the Bar X Ranch Subdivision at 29°7′53.41″N, 95°34′6.35″W. The Mills cemetery at Bynum is located adjacent to the ruins of the sugar mill. The Munson Cemetery is located at 29°8′47.68″N, 95°31′21.16″W. Brazosport Archaeology Society, "Bynum Plantation," http://lifeonthebrazosriver.com/Bynum-Plantation.pdf (accessed April 6, 2019); Craig H. Roell, "Sayre, Charles D.," *Handbook of Texas Online* (accessed April 6, 2019), https://www.tshaonline.org/handbook/entries/ sayre-charles-d; Merle Weir, "Bailey, James Briton," *Handbook of Texas Online*, accessed April 6, 2019, https://www.tshaonline.org/handbook/entries/bailey-james-briton.

17. After the Civil War, Chenango lent its name to the stop on the Columbia Tap Railroad. Today, the town of Chenango lies about a mile east of the old plantation, at the eastern edge of the Ramsey State Prison Farm. Hurricane Ike destroyed much of the ruins of the Chenango sugar mill in 2008, and the owner of the property demolished the rest of the mill in 2014. The sugar mill was approximately at 29°15′32.82″N, 95°28′52.87″W. The plantation was named after Chenango County, New York, by Monroe Edwards. Abner J. Strobel, *The Old Plantations and Their Owners of Brazoria County, Texas*, 66–68; Brazosport Archaeological Society "Chenango Plantation," http:// lifeonthebrazosriver.com/Chenango%20Plantation.htm (accessed April 12, 2019). The other eleven plantations in this neighborhood included Waverly, Drayton, Quarl's, Palo Alto, Tankersly, George A. Smith, Compton, Coffee, Willow Glen, Bingham, and Van plantations. Waverly, Drayton, Quarl's, and Palo Alto are now part of the Ramsey State Prison Farm.

18. William Preston Johnston, *The Life of Albert Sidney Johnston* (New York: D. Appleton & Co., 1876), 146–148.

19. Strobel, *The Old Plantations and Their Owners of Brazoria County, Texas*, 70; Brazosport Archaeological Society, "Warren D. C. Hall-Albert Sidney Johnston-William Preston Johnston-William J. Hutchins China Grove Plantation," http://lifeonthebra-zosriver.com/ChinaGroveWarrenDCHall.pdf (accessed April 12, 2019). China Grove also sat east of Oyster Creek. The historical marker for the Johnston residence is at 29°18′48.55″N, 95°27′1.06″W, along Texas State Highway 521 south of Bonney, Texas.

20. Strobel, *The Old Plantations and Their Owners of Brazoria County, Texas*, 71–72; Brazosport Archaeological Society "Darrington Plantation," http://lifeonthebrazosriver. com/DarringtonPlantation.htm (accessed April 13, 2019). In 1918, the state of Texas acquired Darrington, and it now serves as the heart of the Darrington State Prison Farm at 59 Darrington Rd #59, Rosharon, TX 77583.

21. Lewis Strobel is the father of Abner Strobel, the chronicler of Brazoria County plantations, who grew up on his father's plantation.

22. After the Civil War, Thomas W. House, a wealthy Houston merchant, acquired Arcola. His son, Edward M. House, the famous Texan political operator, grew up on the plantation. Thomas House employed a great deal of convict labor on the plantation. He also constructed a second sugar mill, the ruins of which were discovered in 2011 as a road crew was building Waters Lake Boulevard in front of the future site of Ridge Point High School. After an archaeological investigation, the road crew paved over the second sugar mill, which lies at precisely 29°29'6.43"N, 95°30'40.40"W, beneath the eastbound lane of Waters Lake Boulevard. Around 1929, Thomas H. Scanlan, former mayor of Houston, acquired the plantation, and the Scanlan daughters moved their plantation house from Houston to the property, naming it Cenacle Retreat, later renaming it Sienna plantation. In the 1970s, when developers began surveying the property for a master-planned community, they inventoried the plantation for its historical and archaeological significance. At that time, the Scanlan house was still standing, although nothing but ruins remained of the original Waters home site. Today, Sienna plantation is a wealthy master-planned community, but in the woods behind the ballfields, the Waters family cemetery still stands, complete with the shaft of Italian marble that marks the grave of Clara Byne Waters. The Waters cemetery is at 29°29'51.50"N, 95°33'10.05"W. The home site existed 200 yards west of the cemetery, approximately 150 yards from the bank of the Brazos, near where the railroad bridge stands today. Incredibly, the two-story original Waters sugar mill remains to this day, approximately 6,468 yards southeast of the Waters home site with a heading of 295 degrees, at 29°28'27.22"N, 95°29'56.30"W, adjacent to Oyster Creek. The Waters sugar mill is the only antebellum sugar mill still standing in Texas. The Waters brick yard was located 3,400 yards south of the Waters home site, on the east bank of the Brazos, at approximately 29°28'11.00"N, 95°32'35.37"W. Unfortunately, the slave cabins could not be located, although, judging by the tenant houses found on the property, they were probably constructed of wood and were located in the vicinity of the Waters sugar mill. Clarence R. Wharton, *History of Fort Bend County* (San Antonio: The Naylor Company, 1939), 138–139; http://lifeon thebrazosriver.com/WatersColJonathanDawson-House.pdf (accessed April 21, 2019); the Cultural Resources Survey of Sienna Plantation at http://lifeonthebrazosriver.com/ siennabounda.PDF (accessed April 21, 2019).

23. Smada is Adams spelled backwards. The plantation was in what is today Missouri City, Texas, at 29°34'52.85"N, 95°34'48.80"W. The Stafford plantation was located near the Stafford family cemetery at 29°36'20.72"N, 95°35'9.47"W. Note that the plantation was located 1.9 miles south of Stafford's Point, which is near the center of the city of Stafford today. The Stafford family cemetery is located within the city limits of Sugar Land, Texas. William Stafford spent winter, spring, and fall at the plantation near Oyster Creek, and summers at Stafford's Point. It was at the latter place that he erected the sugar mill and his horse-powered cotton gin. A. J. Sowell, *A History of Fort Bend County* (Houston: W. H. Coyle & Co. Stationers and Printers, 1904), 237.

24. Many sources claim that Kyle and Terry struck gold in California and used that money to purchase Oakland, but there is no hard evidence for this claim. The Austin *Texas Democrat* noted in April 1849 that a group of Texans was headed to California, and listed Frank Terry and William J. Kyle. It appears, however, that Kyle either returned

before the others or never made it to California, as he is not listed with the others on the 1850 Census. The 1850 Census, taken on November 11, 1850, shows Thomas S. Lubbock serving as a hotel keeper, Frank Terry working as a "trader," a younger Terry brother, David, working as an attorney at law, and a third brother, Riley Terry, assisting Lubbock as a hotel keeper in Stockton, California. Thomas Lubbock and Frank Terry returned to Texas permanently, while David Terry remained in California and became the first chief justice of the California Supreme Court. Another famous resident of the lowcountry who never returned from California was Henry Smith, the original *alcalde* (i.e., "mayor") of Brazoria and provisional president of the Republic of Texas; he died in a mining camp in Los Angeles County in 1851. Kyle and Terry purchased Oakland in March 1853 but did not fully pay off the mortgage to the property until August 1859, so if Frank Terry did strike gold in California, it was not much. The Terry mansion at Oakland stood approximately where Sugar Mill Elementary school is located today in Sugar Land, Texas, at 29°38′0.60″N, 95°37′29.90″W. The Imperial Sugar Company Sugar Mill on the south bank of Oyster Creek was the location of the sugar mill constructed in 1843 at 29°37′16.09″N, 95°38′12.45″W. The slave quarters were located 800 yards north of the sugar mill in what is now the Mayfield Park neighborhood at 29°37′37.60″N, 95°38′12.97″W. Although the resting places of many of those who died during the convict leasing period were discovered at the corner of University Boulevard and Chatham Lane in Sugar Land at 29°36′14.20″N, 95°38′53.49″W in 2018, it is unlikely that this was also the slave cemetery, as this newly found burial ground is 1.77 miles south of the slave quarters. The location of the slave cemetery at Oakland remains unknown. However, in May 1880, the remains of the members of the Terry family were removed to Glenwood Cemetery Plot E-1 in Houston at 2525 Washington Avenue. Those buried now in Glenwood Cemetery include Frank Terry, who was originally interred on the plantation in 1862 after his death in the Civil War. William J. Kyle took over management of Oakland after Terry's death, and he himself passed away in January 1864. Kyle is buried in the Sandy Point Cemetery in Brazoria County near Rosharon at 29°22′34.75″N, 95°29′5.60″W. Oakland was renamed Sugar Land sometime after Kyle's death, as his will calls the plantation Oakland. R. M. Armstrong, *Sugar Land, Texas and the Imperial Sugar Company* (Houston: D. Armstrong & Co. 1991), 15–17; Fort Bend County Deed Records Book C p.115; 1850 US Census for California; (Austin) *Texas Democrat*, April 21, 1849; A. Russell Buchanan, *David S. Terry of California: Dueling Judge* (San Marino, CA: The Huntington Library), 1956.

25. Mrs. Roberts's account can be found at http://lifeonthebrazosriver.com/Nibbs HouseArticle.pdf (accessed May 10, 2019). The mansion at Walnut Grove deterio-rated and was used to store hay for many years before being razed in the 1970s. The plantation house was in what is now Orchard Lake Estates. Other plantations in the Stafford-Oakland neighborhood included the Henry Dunleavy, Patrick Perry, and F. G. Sonst plantations, all on the M. M. Battle League between Oakland and Walnut Grove, the Dan A. Connor and Randolph Foster plantations on the J. H. Cartwright League near Walnut Grove, the John Thatcher plantation on the E. Alcorn League south-east of Oakland, the Ezekiel Varney plantation on the William Neel League, northeast of Smada, the William Freeman plantation on the Alex Hodges League, immediately northwest of Oakland, and the Ebenezer Cheney plantation on Oyster Creek. The final

plantation in the neighborhood, named Harlem, belonged to William W. McMahon on the William Morton League, southwest of Oakland. The McMahon plantation is now occupied by the Jester State Prison Farm (named the Harlem plantation when purchased by the state of Texas in 1885), *Handbook of Texas Online*, Stephen L. Hardin, "JESTER STATE PRISON FARM," accessed May 10, 2019, http://www.tshaonline.org/handbook/online/articles/acj01. Fort Bend County Tax Records, 1860. For the name of the Harlem plantation, see Fort Bend County Deed Records Deed Book I, pp. 117–118.

26. The Foster plantation was located where the town of Foster, Texas, is now located, in the Foster Creek Estates neighborhood on the east bank of Oyster Creek. The Fulshear plantation was located where the town of Fulshear, Texas, stands today. The Fulshear Black Cemetery at 29°41′17.69″N, 95°54′16.16″W began as the slave cemetery on the Fulshear plantation. The white Fulshear Cemetery is located 1,368 yards to the north. The Lake Hill Plantation was likely located on the banks of Lake Fulshear, just south of the current town of Fulshear at 29°41′10.66″N, 95°53′43.88″W. The mansion was razed in about 1933. Pittsville was located 1.85 miles northwest of the white Fulshear Cemetery, near where the historical marker stands today. Churchill Fulshear Jr. bred racehorses at Churchill Downs, and his pupil, John Huggins, son of the plantation owner, became one of the best horse trainers in the world. The Simonton plantations were located four miles west of Fulshear, where Simonton, Texas, is located now. In addition, L. J. Pool opened a large plantation on the N. F. Roberts League, east of and near Simonton in the late 1850s, near the Pool Hill Cemetery at 29°40′48.18″N, 95°56′41.24″W. The last plantation in the neighborhood was the Edward L. Walker plantation on the E. Latham League, immediately east of Fulshear. *Handbook of Texas Online*, Ann Fears Crawford, "FULSHEAR, TX," accessed May 11, 2019, http://www.tshaonline.org/handbook/online/articles/hlf34; *Handbook of Texas Online*, Sethora West, "PITTSVILLE, TX," accessed May 11, 2019, http://www.tshaonline.org/handbook/online/articles/hxput; "Veteran Trainer John Huggins Dies," *Daily Racing Form* May 11, 1917 at https://drf.uky.edu/catalog/1910s/drf1917051101/drf1917051101_1_2 (accessed May 11, 2019).

27. The Henry Jones plantation is now the George Ranch Historical Park in Fort Bend County. https://www.georgeranch.org/ (accessed May 13, 2019). The Kuykendall, Pettus, and Vail plantations were in what is now the Greatwood neighborhood of Fort Bend County centering on approximately 29°32′59.25″N, 95°41′36.18″W. The Bohannon plantation became the town of Thompson's Texas and is now underneath Smither's Lake in Fort Bend County. *Handbook of Texas Online*, "JONES, HENRY," accessed May 13, 2019, http://www.tshaonline.org/handbook/online/articles/fjo50; *Handbook of Texas Online*, Mark Odintz, "THOMPSONS, TX," accessed May 13, 2019, http://www.tshaonline.org/handbook/online/articles/hlt14.

28. Mirabeau Lamar, who lived in a Greek Revival-style house on the outskirts of Richmond, passed away in 1859 and was buried in the Morton Cemetery. His house still stands at 29°34′36.22″N, 95°45′1.85″W.

29. Mary McAllister Ingram, *Canebrake Settlements: Colonists, Plantations, Churches 1822–1870 Matagorda County, Texas* (Bay City, TX: Lyle Printing, 2006), 33.

30. Ingram, *Canebrake Settlements*, 70–75; The McCormick residence was located at approximately 28°50′50.20″N, 95°40′8.13″W, less than a mile north of the current town

of Sargent, the location of the home of early Anglo colonist George Sargent. *Handbook of Texas Online*, Will Branch, "SARGENT, TX," accessed May 24, 2019, http://www.tshaonline.org/handbook/online/articles/hns21. The Ewing plantation was located at approximately 28°51′39.58″N, 95°40′6.09″W, and the Sanborn plantation at approximately 28°52′14.11″N, 95°40′17.65″W. The village of Cedar Lake grew up on the old Ewing plantation. *Handbook of Texas Online*, Diana J. Kleiner, "CEDAR LAKE, TX," accessed May 25, 2019, http://www.tshaonline.org/handbook/online/articles/hlc15.

31. Margaret Lewis Furse, *The Hawkins Ranch in Texas: From Plantation Times to the Present* (College Station: Texas A&M University Press 2014), 24–25, 31. The Hawkins plantation house was located 327 yards from current F. M. 457 and 20 yards from the east bank of Caney Creek near the village of Hawkinsville at 28°53′9.41″N, 95°40′19.72″W. The Hawkins family cemetery, where James B. Hawkins and his family are buried, is 44 yards west of the house, on the bank of Caney Creek, under a giant pecan tree at 28°53′8.29″N, 95°40′21.97″W. The ruins of the house were razed in 2011, but photographs of the interior, taken in 2008, can be found at http://www.usgenwebsites.org/TXMatagorda/family_hawkins_home2.htm (accessed May 16, 2019).

32. Furse, *The Hawkins Ranch in Texas*, 26. At least one of the slave cabins was still standing on the west side of Caney Creek, in 1975, a mile south of the plantation house. The wooden cabin was thirteen feet by thirty-two feet by thirteen feet high. Gayle Fritz, *Matagorda Bay Area, Texas: A Survey of the Archaeological and Historical Resources* (Austin: Texas Archaeological Survey, The University of Texas at Austin Research Report No. 45, June 1975), 98–99.

33. James B. Hawkins to Dr. William J. Hawkins, January 16, 1847, in the Hawkins Ranch File of Historical Data, as quoted in Furse, *The Hawkins Ranch in Texas*, 29–30. The Hawkins family and descendants maintain this file of primary documents and information at Hawkins Ranch Ltd. 2020 Avenue H Bay City, Texas 77414. A hogshead of sugar in Texas consisted of 450–500 pounds of granulated sugar. In the decade before the Civil War, sugar averaged 11 cents per pound, making a crop of six hundred hogsheads worth potentially as much as $33,000. The sugar mill was located several hundred yards southeast of the plantation house, but no above-ground ruins remain because more than 250,000 bricks were removed to build houses in Bay City or California. Fritz, *Matagorda Bay Area, Texas*, 98–99.

34. James B. Hawkins to John D. Hawkins December 25, 1848, Hawkins Ranch File of Historical Data, as quoted in Furse, *The Hawkins Ranch in Texas*, 30.

35. James D. Hawkins to Sarah Alston, January 12, 1854, Archibald D. Alston Papers, Southern Historical Collection, Wilson Library, University of North Carolina at Chapel Hill, as quoted in Furse, *The Hawkins Ranch of Texas*, 49–51. The Hawkins family and descendants still own and maintain the Lake Austin house, using it for periodic family gatherings. It is located three miles south of Texas State Farm Road 521 at 28°49′37.55″N, 95°47′35.31″W. The Oak trees planted by Mrs. Hawkins, now 167 years old, still stand along both sides of the front walkway leading to the house. Matagorda County Book Committee, *Historic Matagorda County* (Houston: D. Armstrong, 1986), Vol. 1, p. 116. After the Civil War, a small community grew up around the old Hawkins plantation called Hawkinsville. The town site still appears on maps at the intersection of F. M. 457 and 2611, 1,660 yards south of the site of the Hawkins

plantation house at 28°52′22.63″N, 95°40′2.00″W. *Handbook of Texas Online*, Rachel Jenkins, "HAWKINSVILLE, TX," accessed May 16, 2019, http://www.tshaonline.org/handbook/online/articles/hvh34.

36. Ingram, *Canebrake Settlements*, 61–65; the Hebert plantation was located at approximately 28°54′49.66″N, 95°41′9.04″W; The Jones plantation was also located on the Morrison & Cooper League at approximately 28°55′10.45″N, 95°41′29.22″W; the Nancy Thompson plantation was located at approximately 28°55′54.53″N, 95°41′6.66″W.

37. Ingram, *Canebrake Settlements*, 54–56; the Margaret Gibson plantation was located at approximately 28°56′24.68″N, 95°41′41.60″W; The Chinn plantation was near where Farm to Market Road 521 crosses Caney Creek today at 28°56′27.82″N, 95°43′21.34″W.

38. George J. Bowie to Frances Bowie, March 13, 1850, as quoted in Ingram, *Canebrake Settlements*, 57; The Bowie plantation was located near Lake Bowie at 28°56′31.22″N, 95°44′20.73″W. An unknown cemetery near the lake probably belonged to the plantation at 28°56′28.93″N, 95°44′7.30″W. The community of Sugar Land grew up around a plantation store (it is unclear which plantation) where customers approached the store through a lane of cedar trees. Today, the town is known as Cedar Lane, Texas. *Handbook of Texas Online*, Stephen L. Hardin, "CEDAR LANE, TX," accessed May 24, 2019, http://www.tshaonline.org/handbook/online/articles/hnc30.

39. Ingram, *Canebrake Settlements*, 64–65. The Henry Gibson plantation was located at approximately 28°56′39.51″N, 95°45′3.50″W.

40. Ingram, *Canebrake Settlements*, 40–47. Caney Crossing was located at approximately 28°57′39.82″N, 95°47′58.98″W. Ingram, *Canebrake Settlements*, 49–53. The Stewart plantation was located at approximately 28°56′18.06″N, 95°47′38.95″W. The Warren family cemetery is located 125 yards east of Caney Creek at 28°56′35.13″N, 95°47′52.97″W; remnants of the slave quarters include brick cisterns directly across the creek. Five hundred yards northwest of the slave quarters is Mount Pilgrim Missionary Baptist Church, where the enslaved on the nearby plantations gathered to worship before emancipation. The church was formally established in the 1880s. The village of Caney Crossing, three miles west of the Caney Crossing plantation, is now simply named Caney. Williams served as the postmaster at Caney Crossing in the late 1830s and early 1840s. *Handbook of Texas Online*, Stephen L. Hardin, "CANEY, TX (MATAGORDA COUNTY)," accessed May 24, 2019, http://www.tshaonline.org/handbook/online/articles/hlc06.

41. Ingram, *Canebrake Settlements*, 36–37, 49–51. The Thorp plantation was located at 28°56′40.08″N, 95°47′1.97″W on the west bank of Caney Creek. The Sheppard plantation was located at approximately 28°53′18.61″N, 95°48′46.35″W.

42. Ingram, *Canebrake Settlements*, 35–36. The John Gibson plantation was located at approximately 29°1′20.68″N, 95°51′18.53″W. The Talbot plantation was located at approximately 29°0′56.50″N, 95°50′25.47″W. Caney Creek does not flow through the George League, and it is unclear where Rugeley located his plantation.

43. In 1986, descendants of the Hardeman family published a book of letters from the Hardemans between the 1840s and the 1880s titled *The Saga of Caney Creek* (Fresno, CA: Pioneer Publishing, 1986). Edward or Ned Rugeley's plantation also extended onto the Thomas M. Duke and George Freeman Leagues. The village of Sugar Valley, Texas, grew

up around the remnants of the Rugeley sugar fields. Matagorda County Deed Record Book, Vol. I, p.555. The Pearson plantation was located at approximately 29°2′14.08″N, 95°52′0.06″W; the Wiggins plantation at approximately 29°3′0.10″N, 95°51′41.88″W; the Hardeman plantation at approximately 29°3′18.93″N, 95°52′11.44″W; the Ned Rugeley plantation at approximately 29°3′18.83″N, 95°51′6.68″W; and the Irvin Rugeley plantation at approximately 29°3′51.72″N, 95°51′46.99″W. The village of Rugeley grew up between the Ned and Irvin Rugeley plantations. *Handbook of Texas Online*, Rachel Jenkins, "RUGELEY, TX," accessed May 29, 2019, http://www.tshaonline.org/handbook/online/articles/hrr83.

44. The John Rugeley house was located 862 yards southeast of the C. L. Smith house at 29°5′30.97″N, 95°52′17.47″W. The Smith house, a Greek Revival-style home built in 1910, now serves as Caney House Weddings and Events at 7837 Co. Rd 112, Van Vleck, TX 77482. A photograph of the Smith house in *Historic Matagorda County*, Vol. 1, 118, identifies a building in the background as the Ned Rugeley House, but this is highly unlikely as the John Rugeley plantation sat on the Amos Rawls League. The Rugeley slave quarters stood near a probable brickworks on the plantation, 683 yards southeast of the Rugeley residence at 29°5′24.61″N, 95°51′55.24″W. The Rugeley Cemetery is across the creek, at the tip of a "horseshoe" bend in the creek at 29°5′20.34″N, 95°52′10.18″W. The cemetery is 416 yards south of the home site. Author interview and tour of the old plantation site with the property owner, Bill Pendergast, June 19, 2019.

45. As a business partner of James Fannin, John Duncan engaged in the illegal African slave trade from Cuba. In addition to Podo, the other African men enslaved by Duncan included Darda, Byoman, Bion, John, Walowa, Fadara, Bob, Caley, Bato, Joe, and Shade. Podo remained on the land after John Duncan's death, after which he worked for Abel Head "Shanghai" Pierce, the new owner of the land. Tall and imposing, Podo "moved about the [Pierce] ranch with a dignity in keeping with his pastoral people. Taller than Mr. Pierce, carrying a staff even taller than himself, and wearing abbreviated pants in lieu of a breechcloth, Podo would wend his way unhurried over the ranch in contrast to the general bustle found there. He was, however, a source of constant annoyance to John McCroskey, for upon him fell the responsibility of keeping Podo supplied with liquor." There are claims that Podo came from the "Kaffir" tribe of Zululand, South Africa, but this is almost certainly incorrect. Podo was most likely smuggled into Texas by James Fannin in May 1835 and taken away from African Landing by John Duncan, Fannin's business partner, along with thirty-seven or so other Africans. Podo was probably a Yoruba speaker who originated from the collapsing Oyo Empire in what is today western Benin and eastern Nigeria. When the New York, Texas, and Mexican Railroad came through the area in 1900, Shanghai Pierce named a railroad switch for Podo, and a small settlement grew up around the old Duncan residence called Podo. In 1936, the state of Texas placed a centennial marker to John Duncan at his grave. The land is now part of the Runnells-Pierce Ranch. The Texas Centennial marker over Duncan's grave is located at 29°6′52.28″N, 95°54′34.43″W. The marker faces west, away from Caney Creek. One of the crepe myrtles in front of the Duncan house still stands 192 yards southeast of the centennial marker at 29°6′48.98″N, 95°54′29.03″W. The slave quarters were located 1,073 yards to the south at 29°6′23.90″N, 95°54′6.00″W. A brick cistern still marks the location of "Slave Row." Podo's house stood near the old slave quarters, under

a "spreading oak tree." The railroad bridge over the creek, known as "Podo's Bridge," was located at 29°6′42.90″N, 95°53′41.60″W. Old wooden trestles are still in place there. There is also an old sugar kettle still on the property, which is now used as a watering trough for cattle at 29°6′47.01″N, 95°54′3.90″W. The cotton gin was located on the east side of the creek, at approximately 29°7′38.48″N, 95°54′33.46″W. The slave cemetery on the Duncan plantation has been lost, but it is known to have stood 337 yards south of the slave quarters at approximately 29°6′13.97″N, 95°54′8.23″W. 1867 Voter Rolls, Matagorda County; Ingram, *Canebrake Settlements*, 30–31; Chris Emmett *Shanghai Pierce: A Fair Likeness* (Norman: University of Oklahoma Press, 1953), 106–108; *Handbook of Texas Online*, Rachel Jenkins, "PODO, TX," accessed May 26, 2019, http://www.tshaonline.org/handbook/online/articles/hrpbe; Thelma Smith, "Duncan Plantation Influence Continues through the Present," *Bay City Sentinel*, February 28, 2019; Author interview and tour of the Runnells-Pierce Ranch with the owner, John S. Runnells III, June 20, 2019; map of the Duncan property in the possession of John S. Runnells III.

46. The Gordon plantation was located on the Rawls and Stout League north of the Duncan plantation. The slave quarters for the Gordon plantation are clearly marked on an 1880s map, 1,689 yards north of the Duncan home site at 29°7′32.90″N, 95°54′57.44″W. The Matthews plantation was about 2 1/2 miles north of the Gordon plantation, although it is unclear which side of Caney Creek Matthews resided on. The John Walton Brown home sat on the west bank of Caney Creek at 29°11′1.96″N, 95°54′37.10″W. The small settlement that grew up around the plantation received a post office in 1880, which Brown named Pledger in honor of his late wife, Narcissa Pledger, and her family. The Grove Hill Missionary Baptist Church, organized in 1884, served as a school for the African American children on the nearby plantations. The historical marker at the church today is at 29°10′51.54″N, 95°54′26.57″W. Caney Creek does not flow through the Ramsey League, and it is unclear where Ann Eliza Pledger might have located her plantation. *Handbook of Texas Online*, Will Branch, "PLEDGER, TX," accessed May 26, 2019, http://www.tshaonline.org/handbook/online/articles/hlp32.

47. William H. Wharton, the owner of Eagle Island plantation in Brazoria County, died on March 14, 1839, at the age of thirty-six after accidentally shooting himself as he dismounted his horse at the home of his father-in-law, Leonard Groce Bernardo. His brother, John A. Wharton, who fought at San Jacinto, died at the age of thirty-two from fever while serving in the Third Congress of the Republic of Texas on December 17, 1838. *Handbook of Texas Online*, Merle Weir, "WHARTON, WILLIAM HARRIS," accessed May 28, 2019, http://www.tshaonline.org/handbook/online/articles/fwh08; *Handbook of Texas Online*, "WHARTON, JOHN AUSTIN [1806–38]," accessed May 28, 2019, http://www.tshaonline.org/handbook/online/articles/fwh03.

48. Annie Lee Williams, *The History of Wharton County 1846–1961* (Austin, TX: Von Boeckman-Jones Company, 1964), 88. The Cardwell plantation was located near Cardwell Road at 29°12′44.42″N, 95°54′49.54″W. The Galbraith plantation was near the town of Don Tol at 29°13′32.89″N, 95°54′49.09″W.

49. Williams, *The History of Wharton County*, 88. The site of Preston is now the town of Iago. All that is left of Preston is the Preston Cemetery, in a cow pasture, about three hundred feet west of FM 1096 at 29°16′45.09″N, 95°57′51.04″W. Lalla Rookh was located at approximately 29°16′47.16″N, 95°57′29.89″W. Bear Camp occupied the "northern

half of Boling, all the way to the Needville Highway," at approximately 29°16′0.62″N, 95°56′35.80″W. Streets in Boling are named Lalla Rookh, Stith, and Alexander.

50. Other than placing the plantations on the league, the exact locations are unclear.

51. Calloway was apparently the matriarch of a large clan of Calloways who came from Alabama, four of whom counted themselves as enslavers in 1860. 1860 Slave Schedule, Wharton County, 1860 Census. The exact location of the plantations on the Parker League is unclear.

52. Lawson's Corner is now known as the town of Burr, Texas, in honor of Burr Albert Harrison at 29°18′29.26″N, 96°0′27.68″W. *Handbook of Texas Online*, Claudia Hazlewood, "BURR, TX," accessed May 26, 2019, http://www.tshaonline.org/handbook/online/articles/hrb68. Two other planters, W. C. Brooks and W. H. Davis, also apparently had plantations along Caney Creek, but the author could not find the exact location of their landholdings or residences. Brooks enslaved thirty-five people, while Davis enslaved fifty-nine. See 1860 Slave Schedule, Wharton County, 1860 Census. It also appears that a man named Booth, a stock driver who enslaved seventy-four African Americans in 1860, may also have raised cotton on some land owned by Burr Harrison, as he is listed in Harrison's household in 1860. Booth reported 550 improved acres and 300 bales of cotton on the 1860 Agricultural Census of Wharton County. Booth is listed with $30,000 in his personal estate on the census but withno real estate.

53. The Wharton City Cemetery is located at 29°18′38.77″N, 96°5′30.47″W. The Anderson plantation was approximately 2,450 yards east of the city cemetery along Caney Creek. The locations of the other three plantations on the Kincheloe League are unclear. The only plantation in Wharton County that stood isolated was the Shadrach Cryer plantation, with twenty-eight enslaved African Americans, on the Sylvanius Castleman League, on the east bank of the Colorado, roughly nine miles south of the city of Wharton. *Handbook of Texas Online*, Ray Spitzenberger, "WHARTON, TX," accessed May 30, 2019, http://www.tshaonline.org/handbook/online/articles/hfw01.

54. Albert Clinton Horton served as the first lieutenant governor of the state of Texas, and he was the largest enslaver in the county. The Horton Cemetery is located at 29°18′40.32″N, 96°4′31.82″W. The Sycamore Grove house stood along Caney Creek, 600 yards southeast of the cemetery at 29°18′30.10″N, 96°4′48.01″W near the historical marker to Albert Clinton Horton in what is now a residential subdivision of Wharton. The historical marker is in the rear of the house at 324 Croom Street, Wharton. The Horton residence was razed in 1960, at the same time the house on Croom Street was built. Pulitzer Prize-winning playwright and author Horton Foote grew up in Wharton and twice visited the home of his great-great-grandfather at Sycamore Grove. Horton Foote, *Farewell: A Memoir of a Texas Childhood* (New York: Scribner, 1999), 35–36; Williams *The History of Wharton County*, 88; *Handbook of Texas Online*, Matthew Ellenberger, "HORTON, ALBERT CLINTON," accessed May 30, 2019, http://www.tshaonline.org/handbook/online/articles/fho62.

55. George Quinan, who began his career by serving as a clerk for R. & D. G. Mills in Brazoria, then studied law and served for many years as a Texas attorney and jurist. He was a founding member of the Texas Bar Association and delivered the dedication speech for the new Texas State Capitol in Austin in 1885. Quinan is buried on his plantation, although the exact location of neither his grave nor the nearby slave cemetery

could be determined. The village of Peach Creek eventually gave way to the village of Quinan (founded in 1872), four miles north of Quinan's residence. Ten years later, the town of Hungerford replaced Quinan. There is a historical marker at the site of Quinan at 29°23′56.20″N, 96°4′37.66″W. The middle of the Peach Creek neighborhood, on the Kincheloe League, was centered on 29°22′8.97″N, 96°4′33.32″W. The Hudgins plantations, on the Jackson League, were located near 29°21′58.57″N, 96°6′8.22″W; the Crisp plantation, on the Phillips League, near 29°21′29.36″N, 96°3′42.93″W; and the Sorrell plantation in the vicinity of 29°22′30.51″N, 96°6′56.57″W. *Handbook of Texas Online*, Merle R. Hudgins, "PEACH CREEK, TX (WHARTON COUNTY)," accessed June 1, 2019, http://www.tshaonline.org/handbook/online/articles/hvp23; *Handbook of Texas Online*, Merle R. Hudgins, "QUINAN, GEORGE E.," accessed June 01, 2019; http://www.tshaonline.org/handbook/online/articles/fqu10; Williams, *History of Wharton County*, 214, 88.

56. Williams, *History of Wharton County*, 89. The location of the Jackson residence at Fleetwood is unclear, but Valhalla lay at 29°20′55.78″N, 96°6′34.21″W, along Old Bolton Place Road.

57. Williams, *History of Wharton County*, 89. Gordon most likely located his residence along Caney Creek, a little less than 2 miles east of the Colorado. There are two Robert Kuykendall Leagues in the Glen Flora neighborhood, one on the west side of the Colorado, and one on the east. The Robert Kuykendall League owned by Gordon is Abstract 39 on the west side of the river. Many of the other plantations in the neighborhood were located on the Robert Kuykendall League Abstract 40, on the east side of the river.

58. The Glen Flora House, designated a Texas historic landmark in 1967, still stands, along with a historical marker, on FM 640 at 29°21′9.23″N, 96°10′21.91″W. Williams, *History of Wharton County*, 224; Application for Historical Marker at Glen Flora at https://texashistory.unt.edu/ark:/67531/metapth477863/m1/ (accessed June 2, 2019). The town of Glen Flora, founded in the 1890s, is 1.34 miles southwest of the home site. *Handbook of Texas Online*, Merle R. Hudgins, "GLEN FLORA, TX," accessed June 01, 2019, http://www.tshaonline.org/handbook/online/articles/hlg42.

59. The Sanford, Thompson, Walker, and Williams plantations existed on the Robert Kuykendall League Abstract 40, on the east side of the Colorado, in the vicinity of what is now the town of Glen Flora.

60. *Handbook of Texas Online*, "CLARK, JOHN C.," accessed June 2, 2019, http://www.tshaonline.org/handbook/online/articles/fcl09. John C. Clark Probate Records, Wharton County Probate Records Vol. A-C2, pp. 458–467. Even though Clark's estate amounted to more than $478,000, he always lived in the same simple log cabin that he first built when he moved onto his league in 1824.

61. *Handbook of Texas Online*, Joe B. Frantz, "BORDEN, GAIL, JR.," accessed June 2, 2019, http://www.tshaonline.org/handbook/online/articles/fbo24. *Handbook of Texas Online*, Vernon P. Crockett, "MERCER, ELI," accessed June 2, 2019, http://www.tshaonline.org/handbook/online/articles/fme24. This is the same Gail Borden who invented condensed milk.

62. *Handbook of Texas Online*, Thomas W. Cutrer, "HEARD, WILLIAM JONES ELLIOTT," accessed June 2, 2019, http://www.tshaonline.org/handbook/online/articles/fhe04. The Heard plantation house still stands at 29°24′18.42″N, 96°14′20.04″W. In

1839, a man named Andrew Northington ran a stagecoach line at Egypt. The Heard and Northington families intermarried, and six generations later, members of the family still live in the original Heard residence at Egypt. The current occupants possess a wealth of historical documents, artifacts, and materials but have fallen on hard economic times. If Egypt is not preserved soon, all the materials, relics, artifacts, and the house might be lost to posterity permanently. There is also a slave cabin still standing behind the Heard residence. It is one of only two extant slave cabins, brick or wood, in the Texas lowcountry to the author's knowledge. The other cabin is the Sweeney-Waddy log cabin in old East Columbia in Brazoria County at 29°8′24.82″N, 95°37′0.93″W. The white cemetery at Egypt was located 342 yards southeast of the house at 29°24′12.74″N, 96°14′10.32″W. The slave cemetery is located 235 yards southwest of the house at 29°24′17.49″N, 96°14′27.68″W. *Handbook of Texas Online*, Barbara L. Young, "EGYPT, TX (WHARTON COUNTY)," accessed June 2, 2019, http://www.tshaonline.org/hand book/online/articles/hne08.

63. The exact locations of these last four plantations are unclear.

Chapter 6

1. Edwin Waller to Robert Mills, February 26, 1840, Brazoria County Deed Book B, Volume A, p. 237.

2. The study of capitalism and slavery has received renewed interest from historians in the last decade and is a vibrant and growing field of scholarship. The classic study is Eric Williams, *Capitalism and Slavery* (Chapel Hill: University of North Carolina Press, 1944). More recently, Edward E. Baptist in *The Half Has Never Been Told: Slavery and the Making of American Capitalism* (New York: Basic Books, 2014) makes a compelling case for slavery as the foundation of American capitalism. Joining Baptist is Calvin Schermerhorn's *The Business of Slavery and the Rise of American Capitalism, 1815–1850* (New Haven, CT: Yale University Press, 2015). Other notable contributions to this field include Sven Beckert and Seth Rockman (eds.), *Slavery's Capitalism: A New History of American Economic Development* (Philadelphia: University of Pennsylvania Press, 2016); Gavin Wright, *Slavery and American Economic Development* (Baton Rouge: Louisiana State University Press, 2006); Kathleen M. Hilliard, *Masters, Slaves, and Exchange: Power's Purchase in the Old South* (New York: Cambridge University Press, 2014); Caitlin Rosenthall, *Accounting for Slavery: Masters and Management* (Cambridge. MA: Harvard University Press, 2018); Daina Ramey Berry, *The Price for Their Pound of Flesh: The Value of the Enslaved, From Womb to Grave, in the Building of a Nation* (Boston: Beacon Press, 2017); and Jeff Forret and Christine E. Sears (eds.), *New Directions in Slavery Studies: Commodification, Community, and Comparison* (Baton Rouge: Louisiana State University Press, 2015). Antebellum Texas has never received scholarly coverage in the context of this growing literature on capitalism and slavery.

3. Although these banks allowed slavery and agriculture to flourish in the lowcountry, they failed to attract outside capital or international investors, limiting economic development to slavery and agriculture before the Civil War. Enslavers constructed railroads and canals around Houston solely for the purpose of more expeditiously

transporting their crops to market. See Suzanne Lynn Summers, "The Role of Merchants in Promoting Economic Development in the Houston-Galveston Region, 1836–1860" (PhD dissertation, University of Texas at Austin, 1996).

4. Earl Wesley Fornell, *The Galveston Era: The Texas Crescent on the Eve of Secession* (Austin: University of Texas Press, 1961), 39–50; Avery Luvere Carlson, *A Banking History of Texas 1835–1929* (Rockport, TX: Copano Bay Press, 2007), 25–34. In speaking to the importance of the banking conducted by the Commercial and Agricultural Bank and the firm of R. & D. G. Mils, Judge James Bell of the Texas Supreme Court noted: "The commission business is the creature of agriculture and commerce, and has grown up in all the great centers of trade throughout the United States. The commission merchant finds his proper and necessary place between the farmer or planter . . . and those by whom the productions of the earth are manufactured or consumed." *Robert Mills v. Alexander S. Johnston and Another* (1859). *Reports of Cases Argued and Decided in the Supreme Court of the State of Texas* (Philadelphia: Kay & Brother, 1860), Vol. 23, p. 324.

5. Fornell, *The Galveston Era*, 45–50; Carlson, *A Banking History of Texas*, 36–37. Bynum plantation was located where the Bar X Ranch Subdivision stands now in Brazoria County. The chimneys from the sugar mill there still stand in a public park. Robert Mills's homesite in Galveston is now Garten Verein and Kempner Park off Avenue O. Brazosport Archaeological Society, "Bynum Plantation," http://lifeonthebrazosriver.com/Bynum-Plantation.pdf (accessed July 27, 2019).

6. Fornell, *The Galveston Era*, 51–57. After the Commercial and Agricultural Bank failed, its business passed to Ball, Hutchings & Company, the firm founded by John Hutchings, John Sealy, and George Ball. The institution was known as the First Hutchings Sealy National Bank, but in 1988 the bank failed, and Bank of America acquired the business. https://research.fdic.gov/bankfind/detail.html?bank=3209&name=First+Hutchings-Sealy+National+Bank_8 (accessed July 27, 2019). The relevant court cases are *Commercial and Agricultural Bank v. Simon L. Jones*. 18 Texas (1857), *R. & D. G. Mills and Others v. The State of Texas*. 23 Texas (1859), *Samuel Mav Williams and Others v. The State of Texas*, 23 Texas 264 (1859), *State of Texas v. Samuel May Williams and Others*, 8 Texas 255 (1852), and *Robert Mills v. Alexander S. Johnston and Another*, 23 Texas (1859).

7. Ralph A. Wooster, "Notes on Texas' Largest Slaveholders, 1860," *The Southwestern Historical Quarterly*, Vol. 65, No. 1 (July 1961), 72–79; 1860 US Census for Brazoria and Galveston Counties, 1860 Tax Rolls for Brazoria and Galveston Counties. *Handbook of Texas Online*, Marie Beth Jones, "MILLS, ROBERT," accessed July 28, 2019, http://www.tshaonline.org/handbook/online/articles/fmi39. *Handbook of Texas Online*, René Harris, "MILLS, DAVID GRAHAM," accessed July 28, 2019, http://www.tshaonline.org/handbook/online/articles/fmi64.

8. Fornell, *The Galveston Era*, 49–50; *Houston Telegraph*, October 19 and 21, 1857; *Galveston Daily News*, October 20, 1857. Margaret Swett Henson, *Samuel May Williams: Early Texas Entrepreneur* (College Station: Texas A&M University Press, 1976), 162.

9. J. D. B. DeBow *Debow's Review, Agricultural, Commercial, Industrial Progress and Resources* (New Orleans, LA), Vol. 4, No. 3, (1847), pp. 325. 1850 and 1860 Agricultural Censuses of the United States.

10. J. D. Waters to W. Richardson dated "Arcola," July 13, 1858, in the 1859 *Texas Almanac*, pp. 77–80; for the price of cotton, costs of shipping and the weight of cotton bales, see Richard G. Lowe and Randolph B. Campbell, *Planters and Plain Folk: Agriculture in Antebellum Texas* (Dallas: Southern Methodist University Press, 1987), 164.

11. J. D. Waters to W. Richardson dated "Arcola," July 13, 1858, in the 1859 *Texas Almanac*, pp. 77–80; J. D. B. DeBow, *Debow's Review, Agricultural, Commercial, Industrial Progress and Resources* (New Orleans, LA), Vol. 4, No. 3, (1847), pp. 325; P. A. Champomier, *Statement of the Sugar Crop Made in Louisiana in 1851–52, 1852–53, 1853–54, 1854–55, 1855–56, 1856–57, 1857–58, and 1858–59* (Cook, Young, and Co., 1852–1858). Champomier included the sugar production statistics for Texas for these years as well. The 1850 and 1860 Agricultural Censuses of the United States.

12. For an example of enslavers using cattle to satisfy debts, see Joseph Kuykendall to James F. Perry, April 28, 1835, in Eugene C. Barker (ed.), *The Austin Papers*, October 1834–January 1837, Vol. III (Austin: University of Texas Press, 1924), 67; Cummins, *Emily Austin of Texas*, 196. Sam Jones Washington was 88 when the Works Progress Administration (WPA) interviewer recorded his story in 1936. Washington worked as a cowboy until 1868 and then farmed until 1905. At that time, he went to work in the meatpacking plant at Fort Worth. When the interviewer found him, he was living at 3520 Columbus Avenue, Fort Worth. WPA, *Slave Narratives: A Folk History of the United States from Interviews with Former Slaves* (Washington, DC: Government Printing Office, 1941), Vol. 16, Texas Narratives, Part 4, pp. 138–140; tax rolls of Brazoria, Fort Bend, Matagorda, and Wharton Counties. The fact that cattle already existed as an industry before the Civil War allowed for the smooth transition to a reliance on bovine after abolition in much of the Texas lowcountry.

13. 1850 and 1860 Agricultural Censuses of the United States and the Tax Rolls of Brazoria, Fort Bend, Matagorda, and Wharton Counties.

14. "Sugar Culture in Texas," in J. D. B. DeBow, *Industrial Resources of the Southern and Western States* (New Orleans, 1853), 284–285. Champomier, *Statement of the Sugar Crop Made in Louisiana in 1852–53*, 193. *The Texas Planter* (Columbia), January 24, 1856. Even excluding the cost of feeding and housing enslaved persons, which would amount to approximately $17.50 per year per person, a 41 percent profit in one year represented a substantial return on investment.

15. The data in this section come from a database of 964 enslaved persons in the four counties of the Texas lowcountry compiled by the author from wills, probates, and deeds titled "The Enslaved of the Lowcountry." The numbers referenced in this section refer to the monetary amounts adjusted for the 1860 Consumer Price Index mostly from appraisals. The national averages and age groupings come from Daina Ramey Berry, *The Price for Their Pound of Flesh: The Value of the Enslaved, from Womb to Grave, in the Building of a Nation* (Boston: Beacon Press, 2017).

16. Lundberg "The Enslaved of the Lowcountry"; Berry *The Price for Their Pound of Flesh*, 33.

17. Lundberg "The Enslaved of the Lowcountry"; Berry *The Price for Their Pound of Flesh*, 58.

18. Lundberg, "The Enslaved of the Lowcountry"; Berry, *The Price for Their Pound of Flesh*, 91.

19. Lundberg, "The Enslaved of the Lowcountry"; Berry, *The Price for Their Pound of Flesh*, 129.

20. Lundberg "The Enslaved of the Lowcountry."

21. *The Federal Writers Project Slave Narratives A Folk History of Slavery in the United States from Interviews with Former Slaves*, Vol. 16: Texas Narratives, pt. 4, p. 138 (Washington, DC), Vol. 16, pt. 2, pp. 253 (Kelly), and Vol. 16, pt. 2, p. 42 (Ford.) Scholars have spent a great deal of time on the idea of slave "breeding." In the article "The Slave Breeding Hypothesis," Randolph Campbell and Richard Lowe concluded that "[t]here is little or no documentary evidence of such 'slave breeding,' so conclusive proof of the idea has been impossible." The authors determined that demographic evidence did not support the idea of forced procreation either, but the anecdotal evidence from the slave narratives in the Texas lowcountry defy these conclusions and point to the fact that, at least in this region of Texas, enslavers forced the enslaved to procreate, denying them their last shred of humanity. Randolph Campbell and Richard Lowe, "The Slave Breeding Hypothesis: A Demographic Comment on the 'Buying,' and 'Selling' States," *The Journal of Southern History*, Vol. 42, No. 3 (August 1976), pp. 401–412.

22. John T. Bolton Papers, Dolph Briscoe Center for American History, The University of Texas at Austin. *Slave Narratives*, Vol. 16, pt. 2, p. 42 (Ford), Series 2, Vol. 3, p. 719 (Anthony). For more on the practice of whipping, see Edward Baptist, *The Half Has Never Been Told: Slavery and the Making of American Capitalism* (New York: Basic Books, 2014), 131–134. The detailed daily logs kept by overseers speak to the terrible precision with which enslavers extracted every possible ounce of profit from the bodies and labor of the enslaved.

23. Galveston County Deed Books, Volume C, p. 137.

24. See Galveston County Deed Book C, pp. 33, 430, and 370 for bills of sale on slaves and H pgs. 584 and 165 for the prices on town lots and houses. Bonnie Martin, "Slavery's Invisible Engine: Mortgaging Human Property," *The Journal of Southern History*, Vol. 76, No. 4 (November 2010), pp. 817–866.

25. *Tilley v. Scranton* (16 Texas 183), 1856.

26. *Brown v. McNeel* April 22, 1851. Accession: #21585114 Records of the District Court for the First Judicial District of Texas, Brazoria County Courthouse, Angleton, Texas. The most comprehensive treatment of the laws regarding slavery in Texas remains Randolph B. Campbell (ed.), William P. Pugsley and Marilyn R. Duncan (comps.), *The Laws of Slavery in Texas* (Austin: University of Texas Press, 2010).

27. Allan D. Meyers, "Brazos Canal: Early Intracoastal Navigation in Texas," *The Southwestern Historical Quarterly*, Vol. 103, No. 2 (October 1999), pp. 174–189. The remains of the Brazos Canal are still clearly visible through the city of Lake Jackson. There is a historical marker on Crepe Myrtle Street at 29°3′25.47″N, 95°25′54.32″W marking the old waterway. The so-called slave ditch serves the city of Lake Jackson as a drainage ditch today. Although Meyers speculates that Irish laborers may have been hired to dig the canal, this seems unlikely. It seems more likely that Jackson, Hill, and Perry would have detailed some of the enslaved persons they possessed to dig the canal.

28. Meyers, "Brazos Canal," 187. The Brazos and Galveston Canal now serves as part of the Gulf Intracoastal Waterway between Brazosport and Drum Bay.

29. P. Briscoe, "The First Texas Railroad," *The Quarterly of the Texas State Historical*

Association, Vol. 7, No. 4 (April 1904), pp. 279–285. The BBB&C Railroad still serves today as the oldest section of the present Southern Pacific Railroad. The slight northward bend in the railroad that passes through Sugar Land, Texas today can still be seen on the map. The proximity of the railroad allowed the Imperial Sugar Company to form so successfully after the Civil War. *Handbook of Texas Online*, George C. Werner, "BUFFALO BAYOU, BRAZOS AND COLORADO RAILWAY," accessed October 2, 2019, http://www.tshaonline.org/handbook/online/articles/eqb16.

30. *Handbook of Texas Online*, George C. Werner, "HOUSTON TAP AND BRAZO RIA RAILWAY," accessed October 2, 2019, http://www.tshaonline.org/handbook/online/articles/eqh13. Andrew Forrest Muir, "The Railroads Come to Houston 1857–1861," *The Southwestern Historical Quarterly*, Vol. 64, No. 1 (July 1960), pp. 42–63.

Chapter 7

1. *Sarah H. Black v. James E. Black*, March 26, 1855, Records of the First Judicial Court of Texas, Brazoria County Courthouse, Angleton, Texas. Born in 1798 in South Carolina, James Elliott Black married 26-year-old Sarah Ann Waddy of Huntsville, Alabama, on September 20, 1837, in Tennessee. (Marriage records state San Antonio, but in her divorce petition, Sarah Black named Tennessee as their place of marriage. It appears that they registered their marriage in San Antonio upon arriving in Texas.) The Blacks moved to Brazoria County in 1838 or 1839. In 1845, James E. Black purchased one thousand acres of land from David McCormick on McCormick's League on the west bank of the San Bernard River between what is now Sweeney and Old Ocean. By 1855, Black also owned seventy enslaved African Americans and a sugar mill on his plantation. McCormick had operated a ferry at an earlier date, and Black continued to operate the ferry, named Black's Ferry, where FM 22, the Damon Black Ferry Road, crosses the San Bernard today at 29°4′42.97″N, 95°40′58.22″W. James E. Black died intestate on March 6, 1858, and Sarah Black, along with James Black's adult children from a previous marriage inherited his estate. He was buried in Columbia Cemetery, West Columbia, Texas. Sarah Black died on May 5, 1864, and was buried in the Black family cemetery on the plantation. The Black cemetery is located on County Road 359, 1.5 miles west of FM 1459 at 29°4′44.56″N, 95°42′34.82″W. The grave has evidently been lost, as there is a memorial stone to Sarah Black in the Munson Cemetery at Bailey's Prairie, Brazoria County. Sarah Black's divorce petition provides a window into white women's role in enslaving. It fits with the patterns identified by Stephanie E. Jones-Rogers in *They Were Her Property: White Women as Slave Owners in the American South* (New Haven, CT: Yale University Press, 2019). The central point of Black's divorce petition was that her husband did not allow her to fully be a "master" to the enslaved people on their plantation. Other litigation in the Texas lowcountry involving interracial relationships includes *Bonds v. Foster*, 36 Texas 68 (1872), in which Leah Foster, the formerly enslaved wife of F. H. Foster of Fort Bend County, successfully sued for ownership of his estate after his death in 1867, based on the fact that he had taken them to Ohio in 1847, freed her and their children, and then legally married her there before moving to Texas, and *Smelser v. State* 31 Texas 95 (1868), in which authorities in Brazoria County fined John Smelser, a former enslaver, $100 for cohabitating with Mary Ann Franks,

an African American woman. Smelser appealed to the Texas Supreme Court, and the court reversed the decision of the lower court on the grounds that the state had proved that the couple lived in the same house but not in the same room. For other examples of complex households created by slavery in Texas and the resulting legal battles, see Dale Baum, *Counterfeit Justice: The Judicial Odyssey of Texas Freedwoman Azeline Hearne* (Baton Rouge: Louisiana State University Press, 2009), and Caleb W. McDaniel, *Sweet Taste of Liberty: A True Story of Slavery and Restitution in America* (New York: Oxford University Press, 2019).

2. Quotations are from Brenda E. Stevenson, "What's Love Got to Do with It? Concubinage and Enslaved Women and Girls in the Antebellum South," *The Journal of African American History*, Vol. 98, No. 1, Special Issue: "Women, Slavery, and the Atlantic World" (Winter 2013), pp. 99–125. For more information on these relationships, see Deborah Gray White, *A'rn't I a Woman: Women and Plantation Slavery* (New York: W. W. Norton, 1985); Darlene Clark Hine, "Rape and the Inner Lives of Black Women in the Middle West," *Signs* 14 (Summer 1989), 912–920; Helene Lecaudey, "Behind the Mask: Ex-Slave Women and Interracial Sexual Relations," in Patricia Morton (ed.), *Discovering the Women in Slavery* (Athens: University of Georgia Press, 1996), 260–277; Catherine Clinton and Michelle Gillespie, (eds.), *The Devil's Lane: Sex and Race in the Early South* (Oxford: Oxford University Press, 1997); Martha Hodes, *White Women, Black Men: Illicit Sex in the Nineteenth Century South* (New Haven, CT: Yale University Press, 1999); and Joshua Rothman, *Notorious in the Neighborhood: Sex and Families across the Color Line in Virginia, 1787–1861* (Chapel Hill: University of North Carolina Press, 2007).

3. Columbus R. Patton to Stephen F. Austin, July 12, 1831, in *The Austin Papers*, The Dolph Briscoe Center for American History, The University of Texas at Austin. William Patton participated in the battles of Velasco and San Jacinto and was head of the detachment that guarded Santa Anna after his capture. *Handbook of Texas Online*, Thomas W. Cutrer, "Patton, William Hester," accessed November 3, 2019, http://www.tshaonline. org/handbook/online/articles/fpa54. Inventory of the estate of John D. Patton, Brazoria County Will Book, Vol. A, pp. 356–357.

4. Answers of A. S. Tyler, March 31, 1857, Probate Case 453, "Columbus R. Patton *non compos mentis*," Brazoria County Courthouse Angleton, Texas. How Tyler transferred Rachel to the Pattons is unclear. He may very well have "gifted" her to the family.

5. Martin Varner to Columbus R. Patton Brazoria County Deed Book SR "Spanish," pp. 356 (recording date March 31, 1838). Some dispute has arisen as to whether John D. Patton died in Hopkinsville or Brazoria County. His probate records indicate Hopkinsville, but he is buried in the Patton family cemetery on the edge of the Varner Hogg State Historic Site today. Inventory of the estate of John D. Patton, Brazoria County Will Book, Vol. A, pp. 356–357.

6. Answers of Charles Grimm and A. S. Tyler in Probate Case 453, "Columbus R. Patton ncm," Brazoria County Courthouse, Angleton, Texas. Ardenia is listed on the inventory of John D. Patton's estate at age 16. In his slave narrative, Christopher Anthony talked about his sister "Deenie" who was Charles Patton's "girl." When he died in 1870, Charles Patton left Ardenia, "a freedwoman," $50 in gold and his horse. *Slave Narratives*, Series 2, Vol. 3, p. 719. Will of Charles Fox Patton, April 25, 1870, Probate

Case 904, Brazoria County Will Book, p, 150. The Greek Revival mansion still stands as the Varner-Hogg State Historic Site. The Hoggs stuccoed over the original brickwork sometime in the twentieth century. They also reversed the facing of the house and removed the upstairs porch on both sides of the house.

7. Answers of George O. Jarvis Probate Case 453, "Columbus R. Patton ncm," Brazoria County Courthouse, Angleton, Texas. After the death of William Aldridge, America married Dr. Edward Ragland in 1850 in Victoria, Texas, and she died in 1858.

8. Answers of Isaac Tinsley, Probate Case 453, "Columbus R. Patton ncm," Brazoria County Courthouse, Angleton, Texas.

9. Answers of E. S. Jackson and Charles Grimm, Probate Case 453, "Columbus R. Patton ncm," Brazoria County Courthouse, Angleton, Texas.

10. The nature of Columbus Patton's illness remains unclear, although possible causes include a brain tumor or some neurological illness. Although Patton certainly suffered from an illness, it is unlikely that his family would have petitioned to find him insane if he had remained on good terms with his nephew, Matt, thereby preserving the family line of succession. In his book *Homesteads Ungovernable*, Mark M. Carroll suggests that Charles and Matt entered a conspiracy to have Columbus declared insane, although he presents no evidence for this claim. It would have to be a rather large conspiracy involving the county court and twelve jurors, which seems unlikely. Columbus Patton was unquestionably ill, but the exact nature of his affliction, or its severity, remains unknown. Mark M. Carroll, *Homesteads Ungovernable: Families, Sex, Race, and the Law in Frontier Texas, 1823–1860* (Austin: University of Texas Press, 2001), 52. For the idea of this conspiracy, see also Ann Patton Malone, *Women on the Texas Frontier: A Cross-Cultural Perspective* (El Paso: Texas Western Press, 1983), 43–46.

11. Answers of A. S. Tyler and John Adriance in Probate Case 453, "Columbus R. Patton ncm," Brazoria County Courthouse, Angleton, Texas.

12. Answers of John Minard Probate Case 453, "Columbus R. Patton ncm," Brazoria County Courthouse, Angleton, TX. Why Patton and Murphee acted in November 1854 remains unknown.

13. The jury that found Columbus Patton *non compos mentis* was composed of W. G. Hill, George O. Jarvis, George Rounds, Charles Grimm, James L. Rodgers, C. A. Nash, F. W. T. Harrison, E. T. Burston, J. Spencer, G. L. Nash, J. Thrall, and A. R. Parks. Several of these jurors would later give testimony attesting to Columbus Patton's insanity in the battle over his will in 1857. Probate Case 453, "Columbus R. Patton ncm," Brazoria County Probate Minutes, Vol. F, pp. 599–601. Established in 1821 and opened in 1828, the South Carolina Lunatic Asylum, later renamed the South Carolina State Hospital, was the oldest asylum in the South. http://www.scencyclopedia.org/sce/entries/south-carolina-lunatic-asylum-state-hospital (accessed December 6, 2019). Unfortunately, patient records for this period do not exist, so it is impossible to tell how the doctors treated Columbus Patton or what their diagnosis of his illness was.

14. The original building that housed the asylum, built between 1822 and 1827, now known as the "Mills Building," still stands as a National Historic Landmark at 2100 Bull Street in Columbia. South Carolina State Hospital Superintendent's Reports to the Regents (S 19005), November 18, 1854, and South Carolina State Hospital Admissions

Book (S 190025), November 18, 1854, pp. 37–38, Roll ST835, South Carolina State Archives, Columbia, South Carolina.

15. Brazoria County Will Book, p. 528, expenses against the estate of Columbus R. Patton. Sarah Ford Slave Narrative in Benjamin A. Botkin (ed.), *Slave Narratives: A Folk History of Slavery in the United States from Interviews with Former Slaves* (Washington, DC, 1941), Vol. 16, pt. 2, 41–46.

16. Ebenezer Lutheran Church, located at 1301 Richland Street, Columbia, South Carolina, was founded in 1830 and is still operative, although the current church building was not constructed until 1931. The cemetery is located immediately behind the church. Columbus Patton is buried, apparently in an unmarked grave, immediately adjacent to the building that today houses the South Carolina Republican Party at approximately 34°0′42.92″N, 81°2′6.71″W. South Carolina State Hospital Superintendent's Reports to the Regents (S 19005) October 5, 1856, and South Carolina State Hospital Admissions Book (S 190025), pp. 37–38, Roll ST835, South Carolina State Archives, Columbia, South Carolina.

17. Answers of John Adriance in Probate Case 453: "Columbus R. Patton, ncm," Brazoria County Courthouse, Angleton, TX. Brazoria County Probate Minutes Vol. G, p. 270. E. D. Nash, Henry F. Hanson, and Ammon Underwood testified to the authenticity of the handwriting and signature of Columbus Patton on the will, and Underwood stated that he discovered the will and turned it over to Adriance. Brazoria County Deed Book Vol. H, pp. 215–218. Ammon Underwood, like John Adriance, ran a mercantile business. See *Handbook of Texas Online*, "Underwood, Ammon," accessed December 17, 2019, http://www.tshaonline.org/handbook/online/articles/fun01.

18. Will of Columbus Patton dated June 1, 1853, Probate Case 690, "Columbus R. Patton deceased," Brazoria County Courthouse Angleton, TX. The story in this chapter is largely derived from the two probate cases cited here. In 2013, the Brazoria County Clerk's office clumsily digitized all their probate files and destroyed the original papers. Page numbers and files do not exist in these files. Probate Case 453, opened on the finding of Columbus Patton *non compos mentis*, contains 450 pages, and Probate Case 690, opened after Columbus Patton's death, stretches from 1857 to 1883 and contains 1,382 pages. The origin and fate of Henry Patton remain a mystery. He is listed on the 1850 Census as seven years old born in Germany and living with Columbus Patton. In the 1860 Census, he is listed as seventeen years old and living with Charles Patton. That is the last documented trace of Henry Patton located by the present author. Some scholars have suggested that he may have been the son of Columbus Patton and Rachel, but no proof has been found. Not having children, Columbus Patton may have adopted the orphan of German immigrants. Jacob "Big Jake" Steel sometimes served as an overseer for Patton. If we use the Consumer Price Index, Columbus Patton's estate would amount to $4,970,000 in 2018. John W. Brooks was a young merchant living in Brazoria County, Elisha Pease, a resident of Brazoria County, served as governor of Texas from 1853 to 1857. *Handbook of Texas Online*, Roger A. Griffin, "Pease, Elisha Marshall," accessed December 20, 2019, http://www.tshaonline.org/handbook/online/articles/fpe08. It is abundantly clear that Columbus Patton sat down and wrote out this will after he expelled his nephew from the plantation in 1853.

19. "A Hypothetical Statement of the Case," by the attorney for the heirs in Probate Case 453, "Columbus R. Patton, ncm," Brazoria County Courthouse, Angleton, Texas. A "Gyascutus" is a mythical animal invented by New England lumberjacks in the 1840s. By the 1850s, newspapers defined the hunt for a Gyascutus as referring to any foolish pursuit, which is undoubtedly how it was employed in this testimony. Unfortunately, the witness did not go into detail about the exact specifications of Columbus Patton's machine for constructing fences. *The New England Journal of History*, "Before Big Foot the Mysterious Gyascutus of Vermont," http://www.newenglandhistoricalsociety.com/big-foot-mysterious-gyascutus-vermont/ (accessed December 26, 2019).

20. "A Hypothetical Statement of the Case," by the attorney for the heirs in Probate Case 453, "Columbus R. Patton, ncm," Brazoria County Courthouse, Angleton, Texas.

21. Andrew Jackson Davis, "The Poughkeepsie Seer," born in Orange County, New York, in 1826, is considered the father of the American Spiritualist movement. He published his first volume, *The Principles of Nature, Her Divine Revelation, and a Voice to Mankind*, in 1847, and the 800-page tome immediately caused a stir in American religious circles. It is not difficult to see how Columbus Patton's alleged preaching of Davis's ideas would certainly stand out as eccentric in the religiously conservative plantation society of Brazoria County. For more on Davis and Spiritualism, see Robert W. Delp, "Andrew Jackson Davis: Prophet of American Spiritualism," *Journal of American History*, Vol. 54, No. 1 (June 1967), 43–56.

22. "Statement of the Heirs," March 31, 1857, Probate Case 453, "Columbus R. Patton, ncm," Brazoria County Courthouse, Angleton, Texas.

23. Answers of Charles Grimm in Probate Case 453, "Columbus R. Patton, ncm," Brazoria County Courthouse, Angleton, Texas.

24. Answers of E. S. Jackson and George O. Jarvis in Probate Case 453, "Columbus R. Patton, ncm," Brazoria County Courthouse, Angleton, Texas.

25. Answers of John Adriance in Probate Case 453, "Columbus R. Patton, ncm," Brazoria County Courthouse Angleton, Texas.

26. Answers of Horace Cone in Probate Case 453, "Columbus R. Patton, ncm," Brazoria County Courthouse Angleton, Texas.

27. Brazoria County Probate Minutes Vol. G, p. 309.

28. Brazoria County Deed Book, Vol. H, pp. 215–218.

29. Exhibits submitted to the Brazoria County Court dated December 31, 1858, and December 31, 1859, and statement of John Adriance to the court, January 3, 1859, Probate Case 690, "Columbus R. Patton, deceased," Brazoria County Courthouse, Angleton, TX. The list of goods purchased by Rachel offers its own unique insight into her life. They included "black ribbon, gingham, belt, balance on dress for Eliza, 3 yds trimming, 10 yds. Fig. Muslin, 1 pr. Shoes, 1 fan, 2 edging, 3 yds gingham, 2 yds chambra, 2 sin. Hdkfs, 5 fringe, 1 string beads, 1 pr. Silk cord, 1 pr. Spectacles, 10 yds gingham, 4 yds muslin, 3 bar soap, muslin dress for Dress girl, 1 hoop skirt, 1 pr. Shoes, 1 bot. Cologne, 1 fine dress, 6 yds. Cambric, 4 yds. Silk fringe, 4 sks silk, I pr. Edging. Total $79.65," and "grass skirt; sugar box; 11 yds. Print. . . . 10 yds. Poplin; silk trimming; skeins col. Silk; 4 yds paper cambric . . . 2 ½ lb pul. Sugar; 2 yds paper cambric; 1 work basket; 1 lb dried apples. Total: $20.43." Exhibits presented to the court by John Adriance from Ammon Underwood & Co., 1859 in Probate Case 690.

30. Report of John Adriance to the Brazoria County Court, March 1860, in Probate Case 690, "Columbus R. Patton, deceased," Brazoria County Courthouse, Angleton, Texas. Why Charles Patton chose Cincinnati and why she began using the name Bartlett in Ohio are unknown. See also *Bartlett v. Adriance* Brazoria County Cause 2997 (1870).

31. At the time of the auction, Confederate inflation rates stood at 210 percent. It took $3.10 in Confederate currency to purchase $1 in gold in February 1863. This explains the higher purchase price for the individuals in this auction. Wharton County Probate Minutes, Vol. B, pp. 257–261; Eugene M. Lerner, "Money, Prices, and Wages in the Confederacy, 1861–1865," *Journal of Political Economy*, Vol. 63, No. 1 (February 1955), pp. 20–40. The *Houston Tri-Weekly Telegraph* mentioned the auction as noteworthy, holding it up as "evidence of the confidence of the people in the stability of property" and as "a remarkable sign of the times." The buyers at the auction paid in twelve-month mortgages. The *Houston Tri-Weekly Telegraph*, February 20, 1863.

32. J. H. Kuykendall, "Reminiscences of Early Texans: A Collection from the Austin Papers," *The Quarterly of the Texas State Historical Association*, Vol. 7, No. 1 (July 1903), 29–64; *Handbook of Texas Online*, "CLARK, JOHN C.," accessed January 3, 2020, http://www.tshaonline.org/handbook/online/articles/fcl09; Testimony of Reason Byrne and Clarissa Bird, Trial Transcript of *Clark v. Honey* (Wharton District Court, 1871), Texas Supreme Court Case Files Rehoused Box 26 M-5103, M-6471, M-6614, Texas State Archives and Library Commission, Austin, Texas. Hereafter referred to as *Clark v. Honey* transcript, Texas State Library and Archives Commission (TSLAC); Jason A. Gilmer, *Slavery and Freedom in Texas: Stories from the Courtroom, 1821–1871* (Athens: University Press of Georgia, 2017), 13–52.

33. Testimony of Clarissa Bird, Sharp Jackson, and Pleasant Ballard, *Clark v. Honey* transcript, TSLAC. By the time Clark purchased Sobrina, she already had four children: Dan, Louis, Sethe, and Jane. Testimony of Albert Horton, *Clark v. Honey* transcript, TSLAC. Aunt Clarissa's age is unclear, although she remembered being born in South Carolina, and moving to Alabama and then Texas. At the time she testified in 1871, she was likely ninety years old, although her memory had not failed, judging from her testimony.

34. Testimony of Clarissa Bird and James Montgomery, *Clark v. Honey* transcript, TSLAC.

35. Testimony of Albert Horton and Pleasant Ballard in *Clark v. Honey* transcript, TSLAC. Pleasant Ballard did in fact marry Lourinda, but only after the death of her father.

36. Testimony of David Prophet and Dan Owens, *Clark v. Honey* transcript, TSLAC.

37. Testimony of Reason Byrne and David Prophet, *Clark v. Honey* transcript, TSLAC.

38. Wharton County Probate Minutes Vol. B, pp. 257–261; testimony of Isaac Dennis in *Clark v. Honey* transcript, TSLAC. Witnesses in 1871 testified that Clark had made a will naming his children as his heirs and setting them free, but no one ever found the will.

39. Williams, *The History of Wharton County*, 32–33; Wharton County Probate Minutes Vol. B, pp. 257–261; testimony of Isaac N. Dennis, *Clark v. Honey* transcript, TSLAC. Using the CPI, we see that the wealth generated by the auction of John Clark's estate would have amounted to roughly $9.2 million in 2019. With no heirs, the money

accrued as unclaimed property to the state of Texas. In 1871, Bishop, Lourinda, and Nancy would step forward and sue to claim the money as the rightful heirs of their father. This legal action resulted in the case of *Clark v. Honey* (1871) and the appeal to the Texas Supreme Court in *Honey v. Clark* (1872).

Chapter 8

1. Sarah Ford Slave Narrative in Benjamin A. Botkin (ed.), *Slave Narratives: A Folk History of Slavery in the United States from Interviews with Former Slaves* (Washington, DC, 1941), Vol. 16, pt. 2, 41–46. Sarah Ford was probably born c. 1850, which made her roughly fifteen years old when she was emancipated. On January 31, 1866, Brigadier General Edgar Gregory, Assistant Commissioner of the Bureau of Freedmen, Refugees, and Abandoned Lands wrote to his commander in Washington, Major Oliver O. Howard: "I have the honor to report that Since the 10th of Dec I have visited the Lower Brazos Oyster Creek, Old Caney and Colorado Districts." This probably means that Gregory or one of his aides announced the Emancipation Proclamation in person to the freed people in the lowcountry in late December 1865. Edgar M. Gregory to Oliver O. Howard, January 31, 1866, National Archives Record Group 105, Microfilm Publication M821 Reel 1, pp. 122–125.

2. Sam Jones Washington Narrative in Benjamin A. Botkin (ed.), *Slave Narratives: A Folk History of Slavery in the United States from Interviews with Former Slaves* (Washington, DC, 1941), Vol. 16, pt. 4, pp. 138–140.

3. Most of the Texas runaway slave advertisements can be found in the Texas Runaway Slave Project at https://digital.sfasu.edu/digital/collection/RSP (accessed April 24, 2020).

4. The Houston *Weekly Telegraph*, July 28, 1858.

5. The LaGrange *Texas Monument*, July 14, 1852.

6. Sarah Ford Slave Narrative in Benjamin A. Botkin (ed.), *Slave Narratives: A Folk History of Slavery in the United States from Interviews with Former Slaves* (Washington, DC, 1941), Vol. 16, pt. 2, 41–46.

7. Ann Raney Thomas Coleman Papers, "Reminiscences 1810–1887," Part 1, Book 3, pp. 142–143. Box2Q483, The Dolph Briscoe Center for American History, University of Texas at Austin. At the time she wrote about this story, Ann Thomas and her husband were living on the Brit Bailey Plantation in Brazoria County, which they had purchased after Bailey's death in 1832. The story took place sometime between 1833 and 1836.

8. Ginny McNeil Raska and Mary Lynne Gasaway Hill, *The Uncompromising Diary of Sallie McNeill 1858–1867* (College Station: Texas A&M University Press 2009), 110–111. The man who captured Mose with his pack of dogs was F. M. Snead of Matagorda County, who listed his occupation on the 1860 census as "Negro Catcher." The fifty-one-year-old Snead passed away later in October 1861, leaving a widow, six children, and his most valuable property, a pack of nine "Negro" dogs valued at $535. 1860 United States Census; Matagorda County Probate File for F. M. Sneed Volume S4 1838–1885.

9. James A. Creighton, *A Narrative History of Brazoria County* (Waco: Texian Press, 1975), 263; Allen Andrew Platter, "Educational, Social, and Economic Characteristics of the Plantation Culture of Brazoria County Texas" (Ed.D. Dissertation, University of Houston, 1961), 154. After emancipation, Lew came out of hiding and had a blacksmith

remove the collar. As of 1961, a man named Harold Graves who lived across the San Bernard from the old Mims plantation had "Lew's Horns" sitting in the den of his house. "Lew" was probably Lew Taylor, an African American farm laborer, born in 1835 in Virginia, living in Brazoria County in 1870. 1870 United States Census, Brazoria County.

10. *The Galveston Weekly News*, April 10, 1855; *The Houston Telegraph*, March 13, 1844.

11. Brevard owned 965 acres on the E. Alcorn League in Fort Bend County, in between the Terry and Stafford Plantations, on Oyster Creek near the intersection of Highway 59 and Highway 6 today. Nothing remains of the plantation, with houses and shopping malls now concealing the location of any cemeteries or burials. Adeline Marshall was born c.1860 and was living at 3514 Bastrop Street in Houston, three blocks from Emancipation Park, when the WPA interviewer recorded her account. Fort Bend County Tax Records, 1860; 1930 United States Census; Adeline Marshall slave narrative in Benjamin A. Botkin (ed.), *Slave Narratives: A Folk History of Slavery in the United States from Interviews with Former Slaves* (Washington, DC, 1941), Vol. 16, pt. 3, 45–47.

12. H. Mattison, *Louisa Picquet the Octoroon: Or Inside Views of Southern Domestic Life* (New York: Published by the Author, Nos. 5 & 7 Mercer St. 1861), 23–49. The pamphlet also includes the text of many of the letters exchanged between the mother and daughter.

13. Like Eugene Genovese, I will only claim "that the slaves created impressive norms of family life, including as much of a nuclear family norm as conditions permitted." The reality is that in the Texas lowcountry, enslaved families much more closely mirrored those of the Caribbean sugar colonies or the Louisiana sugar cane parishes due to the skewed sex ratio and higher mortality rate than those in the rest of Texas and the southern United States. Eugene D. Genovese, *Roll Jordan Roll: The World the Slaves Made* (New York: Vintage Books, 1972), 451–452, and John W. Blasingame, *The Slave Community: Plantation Life in the Antebellum South* (Oxford: Oxford University Press, 1972), 450.

14. Ginny McNeil Raska and Mary Lynne Gasaway Hill, *The Uncompromising Diary of Sallie McNeill 1858–1867* (College Station: Texas A&M University Press 2009), 100. For more information on slave marriages, see Tera W. Hunter. *Bound in Wedlock: Slave and Free Black Marriage in the Nineteenth Century* (Cambridge, MA: Harvard University Press, 2017).

15. James Perry Papers, Box 2J42, The Dolph Briscoe Center for American History, The University of Texas at Austin.

16. James A. Creighton A Narrative History of Brazoria County (Waco: Texian Press, 1975), 219; Raska and Hill, *The Uncompromising Diary of Sallie McNeill 1858–1867* (College Station: Texas A&M University Press 2009), 98; Sarah Ford Slave Narrative in Benjamin A. Botkin (ed.), *Slave Narratives: A Folk History of Slavery in the United States from Interviews with Former Slaves* (Washington, DC, 1941), Vol. 16, pt. 2, 41–46.

17. Yvonne Chireau, "Conjure and Christianity in the Nineteenth Century: Religious Elements in African American Magic," *Religion and American Culture: A Journal of Interpretation*, Vol. 7, No, 2 (Summer 1997), 225–246; Sharla M. Fett, *Working Cures: Healing, Health, and Power on Southern Slave Plantations* (Chapel Hill: University of North Carolina Press, 2002), 85.

18. Patsy Moses narrative in Benjamin A. Botkin (ed.), *Slave Narratives: A Folk History of Slavery in the United States from Interviews with Former Slaves* (Washington, DC, 1941), Vol. 16, pt. 3, 142–144. For more on Conjure culture, see Yvonne Chireau, "The Uses of the Supernatural: Toward a History of Black Women's Magical Practices," in Susan Juster and Lisa McFarlane (eds.), *A Mighty Baptism: Race, Gender, and the Creation of American Protestantism* (Ithaca, NY: Cornell University Press, 1996), 171–188, and Yvonne Chireau, *Black Magic: Religion and the African American Conjuring Tradition* (Berkeley: University of California Press, 2003). Archaeologists have also uncovered evidence of Conjuring in a slave cabin at the Levi Jordan plantation in Brazoria County. See Kenneth L. Brown, "Material Culture and Community Structure: The Slave and Tennant Community at Levi Jordan's Plantation, 1848–1892," in Larry E. Hudson Jr. (ed.), *Working toward Freedom: Slave Society and Domestic Economy in the American South* (Rochester, NY: University of Rochester Press, 1994), 95–118. The magic and healing traditions of the enslaved of the lowcountry have persisted well into the twenty-first century. A cosmogram drawn in chalk in the middle of the intersection of Andrews and Wilsons Streets in the Fourth Ward in Houston during a Juneteenth celebration in 2007 is an almost exact match for the healer's cosmogram discovered at the Levi Jordan place. See Carol McDavid, Rachel Feit, Kenneth L. Brown, and Fred L. McGhee, "African American Archaeology in Texas: A Planning Document." https://www.thc.texas.gov/public/upload/publications/African-American-Archeology-in-Texas-A-Planning-Document .pdf (accessed June 12, 2020).

19. In 1857, when the fire eater and proslavery advocate Hardin Runnels ran for governor against the more moderate Sam Houston, the lowcountry gave 80 percent of their votes to Runnels, and in 1859 with the same candidates, the region again gave 61 percent of their vote to Runnels. In the pivotal presidential election of 1860, the voters of the region gave 89.4 percent of their vote to John C. Breckenridge over John Bell, and in the vote on secession in 1861, the lowcountry collectively voted 1,505–12 for secession, with Fort Bend County registering no votes against leaving the United States. At the Texas Secession Convention in January 1861, John Rugeley of Matagorda, Frank Terry of Fort Bend, and John A. Wharton of Brazoria represented the region, with all three men voting for secession. Mike Kingston, Sam Attlesey, and Mary G. Crawford (eds.), *The Texas Almanac's Political History of Texas* (Austin: Eakin Press, 1992), 54–57 and 72–75; Harold E. Simpson (ed.), *Texas in the War 1861–1865* (Hillsboro, TX: Hill Junior College Press, 1965), 175–184.

20. *Matagorda Gazette*, August 12, 1860; Raska and Hill, *The Uncompromising Diary of Sallie McNeill 1858–1867* (College Station: Texas A&M University Press 2009), 82, 89; *The Texas State Gazette* August 11, 1860. For more on the Texas Troubles, see Wendell G. Addington, "Slave Insurrections in Texas," in *The Journal of Negro History*, Vol. 35, No. 4 (October 1950), 408–434; Donald E. Reynolds, *Texas Terror: The Slave Insurrection Panic of 1860 and the Secession of the Lower South* (Baton Rouge: Louisiana State University Press, 2007); Walter L. Buenger, *Secession and the Union in Texas* (Austin: University of Texas Press, 1984); Donald E. Reynolds, *Editors Make War: Southern Newspapers in the Secession Crisis* (Nashville: Vanderbilt University Press, 1970); Donald E. Reynolds, "Vigilante Law during the Texas Slave Panic of 1860," in *Locus: An Historical Journal*

of Regional Perspectives 2 (Spring 1990), 259–285; William W. White, "The Texas Slave Insurrection of 1860," in *The Southwestern Historical Quarterly*. Vol. 52 (January 1949).

21. *The Houston Tri-Weekly Telegraph*, September 1, 1863; Philles Thomas narrative in Benjamin A. Botkin (ed.), *Slave Narratives: A Folk History of Slavery in the United States from Interviews with Former Slaves* (Washington, DC, 1941), Vol. 16, pt. 4, 92–94; National Archives Microfilm Series M346, *Confederate Papers Relating to Citizens or Business Firms, Compiled 1874–1899, Documenting the Period 1861—1865*, Roll 1006; F. A. Tankersly, p. 5. For an example of men escaping to US lines, see *The Houston Tri-Weekly Telegraph*, January 18, 1864, in which H. B. Jones of Wharton County seeks two men, Patrick and John, who supposedly made their escape to the Yankees.

22. Edward T. Cotham Jr., *Battle on the Bay: The Civil War Struggle for Galveston* (Austin: University of Texas Press, 1998), 182–185; Robert N. Scott (ed.), *The War of the Rebellion: A Compilation of the Official Records of the Union and Confederate Armies* (Washington, DC: Government Printing Office 1896), Series I, Vol. 48, pt. 2, p. 929. *The Galveston Weekly News*, June 21, 1865. Granger's orders on June 19 are the genesis of the Juneteenth holiday. Local tradition in Galveston holds that Granger read his orders aloud from the balcony of Ashton Villa, the three-story antebellum home of James M. Brown at the corner of Broadway and 24th Street. There is a monument commemorating Juneteenth on the grounds of the house, but there does not appear to be any documentation to support this assertion, or indeed any evidence that Granger ever publicly proclaimed his orders. It is more likely that Granger issued his orders, which circulated through his subordinates and first made their appearance to the public two days later in the Galveston newspapers. Granger's headquarters, the Ostermann House, built in 1857, stood adjacent to John S. Sydnor's slave market between 22nd and 23rd Streets on the Strand, which may have prompted Granger's announcement of the Emancipation Proclamation and freedom. There is a historical marker today in front of the parking lot where the Ostermann House once stood commemorating Juneteenth, which is probably a more appropriate location than Ashton Villa.

23. "An Act to establish a Bureau for the Relief of Freedmen and Refugees," March 3, 1865, *Journal of the United States Senate*, 38th Congress, Session II, Ch. 89, 90, 1865, p. 507; William L. Richter, *Overreached on All Sides: The Freedmen's Bureau Administrators in Texas 1865–1868* (College Station: Texas A&M University Press, 1991), 3–22; Edgar M. Gregory to Oliver O. Howard January 31, 1866, National Archives Record Group 105, Microfilm Publication M821 Reel 1, pp. 122–125.

24. On January 19, 1860, Judge Edward A. Palmer, a native of Virginia who immigrated to Texas in 1846 and served in the Texas Legislature from Houston in the 1850s and then as a district judge beginning in 1860, purchased 640 acres in the southeast corner of the David Bright League in Fort Bend County for $6,000 from J. C. and Bettie Earp. There the twenty-five people he enslaved established a plantation on the east bank of Oyster Creek. Judge Palmer died on January 15, 1862, and his wife, Martha (Branch) Palmer, followed him in death on January 5, 1865, leaving the plantation to their thirteen-year-old daughter Bettie. The other people under the tree that day included Dick, York, Sarah, Elleck, Leroy, Eliza, Tilda, Nelson, Silas, George, Jesse, David, Henry, Ellen, Booker, Caleb, Lewis, Tilda's child, Tony, Tom, Alfred, Betsy, Delphia, and Eliza's

child. The live oak on the Palmer Plantation became known as the Freedom Tree and was preserved in what is now Freedom Tree Park at 4303 Freedom Tree Drive, Missouri City, Texas, 77459. The actual tree is across the street from the park at 29°33'28.51"N, 95°31'41.86"W. The park is in a residential development called Lakeshore Forrest Estates at Lake Olympia. Fort Bend County Deed Book F, p. 219; "Hon. Edward Albert Palmer" in James Terry White, *The National Cyclopædia of American Biography* (New York: J. T. White, 1893), Vol. 8; 1860 and 1870 United States Censuses for Fort Bend and Harris counties; and Harris County Probate Record Vol. L-N 1854–1864, pp. 673–674, 697. The list of the enslaved people comes from the probate record. The story of the Bois d' Arc trees at the Sweeney plantation comes from the Texas Forest Service *Famous Trees of Texas* (College Station: Texas A&M University Press, 1970), 143. In 1970, only one of the two Bois d' Arc trees survived in front of the old Sweeney house, which was in the middle of what is now the city of Old Ocean, Texas. As of 2013, the house and tree still stood on the south side of State Highway 35 at 29°4'49.63"N, 95°45'26.32"W, but in 2014 Phillips 66 purchased the land and bulldozed the house and the tree.

Chapter 9

1. National Archives Microfilm Series M821, roll 32, "Records of the Assistant Commissioner for Texas of the Bureau of Refugees, Freedmen, and Abandoned Lands 1865–1872" and "Miscellaneous Records Relating to Murders and Other Criminal Offenses Committed in Texas 1865–68."

2. The historiography of Reconstruction is extensive, but the first, and in some ways still the most comprehensive, treatment of this pivotal period is *Black Reconstruction in America 1860–1880* by W. E. B. Du Bois (New York: Horace, Harcourt and Brace, 1935). The best modern synthesis of the topic remains Eric Foner's *Reconstruction: America's Unfinished Revolution, 1863–1877* (New York: Harper Collins, 1988). The first history of Reconstruction in Texas was written by a young University of Texas professor, Charles W. Ramsdell, in 1910. Already teaching at UT, Ramsdell completed his PhD in 1910 at Columbia University under William Dunning. Ramsdell, echoing the attitudes of his mentor, published his treatise *Reconstruction in Texas* that same year, in which he portrayed African American voters and white Radical Republicans in Texas as "the rule of a minority, the most ignorant and incapable of her population under the domination of reckless leaders." Not until the 1960s would white scholars begin to challenge Ramsdell and Dunning's assessment. Reconstruction in Texas has received a great deal of attention in the last six decades, with the most notable works being Alwyn Barr, *Reconstruction to Reform: Texas Politics, 1876–1906* (Dallas TX: Southern Methodist University Press, 1971); Carl Moneyhon, *Republicanism in Reconstruction Texas* (College Station: Texas A&M University Press, 1980); Randolph Campbell, *Grass-Roots Reconstruction in Texas 1865–1880* (Baton Rouge: Louisiana State University Press, 1997); Dale Baum, *The Shattering of Texas Unionism: Politics in the Lone Star State during the Reconstruction Era* (Baton Rouge: Louisiana State University Press, 1998), James M. Smallwood, *Time of Hope, Time of Despair: Black Texans during Reconstruction* (Port Washington, NY: Kennikat Press, 1981); James M. Smallwood, Barry A. Crouch, and Larry Peacock *Murder and Mayhem: The War of*

Reconstruction in Texas (College Station: Texas A&M University Press, 2003); Barry A. Crouch, *The Dance of Freedom: Texas and African Americans during Reconstruction* (Austin: University of Texas Press, 2007); and Kenneth W. Howell (ed.), *Still in the Arena of the Civil War.*

3. The history of the Freedmen's Bureau in Texas constitutes an entire subgenre of literature on Reconstruction in the state. Perhaps the best work to date on the role of the bureau in Texas is Christopher B. Bean, *Too Great a Burden to Bear: The Struggle and Failure of the Freedmen's Bureau in Texas* (New York: Fordham University Press, 2016). Other important works include Barry A. Crouch, *The Freedmen's Bureau and Black Texans* (Austin: University of Texas Press, 1992); William L. Richter, *Overreached on All Sides: The Freedmen's Bureau Administrators in Texas 1865–1868* (College Station: Texas A&M University Press, 1991); William L. Richter, *The Army in Texas during Reconstruction 1865–1870* (College Station: Texas A&M University Press, 1987); and Carl Moneyhon, *George T. Ruby: Champion of Equal Rights in Reconstruction Texas* (Fort Worth: Texas Christian University Press, 2020).

4. For the quotations, see Barry A. Crouch, "Hidden Sources of Black History: The Texas Freedmen's Bureau Records as a Case Study," *The Southwestern Historical Quarterly*, Vol. 83, No. 3 (January 1980), 216–217. James Hutchison headed the Columbia office from January 1866 to May 1867. He was replaced by John F. Stokes from May to June 1867, and then by P. F. Duggan from June to October 1867. Duggan was replaced by A. F. N. Rolfe from October to December 1867, and finally Arthur B. Honer commanded the office from January to December 1868. Abner Strobel, in his book *The Old Plantations and Their Owners of Brazoria County Texas*, originally published in 1930, identified Pleasant Grove as the headquarters of what he called the "Negro Bureau." After emancipation, according to Strobel, Leander McNeel would come to West Columbia with his African American coachman driving him and leave town very intoxicated, driving the coach with his driver seated in the carriage, yelling "Bottom Rail on top by God." Alexander Strobel, *The Old Plantations and Their Owners of Brazoria County Texas* (Lake Jackson, TX: Lake Jackson Historical Society, 2006), 24. For the contracts recorded at Columbia, see National Archives and Records Administration, "Records of the Field Offices for the State of Texas, Bureau of Refugees, Freedmen, and Abandoned Lands, 1865–1870," Roll 15 "Register of Contracts, Vol. 79 (1866–1868); see also Sean Kelley, "A Texas Peasantry? Black Smallholders in the Texas Sugar Bowl, 1865–1890," *Slavery and Abolition*, Vol. 28, No. 2 (August 2007), pp. 193–209. Kelley has tabulated the number and nature of the contracts from the Columbia office in table 1 of this article, p. 198. The J. C. Mitchell contract is in NARA, "Records of the Field Offices for the State of Texas," Roll 25, "Contracts, undated."

5. Bean, *Too Great a Burden to Bear*, 189–194; NARA Series M821, roll 15, Texas, Freedmen's Bureau Field Office Records, Register of Complaints (Vol. 80), April 1868–November 1868.

6. John Gorman, "Reconstruction Violence on the Lower Brazos River Valley," in Kenneth W. Howell (ed.), *Still in the Arena of the Civil War*, 387–420; Barry A. Crouch, "A Spirit of Lawlessness: White Violence, Texas Blacks, 1865–1868," *Journal of Social History*, Vol. 18, No. 2 (Winter 1984), 217–232; F. G. Franks to Editor, *Flake's Bulletin*, July 27, 1868, in NARA Series M821, roll 32, "Records of the Assistant Commissioner

for Texas of the Bureau of Refugees, Freedmen, and Abandoned Lands 1865–1872," "Miscellaneous Records Relating to Murders and Other Criminal Offenses Committed in Texas 1865–68." *Flake's Bulletin* was a Galveston newspaper published by Ferdinand Flake, a staunch Unionist. *Handbook of Texas Online*, Randolph Lewis, "Flake, Ferdinand," accessed August 08, 2020, http://www.tshaonline.org/handbook/online/articles/ffl02.

7. NARA Series M821, roll 15, "Texas, Freedmen's Bureau Field Office Records, Register of Complaints (Vol. 80), April 1868–November 1868." Rachel Bartlett v. John Adriance Brazoria County Cause 2997 (1870). Rachel also filed a lawsuit against her neighbor, W. Freund, in 1879 for "erecting a privy" too close to her house. Apparently, the privy blocked the natural light that normally came in through her bedroom window. The jury found in her favor and awarded damages of $25. Cause 3757 *Bartlett v. Freund*, Brazoria County Courthouse. Rachel probably died in 1882 or 1883, as the latter year is when the probate of Columbus Patton's estate was finally closed by the court. *Handbook of Texas Online*, John R. Lundberg, "PATTON, RACHEL," accessed August 8, 2020, http://www.tshaonline.org/handbook/online/articles/fpat1.

8. Randolph Campbell, *Grass-Roots Reconstruction in Texas*, 7–26; William A. Russ Jr., "Radical Disfranchisement in Texas, 1867–1870," *The Southwestern Historical Quarterly*, Vol. 38, No. 1 (July 1934), 40–52.

9. Voter Registration Rolls for Brazoria, Fort Bend, Matagorda, and Wharton counties, *1867 Voter Registration Lists*, Microfilm, 12 rolls, Texas State Library and Archives Commission, Austin, Texas. The numbers of those white men not counted are approximate and come from the 1870 US Census numbers. That census showed 1,573 white men of voting age and 3,461 African Americans.

10. Moneyhon, *Republicanism in Reconstruction Texas*, 61–65; George T. Ruby to Charles Griffin, April 10, 1867, in "Letters Received—Records of the Assistant Commissioner—Texas Bureau of Refugees, Freedmen, and Abandoned Lands," NARA Group 105, MS 821, Roll 7; Carl H. Moneyhon *George T. Ruby: Champion of Equal Rights in Reconstruction Texas* (Fort Worth: Texas Christian University Press, 2020), 83. George Ruby was an African American man born in New York, who grew up in Maine. He settled in Louisiana in 1864 and was employed as a schoolteacher by the Freedmen's Bureau, but he went to Galveston in 1866 after being beaten by a white mob in Louisiana. He helped organize the Union League and the Republican Party in Texas, and later served in the Texas State Senate representing part of the Texas lowcountry. Merline Pitre, "Ruby, George Thompson," *Handbook of Texas Online*, accessed August 29, 2020, https://www.tshaonline.org/handbook/entries/ruby-george-thompson. *Handbook of Texas Online*, published by the Texas State Historical Association. James H. Bell, a white man, was born on his father's plantation at Bell's Landing in 1825. He attended Bardstown College in Kentucky and then Center College, Kentucky. He studied law with William Jack and attended Harvard Law School in 1845. Bell served as associate justice of the Texas Supreme Court from 1858 to 1864, and then as secretary of state to Governor A. J. Hamilton before helping to organize the new Texas Republican Party. Anonymous, "Bell, James Hall," *Handbook of Texas Online*, accessed August 29, 2020, https://www.tshaonline.org/handbook/entries/bell-james-hall. Published by the Texas State Historical Association.

11. The *Tri-Weekly Austin Republican*, October 26, 1867. At least thirty of the delegates to the convention were white, but most of the rest were African American. Both Henry Curtis and Daniel Gregory were listed as "colored voters" in 1867. The *Tri-Weekly Austin Republican* became the party newspaper from 1867 to 1868, only to be replaced by the *Austin Daily Republican* from 1868 to 1870. For the white reaction to the convention, see the *Galveston News*, July 5, 1867.

12. *Journal of the Reconstruction Convention: which met at Austin, Texas. Texas Constitutional Convention (1868–1869)* (Austin: Tracy, Siemering & Co., printers, 1870), 534; Claude Elliott, "Constitutional Convention of 1868–69," *Handbook of Texas Online*, accessed September 1, 2020, https://www.tshaonline.org/handbook/entries/constitutional-convention-of-1868–69. Even though many African American men served as delegates to the meetings of the Texas Republican Party during Reconstruction, few of them served as delegates to the larger conventions.

13. *Proceedings of the Republican State Convention, Assembled at Austin August 12, 1868* (Austin: Printed at the Daily Republican Book and Job Office, 1868), 1–24. Of the lowcountry delegates at the 1868 Republican state convention, Walter Warmly, George Douglass, and Murray Cole were African American.

14. *Journal of the Reconstruction Convention: which met at Austin, Texas. Texas Constitutional Convention (1868–1869)* (Austin: Tracy, Siemering & Co., printers, 1870).

15. Merline Pitre, *Through Many Dangers, Toils and Snares: Black Leadership in Texas, 1868–1898* (College Station: Texas A&M University Press, 2016), 44; J. Mason Brewer, *Negro Legislators of Texas and Their Descendants* (Dallas: Mathis, 1935). A white contemporary wrote that Fort Bend County whites accepted Burton as sheriff and tax collector because of his "character . . . He was always respectful and careful not to annoy or antagonize his white constituents. He had a white deputy who was charged with the duty of arresting all white offenders who must be visited with the displeasure of the law. Although he collected all the County and State taxes no charge of defalcation was ever made against him." Apparently, a man named "Connor" served as Burton's white deputy from 1869 to 1873. Clarence R. Wharton, *History of Fort Bend County* (San Antonio: The Naylor Company, 1939), 181. The Texas lowcountry also produced William A. Price of Matagorda County who became the first African American licensed to practice law in Texas in 1873. He also served as Justice of the Peace in Matagorda County Precinct 2, winning election in 1872 and was elected Fort Bend County Attorney in 1875, becoming the first African American to hold such a post. See John G. Browning and Honorable Carolyn Wright, "And Still He Rose: William A Price, Texas' First Black Judge and the Path to a Civil Rights Milestone," *Journal of the Texas Supreme Court Historical Society*, Vol. 8, No. 2 (Winter 2019), 39–49.

16. Moneyhon, *Republicanism in Reconstruction Texas*, 207–211.

17. The precipitous drop in land value is in line with other slaveholding areas of the South, from a drop of 55 percent in Georgia to 70 percent in Louisiana. Roger L. Ransom and Richard Sutch, *One Kind of Freedom: The Economic Consequences of Emancipation* (Cambridge: Cambridge University Press, 1977), 51. 1870 Tax Rolls for Fort Bend, Matagorda, and Wharton Counties; 1866 Tax Rolls for Brazoria County; 1870 United States Census for Brazoria, Fort Bend, Matagorda, and Wharton Counties. Of

the forty-five real estate owners in 1870, twenty-six of them reported their professions as farmers, sharecroppers, or farm laborers, while the other nineteen reported their occupations as butchers, house carpenters, wood cutters, and the like, indicating that those who worked in the trades probably fared better economically, and probably owned small houses or town lots, than those who engaged in agriculture, where whites remained reticent to sell prime farmland.

18. Moneyhon, *Republicanism in Reconstruction Texas*, 158–164.

19. Moneyhon, *Republicanism in Reconstruction Texas*, 213. The counties included in the Third District were Austin, Bosque, Brazoria, Brazos, Burleson, Falls, Fort Bend, Freestone, Galveston, Grimes, Harris, Hill, Leon, Limestone, McLennan, Madison, Matagorda, Milam, Montgomery, Navarro, Robertson, Walker, Washington, and Wharton. Clark carried a majority of the votes in Brazoria, Falls, Fort Bend, Grimes, Harris, Matagorda, Walker, and Washington Counties. The initial count was 20,270 for Clark, 21,844 for Giddings, and 830 for Stevenson. The lowcountry vote was 2,886 for Clark, 1,739 for Giddings, and 33 for Stevenson.

20. The estimates of voter turnout are based on the 1870 Census. Historians have long suspected that the 1870 Census represented a severe undercount, especially in the South, but this undercount, about 10 percent, was mostly among African Americans. See J. David Hacker, "New Estimates of Census Coverage in the United States, 1850–1930," *Social Science History*, Vol. 37, No. 1 (Spring 2013), pp. 71–100. Notwithstanding any undercount, no logical conclusion from the results in Wharton County point toward anything other than massive voter fraud, without which Clark would have won the election. Historians have focused on areas where Governor Davis and the Republicans alleged fraud but have never compared voter turnout to the vote tallies.

21. *Galveston News*, November 11 and 23, 1871; Moneyhon, *Republicanism in Reconstruction Texas*, 165.

22. C. T. Neu, "Giddings-Clark Election Contest," *Handbook of Texas Online*, accessed September 19, 2020, https://www.tshaonline.org/handbook/entries/giddings-clark-election-contest; Moneyhon, *Republicanism in Reconstruction Texas*, 165–166.

23. F. G. Franks, or Guy Franks, came to Wharton County as a teenager and belonged to a slaveholding family, but after the Civil War he enthusiastically joined the Freedmen's Bureau as a sub-assistant commissioner for Wharton, and later won election to the Texas House of Representatives as a radical Republican, casting one of the first votes to ratify the Fifteenth Amendment. Jason A Gilmer, *Slavery and Freedom in Texas: Stories from the Courtroom, 1821–1871* (Athens: University of Georgia Press, 2017), 27–29.

24. Transcripts of *Clark v. Honey* in the possession of the Texas State Library and Archives Commission.

25. Henry Fleming was a thirty-five-year-old African American man, and the jury may not have included even one white man considering that the population of Wharton County was only 15 percent white at this time. Unfortunately, the story of the Clark children does not have a happy ending. After Isaac Baughman shot and killed Franks in the streets of Wharton in 1874, the children lost their protector and champion. Tilson Barden, a former legal partner of Franks, apparently cheated the heirs out of all but $15,000 of their inheritance. Only Bishop lived into the twentieth century. Transcript of *Clark v. Honey*, TSLAC; Gilmer *Slavery and Freedom in Texas*, 13–52.

26. *Journal of the Senate of Texas during the Session of the Fourteenth Legislature* (Austin: Cardwell & Walker Printers, 1874), 17, 82–83, 87–89. Walter Burton and his wife sometimes paid a high price for their political activism. In response to the Civil Rights Act of 1875, many African American women began demanding equality in public transportation, including accommodations in the ladies' car on trains. Walter Burton's wife was thrown headfirst from a slowly moving train when she refused to leave the ladies' coach in March 1882. Lawrence D. Rice, *The Negro in Texas, 1874–1900* (Baton Rouge: Louisiana State University Press, 1971), 146.

27. Rice, *The Negro in Texas*, 91–92.

Chapter 10

1. These figures come from the 1880 US Agricultural Census for Brazoria, Fort Bend, Matagorda, and Wharton Counties and from random samples of thirty-nine African American farmers from Brazoria County, fifty-nine from Fort Bend County, and thirty-four from Wharton County. For more on African American land owner-ship, see Loren Schweninger, *Black Property Owners in the South 1790–1915* (Urbana: University of Illinois Press, 1997.) and Debra Reid "Furniture Exempt from Seizure: African-American Farm Families and Their Property in Texas 1880s-1930s," *Agricultural History*, Vol. 80, No. 3 (Summer 2006), 336–357. For more information on land ownership in Brazoria County, see Sean Kelley, "A Texas Peasantry? Black Smallholders in the Texas Sugar Bowl 1865–1890," *Slavery and Abolition*, Vol. 28, No. 2 (August 2007), 193–209. Kelley, working from a database of seventy-nine African American landholders, suggests that most African American landholders in Brazoria did not possess enough land to be completely self-sufficient and that African ethnicity may have somehow played a role in land acquisition.

2. 1880 Agricultural Census of Brazoria and Fort Bend Counties; Brazoria County Deed Book D, Vol. M, p. 728; Fort Bend County Deed Book J, p. 532. R & DG Mills filed for bankruptcy in December 1873 in the US District Court for the Southern District of Texas at Galveston. The records of their bankruptcy are in the National Archives and Records Administration RG21, Bankruptcy Case Files, 1867–1878 Case 523, Box 95, Kansas City, Missouri. Robert Mills refused to shield even his elegant antebellum Galveston home from seizure, and a group of German immigrants purchased it in 1876 as a social club. They demolished the old house and built a pavilion that survived the 1900 Galveston Hurricane. It is now Garten Verein and Kempner Park at 2704 Avenue O, Galveston, Texas. Andrew G. Mills Jr. was born in Texas in February 1840 to David G. Mills and an unknown enslaved woman who was probably born in Virginia. He lived on his land in Brazoria County into the 1920s. Although the official biographies of David G. Mills note that he never married, they fail to mention his son. René Harris, "Mills, David Graham," *Handbook of Texas Online*, accessed October 29, 2020, https://www.tshaonline.org/handbook/entries/mills-david-graham.

3. Clarence Wharton states that the three brothers arrived from Alabama and Georgia in 1840 and that T. H. McMahon was in Fort Bend County in 1841 to sign a petition to create the county. William W. McMahon was born c. 1803 in Kentucky, T. H. McMahon was born c. 1818 in Kentucky, and G. W. McMahon was born c. 1823 in Alabama. Mary

McMahon, the wife of William W. McMahon, was born c. 1801 in North Carolina. For the purchase of the plantation, see Fort Bend County Deed Book A, p. 191. *Houston Telegraph*, November 23, 1848. For the name "Harlem," see Fort Bend County Deed Book I, pp. 117–118. US Censuses of Fort Bend County for 1850, 1860, and 1870; Clarence R. Wharton, *History of Fort Bend County* (San Antonio: The Naylor Company, 1939), 87, 120–121. The spelling of the name McMahon changes to McMahan at seemingly random points throughout the records, but McMahon appears to be the original and correct spelling. In addition, Thomas H. McMahon is sometimes referred to as "Thompson."

4. US Censuses of 1870 and 1880, Fort Bend County. For parentage, see *Jenola E. Brooks v. Alice Felch, et al.* Cause 3400, Fort Bend County District Court, 1885; Death Certificate of Sydney J. McMahan October 2, 1939, Houston, Texas. The death certificate incorrectly lists his birthdate as 1872, but he is present on the 1870 census as being born in 1862.

5. For the sale of Harlem, see Fort Bend County Deed Book I, pp. 117–118. On June 1, 1869, T. H. McMahan purchased the 1,546 acres of the "Lum Place" from Milton N. Lum, and then sold part of the land to Emma Jane Smith, who is listed in the deed as a "F.W.C." (Free Woman of Color), on December 15, 1869. Fort Bend County Deed Book I, pp. 161, 467. The 105 acres included the Lum house and improvements. The marriage certificate for the union of William W. McMahon and Emma Jane Smith is dated March 3, 1874, number 1372, and was recorded with the county on March 8, 1874. The couple was married by "Elder Jenkins." Neither partner is listed as "colored," indicating that Emma Jane was also the individual listed as a "mulatto" on the 1870 Census and was passing as white. Although such marriage arrangements were common in Texas during this time, this is the only case of a formalized relationship known to me. See Charles F. Robinson II, "Legislated Love in the Lone Star State: Texas and Miscegenation," *The Southwestern Historical Quarterly*, Vol. 108, No. 1 (July 2004), 65–87. William W. McMahon appears on the Fort Bend County Tax Rolls, paying taxes on the 105 acres from 1874 to 1877, and in 1878 "Mrs. Emma Jane McMahon" was listed as paying the taxes. We know from court filings that both parents, along with Cora and Frank Ross, died before 1880.

6. The Thomas H. McMahon estate appears as Case 705, Galveston Probate Records. For the case of *Guion & Williams v. Beven R. Davis* and the subsequent sale of Harlem to the State of Texas, see Galveston County Deed Book 52, p. 472, and Fort Bend County Deed Book S, p. 36. Although the deed was not recorded with Fort Bend County until September 11, 1886, the deed from the Guion & Williams to the state of Texas is dated August 1, 1884.

7. *Jenola E. Brooks v. Alice Felch, et al.* Cause 3400, Fort Bend County District Court, 1885. For the record of the auction, see Fort Bend County Deed Book S, p. 249. Although the author has not located evidence, it certainly seems that Fort Bend County and/or state of Texas officials either instigated or took advantage of the situation to pry the land from the McMahons to complete their acquisition of Harlem and the Lum Place and displace an influential African American landholder. The auction purchase price is also interesting. During the lawsuit, Millard McMahon alleged that

he had constructed a house worth $100 on the land after the death of his mother. The purchase price of $1,330 could *possibly* take into account the original $1,200 paid by Emma Jane Smith in 1869, the $100 house, and a $30 kickback. Today, the land is the part of the Jester State Prison that lies between Harlem and Jester Roads, where the Carol S. Vance Unit is located. In 1888, Sydney McMahon won election as Justice of the Peace for Fort Bend County Precinct 3 and was one of the officeholders ousted in the Jaybird-Woodpecker War.

8. By the time he died in 1920, Charlie Brown owned an estate worth $50,000, the modern equivalent of roughly $640,000. A historical marker today marks the site of Brown's home at the corner of Brown Street and Brazos Avenue in West Columbia. Brazosport Archaeological Society, "Cedar Brake Plantation John Spencer Dance-John Henry Dance-Charles Brown," http://lifeonthebrazosriver.com/Cedar-Brake .pdf (accessed May 25, 2021). The Texas Legislature passed a resolution honoring the life and accomplishments of Charlie Brown in 2015. *The Houston Chronicle* March 15, 2015 https://www.houstonchronicle.com/news/houston-texas/texas/article/Legislature-honors-ex-slave-who-became-6128028.php (accessed May 25, 2021)

9. Thad Sitton, rev. by Andrea Roberts, Grace Kelly, and Schuyler Carter, "Freedmen's Settlements," *Handbook of Texas Online*, accessed November 20, 2020, https://www.tsha online.org/handbook/entries/freedmens-settlements. Freedom Colonies are a subject in Texas history that has often been overlooked; the two main sources are Thad Sitton and James H. Conrad, *Freedom Colonies: Independent Black Texans in the Time of Jim Crow* (Austin: University of Texas Press, 2005), and the Texas Freedom Colony Project under the direction of Andrea Roberts at http://www.thetexasfreedomcoloniesproject .com (accessed November 20, 2020). The best directory of historical African American churches in Texas is Clyde McQueen, *Black Churches in Texas: A Guide to Historic Congregations* (College Station: Texas A&M University Press, 2000).

10. The exact location of the Lake Jackson community is unknown, but it probably began around the slave quarters of the old Lake Jackson Plantation at 29°3'13.74"N, 95°27'24.20"W. Both True Honor Baptist Church (founded in 1867), and Evergreen Baptist Church (founded in 1872) are located today in Clute on the old Evergreen Plantation, at 703 Lazy Lane and Garland Park Street, respectively. McQueen, *Black Churches in Texas*, 142.

11. According to the official history, Laytonia came about from the Laytonia Land Company, which operated from 1876 to 1879, but the African American settlement there predated and persisted past the dissolution of the company. The town, which is now nonexistent, was located at 29°5'37.53"N, 95°37'10.13"W and is clearly visible on maps of Brazoria County from the 1870s. The three churches are today located in Brazoria, where many of the residents relocated as the town declined over time. White Oak Baptist is located on the east side of the Brazos River from Brazoria on FM 508 at 29°4'38.41"N, 95°32'39.38"W. Hall Chappell Baptist is located at the intersection of Travis and Park Streets in Brazoria, and Ministry of Reconciliation is located at the intersection of Travis and Walnut Streets in Brazoria. Wilhite AME Church is located at the intersection of Camp and Chesnut Streets in Brazoria. Diana J. Kleiner, "Laytonia, TX," *Handbook of Texas Online*, accessed November 20, 2020, https://www.tshaonline

.org/handbook/entries/laytonia-tx; McQueen, *Black Churches in Texas*, 140–141. 1870 US Census, Brazoria County Texas.

12. The Island, or Mound Creek Cemetery, marks the location of the original settlement off County Road 450 at 29°10′30.94″N, 95°41′40.10″W. St. Paul's AME Church is still in existence on FM 1301, 1.69 miles south of the cemetery at 29°9′8.47″N 95°42′16.83″W. Blue Run Baptist Church is located at 200 16th Street, West Columbia. McQueen, *Black Churches in Texas*, 141, 143; Anonymous, "Mound Creek (Fort Bend County)," *Handbook of Texas Online*, accessed November 21, 2020, https://www.tshaonline.org/handbook/entries/mound-creek-fort-bend-county.

13. Green Hill AME Church is located on County Road 26 at 29°14′11.81″N, 95°34′34.66″W. McBeth is located at the intersection of 521 and 44 northwest of Angleton, at 29°12′27.78″N, 95°28′26.43″W. McQueen Black Churches of Texas, 140–144; Diana J. Kleiner, "Green Hill, TX (Brazoria County)," *Handbook of Texas Online*, accessed November 21, 2020, https://www.tshaonline.org/handbook/entries/green-hill-tx-brazoria-county. Although the white community of Anchor is gone, McBeth is still in existence. "McBeth" vertical files of the Brazoria County Historical Museum, Angleton, Texas.

14. Providence Missionary Baptist Church, with accompanying cemetery, is located on County Road 34, west of the town of Chenango at 29°15′11.42″N, 95°28′56.85″W. Bethelder Baptist Church is located on FM 1462 west of Rosharon at 29°21′11.86″N, 95°30′25.39″W. Deacons of Bethelder in 1886 included L. G. Cooper, S. L. Lundy, A. Thomas, D. W. Williams, L. V. Williams, S. W. Williams, and C. J. Williams. Trustees included K. J. Dawson Jr. and R. Godley. Merle Weir, "Chenango, TX," *Handbook of Texas Online*, accessed November 23, 2020, https://www.tshaonline.org/handbook/entries/chenango-tx. McQueen, *Black Churches in Texas*, 140–144.

15. St. Mary's AME cemetery and the original Cedar Grove colony are located at 29°8′59.89″N, 95°48′7.17″W off FM 524 near Danciger. Diana J. Kleiner, "Cedar Grove, TX (Brazoria County)," *Handbook of Texas Online*, accessed November 24, 2020, https://www.tshaonline.org/handbook/entries/cedar-grove-tx-brazoria-county. The church has since relocated to FM 524 at 29°8′25.69″N, 95°48′34.28″W, roughly 1,453 yards south of the cemetery. McQueen, *Black Churches in Texas*, 142.

16. Bethlehem AME Church is located near State Highway 35 just west of Old Ocean at 29°4′28.62″N, 95°46′12.59″W. The Mims community took shape near what is now FM 521 on the west bank of the San Bernard. Diana J. Kleiner, "Mims, TX," *Handbook of Texas Online*, accessed November 24, 2020, https://www.tshaonline.org/handbook/entries/mims-tx. Mims still has a community center, and the Zion Temple AME Church is at 29°0′29.38″N, 95°36′9.20″W. The Zion Temple and Mims Community Cemeteries are located 533 yards to the northeast, on the other side of FM 521, at 29°0′35.97″N, 95°35′51.80″W. Grace United Methodist Church is located on the old Levi Jordan plantation on County Road 316 at 28°59′12.88″N, 95°38′18.58″W, and Magnolia Baptist Church (now Magnolia Bible Church) is located on County Road 809 at 28°59′15.31″N, 95°39′58.36″W. Galilee Baptist Church and its accompanying cemetery are located on the east side of the San Bernard, just northeast of Hinkle's Ferry on County Road 311 at 28°57′57.81″N, 95°32′40.86″W. McQueen, *Black Churches in Texas*, 140–144.

17. Linnville was located on County Road 321 at 28°59′21.26″N, 95°45′44.09″W. Diana J. Kleiner, "Linnville, TX (Brazoria County)," *Handbook of Texas Online*, accessed November 24, 2020, https://www.tshaonline.org/handbook/entries/linnville-tx-brazoria-county. Jerusalem Baptist Church and accompanying cemetery is located on County Road 317 at 28°56′30.82″N, 95°36′59.51″W. St. Paul Missionary Baptist Church is located on County Road 318 at 28°55′47.94″N, 95°37′57.25″W. Diana J. Kleiner, "Jerusalem, TX (Brazoria County)," *Handbook of Texas Online*, accessed November 24, 2020, https://www.tshaonline.org/handbook/entries/jerusalem-tx-brazoria-county. McQueen, *Black Churches in Texas*, 140–144.

18. Arcola was located at 29°29′45.85″N, 95°27′56.82″W. DeWalt was located along Oyster Creek, just north of the old Palmer plantation, at 29°33′22.05″N, 95°33′23.45″W. St. John Missionary Baptist Church still stands, just west of DeWalt, at 29°33′8.44″N, 95°33′49.64″W. Mark Odintz, "Arcola, TX," *Handbook of Texas Online*, accessed December 07, 2020, https://www.tshaonline.org/handbook/entries/arcola-tx; Mark Odintz, "Dewalt, TX," *Handbook of Texas Online*, accessed December 7, 2020, https://www.tshaonline.org/handbook/entries/dewalt-tx.

19. Mount Vernon United Methodist Church is located at 601 Travis Street in Richmond; Mt. Carmel Baptist Church sits at 303 N. 10th Street, and Mt. Vernon Missionary Baptist Church is located at 218 N. 3rd Street in what is now Rosenberg. The Hackworth Colony was located on the Sarah Isaacs League at 29°34′10.42″N, 95°48′53.30″W, and Kendleton is located along US Highway 59 at 29°27′2.48″N, 95°59′41.39″W. In 1973, residents incorporated Kendleton, making it the only freedom colony in the lowcountry to receive formal status as a city. The Henry and Ann Green house, built c. 1870, still stands and has been listed on the National Register of Historic Places (NHRP). The house is located at 29°27′0.45″N, 95°59′39.62″W. See also the NRHP application for the Green house at https://atlas.thc.texas.gov/NR/pdfs/96001016/96001016.pdf (accessed December 7, 2020). Powell Point was located at 29°28′45.73″N, 96°1′21.18″W. Vivian Elizabeth Smyrl, "Kendleton, TX," *Handbook of Texas Online*, accessed December 7, 2020, https://www.tshaonline.org/handbook/entries/kendleton-tx. Vivian Elizabeth Smyrl, "Powell Point, TX," *Handbook of Texas Online*, accessed December 07, 2020, https://www.tshaonline.org/handbook/entries/powell-point-tx.

20. Cedar Lake is located along FM 2611 on the Brazoria-Matagorda County line at 28°54′5.15″N, 95°38′11.46″W, but Bethlehem Christian Church is located at the corner of League Line and Murphy Road to the southwest at 28°52′23.73″N, 95°38′50.71″W, and the church probably more accurately represented the center of the historic settlement. Diana J. Kleiner, "Cedar Lake, TX," *Handbook of Texas Online*, accessed December 8, 2020, https://www.tshaonline.org/handbook/entries/cedar-lake-tx. Cedar Lake is located at the intersection of FM 521 and RM 457 at 28°56′8.64″N, 95°43′47.97″W, and Shiloh Missionary Baptist Church is located on Sydney Lane at 28°56′17.91″N, 95°43′11.85″W. Bell Bottom and St. Mark Missionary Baptist Church are located along Bell Bottom Road at 28°56′10.58″N, 95°41′8.23″W. Stephen L. Hardin, "Cedar Lane, TX," *Handbook of Texas Online*, accessed December 8, 2020, https://www.tshaonline.org/handbook/entries/cedar-lane-tx. Rachel Jenkins, "Bell Bottom, TX," *Handbook of Texas Online*, accessed December 8, 2020, https://www.tshaonline.org/handbook/entries/bell-bottom-tx.

21. Fatima and Odo Vann were both smuggled into Texas by James Fannin in May 1835 and landed at African Landing in Brazoria County. Abram Sheppard was one of Fannin's partners in this smuggling, and in 1849 Sheppard sold his entire plantation and dozens of enslaved people, including Odo and Fatima, to Samuel G. Powell in Matagorda County. The deed lists Odo as twenty-four and Fatima as twenty-one, making them born in 1825 and 1828, respectively, and ages seven and ten in 1835 when captured and taken to Cuba and then Texas. These dates conform more closely to the nature of Fannin's smuggling. Odo and Fatitma were almost certainly Yoruba speakers from the collapsing Oyo Empire in what is today eastern Benin and Western Nigeria. Both Odo and King Van registered to vote in 1867, living on the Powell plantation. The 1870 Census spells Udo's name "Udoo Vann" and lists his age as sixty-one, making his birth year in West Africa approximately 1807. The 1880 Census lists him as "Udo Van," as do legal documents filed in Matagorda County. The 1880 Census marks his birth year as approximately 1800. Fatima, his wife, listed her age as seventy in 1870. Her name appears as "Fatomia" and her birth date as 1795 on the 1880 Census. They both evidently passed away between 1890 and 1900 and are probably buried in the cemetery near Berean Missionary Baptist Church. King Van listed his name as "King Vann" on the 1870 Census and his birth year as 1847, with both of his parents born in Africa. On the 1880 Census, he is listed as "King Van," as he is on other legal documents, and his birthplace is listed as Texas in 1848. Odo and Fatima also had a daughter named Louise who was born on September 15, 1860, and did not die until November 10, 1956. Death certificate of Louise Edison, 161-1-0-1, Bay City Texas, November 18, 1956. The Vann community was located off Powell Road at 28°54′47.04″N, 95°45′55.59″W where the cemetery, previously known as the Buckner's Prairie Cemetery, is now located. Berean Missionary Baptist Church is located on Hawkinsville Road at 28°54′38.01″N, 95°46′21.63″W. Liveoak was located around the Vine Grove Christian Church off FM 2540 at 28°53′55.29″N, 95°48′26.11″W. The Vann Settlement was sometimes also known as simply "Vann," "Vann African," or "King Vann African." Matagorda County Deed Records Vol. 2, p. 10, Vol. 5, p. 293; Matagorda County Deed Records Vol. G, pp. 481–482. Rachel Jenkins, "Vann Settlement, TX," *Handbook of Texas Online*, accessed December 8, 2020, https://www.tshaonline.org/handbook/entries/vann-settlement-tx. Rachel Jenkins, "Liveoak Community, TX," *Handbook of Texas Online*, accessed December 9, 2020, https://www.tshaonline.org/handbook/entries/liveoak-community-tx.

22. Mount Pilgrim Missionary Baptist Church is located off Grisham Road at 28°56′51.04″N, 95°48′4.63″W. Hudgins was located near the Hudgins Cemetery off Hudgins Road at 28°58′38.68″N, 95°49′37.96″W. Rachel Jenkins, "Mount Pilgrim, TX (Matagorda County)," *Handbook of Texas Online*, accessed December 9, 2020, https://www.tshaonline.org/handbook/entries/mount-pilgrim-tx-matagorda-county. Rachel Jenkins, "Hudgins, TX," *Handbook of Texas Online*, accessed December 9, 2020, https://www.tshaonline.org/handbook/entries/hudgins-tx. Freed people also established Mother Zion Missionary Baptist Church in 1887 near Caney Creek, but at some point, the congregation moved to Bay City, where they are located today at 2700 Avenue B, Bay City. McQueen, *Black Churches in Texas*, 162.

23. Podo was located at 29°6′23.90″N, 95°54′6.00″W. For more on Podo, see chapter 5. Grove Hill Missionary Baptist Church still stands at 29°10′51.98″N, 95°54′26.68″W.

See also chapter 5 for the origin of Pledger. Rachel Jenkins, "Grove Hill, TX (Matagorda County)," *Handbook of Texas Online*, accessed December 21, 2020, https://www.tsha online.org/handbook/entries/grove-hill-tx-matagorda-county. After founding Grove Hill, Jack Yates moved to Freedman's Town in Houston's Fourth Ward and founded Antioch Missionary Baptist Church. In 1872, the church, under the leadership of Yates, purchased Emancipation Park, the first public park for African American Houstonians. Yates purchased several lots of land on Andrews Street in Houston and built a house, which still stands, although the house has been moved to Sam Houston Park in Houston. Jack Yates High School in Houston is named in his honor. Olee Yates McCullough, "Yates, John Henry [Jack]," *Handbook of Texas Online*, accessed March 9, 2021, https://www.tshaonline.org/handbook/entries/yates-john-henry-jack.

24. Claudia Hazlewood, "Burr, TX," *Handbook of Texas Online*, accessed December 21, 2020, https://www.tshaonline.org/handbook/entries/burr-tx. Burr was located at approximately 29°18'29.01"N, 96°0'27.33"W. Shiloh Baptist Church is located at 29°15'33.33"N, 95°56'50.44"W. According to tradition, Isam Davenport would get free labor by convicting other African American men of "drunkenness" or "shooting craps," and would sentence them to "ten days hard labor in Isam Davenport's cotton patch." Williams, *The History of Wharton County*, 231.

25. Merle R. Hudgins, "Dinsmore, TX," *Handbook of Texas Online*, accessed December 21, 2020, https://www.tshaonline.org/handbook/entries/dinsmore-tx. Dinsmore was located at 29°19'1.65"N, 96°3'2.97"W.

26. Sorrell was located at 29°20'24.48"N, 96° 9'47.89"W; Diana J. Kleiner, "Sorrelle, TX," *Handbook of Texas Online*, accessed December 22, 2020, https://www.tsha online.org/handbook/entries/sorrelle-tx. Old Jerusalem and the Jerusalem Missionary Baptist Church were located near the cemeteries of those names at 29°23'40.99"N, 96°10'0.81"W (church), and 29°22'52.42"N, 96°10'7.36"W (community). Spanish Camp was located at 29°23'2.63"N, 96°10'44.18"W. Rising Star Baptist Church is located at 29°23'11.63"N, 96°10'36.87"W; Camp Zion Missionary Baptist Church was located at 29°23'18.00"N, 96°11'42.27"W. The church is gone, but the historical marker at the site reads: "The Rev. Hillary Hooks, formerly a slave on the James E. Winston plantation, organized Camp Zion Baptist Church in 1870. Winston granted land to Camp Zion trustees in 1887. A segment of the membership left and organized Rising Star Baptist Church in 1888. The Camp Zion church structure served as a school, a refuge during floods, and as a Red Cross chapter location during World War I. The Camp Zion Community Cemetery was established on land donated by the Duncan family in 1905. In 1998, the Camp Zion and Rising Star Baptist congregations reunited into a single church family, which continues to include descendants of the former slave families who founded the church. Sand Ridge was located just northwest of Egypt at 29°25'5.85"N, 96°15'7.67"W, with the cemetery there located on the north side of FM 102. Elm Grove was located at 29°27'26.65"N, 96°18'37.67"W. Diana J. Kleiner, "Sand Ridge, TX (Wharton County)," *Handbook of Texas Online*, accessed December 22, 2020, https://www.tshaonline.org/handbook/entries/sand-ridge-tx-wharton-county. Diana J. Kleiner, "Elm Grove, TX (Wharton County)," *Handbook of Texas Online*, accessed December 22, 2020, https://www.tshaonline.org/handbook/entries/elm-grove-tx-wharton-county.

27. Convict leasing in Texas has received increased scholarly interest in the recent past. The first full work to consider the topic was Donald R. Walker, *Penology for Profit: A History of the Texas Prison System 1867–1912* (College Station: Texas A&M Press, 1988). Other notable works include Robert Perkinson, *Texas Tough: The Rise of America's Prison Empire* (New York: Picador Press, 2010), and Theresa R. Jach, "'It's Hell in a Texas Pen': Life and Labor in the Texas Prison System 1840–1929" (PhD dissertation, University of Houston, 2009); Thomas Michael Parrish, "'This Species of Slave Labor': The Convict Lease System in Texas 1871–1914" (MA Thesis Baylor University, 1976), and Theresa R. Jach, "Reform versus Reality in the Progressive Era Texas Prison," *Journal of the Gilded Age and Progressive Era* (Vol. 4, No. 1, January 2005), pp. 53–67. See also Reign Clark, Catrina Banks Whitley, Ron Ralph, Helen Graham, Theresa Jach, Abigail Eve Fisher, Valerie Tompkins, Emily van Zanten, and Karissa Basse, "Back to Bondage: Forced Labor in Post Reconstruction Era Texas The Discovery, Exhumation, and Bioarcheological Analysis of Bullhead Convict Labor Camp Cemetery" (41FB355) James Reese Career and Technical Center Campus, 12300 University Boulevard, Sugar Land, Texas (August 2020), https://www.fortbendisd.com/Page/131568 (accessed January 24, 2021). Convict leasing, of course, was not unique to Texas. For a more national treatment, see Douglas A. Blackmon, *Slavery by Another Name: The Re-Enslavement of Black Americans from the Civil War to World War II* (New York: Doubleday Press, 2009), and Michelle Alexander, *The New Jim Crow: Mass Incarceration in the Age of Colorblindness* (New York: The New Press, 2010). Governor Throckmorton, in addressing the state of the penitentiary to the Eleventh Legislature, noted that the prison population had skyrocketed from just 146 to 264 in just a few months, and he suggested a revision of the penal code to change the definitions of grand and petty larceny. The legislature ignored him. *Journal of the House of Representatives, Eleventh Legislature, State of Texas* (Austin: Office of the State Gazette, 1866), 86–87. For the number of prisoners by year and their racial makeup, see Walker, *Penology for Profit*, Tables 1–2, pp. 113–114.

28. Walker, *Penology for Profit*, 19–20. For examples of the suggested segregated role of prisoners by race, see the address of Governor Richard Coke in *Texas Penitentiary Report of the Commission Appointed by the Governor of Texas April 10, 1875 to Investigate the Alleged Mismanagement and Cruel Treatment of the Convicts* (Houston: A. C. Gray, State Printer, 1875), 67.

29. Nathan Patton had close political ties to Governor Davis and served as the preeminent partner in securing the lease for Ward, Dewey & Company. Walker *Penology for Profit*, 28–31.

30. William R. Johnson *A Short History of the Sugar Industry in Texas* (Texas Gulf Coast Historical Publications, Vol. 5, No. 1, April 1961), 39–40.

31. *Texas Penitentiary Report of the Commission Appointed by the Governor of Texas April 10, 1875 to Investigate the Alleged Mismanagement and Cruel Treatment of the Convicts* (Houston: A. C. Gray, State Printer, 1875), 57, 89–90. By this time, Arcola was owned by Thomas W. House of Houston, and in the report he was mistakenly identified as existing in Matagorda County. The other two plantations in Fort Bend County are unknown, but considering that the T. H. McMahon Company was one of the sublessees, it is almost certain that Harlem was one of the unnamed plantations.

32. Clark et al., "Back to Bondage," 180.

33. *Texas Penitentiary Report of the Commission Appointed by the Governor of Texas April 10, 1875*, 104; Clark et al., "Back to Bondage," 183–187.

34. Clark et al., "Back to Bondage," 186–187.

35. Clark et al., "Back to Bondage," 189.

36. Walker *Penology for Profit*, 46–48.

37. Many sources state that L. A. Ellis and Ed Cunningham, both of whom were referred to as "colonel" after the Civil War, met while serving in Hood's Texas Brigade, but that assertion is incorrect. Ellis was the nephew of Richard Ellis, signatory to the Texas Declaration of Independence and resident of Bowie County. It seems likely that L. A. Ellis moved to Bowie County to join some of his family in 1859. Why he joined Scott's Tennessee Battery at Lewisville, Arkansas, just east of Bowie County, remains a mystery. Edward Cunningham made his fortune in cattle after the Civil War before joining Ellis in the partnership. Cunningham's ranch house in Bexar County later became the base hospital at Camp Travis, the World War I era training camp that is now part of Fort Sam Houston. Confederate Compiled Service Records of Edward H. Cunningham and L. A. Ellis in "Compiled Service Records of Confederate General and Staff Officers, and Nonregimental Enlisted Men," National Archives and Records Administration RG 109; 1860 and 1870 Censuses of the United States; R. M. Armstrong *Sugar Land Texas and the Imperial Sugar Company* (Houston: D. Armstrong Co. Inc., 1991), 25–44; Joe E. Ericson, "Ellis, Richard," *Handbook of Texas Online*, accessed February 07, 2021, https://www.tshaonline.org/handbook/entries/ellis-richard.

38. In the records, L. A. Ellis No. 1 refers to the old coffee plantation, and L. A. Ellis No. 2 is Sartartia. M. B. Dunlavy is M. B. Dunleavy of Fort Bend County, and of course David Terry owned the Oakland, later Sugar Land plantation previously owned by his late father, Frank Terry. Quigg and Pendall owned an old sugar plantation in the Cartwright League in Fort Bend County, although which one is unclear. *Biennial Reports of the Directors and Superintendent of the Texas State Penitentiary at Huntsville, Texas with the Report of the Prison Physician, Commencing December 1, A. D. 1878 and Terminating October 31, A. D. 1880* (Galveston: The News Book and Job Office, 1881), 51; Walker, *Penolgy for Profit*, 113–114; for the quotation, see Armstrong *Sugar Land, Texas and the Imperial Sugar Company*, 25.

39. $73,468 in 1883 would equal roughly $1.93 million today. Clarence Wharton, an early historian of Fort Bend County, put it bluntly: "[Cunningham and Ellis's] success was so spectacular that the State decided to embark on the convict farm business." By 1930, the state of Texas owned twelve prison farms, seven of which were in Fort Bend and Brazoria counties. In Brazoria County, the state owned the Clemens, Darrington, Ramsey and Retrieve State Prison Farms on old sugar plantations (see chapter 5). In Fort Bend County, the state owned Harlem, Imperial, and Blue Ridge State Prison Farms. Blue Ridge, owned by the W. Allen Robinson family and worked by enslaved people before emancipation, was located on a small ridge on the north bank of Oyster Creek, just southeast of Missouri City on the Drew League at approximately 29°34′27.67″N, 95°29′38.32″W. Wharton, Wharton's *History of Fort Bend County*, 228; Jach "Reform Versus Reality," 57; Walker, *Penology for Profit*, 97; Clark et al., "Back to Bondage," 195; Armstrong, *Sugar Land, Texas, and the Imperial Sugar Company*, 24–25. The Imperial Sugar Company, built on the backs of enslaved and then imprisoned Af-

rican Americans, is the oldest continuously operating business in Texas and a Fortune 500 Company. Today (in 2021), bags of Imperial Sugar and boxes of Imperial Sugar Cubes ironically bear the phrase "since 1843," the year that the enslaved built the first sugar mill on Samuel May Williams's Oakland Plantation. Diana J. Kleiner, "Imperial Sugar Company," *Handbook of Texas Online*, accessed February 7, 2021, https://www .tshaonline.org/handbook/entries/imperial-sugar-company.

Chapter 11

1. The Vann Massacre has received no scholarly treatment despite its importance and nationwide news coverage it received at the time. Matagorda County Historical Commission, *Historic Matagorda County Vol. 1* (Houston: D. Armstrong Company, 1986), 174; *The Fort Worth Gazette*, September 30, 1887; *The Austin Weekly Statesman*, September 28, 1887; *The Dallas Daily Herald*, September 27, 1887; *The Galveston Daily News*, September 29, 1887; *The Chicago Tribune*, September 27, 1887; *The Champaign Daily Gazette*, September 27, 1887; *The Buffalo Times*. September 27, 1887.

2. For more on the Republican Party and its attitudes toward African American suffrage in this period, see Xi Wang, *The Trial of Democracy: Black Suffrage and Northern Republicans, 1860–1910* (Athens: University of Georgia Press, 1997); Charles W. Calhoun, *Conceiving a New Republic: The Republican Party and the Southern Question, 1869–1900* (Lawrence: University Press of Kansas, 2006); and Thomas Adams Upchurch, *Legislating Racism: The Billion Dollar Congress and the Birth of Jim Crow* (Lexington: University Press of Kentucky, 2004). In terms of the white man's union associations in Texas, only the association in Harrison County, The Citizen's Party, formed in 1878, predated the formation of the white man's unions in the lowcountry. Merlene Pitre *Through Many Dangers, Toils and Snares: Black Leadership in Texas, 1868–1898* (College Station: Texas A&M University Press, 2016), 158–162; Christopher Long, "White Man's Union Associations," *Handbook of Texas Online*, accessed March 10, 2021, https://www.tshaonline.org/handbook/entries/ white-mans-union-associations.

3. In 1884, Texans gave 69 percent of their vote to Cleveland, 225,309 to 93,141. In contrast, the lowcountry gave 77 percent of their vote to Blaine, 3,948 to 1,159; Brazoria County 1,128 to 430; Fort Bend County, 1,588 to 317; Matagorda County, 476–248; and Wharton County, 756 to 164, showing the continued dominance of the African American Republican vote. Mike Kingston, Sam Attlesey, and Mary G. Crawford, *The Texas Almanac's Political History of Texas* (Austin, TX: Eakin Press, 1992), 76–79; Pitre, *Through Many Dangers, Toils and Snares*, 162; Pauline Yelderman, *The Jay Birds of Fort Bend County: A White Man's Union* (Waco: Texian Press, 1979), 60–61; Wharton, *History of Fort Bend County*, 192–193. Benjamin F. Williams, enslaved in Colorado County at emancipation, established the Wesley Methodist Chapel in Austin and became a strident spokesman for African Americans. He rose to the vice presidency of the Loyal Union League and won a seat to the Constitutional Convention of 1869, where he was an outspoken proponent of desegregation and suffrage. He refused to sign the final document because he felt it did not go far enough in protecting the rights of African Americans. He served in the Twelfth Legislature from Lavaca and Colorado counties, where he balloted

third for Speaker of the House, represented Waller, Fort Bend, and Wharton counties in the Sixteenth Legislature, and then won his last election to office in 1884. He helped establish Kendleton and suffered from illness through much of his last legislative term. He returned home and died in office on February 27, 1886. He is buried in the Old Kendleton Cemetery off Charlie Roberts Lane at 29°26′1.83″N, 96°0′19.15″W. Merline Pitre, "Williams, Benjamin Franklin," *Handbook of Texas Online*, accessed March 15, 2021, https://www.tshaonline.org/handbook/entries/williams-benjamin-franklin. https://lrl. texas.gov/mobile/memberDisplay.cfm?memberID=4193 (accessed March 15, 2021).

4. See Robert W. Shook "The Texas 'Election Outrage' of 1886," *East Texas Historical Journal*, Vol. 10, Issue 1 (1972), 20–30; Senate, 50th Congress, 2nd Session, Misc. Doc. 62 "Testimony on the Alleged Election Outrages in Texas Reported From the Committee on Privileges and Elections of the Senate of the United States February 4, 1889" (Washington, DC: Government Printing Offices), 1889.

5. Matagorda County Historical Commission, *Historic Matagorda County Vol. 1* (Houston: D. Armstrong Company, 1986), 174; *The Fort Worth Gazette*, September 30, 1887. The Houston Light Guards was the first militia company raised in Texas during Reconstruction. Bruce A. Olson, "Houston Light Guards," *Handbook of Texas Online*, accessed March 22, 2021, https://www.tshaonline.org/handbook/entries/houston-light-guards. On November 10, 1886, Oliver Sheppard married Faltoumber Van, one of the daughters of the Van family, making him a community leader. Sheppard evidently escaped to the Fourth Ward of Houston, because he and his wife gave birth to a daughter there, Sallie, on September 20, 1901. Death Certificate of Sallie S. Collins, daughter of "Fatima" Van and Oliver Sheppard, August 18, 1967.

6. *The San Marcos Free Press*, March 15, 1888; *The Austin American Statesman*, March 21, 1888; *The Chicago Tribune*, March 3, 1888; *The Vicksburg Evening Post*, March 5, 1888; and *The Galveston Daily News*, March 4, 1888. The Republican Party of Brazoria County issued a statement praising Governor Ross for his actions in sending the Rangers to Wharton County, but on Tuesday, March 20, two more African American men were murdered on the Battle Plantation in the continuing "feud." In all, at least eighteen men died in the vicinity of Spanish Camp through the first half of 1888. *Wichita Eagle* (Kansas) June 7, 1888. The Texas Rangers arrested W. A. Hughes, Allen Stratton, James Beatty, Lee Andrews, and Arch Andrews on March 30, 1888, and charged them with the murders. After a trial, the Rangers also arrested George Dorman. The author was not able to locate the court case that led to the massacre or the names of the victims. *The Galveston Daily News*, March 31, 1888. All credit for identifying the Spanish Camp Massacre and tying it to the demise of the Republican Party in Wharton County goes to Katherine Kuehler Walters.

7. Petrie, *Through Many Dangers, Toils and Snares*, 160; Pauline Yelderman, *The Jay Birds of Fort Bend County: A White Man's Union* (Waco: Texian Press, 1979), 63–65.

8. Yelderman, *The Jay Birds of Fort Bend County*, 66–75. On Tuesday, November 3, 2020, the voters of Fort Bend County elected Eric Fagan county sheriff, the first African American man to hold that position since the ouster of Henry Ferguson in 1888. The *Houston Chronicle*, https://www.houstonchronicle.com/politics/election/article/Fort-Bend-elects-first-Black-sheriff-in-150-years-15701895.php (accessed April 20, 2021).

9. Yelderman, *The Jay Birds of Fort Bend County*, 77–78.

10. Kyle Terry was the son of Benjamin F. "Frank" Terry, owner of Oakland plantation and organizer of Terry's Texas Rangers, the famed rebel cavalry regiment. The assassination of Gibson ultimately cost Kyle Terry his life when Volney Gibson shot and killed Terry on the courthouse steps in Galveston on January 21, 1890, as Terry arrived to stand trial for the murder of Ned Gibson. *Galveston Daily News*, January 22, 1890.

11. For a bullet-by-bullet account of the battle of Richmond, see Yelderman, *The Jay Birds of Fort Bend County*, 95–111. In 1896, the white people of the county dedicated a statue to the Jay Birds, which stood "as a symbol of white man's control over county politics." On October 27, 2020, the Fort Bend County commissioners voted unanimously to move the symbol of white supremacy from its spot across the street from the county courthouse to Morton Cemetery in Richmond. *The Houston Chronicle*, October 27, 2020. https://www.houstonchronicle.com/news/houston-texas/houston/article/Fort-Bend-County-Richmond-city-agree-to-move-15679001.php (accessed April 17, 2021).

12. Pauline Yelderman's history of the Jaybirds is a detailed, white supremacist apologia, although her honesty about the centrality of white supremacy to the Jaybirds is instructive. For a more modern view of the Jaybird–Woodpecker War, see Leslie Ann Lovett, "The Jaybird-Woodpecker War: Reconstruction and Redemption in Fort Bend County" (MA Thesis, Rice University, 1994). For a more condensed version of Yelderman's narrative, see Pauline Yelderman, "Jaybird-Woodpecker War," *Handbook of Texas Online*, accessed April 17, 2021, https://www.tshaonline.org/handbook/entries/jaybird-woodpecker-war.

13. Annie Lee Williams, *The History of Wharton County 1846–1964* (Austin: Von Boeckman-Jones, 1964), 133–137. Both Yelderman and Williams include the constitutions for the respective white man's union associations in their respective monographs.

14. Haller's official biography lists his birth date as July 8, 1845, but his death certificate states that he was born on July 8, 1840. Texas Legislative Reference Library, https://lrl.texas.gov/legeLeaders/members/memberDisplay.cfm?memberID=3450 (accessed April 20, 2021); Nathan Haller death certificate, Harris County Texas February 17, 1917. Haller died at his home at 3219 Dowling Street in Houston's Third Ward. For Haller's residence in Matagorda County, see Journal of the Texas House of Representatives Twenty-Third Texas Legislature, Regular Session, p. 1. Paul M. Lucko, "Haller, Nathan H.," *Handbook of Texas Online*, accessed April 20, 2021, https://www.tshaonline.org/handbook/entries/haller-nathan-h. There is some debate about whether Haller lived in Matagorda or Brazoria counties in 1892, but he claimed Matagorda as his home county when representing the district in the legislature.

15. The Texas State Capitol building was a little less than five years old when Nathan Haller took his first oath of office, and the University of Texas was less than ten years old in January 1893, housed in the Victorian-style Old Main building just blocks north of the Capitol in Austin. For the text of Haller's Bill and his introduction of the protest against dividing Brazoria County, see *Texas House of Representatives Twenty-Third Texas Legislature, Regular Session*, pp. 278–279 and 341. For more detail on the battle over the seat of government in Brazoria County, see James A. Creighton, *A Narrative History of Brazoria County* (Waco. TX: Texian Press, 1975), 287–291.

16. Matagorda County Historical Commission *Historic Matagorda County Vol. 1* (Houston: D. Armstrong Company Inc., 1986), 174, 212–213. The other African American member of the legislature that year was Robert L. Smith of Colorado County.

17. A. R. Masterson later served as one of the chief organizers of the Taxpayers' Union of Brazoria County. For the reports of the Committee on Elections and Privileges, see *The Journal of the House of Representatives Being the Regular Session Twenty-Fourth Legislature Begun and Held at the City of Austin, Texas January 8, 1895* (Austin: Ben C. Jones & Co., State Printers, 1895), 127, 269–277; *Galveston Daily News*, November 15, 1894, and December 23, 1894.

18. Nathan Haller owned a town lot in the city of Brazoria worth $400 according to the 1895 Brazoria County tax rolls. Ida Brandon, "Tax Payer's Union in Brazoria County," *The Texas History Teachers' Bulletin*, Vol. XIV, No. 1, in *University of Texas Bulletin* No. 2746: December 8, 1927, pp. 86–92. Brandon wrote: "A candid statement of the matter, however, requires the admission that the 'T.P.U.' recognizes the fact that this is a white man's country and that white supremacy must obtain." Brandon also included the 1919 version of the constitution of the Taxpayers' Union in her article. Creighton, *A Narrative History of Brazoria County*, 291–292. The Brazoria County Courthouse in Brazoria was demolished in 1930.

19. Nathan Haller was the penultimate African American officeholder in Texas in the nineteenth century. Robert L. Smith of Colorado County won reelection to the Twenty-Fifth Legislature in 1896 because of a split between the Populists and Democrats that year. Smith left office in January 1899, and no African American held office in Texas again until the election of Barbara Jordan to the Texas Senate in 1966. Lawrence D. Rice, "Smith, Robert Lloyd," *Handbook of Texas Online*, accessed April 20, 2021, https://www.tshaonline.org/handbook/entries/smith-robert-lloyd.

Conclusion

1. Charles Wolfe and Kip Lornell, *The Life and Legend of Leadbelly* (New York: Da Capo Press, 1999), 87, 112.

2. For more on the African American exodus to Houston, see Bernadette Pruitt, *The Other Great Migration: The Movement of Rural African Americans to Houston, 1900–1941* (College Station: Texas A&M University Press, 2013).

3. For more on the Texas white primary and the case of *Smith v. Allwright*, see Darlene Clark Hine, *Black Victory: The Rise and Fall of the White Primary in Texas* (Millwood, NY: KTO Press, 1979).

4. Today there is a historical marker in Kendleton describing the case of *Terry v. Adams* near the former home of Willie Melton. Bonni C. Hayes, "Fleming, Arizona," *Handbook of Texas Online*, accessed May 20, 2021, https://www.tshaonline.org/handbook/entries/fleming-arizona.

5. William R. Johnson, *A Short History of the Sugar Industry in Texas*, Texas Gulf Coast Historical Publications, Vol. 5, No. 1 (April 1961).

6. Michel-Rolph Trouillot, *Silencing the Past: Power and the Production of History* (Boston: Beacon Press, 1995), xix, 26.

Bibliography

Primary Sources

Books

Affleck, Thomas. *Affleck's Southern Rural Almanac*. Brenham, TX: New Year's Creek Settler's Association, 1986.

Barker, Eugene C. (ed.). *The Austin Papers*, Vol. I. Washington, DC: Government Printing Office, 1924.

Barker, Eugene C. (ed.). *The Austin Papers*, Vol. II. Washington, DC: Government Printing Office, 1924.

Barker, Eugene C. (ed.). *The Austin Papers*, Vol. III. Washington, DC: Government Printing Office, 1928.

Biennial Reports of the Directors and Superintendent of the Texas State Penitentiary at Huntsville, Texas with the Report of the Prison Physician, Commencing December 1, A. D. 1878 and Terminating October 31, A. D. 1880. Galveston, TX: The News Book and Job Office, 1881.

Breeden, James O. (ed.). *Advice among Masters: The Ideal of Slave Management in the Old South*. Westport, CT: Greenwood Press, 1980.

Braman, D. E. E. *Braman's Information about Texas. Carefully Prepared by D. E. E. Braman, OP Matagorda, Texas*. Philadelphia: J. B. Lippincott, 1858.

Casteneda, Carlos E. (ed.). *The Mexican Side of the Texas Revolution*. New York: Graphic Ideas, Inc., 1970.

Celebrated and Extraordinary Trial of Col. Monroe Edwards for Forgery and Swindling. Austin, TX: Pemberton Press, 1970.

Champomier, P. A. *Statement of the Sugar Crop Made in Louisiana in 1852–1858*. New Orleans: Cook, Young, & Co., 1852–1858.

de la Pena, Jose Enrique. *With Santa Anna in Texas: A Personal Narrative of the Texas Revolution*, Carmen Perry (trans. and ed.). College Station: Texas A&M University Press, 1975.

Dewees, William B. *Letters from an Early Settler of Texas*. Louisville, KY: Hull and Brother, 1852.

The Federal Writer's Project. *Slave Narratives: A Folk History of Slavery in the United States From Interviews with Former Slaves*, Vol. 16, Series 2, Vol. 3. Washington, DC: Government Printing Office, 1941.

Fiske, M. *A Visit to Texas: Being the Journal of a Traveler Through Those Parts Most Interesting to American Settlers with Descriptions of Scenery and Habits &c &c.* New York: Goodrich & Wiley, 1834.

Garrison, George P. (ed.). *Diplomatic Correspondence of the Republic of Texas*, Vol. I. Washington, DC: Government Printing Office, 1909.

Garrison, George P. (ed.). *Diplomatic Correspondence of the Republic of Texas*, Vol. II. Washington, DC: Government Printing Office, 1911.

Garrison, George P. (ed.). *Diplomatic Correspondence of the Republic of Texas*, Vol. III. Washington, DC: Government Printing Office, 1911.

Gray, William Fairfax. *From Virginia to Texas, 1835: Diary of Col. William F. Gray.* Houston, TX: Gray, Dillaye & Co., 1909.

Gretchen, Mark. *Slave Transactions of Guadalupe County, Texas.* Santa Maria, CA: Janaway Publishing, 2009.

The Hardeman Historians of Madera, California and Bay City, Texas. *The Saga of Caney Creek.* Fresno, CA: Pioneer Publishing, 1986.

Hayes, Rutherford Birchard. *The Diary and Letters of Rutherford B. Hayes, Nineteenth President of the United States,* Vol. 1. Charles Richard Williams (ed.). Columbus: Ohio State Archeological and Historical Society, 1922.

Jackson, Jack (ed.), and Wheat John (trans.). *Almonte's Texas: Juan N. Almonte's 1834 Inspection, Secret Report & Role in the 1836 Campaign.* Austin: Texas State Historical Association, 2003.

Jenkins, John H. (ed.). *The Papers of the Texas Revolution 1835–1836.* Austin: Presidial Press, 1973. 10 Vols.

Jones, Anson. *Memoranda and Official Correspondence Relating to the Republic of Texas, Its History and Annexation.* New York: Arno Press, 1973.

Johnston, William Preston. *The Life of Albert Sidney Johnston.* New York: D. Appleton & Co., 1876.

Journal of the Reconstruction Convention: which met at Austin, Texas. Texas Constitutional Convention (1868–1869). Austin: Tracy, Siemering & Co., printers, 1870.

Journal of the Senate of Texas during the Session of the Fourteenth Legislature. Austin: Cardwell & Walker Printers, 1874.

Journal of the Texas House of Representatives Being the Regular Session Twenty-Fourth Legislature Begun and Held at the City of Austin, Texas January 8, 1895. Austin: Ben C. Jones & Co., State Printers, 1895.

Lack, Paul D. (ed.). *The Diary of William Fairfax Gray: From Virginia to Texas, 1835–1837.* Dallas: Southern Methodist University Press, 1997.

Letter from the Secretary of the Treasury, Transmitting in Obedience to a Resolution of the House of Representatives, of the 31st Ultimo. Information in Relation to the Illicit Introduction of Slaves into the United States: With a Statement of the Measures which have Been Taken to Prevent the Same, January 13, 1820. Washington, DC: Gales and Seaton, 1820.

Life and Adventures of the Accomplished Forger and Swindler Colonel Monroe Edwards. New York: H. Long & Brother, 1848.

Lubbock, Francis R. *Six Decades in Texas; or Memoirs of Francis Richard Lubbock, Governor of Texas in War Time, 1861–1863. A Personal Experience in Business, War and Politics.* Austin, TX: B. C. Jones & Co., 1900.

Lundy, Benjamin. *The War in Texas*. Philadelphia: Merriweather and Gunn, 1837.

Lundy, Benjamin. *The Life, Travels and Opinions of Benjamin Lundy*. Philadelphia: W. M. Parrish, 1847.

Mattison, Hiram. *Louisa Picquet the Octoroon, or Inside Views of Southern Domestic Life*. New York: Hiram Mattison, 1861.

McCormick, Andrew Phelps. *The Scotch-Irish in Ireland and America*. Andrew P. McCormick, 1897.

Mullins, Marion Day. *The First Census of Texas, 1829–1836: to which are added, Texas Citizenship lists, 1821–1845, and other early records of Republic of Texas*. Washington, DC: National Genealogical Society, 1959.

Olmstead, Frederick Law. *A Journey Through Texas: Or a Saddle Trip on the Southwestern Frontier*. New York: Dix, Edwards, 1857.

Pratt, Willis W (ed.). *Galveston Island: Or a Few Months off the Coast of Texas: The Journal of Francis C. Sheridan*. Austin: University of Texas Press, 1954.

Proceedings of the Republican State Convention, Assembled at Austin August 12, 1868. Austin: Printed at the Daily Republican Book and Job Office, 1868.

Raska, Ginny McNeill, and Hill, Mary Lynne Gasaway (eds.). *The Uncompromising Diary of Sally McNeill 1858–1867*. College Station: Texas A&M University Press, 2009.

Reports of Cases Argued and Decided in the Supreme Court of the State of Texas. Vol. 23. Philadelphia: Kay & Brother, 1860.

Scott, Robert N. (ed.). *Reports of Cases Argued and Decided in the Supreme Court of the State of Texas*. Philadelphia: Kay & Brother, 1860.

Scott, Robert N. (ed.). *The War of the Rebellion: A Compilation of the Official Records of the Union and Confederate Armies*. 125 vols. Washington, DC: Government Printing Office 1896.

Smithwick, Noah. *The Evolution of a State: Or Recollections of Old Texas Days*. Austin, TX: Gammel Book Co., 1900.

Stevens, Kenneth R. (ed.). *The Texas Legation Papers 1836–1845*. Fort Worth: Texas Christian University Press, 2012.

Strobel, Abner J. *The Old Plantations and Their Owners of Brazoria County, Texas*. Lake Jackson, TX: Lake Jackson Historical Society, 1930.

Texas Almanac for the Year 1857. Galveston, TX: Richardson, 1857.

Texas Penitentiary Report of the Commission Appointed by the Governor of Texas April 10, 1875 to Investigate the Alleged Mismanagement and Cruel Treatment of the Convicts. Houston: A. C. Gray, State Printer, 1875.

Tyler, Ronnie C., and Murphy, Lawrence W. (eds.). *The Slave Narratives in Texas*. Austin, TX Encino Press, 1974.

United States Senate. *Journal of the Senate of the United States Senate*, 38th Congress Sess. II. December 3, 1864–March 3, 1865. Washington: Government Printing Office, 1865.

United States Senate, 50th Congress, 2nd Session, Misc. Doc. 62. *Testimony on the Alleged Election Outrages in Texas Reported From the Committee on Privileges and Elections of the Senate of the United States February 4, 1889*. Washington, DC: Government Printing Office, 1889.

Wallis, Jonnie Lockhart. *Sixty Years on the Brazos: The Life and Letters of Dr. John Washington Lockhart 1824–1900*. Los Angeles, 1930.

Watson, William. *The Civil War Adventures of a Blockade Runner*. College Station: Texas A&M University Press, 2001.

Wharton, William H., and Austin, Stephen F. *Address of the Honorable Wm. H. Wharton, delivered in New York on Tuesday, April 26, 1836. Also, Address of the Honorable Stephen F. Austin, delivered in Louisville, Kentucky, on the 7th March, 1836. Together with other documents explanatory of the origin, principles, and objects of the contest in which Texas is at present engaged*. Tarrytown, NY: W. Abbott, 1922.

Articles

Adams, Ephraim D. (ed.). "Correspondence from the British Archives Concerning Texas 1837–1845." *The Southwestern Historical Quarterly*, Vol. 15, No. 3–Vol. 21, No. 2 (1911–1917), 1–24.

Bowie, John. "Early Life in the Southwest—the Bowies." *De Bow's Review of the Southern and Western States*, (New Orleans, 1852), 378–382.

Brandon, Ida. "Tax Payer's Union in Brazoria County." *The Texas History Teachers' Bulletin* Vol. XIV, No. 1, in *University of Texas Bulletin* No. 2746: December 8, 1927, pp. 86–92.

Bryan, Guy M., and Hayes, Rutherford B. "The Bryan-Hayes Correspondence, I." *The Southwestern Historical Quarterly*, Vol. 25, No. 2 (October 1921), 98–120.

Harris, Dilue. "The Reminiscences of Mrs. Dilue Harris. I." *The Quarterly of the Texas State Historical Association*, Vol. 4, No. 2 (October 1900), 85–127.

Harris, Dilue. "The Reminiscences of Mrs. Dilue Harris. II." *The Quarterly of the Texas State Historical Association*, Vol. 4, No. 3 (January 1901), 155–189.

Kuykendall, J. H. "Reminiscences of Early Texans: A Collection from the Austin Papers." *The Quarterly of the Texas State Historical Association*, Vol. 6, No. 3 (January 1903), 236–253.

Pearson, P. E. "Reminiscences of Judge Edwin Waller." *The Quarterly of the Texas State Historical Association*, Vol. 4, No. 1 (July 1900), 33–53.

Winkler, E. W. "The Bryan-Hayes Correspondence, II." *The Southwestern Historical Quarterly*, Vol. 25, No. 3 (January 1922), 198–221.

Winkler, E. W. "The Bryan-Hayes Correspondence III." *The Southwestern Historical Quarterly*, Vol. 25, No. 4 (April 1922), 274–299.

Secondary Sources

Books

Adams, Ephraim Douglass. *British Interest and Activities in Texas 1838–1846*. Gloucester, MA: Peter Smith, 1963.

Aitken, Hugh G. J. *Did Slavery Pay?: Readings in the Economics of Black Slavery in the United States*. Boston: Houghton Mifflin, 1971.

Alexander, Michelle. *The New Jim Crow: Mass Incarceration in the Age of Colorblindness*. New York: The New Press, 2010.

Armstrong, R. M. *Sugar Land, Texas and the Imperial Sugar Company*. Houston: D. Armstrong Co., 1991.

Astor, Aaron, and Buchanan, Thomas C. (eds.). *Slavery: Interpreting American History.* Kent, OH: Kent State University Press, 2021.

Austin, Peter E. *Baring Brothers and the Birth of Modern Finance.* London: Pickering and Chatto, 2007.

Bancroft, Frederick. *Slave Trading in the Old South.* Columbia: University of South Carolina Press, 1996.

Baptist, Edward E. *The Half Has Never Been Told: Slavery and the Making of American Capitalism.* New York: Basic Books, 2014.

Barker, Eugene C. *The Life of Stephen F. Austin, Founder of Texas, 1793–1836.* Austin: University of Texas Press, 1926.

Barker, Eugene C., Potts, Charles S., and Ramsdell, Charles W. *A School History of Texas.* Chicago: Row, Peterson & Co., 1913.

Barr, Alwyn. *Reconstruction to Reform: Texas Politics 1876–1906.* Austin: University of Texas Press, 1971.

Barr, Alwyn. *Black Texans: A History of African Americans in Texas, 1528–1995,* 2nd ed. Norman: University of Oklahoma Press, 1996.

Barr, Alwyn. *The African Texans.* San Antonio: University of Texas Institute of Texan Cultures, 2004.

Barr, Alwyn, and Calvert, Robert A. (eds.). *Black Leaders: Texans for Their Times.* Austin: Texas State Historical Association, 1981.

Bass, Feris A., Jr., and Brunson, B. R.. *Fragile Empires: The Texas Correspondence of Samuel Swartout and James Morgan, 1836–1856.* Austin, TX: Shoal Creek Publisher, 1978.

Baughman, James P. *Charles Morgan and the Development of Southern Transportation.* Nashville: Vanderbilt University Press, 1968.

Baum, Dale. *Counterfeit Justice: The Judicial Odyssey of Texas Freedwoman Azeline Hearne.* Baton Rouge: Louisiana State University Press, 2009.

Baum, Dale. *The Shattering of Texas Unionism: Politics in the Lone Star State during the Reconstruction Era.* Baton Rouge: Louisiana State University Press, 1998.

Baumgartener, Alice. *South to Freedom: Runaway Slaves to Mexico and the Road to the Civil War.* New York: Basic Books, 2020.

Bean, Christopher B. *Too Great a Burden to Bear: The Struggle and Failure of the Freedmen's Bureau in Texas.* New York: Fordham University Press, 2016.

Beckert, Sven. *Empire of Cotton: A Global History.* New York: Vintage Books, 2014.

Beckert, Sven, and Rockman, Seth (eds.). *Slavery's Capitalism: A New History of American Economic Development.* Philadelphia: University of Pennsylvania Press, 2016.

Bergard, Laird W., Garcia, Felix Iglesias, and Barcia, Maria del Carmen. *The Cuban Slave Market, 1790–1800.* New York: Cambridge University Press, 1995.

Bernard, Lora-Marie. *The Counterfeit Prince of Old Texas: Swindling Slaver Monroe Edwards.* Charleston, SC: The History Press, 2017.

Berry, Daina Ramey. *The Price for the Pound of Their Flesh: The Value of the Enslaved From Womb to Grave, in the Building of a Nation.* Boston: Beacon Press, 2017.

Bevill, James P. *The Paper Republic: The Struggle for Money, Credit, and Independence in the Republic of Texas.* Houston, TX: Bright Sky Press, 2009.

Blackmon, Douglas A. *Slavery by Another Name: The Re-Enslavement of Black Americans from the Civil War to World War II.* New York: Doubleday Press, 2009.

Blasingame, John W. *The Slave Community: Plantation Life in the Antebellum South*. New York: Oxford University Press, 1979.

Boddie, Mary D. *Thunder on the Brazos: The Outbreak of the Texas Revolution at Fort Velasco, June 26, 1832*. Lake Jackson, TX: Historical Research Center, 1979.

Brewer, J. Mason. *Negro Legislators of Texas and Their Descendants*. Dallas: Mathis, 1935.

Brown, Gary. *James Walker Fannin: Hesitant Martyr in the Texas Revolution*. Plano, TX: Republic of Texas Press, 2000.

Buchanan, Russell. *David S. Terry of California: Dueling Judge*. San Marino, CA: The Huntington Library, 1956.

Buenger, Walter L. *Secession and the Union in Texas*. Austin: University of Texas Press, 1984.

Calhoun, Charles W. *Conceiving a New Republic: The Republican Party and the Southern Question, 1869–1900*. Lawrence: University Press of Kansas, 2006.

Campbell, Randolph B. *An Empire for Slavery in Texas: The Peculiar Institution in Texas*. Baton Rouge: Louisiana State University Press, 1989.

Campbell, Randolph B. *Grass-Roots Reconstruction in Texas, 1865–1880*. Baton Rouge: Louisiana State University Press, 1997.

Campbell, Randolph B. (ed.). *The Laws of Slavery in Texas*. Austin: University of Texas Press, 2010.

Campbell, Randolph B., and Lowe, Richard G. *Wealth and Power in Antebellum Texas*. College Station: Texas A&M University Press, 1977.

Cantrell, Gregg. *Stephen F. Austin: Empresario of Texas*. New Haven, CT: Yale University Press, 1999.

Carlson, Avery Luvere. *A Banking History of Texas 1835–1929*. Rockport, TX: Copano Bay Press, 2007.

Carroll, Mark M. *Homesteads Ungovernable: Families, Sex, Race, and the Law in Frontier Texas, 1823–1860*. Austin: University of Texas Press, 2001.

Cartwright, Gary. *Galveston: A History of the Island*. Fort Worth: Texas Christian University Press, 1991.

Chireau, Yvonne. *Black Magic: Religion and the African American Conjuring Tradition*. Berkeley: University of California Press, 2003.

Clinton, Catherine, and Gillespie, Michelle (eds.). *The Devil's Lane: Sex and Race in the Early South*. Oxford: Oxford University Press, 1997.

Cotham, Edward T., Jr. *Battle on the Bay: The Civil War Struggle for Galveston*. Austin: University of Texas Press, 1998.

Cotham, Edward T., Jr. *Juneteenth: The Story Behind the Celebration*. Kerrville, TX: State House Press, 2021.

Creighton, James A. *A Narrative History of Brazoria County*. Angleton, TX: Brazoria County Historical Commission, 1975.

Crouch, Barry A. *The Freedmen's Bureau and Black Texans*. Austin: University of Texas Press, 1992.

Crouch, Barry A. *The Dance of Freedom: Texas and African Americans during Reconstruction*. Austin: University of Texas Press, 2007.

Cummins, Light Townsend. *Emily Austin of Texas 1795–1851*. Fort Worth: Texas Christian University Press, 2009.

Davis, William C. *Three Roads to the Alamo: The Lives and Fortunes of David Crockett, James Bowie, and William Barret Travis*. New York: Harper Collins, 1998.

Davis, William C. *Lone Star Rising: The Revolutionary Birth of the Texas Republic*. New York: Free Press, 2004.

Deyle, Steven. *Carry Me Back: The Domestic Slave Trade in American Life*. Oxford: Oxford University Press, 2005.

Diouf, Sylviane A. *Slavery's Exiles: The Story of the American Maroons*. New York: New York University Press 2014.

Du Bois, W. E. B. *Black Reconstruction in America 1860–1880*. New York: Horace, Harcourt and Brace, 1935.

Dyer, J. O. *The Early History of Galveston*. Galveston, TX: Oscar Springer Printers, 1916.

Erickson, Joe E. and Erickson, Carolyn R. (comps.). *They Came to East Texas, 1500–1850: Immigrants and Immigration Patterns*. Westminster, MD: Heritage Books, 2005.

Emmett, Chris. *Shanghai Pierce: A Fair Likeness*. Norman: University of Oklahoma Press, 1953.

Falola, Toyin, and Childs, Matt D. (eds.). *The Yoruba Diaspora in the Atlantic World*. Bloomington: Indiana University Press, 2004.

Fett, Sharla M. *Working Cures: Healing, Health, and Power on Southern Slave Plantations*. Chapel Hill: University of North Carolina Press, 2002.

Few, Joan. *Sugar, Planters, Slaves, and Convicts: The History and Archeology of Lake Jackson Plantation Brazoria County, Texas*. Gold Hill, CO: Few Publications, 2006.

Finley, Alexandra J. *An Intimate Economy: Enslaved Women, Work, and America's Domestic Slave Trade* (Chapel Hill: University of North Carolina Press), 2020.

Fogel, Robert W. *Without Consent or Contract: The Rise and Fall of American Slavery*. New York: W. W. Norton, 1989.

Fogel, Robert William, and Engerman, Stanley L. *Time on the Cross: The Economics of American Negro Slavery*. New York: W. W. Norton, 1974.

Follett, Richard. *The Sugar Masters: Planters and Slaves in Louisiana's Cane World, 1820–1860*. Baton Rouge: Louisiana State University Press, 2005.

Follett, Richard, Beckert, Steven, Coclanis, Peter, and Hahn, Barbara. *Plantation Kingdom: The American South and its Global Commodities*. Baltimore, MD: Johns Hopkins University Press, 2016.

Foner, Eric. *Reconstruction: America's Unfinished Revolution, 1863–1877*. New York: Harper & Row, 1988.

Foote, Horton. *Farewell: A Memoir of a Texas Childhood*. New York: Scribner, 1999.

Fornell, Earl V. *The Galveston Era: The Texas Crescent on the Eve of Secession*. Austin: University of Texas Press, 1961.

Forrett, Jeff. *Williams' Gang: A Notorious Slave Trader and His Cargo of Black Convicts*. Cambridge: Cambridge University Press, 2020.

Forrett, Jeff, and Sears, Christine L. (eds.). *New Directions in Slavery Studies: Commodification, Community, Comparison*. Baton Rouge: Louisiana State University Press, 2015.

Francaviglia, Richard V. *From Sail to Steam: Four Centuries of Texas Maritime History 1500–1900*. Austin: University of Texas Press, 1998.

Frantz, Joe B. *Gail Borden: Dairyman to a Nation*. Norman: Oklahoma University Press, 1951.

Franklin, John Hope, and Schweninger, Loren. *Runaway Slaves: Rebels on the Plantation.* Oxford: Oxford University Press, 1999.

Fritz, Gayle. *Matagorda Bay Area, Texas: A Survey of the Archaeological and Historical Resources.* Austin: Archaeological Survey, University of Texas at Austin Research Report No. 45, June 1975.

Furse, Margaret Lewis. *The Hawkins Ranch in Texas: From Plantation to the Present.* College Station: Texas A&M University Press, 2014.

Gambrell, Herbert. *Anson Jones: Last President of the Republic of Texas.* Austin: University of Texas Press, 1947.

Genovese, Eugene. *Roll, Jordan, Roll: The World the Slaves Made.* New York: Vintage Books, 1972.

Gilmer, Jason A. *Slavery and Freedom in Texas: Stories from the Courtroom, 1821–1871.* Athens: University of Georgia Press, 2017.

Glasrud, Bruce A. (ed.). *African Americans in South Texas History.* College Station: Texas A&M University Press, 2011.

Glasrud, Bruce A., and McDonald, Archie P. (eds.). *Blacks in East Texas History.* College Station: Texas A&M University Press, 2008.

Glasrud, Bruce A., and Smallwood, James, M. (eds.). *The African American Experience in Texas: An Anthology.* Lubbock: Texas Tech University Press, 2007.

Gordon-Reed, Annette. *On Juneteenth.* New York: Liveright Publishing Corporation, 2021.

Gouge, William M. *The Fiscal History of Texas.* Philadelphia: Lippincott, Grambo and Compay, 1852.

Gudmestad, Robert H. *A Troublesome Commerce: The Transformation of the Interstate Slave Trade.* Baton Rouge: Louisiana State University Press, 2003.

Gutman, Herbert G. *Slavery and the Numbers Game: A Critique of Time on the Cross.* Urbana: University of Illinois Press, 1975.

Hahn, Stephen. *A Nation under Our Feet: Black Political Struggles in the Rural South from Slavery to the Great Migration.* Cambridge, MA: Harvard University Press, 2005.

Hall, Andrew W. *The Galveston-Houston Packett: Steamboats on Buffalo Bayou.* Charleston, SC: The History Press, 2012.

Haynes, Sam W., and Saxon, Gerald D. (eds.). *Contested Empire: Rethinking the Texas Revolution.* College Station: Texas A&M Press, 2015.

Henson, Margaret Swett. *Samuel May Williams: Early Texas Entrepreneur.* College Station: Texas A&M University Press, 1976.

Henson, Margaret Swett. *Juan Davis Bradburn: A Reappraisal of the Mexican Commander at Anahuac.* College Station: Texas A&M University Press, 1982.

Hilde, Libra R. *Slavery, Fatherhood, and Parental Duty in African American Communities over the Long Nineteenth Century.* Chapel Hill: University of North Carolina Press, 2020.

Hilliard, Kathleen M. *Masters, Slaves, and Exchange: Power's Purchase in the Old South.* New York: Cambridge University Press, 2014.

Hine, Darlene Clark. *Black Victory: The Rise and Fall of the White Primary in Texas.* Millwood, NY: KTO Press, 1979.

Hodes, Martha. *White Women, Black Men: Illicit Sex in the Nineteenth Century South.* New Haven, CT: Yale University Press 1999.

Hogan, William Ransom. *The Texas Republic: A Social and Economic History.* Norman: University of Oklahoma Press, 1946.

Howell, Kenneth W. (ed.). *Still in the Arena of the Civil War: Violence and Turmoil in Reconstruction Texas 1865–1874.* Denton: University of North Texas Press, 2012.

Howell, Kenneth W., and Swanlund, Charles (eds.). *Single Star of the West: The Republic of Texas, 1836–1845.* Denton: University of North Texas Press, 2017.

Hudson, Larry E., Jr. *Working toward Freedom: Slave Society and Domestic Economy in the American South.* Rochester, NY: Rochester University Press, 1964.

Hunter, Tera W. *Bound in Wedlock: Slave and Free Black Marriage in the Nineteenth Century.* Cambridge, MA: Harvard University Press, 2017.

Ingram, Mary McAllister. *Canebrake Settlements: Colonists, Plantations, Churches 1822–1870 Matagorda County Texas.* Mary McAllister Ingram, 2006.

Jackson, Ron, Jr., and White, Lee Spencer. *Joe: The Slave Who Became an Alamo Legend.* Norman: University of Oklahoma Press, 2015.

Johnson, Walter. *Soul by Soul: Life Inside the Antebellum Slave Market.* Cambridge, MA: Harvard University Press, 1999.

Johnson, Walter. *River of Dark Dreams: Slavery and Empire in the Cotton Kingdom.* Cambridge, MA: Harvard University Press, 2013.

Jones, C. Allan. *Texas Roots: Agricultural and Rural Life before the Civil War.* College Station: Texas A&M University Press, 2005.

Jones, Mary Beth. *Peach Point Plantation: The First 150 Years.* Waco, TX: Texian Press, 1982.

Jones-Rogers, Stephanie E. *They Were Her Property: White Women as Slave Owners in the American South.* New Haven, CT: Yale University Press, 2019.

Jordan, Terry G. *German Seed in Texas Soil: Immigrant Farmers in Nineteenth Century Texas.* Austin: University of Texas Press, 1966.

Kaye, Anthony E. *Joining Places: Slave Neighborhoods in the Old South.* Chapel Hill: University of North Carolina Press, 2007.

Kearney, James C. *Nassau Plantation: The Evolution of a Texas German Slave Plantation.* Denton: University of North Texas Press, 2010.

Kelley, Sean M. *Los Brazos de Dios: A Plantation Society in the Texas Borderlands 1821–1865.* Baton Rouge: Louisiana State University Press, 2010.

Kennedy, Roger G. *Cotton and Conquest: How the Plantation System Acquired Texas.* Norman: University of Oklahoma Press, 2013.

Kingston, Mike, Attlesey, Sam, and Crawford, Mary G. (eds.). *The Texas Almanac's Political History of Texas.* Austin, TX: Eakin Press, 1992.

Lack, Paul D. *The Texas Revolutionary Experience: A Political and Social History 1835–1836.* College Station: Texas A&M University Press, 1992.

Lathrop, Barnes F. *Migration into East Texas, 1835–1860.* Austin: Texas State Historical Association, 1949.

Leonard, A. B., and Pretel, David (eds.). *The Caribbean and the Atlantic World Economy.* New York: Palgrave Macmillan, 2015.

Lichtenstein, Alexander C. *Twice the Work of Free Labor: The Political Economy of Convict Labor in the New South.* Brooklyn, NY: Verso Books, 1996.

Lowe, Richard G., and Campbell, Randolph B. *Planters and Plain Folk: Agriculture in Antebellum Texas.* Dallas, TX: Southern Methodist University Press, 1987.

Malone, Ann Patton. *Women on the Texas Frontier: A Cross-Cultural Perspective.* El Paso: Texas Western Press, 1983.

Mancini, Matthew J. *One Dies, Get Another: Convict Leasing in the American South, 1866–1928.* Chapel Hill: University of North Carolina Press, 1996.

Martin, Jonathan. *Divided Mastery: Slave Hiring in the Antebellum South.* Cambridge, MA: Harvard University Press, 2004.

Massey, Sara G. (ed.). *Black Cowboys of Texas.* College Station: Texas A&M University Press, 2004.

Matagorda County Historical Commission. *Historic Matagorda County.* 3 Vols. Houston: D. Armstrong Company, 1986.

McCaslin, Richard, Chipman, Donald E., and Torget, Andrew (eds.). *This Corner of Canaan: Essays on Texas in Honor of Randolph B. Campbell.* Denton: University of North Texas Press, 2013.

McComb, David G. *Galveston: A History.* Austin: University of Texas Press, 1986.

McDaniel, Caleb W. *Sweet Taste of Liberty: A True Story of Slavery and Restitution in America.* New York: Oxford University Press, 2019.

McDonald, Archie P. *William Barrett Travis: A Biography.* Austin, TX: Eakin Press, 1976.

McQueen, Clyde. *Black Churches in Texas: A Guide to Historic Congregations.* College Station: Texas A&M University Press, 2000.

Merk, Frederick. *Slavery and the Annexation of Texas.* New York: Alfred A. Knopf, 1972.

Miller, Edward L. *New Orleans and the Texas Revolution.* College Station: Texas A&M University Press, 2004.

Moneyhon, Carl H. *Republicanism in Reconstruction Texas.* Austin: University of Texas Press, 1980.

Moneyhon, Carl H. *Texas after the Civil War: The Struggle for Reconstruction.* College Station: Texas A&M University Press, 2004.

Moneyhon, Carl H. *George T. Ruby: Champion of Equal Rights in Reconstruction Texas.* Fort Worth: Texas Christian University Press, 2020.

Moneyhon, Carl H. *The Union League and Biracial Politics in Reconstruction Texas.* College Station: Texas A&M University Press, 2021.

Moretta, John Anthony. *William Pitt Ballinger: Texas Lawyer, Southern Statesman, 1825–1888.* Austin: Texas State Historical Association, 2000.

Oakes, James. *The Ruling Race: A History of American Slaveholders.* New York: W. W. Norton, 1998.

Obadale-Starks, Ernest. *Freebooters and Smugglers: The Foreign Slave Trade in the United States After 1808.* Fayetteville: University of Arkansas Press, 2007.

Painter, Nell Irvin. *Southern History across the Color Line.* Chapel Hill: University of North Carolina Press, 2021.

Pargas, Damian Alan. *Slavery and Forced Migration in the Antebellum South.* Cambridge: Cambridge University Press, 2015.

Pargas, Damian Alan. *Fugitive Slaves and Spaces of Freedom in America*. Gainesville: University of Florida Press, 2020.

Perkinson, Robert. *Texas Tough: The Rise of America's Prison Empire*. New York: Picador Press, 2010.

Pitre, Merline. *Through Many Dangers, Toils and Snares: Black Leadership in Texas, 1868–1898*. College Station: Texas A&M University Press, 2016.

Pruitt, Bernadette. *The Other Great Migration: The Movement of Rural African Americans to Houston, 1900–1941*. College Station: Texas A&M University Press, 2013.

Puryear, Pamela, and Winfield, Nath, Jr. *Sandbars and Sternwheelers: Steam Navigation on the Brazos*. College Station: Texas A&M University Press, 1976.

Ramsdell, Charles W. *Reconstruction in Texas*. New York: Columbia University, Longmans, Green & Co. Agents, 1910.

Ransom, Roger L., and Sutch, Richard. *One Kind of Freedom: The Economic Consequences of Emancipation*, 2nd ed. Cambridge: Cambridge University Press, 2001.

Reed, S. G. *A History of Texas Railroads*. 1941. Reprint, New York, Arno Press, 1981.

Reynolds, Donald E. *Texas Terror: The Slave Insurrection Panic of 1860 and the Secession of the Lower South*. Baton Rouge: Louisiana State University Press, 2007.

Reynolds, Donald E. *Editors Make War: Southern Newspapers in the Secession Crisis*. Nashville: Vanderbilt University Press, 1970.

Rice, Lawrence D. *The Negro in Texas 1874–1900*. Baton Rouge: Louisiana State University Press, 1971.

Richter, William L. *The Army in Texas during Reconstruction 1865–1870*. College Station: Texas A&M University Press, 1987.

Richter, William L. *Overreached on All Sides: The Freedmen's Bureau Administrators in Texas, 1865–1868*. College Station: Texas A&M University Press, 1991.

Rosenthal, Caitlyn. *Accounting for Slavery: Masters and Management*. Cambridge, MA: Harvard University Press, 2018.

Rothman, Joshua D. *Notorious in the Neighborhood: Sex and Families Across the Color Line in Virginia, 1787–1861*. Chapel Hill: University of North Carolina Press 2007.

Rothman, Joshua D. *Flush Times and Fever Dreams: A Story of Slavery and Freedom in the Age of Jackson*. Athens: University of Georgia Press, 2014.

Rothman, Joshua D. *The Ledger and the Chain: How Domestic Slave Traders Shaped America*. New York: Basic Books, 2021.

Ruef, Martin. *Between Slavery and Capitalism: The Legacy of Emancipation in the American South*. Princeton, NJ: Princeton University Press, 2014.

Russell, James W. *Escape from Texas: A Novel of Slavery and the Texas War of Independence*. Cornwall-on-Hudson, NY: Sloan Publishing, 2012.

Schermerhorn, Calvin. *The Business of Slavery and the Rise of American Capitalism, 1815–1860*. New Haven, CT: Yale University Press, 2015.

Schmidt, James M. *Galveston and the Civil War: An Island City in the Maelstrom*. Charleston, SC: The History Press, 2012.

Schwartz, Rosalie. *Across the Rio Grande to Freedom: U.S. Negroes in Mexico*. El Paso: Texas Western University Press, 1975.

Schweninger, Loren. *Black Property Owners in the South 1790–1915*. Urbana: University of Illinois Press, 1997.

Sibley, Mary McAdams. *Lone Stars and State Gazettes: Texas Newspapers before the Civil War*. College Station: Texas A&M University Press, 1983.

Siegel, Stanley A. *A Political History of the Republic of Texas, 1836–1845*. Austin: University of Texas Press, 1956.

Silbey, Joel H. *Storm over Texas: The Annexation Controversy and the Road to Civil War*. Oxford: Oxford University Press, 2005.

Silverthorne, Elizabeth R. *Plantation Life in Texas*. College Station: Texas A&M University Press, 1986.

Simpson, Harold E. (ed.). *Texas in the War 1861–1865*. Hillsboro, TX: Hill Junior College Press, 1965.

Sitterson, J. Carlyle. *Sugar Country: The Cane Sugar Industry in the South, 1753–1950*. Westport, CT: Greenwood Press, 1953.

Sitton, Thad, and Conrad, James H. *Freedom Colonies: Independent Black Texans in the Time of Jim Crow*. Austin: University of Texas Press, 2005.

Sitton, Thad, and Utley, Dan K. *From Can See to Can't: Texas Cotton Farmers on the Southern Prairies*. Austin: University of Texas Press, 1997.

Smallwood, James M. *Time of Hope, Time of Despair: Black Texans During Reconstruction*, Port Washington, NY: Kennikat Press, 1981.

Smallwood, James M. Crouch, Barry A., and Peacock Larry. *Murder and Mayhem: The War of Reconstruction in Texas*. College Station: Texas A&M Press, 2003.

Sowell, A. J. *History of Fort Bend County*, Waco, TX: W. M. Morrison, 1964.

Spratt, John Stricklin. *The Road to Spindletop: Economic Change in Texas 1875–1901*. Austin: University of Texas Press, 1955.

Stampp, Kenneth. *The Peculiar Institution: Slavery in the Antebellum South*. New York: Alfred Knopf, 1972.

Tadman, Michael. *Speculators and Slaves: Masters, Traders, and Slaves in the Old South*. Madison: University of Wisconsin Press, 1996.

The Texas Forest Service. *Famous Trees of Texas*. College Station: Texas A&M University Press, 1970.

Thomas, Hugh. *The Slave Trade: The Story of the Atlantic Slave Trade, 1440–1870*. New York: Simon & Schuster, 1997.

Tinkler, Robert. *James Hamilton of South Carolina*. Baton Rouge: Louisiana State University Press, 2004.

Torget, Andrew J. *Seeds of Empire: Cotton, Slavery, and the Transformation of the Texas Borderlands, 1800–1850*. Chapel Hill: University of North Carolina Press, 2015.

Trouillot, Michel-Rolph. *Silencing the Past: Power and the Production of History*. Boston: Beacon Press, 1995.

Turner, Martha Anne. *The Life and Times of Jane Long*. Waco, TX: Texian Press, 1969.

Upchurch, Thomas Adams. *Legislating Racism: The Billion Dollar Congress and the Birth of Jim Crow*. Lexington: University Press of Kentucky, 2004.

Walker, Donald R. *Penology for Profit: A History of the Texas Prison System 1867–1912*. College Station: Texas A&M University Press, 1988.

Wang, Xi. *The Trial of Democracy: Black Suffrage and Northern Republicans, 1860–1910*. Athens: University of Georgia Press, 1997.

Weber, David J. *The Mexican Frontier, 1821–1846: The American Southwest under Mexico*. Albuquerque: University of New Mexico Press, 1982.

Wharton, Clarence R. *Wharton's History of Fort Bend County*. San Antonio, TX: The Naylor Co., 1939.

White, Deborah Gray. *A'rn't I a Woman? Female Slaves in the Plantation South*. New York: W. W. Norton, 1985.

White, James Terry. *The National Cyclopædia of American Biography*. New York: J. T. White, 1893.

Willett, Donald, and Curley, Stephen (eds.). *Invisible Texans: Women and Minorities in Texas History*. New York: McGraw-Hill, 2005.

Williams, David A. *Bricks Without Straw: A Comprehensive History of African Americans in Texas*. Austin, TX: Eakin Press, 1997.

Williams, Eric. *Capitalism and Slavery*. Chapel Hill: University of North Carolina Press, 1994.

Winegarten, Ruthe. *Black Texas Women: 150 Years of Trial and Triumph*. Austin: University of Texas Press, 1995.

Wolfe, Charles, and Lornell, Kip. *The Life and Legend of Leadbelly*. New York: Da Capo Press, 1999.

Woodman, Harold D. *King Cotton and His Retainers: Financing and Marketing the Cotton Crop of the South, 1800–1925*. Lexington: University of Kentucky Press, 1969.

Woodrick, James V. *Bernardo: Crossroads, Social Center and Agricultural Showcase of Early Texas*. Austin, TX: James V. Woodrick, 2011.

Wright, Gavin. *The Political Economy of the Cotton South: Households, Markets, and Wealth in the Nineteenth Century*. New York: W. W. Norton, 1978.

Wright, Gavin. *Slavery and American Economic Development*. Baton Rouge: Louisiana State University Press, 2006.

Yelderman, Pauline. *The Jaybird Democratic Association of Fort Bend County*. Waco, TX: Texian Press, 1979.

Articles

Addington, Wendell G. "Slave Insurrections in Texas." *Journal of Negro History*, No. 35, (October 1950), 408–434.

Barker. Eugene C. "The African Slave Trade in Texas." *The Quarterly of the Texas State Historical Association*, Vol. 6, No. 2 (October 1902), 145–158.

Barker. Eugene C. "Stephen F. Austin and the Independence of Texas," *The Quarterly of the Texas State Historical Association*, Vol. 13, No. 4 (April 1910), 257–284.

Barr, Alwyn. "Reconstruction Change and Continuity in Brazoria County, Texas" *The Houston Review* 18 (Spring 1996), 114–123.

Barr. Alwyn. "The Texas Black Uprising Scare of 1883." *Phylon* No. 41 (June 1980), 179–186.

Bertleth, Rosa Groce. "Jared Ellison Groce." *The Southwestern Historical Quarterly*, Vol. 20 No. 4 (April 1917), 358–368.

Briscoe, P. "The First Texas Railroad." *The Quarterly of the Texas State Historical Association* Vol. 7, No. 4 (April 1904), pp. 279–285.

Browning, John G., and Wright, Hon. Carolyn. "And Still He Rose: William A Price, Texas' First Black Judge and the Path to a Civil Rights Milestone." *Journal of the Texas Supreme Court Historical Society*, Vol. 8, No. 2 (Winter 2019), 39–49.

Buenger, Walter L. "Making Sense of Texas and Its History." *The Southwestern Historical Quarterly*, Vol. 121, No. 1 (July, 2017), 1–28.

Bugbee, Lester G. "The Old Three Hundred: A List of Settlers in Austin's First Colony." *The Quarterly of the Texas State Historical Association*, Vol. 1, No. 2 (October 1897), 108–117.

Bugbee, Lester G. "Slavery in Early Texas. I." *Political Science Quarterly*, Vol. 13, No. 3 (September 1898), 389–412.

Bugbee, Lester G. "Slavery in Early Texas. II." *Political Science Quarterly*, Vol. 13, No. 4 (December 1898), 648–668.

Bugbee, Lester G. "What Became of the Lively?" *The Quarterly of the Texas State Historical Association*, Vol. 3, No. 2 (October 1899), 141–148.

Campbell, Randolph. "Intermittent Slave Ownership: Texas as a Test Case." *The Journal of Southern History*, No. 60 (February 1985), 15–23.

Campbell, Randolph. "Slave Hiring in Texas." *The American Historical Review*, Vol. 93 (February 1988), 107–114.

Carrigan, William Dean. "Slavery and the Frontier: The Peculiar Institution in Central Texas." In Bruce A. Glasrud and Deborah M. Liles (eds.), *African Americans in Central Texas History: From Slavery to Civil Rights* (College Station: Texas A&M University Press, 2019), 41–69.

Carlson, Avery L. "High Lights in Texas Banking History." *The Southwestern Political and Social Science Quarterly*, Vol. 11, No. 1 (June 1930), 79–85.

Chen, Cheryl Rhan-Hsin, and Simon, Gary. "Actuarial Issues in Insurance on Slaves in the United States South." *The Journal of African American History*, Vol. 89, No. 4 (Autumn 2004), 348–357.

Chireau, Yvonne. "Conjure and Christianity in the Nineteenth Century: Religious Elements in African American Magic." *Religion and American Culture: A Journal of Interpretation*, Vol. 7, No. 2 (Summer 1997), 225–246.

Chireau, Yvonne. "The Uses of the Supernatural: Toward a History of Black Women's Magical Practices." Susan Juster and Lisa McFarlane (eds.), *A Mighty Baptism: Race, Gender, and the Creation of American Protestantism*. Ithaca, NY: Cornell University Press, 1996, 171–188.

Cornell, Sarah E. "Citizens of Nowhere: Fugitive Slaves and Free African Americans in Mexico, 1833–1857." *Journal of American History*, Vol. 100, No. 2 (September 2013), 351–374.

Crouch, Barry A. "The 'Chords of Love': Legalizing Black Marital and Family Rights in Postwar Texas," *Journal of Negro History*, Vol. 79 (September 1994), 334–351.,

Crouch, Barry A. "Crisis in Color: Racial Separation in Texas during Reconstruction." *Journal of Civil War History*, Vol. 16 (March 1970), 37–49.

Crouch, Barry A. "Hidden Sources of Black History: The Texas Freedmen's Bureau Records as a Case Study." *The Southwestern Historical Quarterly*, Vol. 83, No. 3 (January 1980), 216–217.

Crouch, Barry A. "Guardian of the Freedpeople: Texas Freedmen's Bureau Agents and the Black Community." *Journal of Southern Studies*, Vol. 3 (Fall 1992), 185–201.

Crouch, Barry A. "A Spirit of Lawlessness: White Violence, Texas Blacks, 1865–1868." *Journal of Social History*, Vol. 18 (Winter 1984), 217–232.

Crouch Barry A., and Madaras, Larry. "Reconstructing Black Families: Perspective from the Texas Freedmen's Bureau Records." *Prologue*, Vol. 18 (Summer 1986), 109–122.

Curlee, Abigail. "The History of a Texas Slave Plantation 1831–63." *The Southwestern Historical Quarterly*, Vol. 26, No. 2 (October 1922), 79–127.

Delp, Robert W. "Andrew Jackson Davis: Prophet of American Spiritualism." *Journal of American History*, Vol. 54, No. 1 (June 1967), 43–56.

Dienst, Alex. "The New Orleans Newspaper Files of the Texas Revolutionary Period." *The Quarterly of the Texas State Historical Association*," Vol. 4, No. 2 (October 1900), 140–151.

Dillon, Merton L. "Benjamin Lundy in Texas." *The Southwestern Historical Quarterly*, Vol. 63, No. 1 (July 1959), 46–62.

Dobie, J. Frank. "Jim Bowie: Big Dealer." *The Southwestern Historical Quarterly*, Vol. 60, No. 3 (January 1957), 337–357.

Ellenberger, Mathew. "Illuminating the Lesser Lights: Notes on the Life of Albert Clinton Horton." *The Southwestern Historical Quarterly*, Vol. 88 (April 1985), 363–386.

Ellis, L. Tuffey. "The Revolutionizing of the Texas Cotton Trade, 1865–1885." *The Southwestern Historical Quarterly*, Vol. 63 (April 1970), 478–507.

Espey, Huston & Associates. "Cultural Resource Assessment of the Proposed Sienna Plantation Development." (1984). http://lifeonthebrazosriver.com/siennabounda.PDF

Fornell, Earl W. "Agitation in Texas for Reopening the Slave Trade." *The Southwestern Historical Quarterly*, Vol. 60, No. 2 (October 1956), 245–259.

Foust, James D. and Swan, Dale E. "Productivity and Profitability of Antebellum Slave Labor: A Micro-Approach." *Agricultural History*, Vol. 44, No. 1 (January 1970), 39–62.

Hacker, J. David. "New Estimates of Census Coverage in the United States, 1850–1930." *Social Science History*, Vol. 37, No. 1 (Spring 2013), pp. 71–100.

Hamilton, Matthew K. "The Pro-Slavery Argument in Brazoria County, Texas 1840–1865." *The East Texas Historical Journal*, Vol. 52 (Fall 2014), 9–29.

Holbrook, Abigail Curlee. "Cotton Marketing in Antebellum Texas." *The Southwestern Historical Quarterly*, Vol. 73, No. 4 (April 1970), 431–455.

Holbrook, Abigail Curlee. "A Glimpse of Life on Antebellum Slave Plantations in Texas." *The Southwestern Historical Quarterly*, Vol. 76, No. 4 (April 1973), 361–383.

House, Boyce. "An Incident at Velasco, 1832." *The Southwestern Historical Quarterly*, Vol. 64, No. 1 (July 1960), 92–95.

Howern, Aileen. "Causes and Origin of the Decree of April 6, 1830." *The Southwestern Historical Quarterly*, Vol. 16, No. 4 (April 1913), 378–422.

Hine, Darlene Clark. "Rape and the Inner Lives of Black Women in the Middle West." *Signs* 14 (Summer 1989), 912–920.

Huston, James L. "Slavery, Capitalism and the Interpretations of the Antebellum United States: The Problem of Definition." *Journal of Civil War History*, Vol. 65 (June 2019), 119–156.

Hyman, Harold. "William Marsh Rice's Credit Ratings, 1846–1866." *The Houston Review*, Vol. 6 (1984), 91–96.

Jach, Theresa R. "Reform versus Reality in the Progressive Era Texas Prison." *Journal of the Gilded Age and Progressive Era*, Vol 4, No. 1 (January 2005), 53–67.

Jackson, Susan. "Slavery in Houston: The 1850s." *The Houston Review*, Vol. 2, No. 2 (Summer 1980), 66–82.

Johnson, William R. "A Short History of the Sugar Industry in Texas." *Texas Gulf Coast Historical Publications*, Vol. 5, No. 1 (April 1961).

Jordan, Gilbert J. "W. Steinert's View of Texas in 1849." *The Southwestern Historical Quarterly*, Vol. 81, No. 1 (July 1977), 45–72.

Kaye, Anthony E. "The Second Slavery: Modernity in the Nineteenth-Century South and the Atlantic World." *The Journal of Southern History*, Vol. 75, No. 3 (August 2009), 627–650.

Kelley, Sean M. "'Mexico in His Head': Slavery and the Texas-Mexico Border, 1810–1860," *Journal of Social History*, Vol. 37 (Spring 2004), 709–723.

Kelley, Sean M. "A Texas Peasantry? Black Smallholders in the Texas Sugar Bowl, 1865–1890." *The Journal of Slavery and Abolition*, Vol. 28, No. 2 (August 2007), 193–209.

Kelley, Sean M. "Blackbirders and *Bozales*: African-Born Slaves on the Lower Brazos River of Texas in the Nineteenth Century." *Civil War History*, Vol. 54, No. 4 (December 2008), 406–423.

Kelley, Sean M., and Lovejoy, Henry B. "The Origins of the African-Born Population of Antebellum Texas: A Research Note." *The Southwestern Historical Quarterly*, Vol. 120, No. 2 (October 2016), 217–233.

Kite, Jared E. "The War and Peace Parties of Pre-Revolutionary Texas, 1835–1836." *East Texas Historical Journal*, Vol. 29, No. 1 (Fall 1991), 11–24.

Lack, Paul D. "Slavery and Vigilantism in Austin Texas 1840–1860." *The Southwestern Historical Quarterly*, Vol. 85, No. 1 (July 1981), 1–20.

Lack, Paul D. "Slavery in the Texas Revolution." *The Southwestern Historical Quarterly*, Vol. 89, No. 2 (October 1985), 181–202.

Lathrop, Barnes F. "Migration into East Texas, 1835–1860 I," *The Southwestern Historical Quarterly*, Vol. 52 (July 1948), 1–29.

Lathrop, Barnes F. "Migration into East Texas, 1835–1860 II," *The Southwestern Historical Quarterly*, Vol. 52 (October 1948), 184–208.

Lathrop, Barnes F. "Migration into East Texas, 1835–1860 III." *The Southwestern Historical Quarterly*, Vol. 52 (January 1949), 325–348.

Lecaudey, Helene. "Behind the Mask: Ex-Slave Women and Interracial Sexual Relations." In Patricia Morton (ed.), *Discovering the Women in Slavery* (Athens: University of Georgia Press, 1996), 260–277.

Ledbetter, Nan Thompson. "The Muddy Brazos in Early Texas." *The Southwestern Historical Quarterly*, Vol. 63, No. 2 (October 1959), 238–262.

Lerner, Eugene M. "Money, Prices, and Wages in the Confederacy, 1861–1865." *Journal of Political Economy*, Vol. 63, No. 1 (February 1955), pp. 20–40.

Lewis, W. S. "Adventures of the Lively Immigrants." *The Quarterly of the Texas State Historical Association*, Vol. 3, No. 1 (July 1899), 1–32.

Lewis, W. S. "Adventures of the 'Lively' Immigrants. II." *The Quarterly of the Texas State Historical Association*, Vol. 3, No. 2 (October 1899), 81–107.

Lovett, Leslie A. "Biracial Politics and Community Development: The Reconstruction Experience in Fort Bend County, Texas 1869–1889." *The Houston Review*, Vol. 16 (Fall 1994), 27–39.

Lowe, Richard, and Campbell, Randolph B. "The Slave-Breeding Hypothesis: A Demographic Comment on the 'Buying' and 'Selling' States," *The Journal of Southern History*, Vol. 42, No. 3 (August 1976), 401–412.

Luskey, Brian P. "Chasing Capital in Hard Times: Monroe Edwards, Slavery, and Sovereignty in the Panicked Atlantic." *Early American Studies*, Vol. 14 (Winter 2016), 82–113.

Martin, Bonnie. "Slavery's Invisible Engine: Mortgaging Human Property." *The Journal of Southern History*, Vol. 86, No. 10 (November 2010), 817–866.

McCandless, Peter. "South Carolina Lunatic Asylum / State Hospital." In *South Carolina Encyclopedia*. Last modified August 24, 2022, https://www.scencyclopedia.org/sce/entries/south-carolina-lunatic-asylum-state-hospital/.

Meyers, Allan D. "Early Intracoastal Navigation in Texas." *The Southwestern Historical Quarterly*, Vol. 103, No. 2 (October 1999), 174–189.

Morris, Christopher. "With 'the Economics-of-Slavery Culture Wars,' It's Déjà vu All over Again." *Journal of the Civil War Era*, Vol. 10 (December 2020), 524–557.

Muir, Andrew Forrest. "The Railroads Come to Houston 1857–1861." *The Southwestern Historical Quarterly*, Vol. 64, No. 1 (July 1960), pp. 42–63.

Narrett, David E. "A Choice of Destiny: Immigration Policy, Slavery, and the Annexation of Texas." *The Southwestern Historical Quarterly*, Vol. 100, No. 3 (January 1997), 271–302.

The New England Journal of History. "Before Big Foot the Mysterious Gyascutus of Vermont." http://www.newenglandhistoricalsociety.com/big-foot-mysterious-gyascutus-vermont/.

Nichols, James David. "The Line of Liberty: Runaway Slaves and Fugitive Peons in the Texas-Mexico Borderlands." *The Western Historical Quarterly*, Vol. 44, No. 4 (Winter 2013), 413–433.

Nichols, Ruth G. "Samuel May Williams." *The Southwestern Historical Quarterly*, Vol. 56, No. 2 (October 1952), 189–210.

Palm, Reba W. "Protestant Churches and Slavery in Matagorda County." *East Texas Historical Journal*, Vol. 14, No. 1 (1976), 3–8.

Petrovich, Alisa V. "The Jacksons of Brazoria County: The Life, the Myth, and the Impact of a Plantation Family." *East Texas Historical Journal*, Vol. 36, No. 2 (1998), 42–49.

Reid, Debra. "Furniture Exempt from Seizure: African-American Farm Families and Their Property in Texas 1880s–1930s." *Agricultural History*, Vol. 80, No. 3 (Summer 2006), 336–357.

Reynolds, Donald E. "Vigilante Law during the Texas Slave Panic of 1860." *Locus: An Historical Journal of Regional Perspectives*, Vol. 2 (Spring 1990).

Robbins, Fred. "The Origin and Development of the African Slave Trade in Galveston Texas and Surrounding Areas." *East Texas Historical Journal*, Vol. 9 (October 1971), 153–162.

Robinson, Charles F., II. "Legislated Love in the Lone Star State: Texas and Miscegenation." *The Southwestern Historical Quarterly*, Vol. 108, No. 1 (July 2004), 65–87.

Russ, William A. Jr. "Radical Disfranchisement in Texas, 1867–1870." *The Southwestern
Historical Quarterly*, Vol. 38, No. 1 (July 1934), 40–52.

Savitt, Todd L. "Slave Life Insurance in Virginia and North Carolina." *The Journal of
Southern History*, Vol. 43, No. 4 (November 1977), 583–600.

Shelton, Robert S. "On Empire's Shore: Free and Unfree Workers in Galveston Texas,
1840–1860." *Journal of Social History*, Vol. 40 (Spring 2007), 717–730.

Shelton, Robert S. "Slavery in a Texas Seaport: The Peculiar Institution in Galveston."
The Journal of Slavery and Abolition, Vol. 28, No. 2 (August 2007), 155–168.

Shook, Robert W. "The Texas 'Election Outrage' of 1886." *East Texas Historical Journal*,
Vol. 10 (Spring 1972), 20–30.

Smith, James. Brazosport Archaeological Society, "Durazno Plantation." (March 2009),
www.lifeonthebrazosriver.com.

Smith, James. Brazosport Archaeological Society, "Bynum Plantation." (January 2010),
www.lifeonthebrazosriver.com.

Smith, James. Brazosport Archeological Society, "Joseph Reese/Charles Keller Reese/
Stephen P. Winston/Fountain Winston/Lafayette Winston Asa E. Stratton Woodlawn
Plantations." www.lifeonthebrazosriver.com (September 2012).

Smith, James. Brazosport Archaeological Society, "Chenango Plantation." www.lifeon
thebrazosriver.com.

Smith, James. Brazosport Archaeological Society, "John McNeel Plantation Ellerslie
Plantation John Greenville McNeel James Marion Huntington Pleasant Grove
Plantation Leander H. McNeel Sugar Plantation of Pleasant D. McNeel (Magnolia)."
(April 2014) www.lifeonthebrazosriver.com.

Smith, James. Brazosport Archeological Society, "Joseph Mims-James Walker Fannin
James Calvin McNeill Plantation." (July 2014), www.lifeonthebrazosriver.com.

Smith, James. Brazosport Archaeological Society, "Alexander John W. Compton Louis
Martin Strobel Plantation." (March 2015), www.lifeonthebrazosriver.com.

Smith, James. Brazosport Archaeological Society, "Eli Manadue Justice John H. Jones
Plantation." (April 2015), www.lifeonthebrazosriver.com.

Smith, James. Brazosport Archaeological Society, "Cedar Brake Plantation John Spencer
Dance-John Henry Dance-Charles Brown." (February 2016), http://lifeonthebrazos
river.com/Cedar-Brake.pdf.

Smith, James. Brazosport Archaeological Society, "Thomas Phillip Crosby-Thomas
Murray Crosby Plantation-Crosby's Landing Reference Aycock's Landing-Perry's
Landing." (March 2016), www.lifeonthebrazosriver.com.

Smith, Ruby Cumby. "James W. Fannin Jr. in the Texas Revolution." *The Southwestern
Historical Quarterly*, Vol. 23, No. 2 (October 1919), 79–90.

Stevenson, Brenda E. "What's Love Got to Do with It? Concubinage and Enslaved
Women and Girls in the Antebellum South." *The Journal of African American History*,
Vol. 98, No. 1, Special Issue "Women, Slavery, and the Atlantic World" (Winter 2013),
pp. 99–125.

Suryanarayan, Pavitha, and White, Steven. "Slavery, Reconstruction, and Bureaucratic Capacity in the American South." *American Political Science Review*, Vol. 115, no. 2 (2021), 568–584.

Tyler, Ronnie. "Fugitive Slaves in Mexico. *The Journal of Negro History*, Vol. 57, No. 1 (January 1972), 1–12.

White, William W. "The Texas Slave Insurrection of 1860." *The Southwestern Historical Quarterly* 52 (January 1949), 259–285.

Winkler, E. W. "Membership of the 1833 Convention of Texas." *The Southwestern Historical Quarterly*, Vol. 45, No. 3 (January 1942), 255–257.

Winston, James E. "New Orleans Newspapers and the Texas Question, 1835–1837." *The Southwestern Historical Quarterly*, Vol. 36, No. 2 (October 1932), 109–129.

Woods, Michael E. "The Dark Underbelly of Jefferson Davis's Camels." *The Journal of Civil War History* (November 2017), https://journalofthecivilwarera.org/2017/11/dark-underbelly-jefferson-daviss-camels/

Woodward, Earl F. "Internal Improvements in Texas in the Early 1850's." *The Southwestern Historical Quarterly*, Vol. 76, No. 2 (October 1972), 161–182.

Woolfolk Michael E. "Cotton Capitalism and Slave Labor in Texas." *The Southwestern Historical Quarterly*, Vol. 37, No. 1 (June 1956), 43–52.

Wooster, Ralph A. "Notes on Texas' Largest Slaveholders, 1860." *The Southwestern Historical Quarterly*, Vol. 65, No. 1 (July 1961), 72–79.

Wright, Gavin. "Slavery and Anglo-American Capitalism Revisited." *Economic History Review*, Vol. 73, No. 2 (2020), 353–383.

Dissertations and Theses

Crane, Robert E. L., Jr. "The Administration of the Customs Service of the Republic of Texas." MA thesis, University of Texas, 1939.

Curlee, Abigail. "A Study of Texas Slave Plantations, 1822 to 1865." PhD dissertation, The University of Texas, 1932.

Harper, Cecil, Jr., "Farming Someone Else's Land: Farm Tenancy in the Texas Brazos River Valley, 1850–1880." PhD dissertation, University of North Texas, 1988.

Ivan, Adrien D. "Masters no More: Abolition and Texas Planters, 1860–1890." PhD dissertation, University of North Texas, 2010.

Jach, Theresa R. "'It's Hell in a Texas Pen': Life and Labor in the Texas Prison System 1840–1929," PhD dissertation, University of Houston, 2009.

Kelly, Sean M. "Plantation Frontiers: Race, Ethnicity and Family along the Brazos River of Texas, 1821–1886." PhD dissertation, The University of Texas at Austin, 2000.

Kite, Jodella. "The War and Peace Parties in Pre-Revolutionary Texas." MA thesis, Texas Tech University, 1986.

Kosary, Rebecca A. "White Violence and the Maintenance of Racial and Gender Boundaries of Reconstruction in Texas, 1865–1868." PhD dissertation, Texas A&M University, 2006.

Lovett Leslie Ann. "The Jaybird-Woodpecker War: Reconstruction and Redemption in Fort Bend County, Texas, 1869–1889." MA Thesis, Rice University, 1994.

Mcghee, Fred L. "The Black Crop: Slavery and Slave Trading in Nineteenth Century Texas." PhD dissertation, The University of Texas at Austin, 2000.

Moore, Michael Rugeley. "Settlers, Slaves, Sharecroppers and Stockhands: A Texas Plantation-Ranch 1824–1896." MA Thesis, University of Houston, 2001.

Neal, Tara Jane. "The Voice of the American Slave: A Quantified Humanistic Study Comparison of Slavery in Texas and South Carolina." PhD dissertation, University of Texas at Dallas, 2001.

Newman, Kurt. "'Hell-Hole on the Brazos: The Origins of Sugar Land, Texas, and the Imperial Sugar Company, 1832–1914." MA thesis, Texas State University, 2006.

Palm, Reba W. "Slavery in Microcosm: Matagorda County, Texas." MS thesis, Texas A&I University, 1971.

Parrish, Thomas, Michael. "This Species of Slave Labor: The Convict Lease System of Texas, 1871–1914." MA thesis, Baylor University, 1976.

Paschal, Christopher B. "'Texas Must Be a Slave Country': The Development of Slavery in Mexican Texas and the Institution's Role in the Coming of Revolution, 1821–1836." MA thesis, Southern Methodist University, 2010.

Platter, Allen Andrew. "Educational, Social, and Economic Characteristics of the Plantation Culture of Brazoria County, Texas." EdD dissertation, University of Houston, 1961.

Purcell, Linda M. "Slavery in the Republic of Texas." MS thesis, North Texas State University, 1982.

Robbins, Fred. "The Origins and Development of the African Slave Trade into Texas, 1816–1860." MA thesis, University of Houston, 1972.

Robbins, Hal. "Slavery in the Economy of Matagorda County, Texas, 1839–1860." MA Thesis, Prairie View A&M College, 1952.

Summers, Suzanne Lynn. "The Role of Merchants in Promoting Economic Development in the Houston-Galveston Region, 1836–1860." PhD dissertation, The University of Texas at Austin, 1996.

Thompson, Ned. "The Origins and Development of the African Slave Trade into Texas." MA thesis, University of Houston, 1972.

Walters, Katherine Kuehler. "The 1920s Ku Klux Klan Revisited: White Supremacy and Structural Power in a Rural County." PhD dissertation, Texas A&M University, 2018.

Ward, Forrest Elmer. "The Lower Brazos Region of Texas, 1820–1845." PhD dissertation, The University of Texas at Austin, 1962.

Watts, Sandra Lee. "A History of the Texas Sugar Cane Industry with Special Reference to Brazoria County." MA thesis, Rice University, 1969.

Government Records

Brazoria County

Will Book Vol. A

Deed Book SR (Spanish)

Deed Records Book A

Deed Records Book B

Deed Records Book C

Deed Records Book D

Deed Records Book H

Probate Minutes Vol. F

Probate Minutes Vol. G

Probate Case 162 (James W. Fannin)

Probate Case 453 (Columbus R. Patton, *non compos mentis*)

Probate Case 690 (Columbus R. Patton, deceased)

Probate Case 904 (Charles Patton)

Brown v. McNeel (1851)

Sarah H. Black vs. James E. Black (1855)

Bartlett v. Adriance Cause 2997 (1870)

Bartlett v. Freund Cause 3757 (1879)

Fort Bend County

Deed Records, Book A

Deed Records, Book F

Deed Records Book I

Deed Records Book S

Jenola E. Brooks v. Alice Felch, et al. Cause 3400 (1885)

Galveston County

Deed Records Book C

Deed Records Book 52

Probate Case 705 (Thomas H. McMahon)

Harris County

Probate Book Vol. L-N

Matagorda County

   Deed Records Book I

Wharton County

   Probate Minutes Vol. B

Newspapers and Periodicals

   The Austin American Statesman
   The Austin Daily Republican
   The Austin Weekly Statesman
   Bay City Sentinel
   The Buffalo Times (New York)
   The Champaign Daily Gazette (Illinois)
   The Chicago Tribune
   The Civilian and Galveston Gazette
   The Dallas Daily Herald
   DeBow's Review
   Democrat and Planter (Brazoria)
   Flake's Bulletin (Galveston)
   The Fort Worth Gazette
   Galveston Daily News
   Galveston Tri-Weekly News
   The Galvestonian
   The Houston Chronicle
   Houston Daily Post
   Lone Star (Washington, TX)
   Matagorda Gazette
   Richmond Democrat
   The San Marcos Free Press (San Marcos, Texas)
   The Semi-Weekly Journal (Galveston)
   Telegraph and Texas Register (Houston)
   Telegraph and Texas Register (San Felipe)
   Texas Advertiser
   The Texas Almanac (1857)

Texas Gazette

Texas Monument (La Grange)

Texas Planter (Brazoria)

Texas Register

Texas Republican (Brazoria)

Texas State Gazette (Austin)

Texian Advocate (Victoria)

The Tri-Weekly Austin Republican

The Vicksburg Evening Post

Washington American (Texas)

The Wichita Eagle (Kansas)

Archival Sources

Brazoria County Historical Museum
Vertical Files

Dolph Briscoe Center for American History, The University of Texas at Austin
Oscar Addison Papers

John Adriance Papers

Moses and Stephen F. Austin Papers

William Pitt Ballinger Papers

James H. Bell Papers

Thomas E. Blackshear Papers

John T. Bolton Papers

Guy M. Bryan Papers

Ann Raney Thomas Coleman Papers

John P. Coles Papers

Thomas Dwyer Papers

John S. "Rip" Ford Papers

William Fairfax Gray Diaries

Albert C. Horton Papers

Mirabeau B. Lamar Papers

Munson Family Papers

Lizzie Scott Neblett Papers

James Perry Papers

Thomas J. Rusk Papers

Ammon Underwood Papers

Hill Memorial Library, Louisiana State University

Thomas Affleck Papers

Baker Library Special Collections, Harvard University

R. G. Dun & Company. R. G. Dun & Company Credit Report Volumes, 1840–1895

Fondren Library, Rice University

William Marsh Rice Papers

National Archives, Fort Worth

Louisiana Slave Ship Manifests, Records of the US Customs Service, RG 36

Texas Slave Ship Manifests, Records of the US Customs Service, RG 36

National Archives, Kansas City

R. & D. G. Mills Case #523, US District Court at Galveston, RG 21

National Archives, Washington, DC.

Microfilm Series M346, Roll 1006 Confederate Papers Relating to Citizens or Business Firms, compiled 1874–1899, documenting the period 1861–1865

Record Group 105, Microfilm Series M821. Records of the Assistant Commissioner for Texas of the Bureau of Refugees, Freedmen, and Abandoned Lands, 1865–1872.

Record Group 105 Records of the Bureau of Refugees, Freedmen and Abandoned Lands.

Rosenberg Library, Galveston, Texas

Thomas Affleck Papers

William Pitt Ballinger Papers

Ball, Hutchings & Co. Records

Memucan Hunt Papers

Samuel May Williams Papers

South Carolina State Archives, Columbia, South Carolina

South Carolina State Hospital Admissions Book (S 190025) November 18, 1854, pp. 37–38, Roll ST835

South Carolina State Hospital Superintendent's Reports to the Regents (S 19005) November 18, 1854

Wharton County Historical Museum, Wharton, Texas

Henry G. Schrock Plantation Diary

Texas General Land Office

Stephen F. Austin's first census of his colony, 1826

http://www.glo.texas.gov/ncu/SCANDOCS/archives_webfiles/arcmaps/webfiles/
landgrants/PDFs/1/0/3/4/1034583.pdf.

Texas State Archives

Bonds v. Foster, 36 Texas 68 (1872)

Clark v. Honey (1871)

Commercial and Agricultural Bank v. Simon L. Jones. 18 Texas (1857)

Honey v. Clark (1872)

Journal of the Texas House of Representatives, Twenty-Third Texas Legislature,
Regular Session (1893)

R. & D. G. Mills and others v. The State of Texas. 23 Texas (1859),

Robert Mills v. Alexander S. Johnston and Another Texas 23 (1859)

Samuel Mav Williams and others v. The State of Texas 23 Texas 264 (1859)

Smelser v. State of Texas 31 Texas 95 (1868)

Tilley v. Scranton 16 Texas 183, (1856)

Voter Registration Rolls, 1867–1868

Websites

Brazosport Archaeological Society

www.lifeonthebrazosriver.com

The Texas General Land Office Atlas

https://gisweb.glo.texas.gov/glomapjs/index.html

The Texas Historical Commission

https://atlas.thc.state.tx.us/Map

Carol McDavid, Rachel Feit, Kenneth L. Brown, and Fred L. McGhee, "African
American Archaeology in Texas: A Planning Document," https://www.thc.texas
.gov/public/upload/publications/African-American-Archeology-in-Texas-A-
Planning-Document.pdf

Texas Freedom Colony Project

http://www.thetexasfreedomcoloniesproject.com

Texas Runaway Slave Project, East Texas Research Center
  http://digital.sfasu.edu/cdm/landingpage/collection/RSP

Texas Slavery Project
  http://www.texasslaveryproject.org/

The Texas Legislative Reference Library
  https://lrl.texas.gov/

Handbook of Texas Online
  https://tshaonline.org/handbook

The Portal to Texas History
  https://texashistory.unt.edu/

Fort Bend County Independent School District
  https://www.fortbendisd.com/

Reign Clark, Catrina Banks Whitley, Ron Ralph, Helen Graham, Theresa Jach, Abigail Eve Fisher, Valerie Tompkins, Emily van Zanten, and Karissa Basse. "Back to Bondage: Forced Labor in Post Reconstruction Era Texas. The Discovery, Exhumation, and Bioarcheological Analysis of Bullhead Convict Labor Camp Cemetery (41FB355) James Reese Career and Technical Center Campus, 12300 University Boulevard, Sugar Land, Texas," (August 2020). https://www.fort bendisd.com/Page/131568

Index